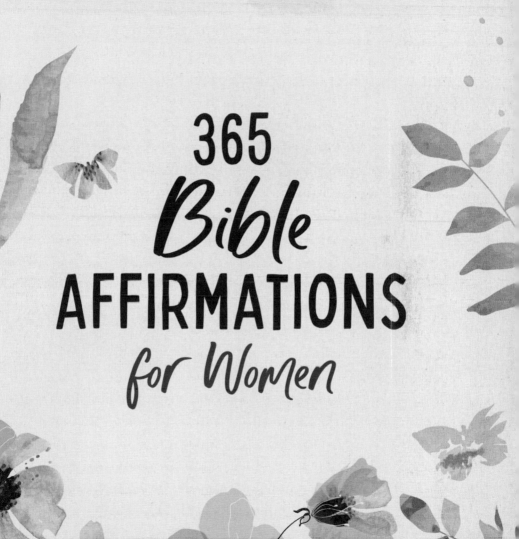

365
Bible
AFFIRMATIONS
for Women

DAILY DEVOTIONS FOR MORNING & EVENING

365
Bible
AFFIRMATIONS
for Women

BARBOUR
PUBLISHING

Member of the
Evangelical Christian
Publishers Association

Printed in China.

MORNING AND EVENING. . .
Bible Wisdom
FOR YOUR SOUL

*Evening, and morning. . .will I pray, and cry
aloud: and he shall hear my voice.*
PSALM 55:17 KJV

365 Bible Affirmations for Women will help you dig deeper into the life-giving
wisdom of God's Word through daily scripture reading, devotional thoughts,
and prayers—twice a day for every day of the year.

Enhance your spiritual journey with the refreshing readings and come to
know just how deeply and tenderly God loves you.

Be blessed!

Morning – JUST BE

*God is our refuge and strength, a very present help in trouble.
Therefore we will not fear. . . . Be still, and know that I am God.*
PSALM 46:1–2, 10 NKJV

Women, born nurturers, are constantly looking to fulfill the needs of others. We are usually the ones who not only plan the meals but also write up the grocery list, do the shopping, then cook them. We are usually the main caregivers, from children to aging parents. In our families, we are usually the go-to person—for missing socks, lost homework or car keys, a ride to soccer practice, etc. Then there are our coworkers who know we pride ourselves on multitasking, taking on big projects while also attending to the details no one else seems to be concerned about. In all these areas, we are running around doing and, as a result, can do ourselves right into the ground. But God wants us to first and foremost just be. He reminds us that because His presence and strength are all we need, fear has no place in our lives. When we believe in those facts, when we trust in Him with all we love, have, and are, we can relax. Be still. Rest in the silence of His presence. So forget about planning tomorrow. Instead, just be in today, knowing He's got it all under control.

Evening – A FRIEND OF GOD

Instead, be filled with the Holy Spirit, singing psalms and hymns and spiritual songs among yourselves, and making music to the Lord in your hearts. And give thanks for everything to God the Father in the name of our Lord Jesus Christ.
EPHESIANS 5:18–20 NLT

In John 15:15, Jesus says that we are His friends. He has given us His Spirit so that we can know His heart and His ways. A great woman of God said that when she spends time with God, He always makes her feel like His favorite daughter. It's so true. You're His favorite daughter too. . .and He wants to be your best friend.

This same woman of God has a very special relationship with her heavenly Father. She sings songs of praise to God throughout the day. If you were to have a conversation with her in the hallway at church, she would likely break into song as God prompted her. Her heart is so full of thanks to God for His faithfulness to her. You wouldn't know by the joy oozing from her that she had many heartbreaking moments, including her husband being taken from her by a freak strike of lightning as he was standing beside her on vacation. She pressed into God during that time instead of pushing Him away. She has allowed God to guide her every step and heal her brokenness. She is always pointing others to the one true God.

Will you be God's friend in joy and sorrow?

DAY 2

Morning – PRAISE WHILE WAITING!

[God says,] "Cease striving and know that I am God; I will be exalted among the nations, I will be exalted in the earth."
PSALM 46:10 NASB

Jamie found herself in a transitional season. It seemed that *everything* was up in the air. Rumors at work suggested changes were coming—there was talk of layoffs and restructure for the organization. God was doing some things in her family—suddenly her parents, sisters, and even cousins were all returning to their home state after everyone being scattered across the nation for more than a decade. On top of that, her very best friend had been unavailable for most of the summer dealing with her mother's health.

Her prayers were constant—asking God to reveal His purpose and plan—but there were no specifics from Him. In her heart she continued to hear the word *wait*! She hated to wait. She planned everything. So she stayed busy doing what she knew to do and kept asking God for more guidance. Jamie knew it was the season she was in, and she had no choice but to embrace it. She determined in her heart to praise Him for what He was about to do—while she was waiting.

Are you in a season of waiting? God is working behind the scenes, preparing His big reveal. Like Jamie, move into a season of praise while waiting.

Evening – SEEKING OF THE FOOLISH

"Then the kingdom of heaven shall be likened to ten virgins who took their lamps and went out to meet the bridegroom. Now five of them were wise, and five were foolish."
MATTHEW 25:1–2 NKJV

The bridegroom is ready. He is adorned in all His wonder, traveling by cloud and to the sound of trumpets, anxiously awaiting union with the bride. But what of her? Christian poets Janette...ikz and Ezekiel Azonwu performed a dramatic reading of the poem "Ready or Not" in which the bride of Christ, representing the Church, is anything but ready.* She busied herself with superfluous actions and forgot the essentials.

Similarly, the women in Jesus' parable were waiting for the bridegroom with lamps in hand. The foolish five readily took their lamps but no oil. They believed He was coming but did little in the way of serious preparation. It is frightening that though they also waited expectantly and claimed to know and love the groom, He did not recognize them. How must we live differently to ensure our seeking and waiting for the Lord is done in the wisdom of the five who entered the feast? Seeking God wisely means being fed with His Word and letting the Spirit work those truths in and through us—invoking His wisdom in all situations.

You can find the performance online: https://www.youtube.com/watch?v=T44LepcRUhk.

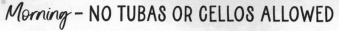

Morning – NO TUBAS OR CELLOS ALLOWED

*Yet to all who did receive him, to those who believed in his
name, he gave the right to become children of God.*
JOHN 1:12 NIV

As teen boys Rick and Ron hefted their orchestra instruments to the bus stop for their first week at a new school, they felt anxious. Most of their high school classmates had been neighbors, teammates, and classmates since kindergarten. Would the students at their new school accept newcomers?

When the bus pulled up, the driver hollered, "Three to a seat! Three to a seat!"

Ron hefted his cello up the steps to the aisle while his brother followed with a violin case.

The driver riveted an unfriendly glare at Ron. "No cellos allowed on this bus! Or tubas! Or drum sets! Or baby grand pianos! That fiddle is too big also."

"How are we supposed to get to school?"

"Walk due north on the dirt road there."

When their mother asked them how their first day was, the boys—who had never been in trouble in school—reported, "We got kicked off the bus!"

Though the driver stopped anyone with too much cargo or who couldn't fit three to a seat, Jesus takes down the restrictions: All who welcome Him into their lives become children of God. All have ahead a new life and a fresh start.

Reflect on the gift of a new beginning. Let go of regrets or mistakes. God forgives you. He still loves you and holds you close as His child.

It doesn't matter if you're a newbie. You're accepted and cherished—always.

Evening – A GOOD DAD

Give thanks to the LORD, for he is good; his love endures forever.
PSALM 107:1 NIV

Our pastor often reminds us that God is a good dad. He is the only perfect parent. Whenever you're tempted to believe the lie that God is just a grumpy old man keeping track of rights and wrongs from heaven, remind yourself that He is good. He loves you with an everlasting love. His Word tells us that it is His kindness that leads us to repentance (see Romans 2:4), not shame and false guilt over our past mistakes.

Did you grow up with loving parents? Or do you consider yourself a loving parent? If you've experienced what it's like to feel secure in that kind of love and give that kind of love. . .how much more does the author and Creator of that love care for you!

In Luke 11:13 (NIV), Jesus says, "If you then, though you are evil, know how to give good gifts to your children, how much more will your Father in heaven give the Holy Spirit to those who ask him!"

God is a good dad who gives us His Spirit to live in us and teach us in each moment. We are never alone. We have a constant, perfect, loving parent and friend with us at all times and in every situation. What an amazing gift to be thankful for this month and always!

DAY 4

Morning – SACRIFICIAL LOVE

For God so loved the world, that he gave.
JOHN 3:16 KJV

Every mother understands sacrifice. We sit on dusty bleachers in 95-degree heat in anticipation of our child's moment up to bat. Crammed between screaming parents, we cheer on our homegrown Michael Jordan. We struggle with an unbridled umbrella and flyaway blanket to repel the cold, pelting rain and whipping wind just to watch our soccer star kick a muddy ball downfield.

For some of us, sports are foreign. But as moms, it doesn't matter if we confuse a hole in one with a slam dunk; we support, love, and cheer our kids on. It matters little if we have to rush from job to gym or if we sit for hours on hard benches. Love impels us to do so.

God's love is similar. Today's scripture declares that God loved us so much that He *gave*. That included so much more than weathering the elements or laundering smelly socks and grimy uniforms. He gave more than His time, efforts, and care. He gave His Son's life. And His love continues. He's never too busy to attend to our needs, and He isn't irritated when we absorb hours of His time.

Someone commented, "We are shaped and fashioned by what we love." God's love for us fashioned Him in the shape of a cruel cross. That's sacrificial love.

Evening – COINCIDENCE OR GOD?

The old has gone, the new is here!
2 CORINTHIANS 5:17 NIV

"Uh-oh!" the young woman breathed. Jana was stranded with a blown engine forty miles from the nearest town. Now she saw a heavyset man stalking her at the rest stop. He was twice her size. Today, one might call on a cell phone and lock the doors. But the new 750cc motorcycle was as wide open as the countryside.

With Jana's communication systems down, how could she call for help? Though raised as a Christian, she'd thumbed her nose at God for ten years. Would He even hear her? "Please, God," she prayed as she saw the man was just twelve feet away, "help me!"

Noise and chaos filled the air as a diesel tow truck pulled up, full of rescuers who cried, "It's true! A lady all the way from Arizona on a motorcycle!" In all the commotion, the stalker turned, got in his truck, and drove away.

Fed and housed at the business owner's house, Jana asked herself, "Coincidence or God?" But deep down she knew God had rescued her—physically and spiritually.

God can make you a new person and set you on an astonishing path. His vision for your life and potential is limitless. No matter where you have been or what you have done, God makes you new and clean when you accept Jesus. He also can guide you to break through the barriers of fear to accomplish new achievements and goals.

If He can transform a cussing motorcycle babe to a Christian writer, what can He do with you? Anything!

Morning – PROMISES OF GOD

"For the LORD your God is living among you. He is a mighty savior. He will take delight in you with gladness. With his love, he will calm all your fears. He will rejoice over you with joyful songs."
ZEPHANIAH 3:17 NLT

Look at all the promises packed into this one verse of scripture! God is with you. He is your mighty savior. He delights in you with gladness. He calms your fears with His love. He rejoices over you with joyful songs. Wow! What a bundle of hope is found here for the believer. Like a mother attuned to her newborn baby's cries, so is your heavenly Father's heart for you. He delights in being your Father. He knows when the storms of life are raging all around you. He senses your need to be held close and for your fears to be calmed. It is in those times that He is for you a prince of peace, a comforter. He rejoices over you with joyful songs. Can you imagine that God loves you so much that you cause Him to sing? God sings over you. And the songs He sings are joyful. He loves you with an unconditional, everlasting love. Face this day knowing that your God is with you. He calms you. And He sings over you. You are blessed to be a daughter of the King.

Evening – STRONG SHEPHERD

Behold, the Lord GOD shall come with a strong hand, and His arm shall rule for Him; behold, His reward is with Him, and His work before Him. He will feed His flock like a shepherd; He will gather the lambs with His arm, and carry them in His bosom, and gently lead those who are with young.
ISAIAH 40:10–11 NKJV

Have you ever watched lambs play? They skip and bounce with newfound joy. It is hard not to smile as you watch their little jig. Today's passage from Isaiah shows some of God's characteristics. He is mighty, and not the fake bodybuilding mighty but a power and strength that is timeless and has no limit. We have only glimpsed the Lord's power in rainstorms and wind. He uses this might and power to lead His flock. What an oxymoron. The God of the universe uses His infinite strength to care for His flock, to "carry them in His bosom, and gently lead those who are with young."

His is not a passive shepherding. Throughout the verses we see God come with might; we see Him rule, tend, gather, carry, and lead. He is our protector. Why would we ever want to stray from this shepherd? Unlike man, God does not abuse His power. Throughout scripture and history we see dictators rise and fall, kings and queens take advantage of the poor; yet our God is just. He rules and leads His flock and nothing is outside of His control, not even the heart and soul of a dictator.

DAY 6

Morning – FEARLESS

God is love. Whoever lives in love lives in God, and God in them. . . .
There is no fear in love. But perfect love drives out fear, because fear
has to do with punishment. The one who fears is not made perfect in love.
1 John 4:16, 18 niv

First John 5:3 says that if we love God, we will do what He commands. It sounds simple enough, but fear can creep in when we consider what it means to show Him complete devotion. Putting Him first in our lives might cost us more than we expect—in our relationships, in our jobs, in how we spend our money or time. We might worry about what others might think of us or fear that we can't accomplish what God calls us to do.

God's unconditional love frees us from fear—the fear of punishment, failure, or harsh judgment from our fellow men and women—because His opinion of us matters most. Through everything, He has promised to be with us and strengthen us. We may feel ashamed of our fear, but God is not angry. Instead, He gives us exactly what we need to strengthen our faith, whether it's the sign of a damp sheepskin (Gideon, Judges 6) or inviting us to touch His wounds (Jesus to Thomas, John 20:24–29).

Do not fear. Christ shows us the vastness of His love to drive out our worries and anxieties. When we rely on Him, we can accomplish *anything* He asks of us.

Evening – GOD GIVES A SOUND MIND

For God hath not given us the spirit of fear;
but of power, and of love, and of a sound mind.
2 Timothy 1:7 kjv

Turn on the evening news and be prepared to see tragedy and chaos. It seems most of the reports we receive are bad ones. Everywhere we turn, something horrific is happening to someone. Crime is rampant and affects all of us, either directly or indirectly. If we're not careful, fear will paralyze us and take over our lives. We must not lose sight of God's promises.

Timothy writes that this spirit of fear did not come from God. God has given us a spirit of power, love, and a sound mind. The mind is fertile ground for every evil thought the devil can bring to you. If we allow those thoughts to take root and grow, fear will overtake us. We must allow God's Spirit to rule our thinking process. We must accept the love He has shown to us and embrace the sound mind He has given us.

As we read God's Word and spend time in prayer with Him, He plants within our minds those things we need to have a sound mind. A sound mind is one the devil can try to attack, but his efforts will be futile. We must be on guard every day to preserve the mind God has given us. Fertilize it with good ideas that glorify God and His purpose.

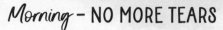

Morning – NO MORE TEARS

" 'He will wipe every tear from their eyes. There will be no more death' or mourning or crying or pain, for the old order of things has passed away."
REVELATION 21:4 NIV

This world is sadly full of sorrow and disappointment. But God doesn't allow our pain to be purposeless. It helps us need Jesus more. It drives us to a closer, more dependent relationship with Him, even when we can't possibly understand the reason for the pain we are experiencing.

Pain, especially when it's seen in our rearview mirror rather than in front of our faces, helps us have greater compassion for others' suffering. It also gives us common ground to give comfort and empathize with others who are in painful circumstances.

It won't always be like this. Someday we will live with Jesus in a perfect life with no sorrow, pain, or disappointment. And we get a "no more tears" promise that is greater than any baby shampoo could deliver. Someday we will have joy greater than anything this earth can offer because it won't be tinged by sin and death. And that is a promise we can hold on to.

Evening – HEAVEN—THE ALWAYS PRESENT

But you must not forget this one thing, dear friends: A day is like a thousand years to the Lord, and a thousand years is like a day.
2 PETER 3:8 NLT

Humans have always been intrigued by what is commonly called the "afterlife." How about the ancient Egyptians who prepared the bodies of their dead pharaohs to live in the great beyond and entombed them with rooms of treasures and foodstuffs to take along? We are still digging up what they buried for the ages. Generations after them also thought about what comes after death. Philosophers offered their best ideas and religions promised peace and reward to their faithful. But only Jesus could offer any concrete evidence that His followers would live forever. He spoke about a place in heaven for those who loved God, and then He rose from the dead to prove He had the power to take them there.

Heaven is the hope of all believers in Christ. Many songs have been written about it, and they bring us comfort when we say goodbye to friends and family members. One written by Billy Sprague has the captivating title "Heaven Is a Long Hello." This lyric encapsulates the thought that there will be no past tense there as we know it here. We will not have to say goodbye or be separated or "leave the party," so to speak. In that land, there is always a glorious "now." We will be beyond the realm of time because we will have stepped into eternity where God dwells.

DAY 8

Morning – BE THE SPARK

*"As surely as I live. . .I take no pleasure in the death of wicked people.
I only want them to turn from their wicked ways so they can live."*
EZEKIEL 33:11 NLT

The Great Awakening was triggered by the evangelist George Whitefield who spent "whole days and even weeks. . .prostrate on the ground in silent or vocal prayer." He said, "[Prayer] is the very breath of the new creature, the fan of the divine life, whereby the spark of holy fire, kindled in the soul by God, is not only kept in, but raised into a flame."

How many believers say they will pray for a situation when all they really do is think about it? Could it be that when we say, "I'll pray for you," we really mean, "I will hope for your sake that things get better"?

God said, "If My people who are called by My name will humble themselves, and pray and seek My face, and turn from their wicked ways, then I will hear from heaven, and will forgive their sin and heal their land" (2 Chronicles 7:14 NKJV).

Prayer for revival should be a daily activity for every Christian. It takes no special talent, no magic words. Prayer doesn't require strength, youth, health, or wealth. You can maintain an attitude of prayer during car trips, meals, or whenever the thought crosses your mind. It is a contrite heart that God loves, and He's waiting for the day His people cry out to Him in desperation. Today, be the spark that starts the fire.

Evening – A WOMAN'S AROMA

*We are a fragrance of Christ to God among those who are
being saved and among those who are perishing.*
2 CORINTHIANS 2:15 NASB

The sense of smell has a strong connection to the brain. A certain fragrance can instantly transport you to a distant memory, maybe even one long forgotten. A person's smell can shape your opinion, even making him or her attractive or repugnant.

The same is true of the spiritual life. Our lives leave an aroma that can be either a pleasing fragrance to God and others or a stench.

In the Old Testament, burnt offerings and incense were used in the temple as a pleasing aroma to God. When King Saul sinned, Samuel chastised him, saying, "Does the LORD delight in burnt offerings and sacrifices as much as in obeying the LORD? To obey is better than sacrifice" (1 Samuel 15:22 NIV).

Just as perfume lingers, you leave behind an aroma of the soul everywhere you go—home, church, work, and public places. Let it be a fragrance people want to keep around.

Here are some ways to leave a pleasing aroma:

- Speak kindly to others.
- Have an attitude of humility.
- Dress modestly.
- Pray continually.
- Don't criticize too sharply.
- Give the benefit of the doubt.
- Speak often about God and His Word.

Life is short. We only have so much time to influence others with our lives. What aroma do you want to leave behind?

Morning – THE PATH TO GOD'S WILL

*All the paths of the Lord are lovingkindness and truth to those
who keep His covenant and His testimonies.*
PSALM 25:10 NASB

It's an age-old question: What is God's will for my life? It's easy to agonize over this question, pondering which path to take and fearfully wondering what will happen if we take a wrong step. But God's will is not necessarily a matter of choosing precisely the right step in each and every situation. This verse teaches that we should focus on God's covenant and His testimony. As we do so, the journey becomes part of the destination.

God doesn't always give us a clear road map, but He does clearly ask us to keep His covenant and His testimonies. When we do so, our individual steps will become clearer, and we will find ourselves more and more in step with His will. As He guides us closer to our destination, we will find much joy in the journey.

Evening – BACK TO THE BEGINNING

*[Abram] went on his journey. . .to the place where his tent had been at the
beginning, between Bethel and Ai, to the place of the altar which he had
made there at first. And there Abram called on the name of the Lord.*
GENESIS 13:3–4 NKJV

Before he was named Abraham, Abram obeyed God by going to a land God said He would show him, uprooting his family and relying on God to show him the way. That took a tremendous amount of faith. But once in Canaan, he discovered a severe famine. So instead of trusting in God to provide, Abram went down to Egypt, where, fearing for his life, he encouraged his wife Sarai to lie and in the process, almost lost her to the pharaoh. Afterward, he was sent out of town and ended up back where he started, to the place where the Lord had initially directed him.

We too can sometimes find ourselves walking out of the Lord's will only to suffer dire consequences. But thank God we have a Lord who is willing to give us a second chance, allowing us to come back, to call on Him once again.

Where have you wandered off to? Are you ready to go back to the beginning, to start again? To get back in God's will and way and see what blessings await?

DAY 10

Morning – HE CARRIES US

In his love and mercy he redeemed them. He lifted them
up and carried them through all the years.
ISAIAH 63:9 NLT

Are you feeling broken today? Depressed? Defeated? Run to Jesus and not away from Him.

When we suffer, He cries. Isaiah 63:9 (NLT) says, "In all their suffering he also suffered, and he personally rescued them. In his love and mercy he redeemed them. He lifted them up and carried them through all the years."

He will carry us—no matter what pain we have to endure. No matter what happens to us. God sent Jesus to be our Redeemer. He knew the world would hate, malign, and kill Jesus. Yet He allowed His very flesh to writhe in agony on the cross—so that we could also become His sons and daughters. He loved me, and you, that much.

One day, we will be with Him. "Beloved," He will say, "no more tears. No more pain." He will lift us up and hold us in His mighty arms, and then He will show us His kingdom, and we will, finally, be whole.

Evening – COMFORT FOR COMFORT

Therefore, in all things He had to be made like His brethren, that He might be a merciful and faithful High Priest in things pertaining to God, to make propitiation for the sins of the people. For in that He Himself has suffered, being tempted, He is able to aid those who are tempted.
HEBREWS 2:17–18 NKJV

God chose to come to earth in human form to be made like us. To understand what it's like to be human. To be able to fully take our place and remove our sins. Because He was fully human while being fully God, He can help. He can comfort. The Bible says that He "comforts us in all our troubles, so that we can comfort those in any trouble with the comfort we ourselves receive from God" (2 Corinthians 1:4 NIV).

It's so encouraging that Jesus was just like us! Our God is not one who wants to remain as a distant high king, out of touch with the commoners. He wants a very personal relationship with each one of us. He lowered Himself to our level so that we could have personal and continual access to Him. His glory knows no bounds, yet He desires to be our friend. Take great comfort in that.

And then when people around you are troubled, you can step in. You can wrap your arms around someone else who needs a friend because of what Jesus has done for you.

Morning – HE MAKES ALL THINGS NEW

Create in me a pure heart, O God, and renew a steadfast spirit within me. Do not cast me from your presence or take your Holy Spirit from me. Restore to me the joy of your salvation and grant me a willing spirit, to sustain me.
PSALM 51:10–12 NIV

King David committed adultery and had the woman's husband killed in battle (see Psalm 51). Talk about guilt! Yet the Bible says David was a man after God's own heart. David truly loved God, and being a king with power, he messed up royally!

David had faith in God's goodness. He was truly repentant and expected to be restored to God's presence. He could not stand to be separated from God. He recognized that he must become clean again through the power of forgiveness.

Perhaps there have been times when you felt distant from God because of choices you made. There is no sin that is too big for God to cover or too small to bother Him with. He is willing to forgive, and He forgets when you ask Him. He expects you to do the same. If you don't let forgiven sin go, it can become a tool for torture for the enemy to use against you. God sent Jesus to the cross for you to restore you to relationship with Him.

Evening – WHEN YOU FEEL LIKE YOU ARE BLOWING IT

For the word of God is alive and active. Sharper than any double-edged sword, it penetrates even to dividing soul and spirit, joints and marrow; it judges the thoughts and attitudes of the heart. Nothing in all creation is hidden from God's sight. Everything is uncovered and laid bare before the eyes of him to whom we must give account.
HEBREWS 4:12–13 NIV

Have you ever had a sense when you read the Bible that you just weren't measuring up? That you were totally blowing it? That happened to me once as I read the New Testament. Then this thought came to mind: *The conviction you are sensing is the purification of the human heart through the Word.* I suddenly remembered Hebrews 4:12–13, which says that God's Word judges the thoughts and intentions of the heart. Suddenly it hit me: *The conviction I feel is God's love in action, transforming me through His Word.*

It's never His desire to burden us down with guilt that leads to death, but to reveal our sin so we can experience life! It's to show us where our thoughts and intentions are wrong so He can lead us to what is right.

Ah! Joyous liberty!

Morning – MY ONE DEFENSE

I will give thanks to the LORD because of his righteousness;
I will sing the praises of the name of the LORD Most High.
PSALM 7:17 NIV

Take a moment and hum through the old hymn "The Solid Rock." Do you remember the words? The songwriter is clear that our hope is built on nothing but the blood of Jesus and His righteousness. And when we stand before the throne, we are dressed in the righteousness of Christ. He is our only defense and the reason we stand before God without fault or stain.

Think about that for a moment. What images come to mind? Do you see yourself hidden in Christ before God? Do you see God looking upon you with love? Can you see that nothing we could possibly do will make God love us any more or less? Do you know for sure that you cannot earn your way to a right relationship with God?

Christ is our one defense. We stand before God without stain or blemish because of Christ. We are made perfect in God's sight because of Christ. We are wholly and dearly loved children of God—completely acceptable in His sight.

All because of Christ.

Evening – CARNAL CHRISTIANS

But put on the Lord Jesus Christ, and make no provision for the flesh in regard to its lusts.
ROMANS 13:14 NASB

Some people believe that a person who stops living like a Christian wasn't one in the first place. But the Bible tells about a prodigal son (who was still a son), men who turned away or strayed from the truth (2 Timothy), disciples who forsook Jesus or denied knowing Him, and carnal believers (1 Corinthians 3). Not to mention the Old Testament saints who messed up big-time.

When we believe in Jesus, we become a child of God (John 1:18), and a child can never undo her parentage. She may legally change her name and never contact her parents again, but that does not cancel her DNA. Even when we act and feel like an unbeliever, that does not negate God's promise of eternal life to everyone who believes. Jesus' death and resurrection paid for our sins so we can have the gift of eternal life and never perish (John 3:16). His promise is as good as His word.

When Christians continue making provisions for the flesh and persist in sinful lifestyles, it does have consequences. If we deny Christ, He will deny us spiritual blessings and the reward of reigning with Him (2 Timothy 2:12–13). We also lose out on fellowship with Him, but we never lose Him. A Christian may turn her back on God, but God will never reject her.

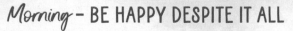

Morning – BE HAPPY DESPITE IT ALL

Light in a messenger's eyes brings joy to the heart,
and good news gives health to the bones.
PROVERBS 15:30 NIV

The apostle Paul had much he could've grumbled about. He was beaten, jailed, shipwrecked, and nearly drowned; yet through it all, he discovered God was the source of his contentment. Paul understood God was in control of his life, even when he was in those overwhelming, tragic situations. Remember his songs of praise from the jail cell (Acts 16)?

Sometimes we find ourselves in hard places, and life isn't going the way we planned. This is the time we have to look for the positive. We have to make the choice to "bloom where we're planted," and God will meet us there. In our songs of praise amid the difficulties, God will come. The Holy Spirit, the comforter, will minister to our needs. The Lord has promised to never leave or forsake us, so if He is present, we should have no fear or worry. Without fear or worry, we can learn to be content. No fretting, no regretting, just trusting the Word is truth.

When we place our hope in Christ and He's our guide, He will give us the ability to walk satisfied, no matter our circumstances. He is our all in all.

Evening – CURE FOR DISCONTENT

Always giving thanks for all things in the name of
our Lord Jesus Christ to God, even the Father.
EPHESIANS 5:20 NASB

Do you struggle with being satisfied with your current situation in life? Discontent is a heart disease that manifests in comparing, coveting, and complaining. What is the cure? The habit of gratitude. Thanking God for everything—the good and the bad—means we accept it as His will, even if we don't like it.

Sometimes we receive birthday or Christmas gifts we have no desire for, but we still thank the giver. God is the good giver of every perfect gift (James 1:17). Failing to thank Him is rebellion against His wisdom and ways. If we expect Him to do things the way we want or to give us more, we forget that God owes us nothing.

When God commands thanksgiving, He is not mandating our feelings but rather our submission. However, because thankfulness changes our attitude and outlook, it does affect our feelings. Discontent and resentment cannot coexist with humble acceptance of what happens to us. Therefore, thanking God must become our lifelong habit. When we turn out the light every night, we can review our day and thank God for each event—good and bad—because He allowed it, and He is good. We can be satisfied with that.

Morning – DECLARING RIGHTEOUSNESS

I do not hide your righteousness in my heart; I speak of your faithfulness and your saving help. I do not conceal your love and your faithfulness from the great assembly.
PSALM 40:10 NIV

A person cannot help but proclaim God's undeserved goodness in everything that she does when she sees what God has done in the lives of the broken. Richard Wurmbrand spent a total of fourteen years in Communist prisons. Despite incarceration, he used every opportunity to tell fellow prisoners of the perfect holy God who came to earth to die for the broken and sinful. Even in solitary confinement Wurmbrand used Morse code to spread the good news of the resurrection and the hope of life after death through Jesus. These are truths that should not and cannot be hidden. If a person refuses to speak God's truth, God will make His Word heard through someone else. The first person will sadly miss out on the beautiful partnership with God and the fruit that is produced. So many things try to discourage Christians from saying confidently that God is completely good and that only He can give lasting help. However, the psalmist encourages Christians to not conceal the great love and awesome faithfulness of God. Personal testimonies have proved to be a powerful tool for revealing the truth. Many prisoners dedicated their lives to Christ through Wurmbrand because he refused to keep silent.

Evening – UNDER VINE AND FIG TREE

" 'And I will remove the iniquity of that land in one day. In that day,' says the LORD of hosts, 'everyone will invite his neighbor under his vine and under his fig tree.' "
ZECHARIAH 3:9–10 NKJV

The context of today's scripture is the prophet Zechariah's vision in which he saw Satan accusing Joshua, the high priest of Israel. Joshua was clothed in filthy garments, which represented his sin and thus revealed his inadequacy in serving as the spiritual leader of God's people. However, God rejected Satan's accusations and commanded that new clothes be given to Joshua. God took away his sins and gave him another chance to be the high priest. He promised to soon send His servant the branch, at which time the sins of the people would be removed in a single day and there would be rejoicing.

About five hundred years later, Jesus came as the promised branch of the family tree of King David. Through His sacrifice, our sins were removed and we were washed clean. In Hebrew the names Joshua and Jesus are the same: Yeshua, meaning "God who saves." Where earthly high priests, like Joshua of Zechariah's time, failed to bring redemption for people, Jesus, as the true High Priest (see Hebrews 7) and as the God who saves, offered Himself and made a way back to God. Now it is time to invite our neighbors to celebrate under our "vine and fig tree."

Morning – STAY TEACHABLE

When Apollos wanted to go to Achaia, the brothers and sisters encouraged him and wrote to the disciples there to welcome him.
ACTS 18:27 NIV

Apollos was a powerhouse for the Lord. The scriptures describe him as "a learned man, with a thorough knowledge of the Scriptures. . . he spoke with great fervor and taught about Jesus accurately" (Acts 18:24–26).

So it's interesting that even with those credentials, Priscilla and Aquila, having heard him, invited him to their house for additional teaching. Afterward, Apollos desired to preach in Achaia, and the couple encouraged him to do so. They immediately contacted the disciples there to welcome him. The result? Apollos refuted the Jews in public debate, proving that Jesus was the Messiah while helping the apostles at the same time (Acts 18:27–28).

We all have room for spiritual growth and godly knowledge no matter how long we have known the Lord. The Bible encourages us to encourage one another. What would happen to advance the kingdom if every believer, despite their position or spiritual seniority, exercised the humility of Apollos? Though scholarly, he accepted more instruction from other believers who, in turn, encouraged his ministry. Jealousy, pride, or one-upmanship didn't exist.

We are to encourage one another, just as God encourages us.

Evening – HE LIFTS YOU UP

Humble yourselves, therefore, under God's mighty hand, that he may lift you up in due time.
1 PETER 5:6 NIV

Nancy's homework for Bible study was to list actions of a humble person and to identify two humble people. Her dictionary app showed descriptive terms like *not proud or arrogant*, *modest*, *courteously respectful*. Those made sense, but what really caught Nancy's attention was the definition of the verb *humble*: "to destroy the independence, power, or will of a person."

Nancy jotted, "Actions: surrender my will to God, give God the power to direct my path, and follow God's will in life." She then thought about people who displayed humble actions. Her son-in-law, Jason, met the criteria. Although he was a medical doctor, he only used his title at his practice. And he routinely volunteered his skills for youth athletic programs and disaster relief.

Next, she thought of Mildred. In her eighties with limited mobility, Mildred still handled hospitality outreach for their church. She called visitors who signed the friendship folder at worship. And she placed regular calls to shut-ins. With both, she would ask if there was anything the church could do and was careful to listen to what was said and sometimes to what wasn't said.

The final section of Nancy's worksheet left space for "Conclusions." Nancy wrote, "Humble people serve others with the unique abilities that God has given them. God rewards a humble person in a way that helps them continue to prosper and serve."

DAY 16

Morning – WHAT'S YOUR GIFT?

Yes, my brother, please do me this favor for the
Lord's sake. Give me this encouragement in Christ.
PHILEMON 20 NLT

Encouragement comes in many forms. A standing ovation and generous applause encourage the performer. Sports teams are uplifted through the cheers of loyal fans. For the Christian, nothing compares to the encouragement we receive from one another through God's love.

The world is full of competition; consequently, words of encouragement are few. Sadly, the body of Christ often does the same, as jealousy blocks the flow of encouragement toward our brothers and sisters in Christ.

Every believer is gifted in different ways. Yet we often covet another's God-given gift. We wish we could sing or recite scriptures or teach like others. Yet God equips every believer with different talents.

Have you found yours? Often the greatest gifts are ones behind the scenes. The intercessors who pray daily for the pastors and leaders are greatly gifted with the power of the Holy Spirit to target and pray for whomever God puts on their hearts. Some possess the gift of giving—not just financially, but of themselves. Others possess God's wisdom and share a word that someone desperately needs. Where would we be without these loving, caring people?

Imprisoned, Paul wrote to Philemon asking him for a favor, indicating it would be of great encouragement to him. Similarly, God encourages us to encourage too.

Evening – MIND AND HEART

Accept instruction from his mouth and lay up his words in your heart.
JOB 22:22 NIV

Although they were sisters, Alice knew she and Sally were as different as day and night. Alice liked to be organized and methodical. She always kept a to-do list and tried to have an overall plan to reach goals. Alice was comfortable evaluating opportunities, determining requirements, and translating everything into a written plan. If something changed, Alice tried to be flexible and revise her plan as needed.

Sally, on the other hand, appeared to make a plan only when all else failed. To Alice, it seemed like Sally put off making a decision until the decision literally made itself. Alice loved her "big sis," but she couldn't understand how Sally had survived, let alone successfully balanced marriage, motherhood, and a career.

At a family reunion, their aunt put things in perspective for Alice. She said, "I am so pleased that you and Sally have both become the women that God intended. It's remarkable how similar you are. It's wonderful to see you both use your minds to listen for God's direction and then act from your heart. It's as evident as the noses on your lovely faces that your hearts for Jesus rule your lives."

Morning – HEAVEN SET

For as he thinketh in his heart, so is he.
PROVERBS 23:7 KJV

*The thing which I greatly feared is come upon me,
and that which I was afraid of is come unto me.*
JOB 3:25 KJV

These two verses are amazing insights into the power of the mind.

According to Proverbs, whatever a woman thinks in her heart, *that* is what she will become. In other words, she is what she thinks! If she is thinking doubt in her heart, that's what she is—doubting. If she's thinking about sad things, that's what she becomes—sad. On the other hand, if she's thinking about joyous things, she cannot help but smile. If she's thinking love, she cannot help but beam with light.

The verse from Job reveals that when a woman is fear-filled, her mind and spirit are focused on her circumstances. Instead of having her eyes on Jesus, she looks at the waves and wind around her and begins to sink. What she feared is what she is focused on and thus what she gets, what she *drowns* in!

It takes the same amount of energy to think of good things as it does bad. But the effect of each is very different. God would have His daughter have a heavenly mindset—thinking of Him, His blessings, His love, and His light. For that not only brightens her outlook and day but shapes her and the world surrounding her.

Evening – REFLECTING (ON) CHRIST'S BEAUTY

*And we all, who with unveiled faces contemplate the Lord's glory,
are being transformed into his image with ever-increasing
glory, which comes from the Lord, who is the Spirit.*
2 CORINTHIANS 3:18 NIV

What are you thinking about? Careful. The act of contemplation is powerful. Why else would teachers chide students when their attention is anywhere but on the lesson? Their daydreams about recess won't fuel their brains for mathematics. Contemplation is a moral and transformative action too. Contemplating the difficulties of a relationship could sway a person's commitment; contemplating wealth (or the lack thereof) can create heart-sinking envy. We pay attention to what we care about; what we care about shapes and changes us.

Throughout scripture, Christians are called to "fix their eyes on Christ" (Hebrews 12:1–2). Here in 2 Corinthians, Paul writes about contemplating Jesus' glory—the Greek word translated into English as "contemplate" means both "to meditate upon" and "to reflect." Dwelling on Christ's life *transforms us* into being more like Him.

Thinking on Jesus means to meditate on the truth we believe about Him. The Word shows us a Savior who gave up His holy, perfect life to restore the undeserving to Himself, who rose again victorious over death! The Holy Spirit enables us to reflect Jesus' loving, sacrificial character in "ever-increasing" measure as we know and love Him better. As God's children, let us know our Savior deeply and reflect Him more and more!.

DAY 18

Morning – EVERYTHING YOU NEED

*And this same God who takes care of me will supply all your needs
from his glorious riches, which have been given to us in Christ Jesus.*
PHILIPPIANS 4:19 NLT

Have you ever gone through a period in your life when you were completely dependent on God to supply everything for you? Perhaps you lost your job or had an extended illness. It can be humbling to be unable to provide for yourself and your family.

The Israelites faced similar circumstances when God freed them from slavery in Egypt. As He led them through the desert toward the Promised Land, He provided water and food in miraculous ways. Every morning, one day's supply of manna would appear. Any attempt to save it until the next day was futile; the manna would rot. God wanted them to rely on Him daily for their provision. Yet the Israelites' response wasn't to be grateful but to complain they didn't have enough variety!

God often takes us through the desert before we get to the Promised Land. It's in the desert that we learn the lessons we will need to use in the Promised Land, most of which involve trusting Him. It's in the desert that we learn God is who He says He is. It's in the desert that we learn to obey Him, not because He says to, but because it's what will ultimately give us the life we were designed to live.

Evening – TRUST AND LEAN

Trust in the LORD with all your heart and do not lean on your own understanding.
PROVERBS 3:5 NASB

This verse contains two commands—trust in the Lord and don't rely on your own understanding.

Do you trust in God? You can rely on God because He is truly trustworthy—He has the strength to sustain, help, and protect you and an incomprehensible love for you that cannot be broken or grow stale. You are not bringing your prayers before someone who is powerful but fickle, or one who is loving and good but weak. You pray to a God who is all-powerful but also good and loving. Therefore, you can be confident that your life is placed firmly in His hands and His control and that He considers it precious.

How often do you lean on your own understanding and strength instead of God's? You are remarkably less capable of controlling your life than God is. Instead of trusting yourself, someone who doesn't know the future and certainly can't control it, lean on the all-powerful God who knows each step you will take. Relinquish all your anxious thoughts over to His control. Trusting God with your future is far more productive than worrying about it. So lean on Him and trust Him with *everything* in your heart. He will sustain you.

Morning – SIMPLE JOY

Yet I am confident I will see the Lord's goodness
while I am here in the land of the living.
PSALM 27:13 NLT

Marie's husband was out of work and unmotivated to find another job. The overdue bills were mounting along with the stressfulness of the situation. For many weeks she had trouble sleeping and needed rest so desperately to make it through her long days at work.

Nearly exasperated, finally one night she got a good night's sleep. She awoke to birds singing just outside her slightly open window where a gentle breeze blew the curtain open enough to let in sunshine and the smell of lavender just now in bloom.

There was much that Marie could not control about the situations in her life, it was a difficult season to be sure, but she decided to enjoy the blessings. She spent a few moments just savoring the simple joys of sleep and morning sunshine.

Evening – REMEMBER THE MIRACLES

He came to Jesus at night and said, "Rabbi, we know that you are
a teacher who has come from God. For no one could perform
the signs you are doing if God were not with him."
JOHN 3:2 NIV

People today are cynical about miracles. Even some Christians wonder if miracles are perhaps a Bible-times phenomenon and no longer part of modern-day life. Disbelief and cynicism are easy emotions. In fact, some of the Israelites felt this way even after they had witnessed many signs and wonders from God. How many miracles does it take for humanity to finally have faith? The kind of belief that doesn't wobble like a tower of Jell-O?

If we will look, we will see miracles—even daily. Miracles come in all shapes and sizes. And when they do come, thank God for them. Tell others about them so that they too might be uplifted. Write them down. Memorize them and keep them close to your heart. That way, when hardships come—and they will come eventually—you can remember all that God has done for you.

Then when the enemy of your soul comes to tempt and discourage you, you will be able to stand strong. You will keep hold of joy. You will live with victory.

Acknowledging and celebrating these wonders from God is part of a contented Christian life. What miracles will you praise God for today?

DAY 20

Morning – A REGULAR OFFERING

*The angel answered, "Your prayers and gifts to the poor
have come up as a memorial offering before God."*
ACTS 10:4 NIV

Jenna dropped off another load of clothes at the Goodwill then swung by the school to help the first-grade class with reading group. She loved this volunteer job! On her way to Mrs. Windom's class, she dropped off her coin collection bank in the office. Her husband and the kids had been helping her save extra change to give to the school's building campaign.

At church on Sunday morning, Jenna asked her children to help her carry in a few bags of canned goods they had packed for the community food pantry drive. It was a simple thing she could do, and the kids seemed to like helping with it.

That evening before bed, their family prayed for the needs they knew of in the lives of their neighbors, friends, and loved ones. Jenna's daughter asked her, "Mommy, why do we do all these nice things? My friends' mommies don't do these things with them."

Jenna didn't think much about any of the acts of kindness; it just felt right to do them.

"Well, I don't know exactly, but when I feel a nudge to do a nice thing, I think I just ought to do it, and I believe God will do something with it someday."

Evening – A RECIPE OF LOVE

*"Give, and you will receive. . . . The amount you
give will determine the amount you get back."*
LUKE 6:38 NLT

A delicious assortment of pies lined the glass showcase in a rudimentary diner nestled in the Ponderosa pines of Mt. Lemmon, Arizona. As a husband and wife entered the door, strangers greeted them with warm hospitality. Soothing classical music played as the couple squeezed into a corner table. Although the type of music seemed out of character for the diner, its significance became clear as the wife chatted with the diner's owner, Pam.

Pam's character matched her music. She appreciated life and the gifts of others. "I can't paint, and I can't compose music," Pam admitted, "but I can bake. It's my way of giving back to the mountain."

Pam discovered her "gift" in 1972 when she first started baking her mother's Pennsylvania Dutch pie recipes for her customers. She explained how her mother demonstrated her love through everything she cooked or baked. "Now my mother touches people through my hands," she explained. "I just want to reach people with God's love, and it begins with giving, sharing the gifts I have."

"I am blessed," Pam shared.

The couple was too. For a moment, their lives became as simple as Pam's unpretentious surroundings and basic philosophy: "Whatever you do, do it with love."

Morning – GOODBYE AND HELLO

Therefore we do not lose heart. Even though our outward man is perishing, yet the inward man is being renewed day by day. For our light affliction, which is but for a moment, is working for us a far more exceeding and eternal weight of glory, while we do not look at the things which are seen, but at the things which are not seen. For the things which are seen are temporary, but the things which are not seen are eternal.

2 CORINTHIANS 4:16–18 NKJV

One of the most difficult things in life is watching a loved one nearing the end of their life. Maybe you know someone who is caring for such a person right now. Those last miles in the earthly journey can be long and hard.

The American author and clergyman Henry van Dyke offers encouragement in his poem "Parable of Immortality." He compares a person to a beautiful and strong ship spreading its sails in the morning breeze and slowly sailing for the horizon. In time, she fades into where the ocean meets the sky, and someone says, "There she goes." But at that exact moment, those on the other side see her appear on the horizon just as strong and powerful as when she began her journey, and they shout joyfully, "Here she comes!"

Isn't it magnificent that God promises Christians eternal life? The journey may be hard, but the destination is magnificent.

Evening – ALWAYS THERE

When I said, "My foot is slipping," your unfailing love, LORD, supported me.
When anxiety was great within me, your consolation brought me joy.

PSALM 94:18–19 NIV

Dayna exited the conference room all smiles and hurried back to her desk. She had just landed a big account, and she wanted to share her news. Imagining just how proud her father would be, she reached for her phone and dialed his number. She stopped, realizing he wouldn't be there. In her excitement she had forgotten, for just a moment, that he was gone. Just six weeks ago she'd stood next to her sister at his memorial service.

Dayna put the receiver down and took a deep breath. She bowed her head and prayed, *Heavenly Father, I miss my dad. Comfort me in his absence. Thank You for blessing me with favor with my new client and giving me inspiration and wisdom to do my job well. Thank You for always being there for me.*

One of the things people grieve most in losing loved ones is trying to overcome that strong desire to reach out, only to find them no longer there. The good news is that God is always there. Through your relationship with Him, you can celebrate the goodness of each new day.

DAY 22

Morning – WITHOUT EXCUSE

Yes, they knew God, but they wouldn't worship him as God or even give him thanks. And they began to think up foolish ideas of what God was like. As a result, their minds became dark and confused.
ROMANS 1:21 NLT

In Romans 1, Paul is reminding us all that we are without excuse (see Romans 1:20). We have a supernaturally created world around us each day, a sun to warm and light our earth and a moon to light our nights. Only our Creator is to thank for those blessings.

But mankind, though they knew God, chose not to worship Him or give Him thanks. This resulted in dark and confused minds. This can be true of our world today. When we choose ourselves over God, life becomes confusing and dark.

If we believe the truth of God and His Word that we are made clean and new in the blood of Christ, then we are without excuse when it comes to thanking Him for all He is and all He has done. We either believe it and it means absolutely everything—changing our entire lives—or we are lukewarm in our faith and the Christian life is really just a supper club. There is great danger in the latter (see Revelation 3:16).

Will you give your thanks and worship to the true God?

Evening – BLESSING AND THANKFULNESS

Give thanks in all circumstances; for this is God's will for you in Christ Jesus.
1 THESSALONIANS 5:18 NIV

"Count your blessings, name them one by one. Count your blessings, see what God has done." As the hymn says, being thankful is a practice. We should take time to contemplate God's blessings to us, especially when there seems to be more trouble than peace in our lives.

No matter how difficult life becomes, God's gifts are still there, abundant and gracious. I knew an artist whose medical conditions caused such terrible pain that she could only stand and walk for a limited time each day. Despite her situation, she made a practice of tracing the threads of God's blessing in her life. If she ate a peach, she would thank God for the peach; the store that sold it; the store's employees; the truck driver; the orchard workers; the farmer who had cared for the trees; and for the soil, air, water, and sunlight. Her spirit radiated thankfulness in the midst of her suffering, even for something as small as a peach.

Our thankfulness is founded on God—He has promised to take care of our needs and to comfort us in our distress. Name what the Father has done for you, blessings big and small, in joyous and in troubled times. All good gifts are from Him (James 1:17). Can you trace the thread of His love in your life?

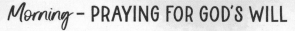

Morning – PRAYING FOR GOD'S WILL

For this reason, since the day we heard about you, we have not stopped praying for you. We continually ask God to fill you with the knowledge of his will through all the wisdom and understanding that the Spirit gives.

COLOSSIANS 1:9 NIV

The apostle Paul reminded the Colossians that he was continuously praying for them to be filled with the knowledge of God's will. Read the verse above closely. How did Paul ask God to fill them with the knowledge of His will? The only way that we can know His will—*through all the wisdom and understanding that the Spirit gives.* Paul was speaking to believers here. Christians have received the Holy Spirit as their counselor and guide. Those who do not have a personal relationship with Christ are lacking the Spirit, and thus, they are not able to discern God's will for their lives. Always take advantage of the wonderful gift that you have been given. If you have accepted Christ as your Savior, you also have the Spirit. One of the greatest things about the Holy Spirit is that it helps us to distinguish God's call on our life from the other voices of the world. Pray that God will reveal His good and perfect will for your life. His Holy Spirit at work in you will never lead you down a wrong path.

Evening – REFUSE TO QUIT

And I will pray the Father, and he shall give you another Comforter, that he may abide with you for ever; even the Spirit of truth; whom the world cannot receive, because it seeth him not, neither knoweth him: but ye know him; for he dwelleth with you, and shall be in you.

JOHN 14:16–17 KJV

There are days when it seems that nothing goes right and you struggle just to put one foot in front of the other. The good news on a day like that is the truth that you are not alone. Whatever obstacle is in your way, you don't have to overcome it in your own power. God is with you. Jesus sent the comforter. The Holy Spirit is your present help in any situation.

The Holy Spirit is the very Spirit of God Himself. He is with you always, ready to care for and guide you. By faith you can rest and rely on the Holy Spirit for strength, wisdom, and inspiration.

The next time you feel like giving up, refuse to quit. Ask the Holy Spirit to intervene, to provide you with the strength and wisdom to continue your journey.

Morning – BEFORE YOU ASK

*"Seek the Kingdom of God above all else, and live righteously,
and he will give you everything you need."*
MATTHEW 6:33 NLT

"Dear God, please. . ."

Do your prayers begin that way? "Dear God, please help me to be patient with my kids." "Dear God, please heal my friend's illness." "Dear God, please provide enough money to pay this month's bills." God wants believers to ask for whatever they need. But Jesus reminds them that there is a right way to pray, and prayer is more than asking.

In the Lord's Prayer, Jesus teaches His followers how to pray. He begins, "Our Father in heaven, may your name be kept holy. May your Kingdom come soon. May your will be done on earth, as it is in heaven" (Matthew 6:9–10 NLT). First, Jesus honors God's holiness. Next, He shows faith in God's promise of reigning over the earth and redeeming His people. Then He accepts God's perfect will. Praise, faith, and acceptance come before asking. Jesus reminds believers to honor God first, put God's will second, and pray for their own needs third. His prayer begins with God and ends with Him: "For thine is the kingdom, and the power, and the glory, for ever. Amen" (Matthew 6:13 KJV).

Bring your requests to God. Ask specifically and confidently, but remember Jesus' model—put God first in your prayers.

Evening – PRAYING FOR ALL PEOPLE

*I urge, then, first of all, that petitions, prayers, intercession and thanksgiving be made
for all people—for kings and all those in authority, that we may live peaceful and
quiet lives in all godliness and holiness. This is good, and pleases God our Savior,
who wants all people to be saved and to come to a knowledge of the truth.*
1 TIMOTHY 2:1–4 NIV

John and Charlie were friends. . .most of the time. It was when they got into a political discussion that observers wondered where their spirited conversation would lead. It seemed that both men thought their point of view was the correct one.

Whether we like the person who is in office or not, God commands us to pray for those He placed in authority over us. In ancient times, this could have meant praying for those who hated Christians and were possibly plotting harm to them. Even today, as issues concerning Christ-followers emerge, we are called to pray for all people, including those with whom we don't see eye to eye politically. Today's verse reminds us that to do so is good and pleasing to the Lord.

Morning – LOOKING ON THE HEART

But the LORD said unto Samuel, Look not on his countenance, or on the height
of his stature; because I have refused him: for the LORD seeth not as man seeth;
for man looketh on the outward appearance, but the LORD looketh on the heart.
1 SAMUEL 16:7 KJV

Everywhere you look, there are beauty products, weight loss programs, and procedures to make you look younger. It seems we never tire of trying to improve our appearance. There's nothing wrong with trying to look our best, but if we're not careful, we can become obsessed with our appearance. Many women worry about how they look to the world around them and whether they live up to the world's standards of beauty.

When God sent Samuel to anoint a new king for Israel, Samuel asked Jesse, the Bethlehemite, to bring out his sons. The sons of Jesse were evidently good-looking men, because Samuel thought that surely the Lord's anointed stood before Him. God said, *"No, I don't look on the outward appearance; I look on the heart."*

In our pursuit of improving our appearance, it's best if we first make sure our hearts are clean. We might look good on the outside, but if our hearts aren't pure before God, then we aren't pleasing to Him. Before we jump on the bandwagon and spend a lot of money on cosmetics, maybe we should ask God about our hearts and make sure He approves. It's far more important to please Him than to please the world.

Evening – UNFADING BEAUTY

You should clothe yourselves instead with the beauty that comes from within,
the unfading beauty of a gentle and quiet spirit, which is so precious to God.
1 PETER 3:4 NLT

Perhaps Sarah was the only elderly woman who was so beautiful that an Egyptian pharaoh wanted her for his harem! Most of us don't have to worry about that. We know that whatever physical beauty we possess is fleeting. Despite the commercials and the boutique counters in the department stores and the advances of Botox and collagen, aging happens to every woman.

God understands that our bodies pay a heavy price for the brokenness caused by sin. He knows that we grieve as we see our youth slipping away. Yet He does not want us to make this temporal body the focus of our living. After all, the body only houses the spirit, and one day we will exchange this primitive model for a glorified one.

I love vintage photos and am intrigued by the youthful beauty seen in the picture albums of the elderly. Looking at them in younger days, full of life and vitality, and then glancing at them today brings one to the stark reality that beauty fades and only a shadow of the former glory exists.

That's why God's Word tells women to spend most of their effort on beautifying the spirit, which can grow lovelier with every passing year. For only eternity will reveal the glories yet to come.

DAY 26

Morning – CONSIDER FORGIVENESS

*Rejoice the soul of Your servant, for to You, O Lord, I lift
up my soul. For You, Lord, are good, and ready to forgive,
and abundant in mercy to all those who call upon You.*
PSALM 86:4–5 NKJV

The beginning of a new year is a good time to consider those to whom you have yet to extend forgiveness. Yes, there are people in our lives who have an amazing capacity to push our buttons. And, yes, there are people who have maimed us by their words and actions. But because God is so willing to forgive those who push His buttons and have harmed His good name, we should be willing to wipe the slate clean of those who have frustrated and offended us. So before you lift up Your soul to God, forgive and bless those who have hurt and upset you. And while you're at it, forgive and bless yourself. Then go to God, ready to have your missteps erased and to be renewed by His amazing mercy and grace.

Evening – THE ULTIMATE ACT OF LOVE

*Bring joy to your servant, Lord, for I put my trust in you. You, Lord,
are forgiving and good, abounding in love to all who call to you.*
PSALM 86:4–5 NIV

The modern theologian Lewis Smedes once said, "You will know that forgiveness has begun when you recall those who hurt you and feel the power to wish them well." It seems the most unnatural thing in the world for us to forgive someone who has hurt us deeply, let alone hoping good things will happen for them. However, that is really the only loving thing to do.

Forgiveness doesn't require that the person who did the hurting apologize or acknowledge what they've done. It's not about making the score even. It doesn't even require forgetting about the incident. But it is about admitting that the one who hurt us is human, just like we are. We surrender our right for revenge and, like God, let go and give the wrongdoer mercy, therefore blessing them.

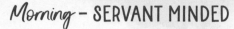

Morning – SERVANT MINDED

Let this mind be in you which was also in Christ Jesus, who, being in the form of God, did not consider it robbery to be equal with God, but made Himself of no reputation, taking the form of a bondservant, and coming in the likeness of men.

PHILIPPIANS 2:5–7 NKJV

If someone were to ask you, "Do you consider yourself equal to God?" your answer would be an emphatic, "No!" But how often do our actions overwrite our answer? Where do you tend to worry, fret, take hold, and micromanage? There are so many small, and at times large, areas of our lives where we prefer to act as a god. We subconsciously think we know best or have the most knowledge of our finances, children, job, husband, or friend. But as scripture constantly reminds us, the Lord knows every aspect of our being.

In his letter to the Philippians, Paul is not merely suggesting that we have a Christlike attitude; he is adamantly instructing us to take this mindset and make it our daily thought process. Notice, Paul doesn't say, "This mind is already in you." Humility is not natural for us; it is at times the hardest part of our walk with the Lord.

If Christ, fully God and fully man, did not consider equality with God a thing to be obtained, why do we? Christ's humility is astounding! He is God, but He became a servant. How effective is a servant who continually wishes to be the master? Until we realize that we—our sinful nature—is what prevents us from entering into a relationship with the Lord and living for His glory, then walking with our Savior is not a thing to be grasped.

Evening – GOD'S UPSIDE-DOWN KINGDOM

"Then, Lord," Simon Peter replied, "not just my feet but my hands and my head as well!"

JOHN 13:9 NIV

This is the well-known scene where Jesus is washing the disciples' feet before His death. Peter, the disciple known for his enthusiastic jump-first-then-look attitude, is having none of it. He is not letting Jesus wash his feet because he doesn't understand the purpose behind what Jesus is doing.

Jesus' reaction here is so different from what we might say. Instead of saying to Peter, "Stop telling me what to do! You have no idea what's going on here," He gently explains the lesson and purpose.

God loves our enthusiasm even if it's misdirected. Often we think we know what God is doing or would want done and so we jump ahead of Him. He calmly pulls us back and reminds us that our thoughts and plans are not His.

His plans can seem counterintuitive to us. They are opposite of the world's definition of success. Jesus was God, and He descended to earth to become man. And not a powerful man, but a poor man. And to His disciples, He became a servant. Our society tells us to push up, to rise to the top. But He descended, came down to save us by dying a criminal's death.

DAY 28

Morning – MAKE IT COUNT

Like arrows in the hand of a warrior, so are the children of one's youth.
PSALM 127:4 NKJV

When a young mom dropped off her children at school each day, she would encourage them, "Hey, let's make today count!"

Most of us realize that children are little sponges, so we get them the best educations and give them lessons in sports and music. But they are also sponges for understanding their purpose in the kingdom. While they are sopping up information, don't forget to instill their purposes as believers. Deuteronomy 6:7 (NIV) says, "Impress [God's principles] on your children. Talk about them when you sit at home and when you walk along the road, when you lie down and when you get up."

Your children are ambassadors for Christ even as young as they are! They are exposed to a mission field at school every day and a variety of differing denominations and beliefs, even at Christian schools. Your child could lead his friends to Christ on the playground. As Jesus said, "I thank You, Father, Lord of heaven and earth, that You have hidden these things from the wise and prudent and have revealed them to babes" (Matthew 11:25 NKJV).

How are you encouraging your kids to make every day count for the Lord? How are you helping them be a light?

Evening – GOD'S WORD ACCOMPLISHES HIS PURPOSES

"As the rain and the snow come down from heaven, and do not return. . .without watering the earth and making it bud and flourish, so that it yields seed for the sower and bread for the eater, so is my word that goes out from my mouth: it will not return to me empty, but will accomplish what I desire and achieve the purpose for which I sent it."
ISAIAH 55:10–11 NIV

Farmers and ranchers settled this country, especially in the move to the West. Many immigrants came into the country looking for land, which was plentiful here. With a general population shift to the cities where people can find jobs, farming and ranching isn't as prominent. For many the experience of planting a field with seed, waiting on God to send the rain at the right times, giving the plants the moisture they need to bud and flourish, and seeing the crop through harvest is only something they read about.

The Lord uses this analogy to describe what happens when God's Word goes out in a sermon, in verses memorized, or in the written word. God promises that when His Word is planted in someone, it doesn't go to waste. It may take a long time to see it take root and grow and be harvested, but it will. For it will not return to God until it has achieved the purpose for which He sent it. So moms of wayward children, take heart. God is still working.

Morning – GOD'S SYSTEM OF JUSTICE

Yet the Lord longs to be gracious to you; therefore he will rise up to show you compassion. For the Lord is a God of justice. Blessed are all who wait for him!
ISAIAH 30:18 NIV

Do you yearn for more of God? This scripture tells us He longs to be gracious to us. If we believe that, our response should be a longing for more of Him, more of His grace, unless pride makes us pull away and try to earn His favor.

That famous line, quoted as though it is scripture, says "God helps those who help themselves." The truth is, when we can't do anything for ourselves, we're in the perfect place for God to pour out His grace.

The world's justice tells us we don't deserve God's graciousness—we've made too many mistakes—but God's justice is wrapped in love and mercy. Instead of pointing to our failures and telling us we're worthless, He forgives our sins and totally forgets them. They're as far from His thoughts as the east is from the west (see Psalm 103:12).

When we run into His arms of love and let His grace overwhelm us, we will long for more of Him. He's too magnificent to ignore. It's impossible to turn our backs on all He does for us. The natural response is to accept His compassion. He longs to give it and waits patiently until we're ready to receive.

Evening – TRUST THE GOOD NEWS

We also have the prophetic message as something completely reliable, and you will do well to pay attention to it, as to a light shining in a dark place, until the day dawns and the morning star rises in your hearts.
2 PETER 1:19 NIV

The beauty of the Old Testament is that it foreshadows the coming of Jesus through the histories that depict humanity's great need for God as rescuer. The apostle Peter knew that God's message was true. Like any good Jewish boy, he had learned the Torah, the first five books of the Bible, and then he actually saw Jesus as the one who made all those images and promises come true. However, there was a time when Peter doubted the role of Jesus as Savior. His denial was the darkest moment of his life. Peter's letters were most likely written to other Jews of his time who also were well acquainted with the Old Testament prophecies about the Messiah. Peter tells the readers to believe the good news of Jesus Christ. It is completely reliable. In the darkest moment of Peter's despair, Jesus—as the incarnate Word of God, Divinity in the flesh—broke the chains of sin holding humans captive since the fall of Adam and Eve. In Jesus' death and resurrection, the awesomeness of God's mysterious rescue plan was revealed. Light came into the hearts of humankind and gave them Life.

DAY 30

Morning – THREE STRINGS

Two are better than one because they have a good return for their labor. For if either of them falls, the one will lift up his companion. But woe to the one who falls when there is not another to lift him up. . . . And if one can overpower him who is alone, two can resist him. A cord of three strands is not quickly torn apart.
ECCLESIASTES 4:9–10, 12 NASB

God uses His people to encourage and strengthen one another. As iron sharpens iron, so a friend sharpens a friend (Proverbs 27:17). We get more accomplished in our own lives—and in the grand scheme of things—when we are open to the help and encouragement of others.

If you see a friend in need of physical, emotional, or spiritual help, ask the Lord to give you the wisdom and understanding to be used in helpful ways. And when a friend offers similar help to you, don't be too proud to accept it.

Ask the Lord to guide you in finding a "three-string" accountability partner. Look for a Christian woman with a strong faith in the Lord who is willing to pray with you, encourage you in your faith, and be honest about your strengths and weaknesses. Meet together several times a month and ask each other the hard questions: Were you faithful to the Lord this week? Did you gossip? Is there anything you're struggling with right now? How can I pray for you?

With God, you, and a trusted Christian friend working together, you become a rope of three strings that is hard to break!

Evening – FOREVER LOVE

Love each other with genuine affection, and take delight in honoring each other.
ROMANS 12:10 NLT

Clara wanted a garden swing. Throughout their fifty years of marriage, she had asked Walter to build one, but other projects took priority. A swing wasn't that important. She wanted it mostly to watch the sun set over the lake and see the stars come out.

One day, Walter decided to surprise his wife. He had discovered something long forgotten, tucked away in the barn, something that would make the perfect swing seat.

When Clara left for a few days to visit her sister, Walter got busy. He built the swing's foundation and then a sturdy lattice roof to which he attached two strong chains. Then, from the barn, he hauled out the front seat from his 1946 Plymouth—the seat where he and Clara had shared their first kiss. He scrubbed it well and fastened it to the chains just minutes before she returned home.

"Oh, my!" Clara gasped when she saw it. "Oh. . .my."

It wasn't the swing that she'd had in mind, but still, it was the most beautiful swing she had ever seen. As the sun set, Clara and Walter sat there together. He wrapped his arm around her shoulder and gently kissed her cheek. "God blessed me with you, dear," he said. "I love you now and forever."

Morning – UPS AND DOWNS

*Casting down arguments and every high thing that exalts
itself against the knowledge of God, bringing every
thought into captivity to the obedience of Christ.*
2 CORINTHIANS 10:5 NKJV

Living according to our fickle feelings is like riding a roller-coaster: one day up, one day down. It's easy to fall into the trap of believing those thoughts more than what God says in His Word. Don't let every emotion that surfaces dictate the direction of the day. Capture loose thoughts with a Christ-centered net.

To begin this process, we should latch on to God's promises and steady our course. We need to line up our feelings with what we know the Bible says. The apostle Paul said, "We walk by faith and not by sight." Sometimes we won't sense God's presence, but because He's promised He'll never leave us, we must believe He's there. Jesus said, "My peace I leave you." Accept that peace. Let it rule in your heart. Concerned about having enough? "My God shall supply all your needs." Proven promises to stand on. Promises we can live by. Search the scriptures for promises. They are there.

God is a God of faithfulness, and He works in ways that faith, not feelings, can discern. Trust Him. We must—even when we don't feel like it.

Evening – WHAT NEXT?

*If any of you lacks wisdom, you should ask God, who gives generously
to all without finding fault, and it will be given to you.*
JAMES 1:5 NIV

Ever been lost in an unfamiliar place? Trees block street signs, and other streets aren't marked at all; construction causes confusing, squiggly detours. Embarrassment or even panic grows as the minutes pass.

In life, we hit unexpected detours that make us unsure where to turn next. They might be difficult decisions involving family, health care, jobs, or relationships at church. Maybe the weight is migrating from the tension in your shoulders to settle in your heart.

The good news is that our heavenly Father knows the way out of our confusion and will help us when we are at our most frantic. James tells us that God promises to give wisdom to those who ask for it in faith; He gives wisdom "generously" and "without fault." Sometimes it's intimidating to ask for advice from others, but God doesn't look down on us for admitting our weakness. He chooses to lavish His love and His gifts on error-prone people because they are a part of His family in Christ. We can entrust ourselves and our lives to our heavenly Father, knowing that through Christ, we have access to "all the treasures of wisdom and knowledge" that our Savior possesses (Colossians 2:3 NIV).

DAY 32

Morning – PRAY THROUGH TROUBLE

Is anyone among you in trouble? Let them pray.
JAMES 5:13 NIV

Mona and her sister argued about their mother. The elderly woman had been self-sufficient, but lately she had trouble caring for herself. Mona's sister decided that putting their mother into a nursing home was the best option. But Mona disagreed. She felt that she and her sister could take turns staying with their mother so she could remain in her house. Communication broke down between the two sisters, and Mona didn't know what to do next—until she remembered the words of Philippians 4:6: "Do not be anxious about anything, but in every situation, by prayer and petition, with thanksgiving, present your requests to God." Mona knelt down in her living room and prayed. "Dear God, help me to mend my relationship with my sister, and help us both to do what is best for Mom."

In everyday life, people get tangled in webs of anxiety, and they sometimes forget to consult God. In Philippians 4:6, Paul reminds Christians not to let that happen. He says in *every* situation, pray. And not only bring requests to God, but bring them with thanksgiving.

The great evangelist and Christian teacher Oswald Chambers said, "We have to pray with our eyes on God, not on the difficulties." How do you handle the difficulties in your life? Do you pray with your eyes on God?

Evening – STRENGTH IN OUR WEAKNESS

"Do you thus repay the LORD, O foolish and unwise people? Is not He your Father who has bought you? He has made you and established you."
DEUTERONOMY 32:6 NASB

Marita suffers from an autoimmune disease. Some days she feels okay, but other days test her reserves. The disease is incurable, chronic, and maddening. Marita often finds herself unable to attend functions or church events because she is too worn out from her part-time job.

She's often begged for healing and continues to pray for a cure. Marita knows God is with her through her struggles, but it's hard for her not to feel frustrated and lonely. She has family who love her unconditionally, but they can't really understand what she goes through on a daily basis.

However, last year, Marita found a lifeline—an internet-based Christian support group that provides a chat room, online articles, and daily devotionals for people with "invisible illnesses." Through networking with other people who deal with debilitating conditions, Marita has found friendship, support—and hope.

Each day when she logs onto the site, Marita hears scripture-based advice, stories, and music that encourage her to keep on keeping on. The site has been a true gift from God, and Marita is thankful.

How could you encourage those with chronic illness? Perhaps you could offer to run errands, babysit their children, or just listen. You might just become a lifeline for someone who feels desperate.

Morning – CLEAR VISION

*So shall the knowledge of wisdom be to your soul; if you have
found it, there is a prospect, and your hope will not be cut off.*
PROVERBS 24:14 NKJV

If you've ever worn glasses, you know what it's like to try to go without them. Talk about a fuzzy world! You take tentative steps, cautiously moving forward, knowing that, at any minute, you might trip over something or knock something down.

Clarity of vision is a wonderful gift. Once you put those glasses on, you can clearly see the road ahead and take bold, big steps. Confidence rises up inside of you as you focus on the path set before you.

In this same way, God can bring clarity/vision to your path when you ask for His wisdom. Picture yourself in a rough situation. You don't know which way to go. You ask for the Lord's wisdom. He offers it, and the road ahead of you is suddenly clear. It's as if you've put on spiritual glasses! That's what His wisdom does—gives definition. Boldness. Confidence. Makes clear the path.

What are you waiting for? No need for a fuzzy road ahead. Put on those glasses, girl, then take a bold step forward!

Evening – WHO AM I IN CHRIST?

For whatever is born of God overcomes the world.
1 JOHN 5:4 NASB

G. K. Chesterton wrote, "The Christian ideal has not been tried and found wanting; it has been found difficult and left untried."

There is a belief today that doing our best to please God is futile and therefore unreasonable. We've even labeled the lack of trying a virtue called "just being me."

Imagine if you applied this philosophy to marriage. A husband stays on the couch, never works, and reasons that he isn't good enough to achieve success, so he isn't going to try. How much more pleased would his wife be if he worked and failed but relentlessly tried anyway?

It is the same in our relationship with Christ. James 1:4 (NASB) admonishes us, "Let endurance have its perfect result, so that you may be perfect and complete, lacking in nothing."

The self on its own can never please God. It will never be more than a sinful personality, and even if that's a relatively "good person," it will always be tainted with a tendency to push pet sins to their limits.

So the real question is not "Who am I?" but rather "Who am I in Christ?"

In Christ you are free; you are an overcomer; you are created for a purpose. You are no longer trapped by the confines of your own abilities because the Holy Spirit empowers you to be so much more.

Morning – ENCOURAGEMENT
FROM THE SCRIPTURES

*For everything that was written in the past was written to teach us,
so that through the endurance taught in the Scriptures and the
encouragement they provide we might have hope.*

ROMANS 15:4 NIV

You know those days when nothing goes right? And sometimes those days stretch into weeks and months? You don't get the promotion. Your car breaks down. Someone you love gets sick. Disappointment settles in and brings its brother, Discouragement. Things are not going according to your plan, and you may wonder if God even hears your prayers.

Looking at the heroes of the Old Testament, you'll see that God's plan for those people wasn't smooth sailing either. Joseph was sold into slavery, falsely accused by Potiphar's wife, and unjustly imprisoned. Moses tended flocks in the wilderness for forty years after murdering a man and before leading God's people out of slavery. David was anointed king but had to run for his life and wait fifteen years before actually sitting on the throne.

Those stories give us hope and encouragement. Our plans are quite different from God's plans, and His ways of doing things are quite different from what we would often choose. We see how things worked out for the people of the Old Testament. We can take encouragement from the fact that the same God is at work in our lives.

Evening – HUNGER FOR GOD'S WORD

*When your words came, I ate them; they were my joy and my
heart's delight, for I bear your name, LORD God Almighty.*

JEREMIAH 15:16 NIV

Why does God tell people to read His Word? He commands this because it is His primary means of communication with His children. Believers are inexorably bound to Him, and because of this great bond, only the will of the Father gives the greatest comfort. Jeremiah's words may seem extreme, but God wants to give a startling picture of what it means to hunger for His words. Jesus while on earth knew the Old Testament scriptures by heart; Paul as a Pharisee may have spent years poring over the books of the law (the first five books of the Bible written by Moses). The disciples too, although mostly poor, came to a deep and saving knowledge of God's words as they listened to Jesus. If people, are God's children, then they also should find delight in reading His Word. They should wrestle with it, analyze it, let it convict and change them; it should be their sustenance just as food and water. Just like earthly hunger cannot be satisfied by eating once a day, His children also continually desire more spiritual growth until they are finally united with Jesus in heaven.

Morning – A HEALTHY BODY

*Beloved, I pray that in all respects you may prosper
and be in good health, just as your soul prospers.*
3 JOHN 2 NASB

If you've ever faced a health crisis or watched a loved one go through a catastrophic illness, you realize the value of good health. There's nothing like almost losing it to realize what you've had all along! In spite of modern technology, great doctors, and the advance of research, health issues persist.

We face seasons where our bodies refuse to cooperate with us. During those times we have to remember who our healer really is. Doctors are great, but ultimately, God is our healer. He longs for us to turn to Him—to trust Him—during our seasons of physical and emotional weakness. He also longs for us to take care of the bodies He's given us. How can we do this? By watching what we put in it and by getting the proper amount of rest and exercise. Our vessels are precious gifts, and we can't afford to wreck them with excessive food or poor nutrition.

If you're in a rough place health-wise, pour out your heart to the Lord. Ask Him to show you the foods that you should be eating and the ones you should avoid. Visit your doctor and get his input, as well. Working as a team, focus on turning your health issues around.

Evening – DO YOU WANT TO BE HEALED?

*When Jesus saw him lying there and learned that he had been in this
condition for a long time, he asked him, "Do you want to get well?"*
JOHN 5:6 NIV

The pool of Bethesda was where disabled people would go, waiting for an angel to stir the waters. The legend went that if someone made it into the water when the angel troubled the waters, that person would be healed. So Jesus' question doesn't seem to make sense. *Of course* the man wants to be healed. He's at a place where people go when they want to be healed.

When Jesus asks a question, it's not because He doesn't know the answer. He asks because He's all-knowing. He's asking it for our benefit.

The man's response to Jesus' question is also interesting. Instead of saying, "Yes, of course! Heal me!" he makes excuses as to why he hasn't been healed.

Isn't that like us? We want to be healed, but we make excuses why we aren't. Jesus is right there waiting to heal us of our wounds, our addictions, our bitterness—anything that keeps us from the best life He has for us. But He doesn't force Himself on us. He asks us, "Do you want to be healed?" We must reach out to Him. We must exercise our faith in Him.

DAY 36

Morning – ENCOURAGE ONE ANOTHER

*Therefore encourage one another and build each
other up, just as in fact you are doing.*
1 Thessalonians 5:11 niv

"Runners, get ready. Set. Go!"

Carol Ann fixed her eyes on the finish line and sprinted ahead in her first-ever Special Olympics race. As she ran, all along the way family members and friends shouted words of encouragement. "Go, Carol Ann! You're doing great! You're almost there!" Carol Ann beamed as she crossed the finish line and fell into the arms of her coach. "Good job!" said the coach as she embraced Carol Ann. "I knew you could do it."

Whether it is a race, a daunting project, or just getting through life, human beings need encouragement. Paul wrote in his letter to the Thessalonians, "Encourage one another. . .build each other up."

Encouragement is more than words. It is also valuing, being tolerant of, serving, and praying for one another. It is looking for what is good and strong in a person and celebrating it. Encouragement means sincerely forgiving and asking for forgiveness, recognizing someone's weaknesses and holding out a helping hand, giving humbly while building someone up, helping others to hope in the Lord, and praying that God will encourage them in ways that you cannot.

Whom will you encourage today? Get in the habit of encouraging others. It will bless them and you.

Evening – DAILY REMINDERS

*[Brothers and sisters,] encourage one another daily, as long as it is called
"Today," so that none of you may be hardened by sin's deceitfulness.*
Hebrews 3:13 niv

Everyone needs reminders about their health. Doctors' offices hang posters to draw attention to healthy habits while patients wait for their appointments—how many minutes of exercise to do, how often to schedule checkups, the right vitamins to take. Though the Bible doesn't have posters, it does remind us how to stay spiritually healthy.

As hard as it is sometimes, sharing our lives with a community of believers is essential to our spiritual health. Hebrews 3 commands us to encourage each other daily, reminding each other of our hope in Christ. Otherwise, we may forget our Savior and turn away from Him in the face of life's difficulties, futilely looking for help elsewhere. Godly encouragement isn't just kind words; its proclamation of truth protects and restores hearts in danger of faltering.

Sometimes it's extremely hard to find the right words to reassure a hurting friend. We all probably recall a time when life was falling to pieces and we weren't eager for a mini-Bible lesson. However, be brave and trust the Spirit; speaking the truth to others as lovingly as we can is a holy duty, a labor of love (Ephesians 4:15). Finally, encouraging others protects us as well—when we share God's goodness and grace with another believer, we remind *ourselves* of the faithful Lord we love and trust.

Morning – FELLOWSHIP

And let us consider how we may spur one another on. . . not giving
up meeting together. . .but encouraging one another.
HEBREWS 10:24–25 NIV

Before his conversion, Paul, then known as Saul, was a thug—a mean-spirited man who hated Christians and wanted them killed. Isn't it amazing that this same man became a great apostle who wrote thirteen books of the New Testament?

The Bible says that immediately after his conversion, Paul spent several days with Jesus' disciples. "At once" he began preaching that Jesus was the Messiah. The Bible also says that Paul became increasingly powerful, and he had followers. He traveled with other Christians, and they encouraged one another in their belief and commitment. Paul enjoyed being with other believers. When in prison, he lamented that he couldn't be with them to share encouragement. Paul understood the importance of fellowship.

Associating with other Christians is more than attending church on Sundays. It is getting to know them on a personal level and discovering what their faith has to offer in fellowship and learning. Paul sought after people whose own gifts would help build his faith. In Romans 1:11–12 (NIV), he writes, "I long to see you so that I may impart to you some spiritual gift to make you strong—that is, that you and I may be mutually encouraged by each other's faith."

Do you have friends who encourage your faith?

Evening – RUN YOUR RACE IN COMMUNITY

Let us draw near to God with a sincere heart. . . . Let us hold unswervingly to
the hope we profess. . . . And let us consider how we may spur one another
on toward love and good deeds, not giving up meeting together, as some
are in the habit of doing, but encouraging one another.
HEBREWS 10:22–25 NIV

God has marked out a journey of faith for each of us. He has also given us a community to help us along this journey. If you look at the verse above, it may seem that the section about "not giving up meeting together" only goes with the "encouraging one another" part. However, grammatically in the Greek, the first three phrases are all the benefit of "not giving up meeting together."

When we remain in community with other believers, we draw near to God. We hold on faithfully to our hope. And we spur each other on.

This section of Hebrews is closely related to Psalm 40:9–10, which talks about sharing with our community how God has saved us, how He has helped us, and how He loves us and is faithful. When we share with each other how God is working in our lives, we are encouraged on our journey. This kind of sharing deepens our faith in God and gives us hope. Take advantage of the community God has placed you in on your journey of faith.

DAY 38

Morning – LOVE IN WORDS AND ACTIONS

" 'Love the Lord your God with all your heart and with all your soul and
with all your mind and with all your strength.' The second is this: 'Love your
neighbor as yourself.' There is no commandment greater than these."
MARK 12:30–31 NIV

I'll let you paint this room in exchange for the guest bed," Marilyn said, "but if you track mud in or get even one drip on the rugs, I'm not giving you the bed. You'll be paying me for the damage!"

"No problem," Jill responded confidently. "The bed looks new. How often did guests sleep in it?"

"Never. Family didn't stay here when they came through town. They didn't stop to visit, either. Some family!"

While Jill worked, she overheard Marilyn with a plumber. "I paid good money for you to fix the clogged drain. A month later, it's clogged again. I expect you to fix this right this time and not charge me more!"

Though it appeared that Jill won in this trade because she got a new bed without a cash outlay and Marilyn won because she could make the guest room into a den by adding furniture, Marilyn is the real loser—in relationships.

As Jesus taught about relationships with others, he took down walls. Jesus gave love, forgiveness, and physical and spiritual healing with- out expecting anything in return from people—men, women, children, the diseased, the poor, or foreigners.

He left us with orders to love all our neighbors—and to show that love in words and actions.

Evening – LOVE YOUR NEIGHBOR AS YOURSELF

" 'And you must love the Lord your God with all your heart, all your soul,
all your mind, and all your strength.' The second is equally important: 'Love
your neighbor as yourself.' No other commandment is greater than these."
MARK 12:30–31 NLT

Look out for number one. It is the message this world sends every day in a million ways. We are bombarded with it. If it feels good, do it. Do what is right for you. But is this the message of God's Word? Nothing could be further from the truth!

We are told to love our neighbors as ourselves. As you would treat your own body, your own heart, treat your neighbor the same. But who is your neighbor? Your neighbor is anyone within your sphere of influence. Those who live near you, certainly. But your neighbors also include your coworkers, friends, relatives, and even strangers on the street. When you make a purchase at a convenience store, treat the clerk as you would like to be treated. When you order dinner at a restaurant, imagine how hard the waitress is working. Treat her with kindness.

Consider others even as Christ considered you on the cross. The greatest commandment of all is to love God, and this goes hand in hand with the second commandment. Love one another. Love your neighbor as yourself.

Morning – SOWING SEEDS

So let's not get tired of doing what is good. At just the right time we will reap a harvest of blessing if we don't give up. Therefore, whenever we have the opportunity, we should do good to everyone—especially to those in the family of faith.

GALATIANS 6:9–10 NLT

Many years ago there was a man named John Chapman. He walked around the United States, planting seeds for apple trees, and so earned the nickname Johnny Appleseed. At the end of his long life, it's reported that he was able to leave his sister over 1,200 acres of nurseries! What a harvest!

In Galatians, the apostle Paul writes that Christians should not get tired of doing good things whenever they have the opportunity. For someday, if they do not give up, *they* will reap a harvest of blessing. The key word in the verses above is *opportunity*. God's daughters are to do good to everyone, *every chance* they get. But to seize that chance, a woman's eyes must be off herself. She must be actively looking around, seeking an opportunity to help someone. When she makes it a habit to survey situations and then serve others—especially fellow believers—she will, like Johnny Appleseed, leave an amazing legacy behind. Not only that, she'll find herself noticing where she can help more and more, all the while reaping a sweet-as-apple-pie reward of God's blessings.

Evening – LEAVING A LEGACY

But the mercy of the LORD is from everlasting to everlasting on those who fear Him, and His righteousness to children's children.

PSALM 103:17 NKJV

Have you given any thought to the legacy you will leave behind after you're gone? If you're a mom or a grandma, you surely have pondered the generations coming up behind you. Maybe you've wondered what, specifically, they will remember about you. If you're not yet married or don't have children of your own, perhaps you could give thought to the legacy you will leave behind to your friends, coworkers, and/or neighbors.

It's an amazing thing to think about God's goodness carrying on from one generation to another, and then another. If you really pause to think it through, the original twelve disciples left a legacy for the early church. Those dedicated believers—in spite of persecution and pain—left a legacy for the next generation, and so on. Without the seeds they planted, the church would surely not have survived.

It's so important to press through. Be a seed planter, no matter how difficult your life. Others are watching and gleaning from your example.

Morning – REJOICE!

Always be full of joy in the Lord. I say it again—rejoice!
PHILIPPIANS 4:4 NLT

Do you feel like life is a fifty-pound backpack? Life can get "heavy" if we aren't careful, with everyday worries wearing us down and making us exhausted. Even small decisions tend to grow in our minds to be more important than they really are. Big decisions can completely take us over so that even the most wonderful news becomes tainted.

Look away from the cares of this world! Rejoice in what the Lord has done! Instead of lending every thought to the troubles at hand, praise God for the ways He has provided in the past and doubtless will again in the future!

Begin to count your blessings, and feel the weight lifting off your shoulders. Feel the freedom you have to enjoy your life. Enjoy your home and the comfort it brings. Enjoy your family, pets, and things you have. Allow yourself to fully feel the joy that comes with the first snow, the first warm breeze of spring, or the first rays of sun in the morning. There are so many wonderful things to enjoy even as you read this!

Life is complicated, yes. But it should never be allowed to rob you of the joy the Lord provides. "I say it again—rejoice!"

Evening – HEART CHECK

Why are you in despair, O my soul? And why have you become disturbed within me?
Hope in God, for I shall yet praise Him, the help of my countenance and my God.
PSALM 42:11 NASB

A woman can be going through her day, minding her own business, and suddenly find herself frowning, discontent. At such times, she would do best to stop whatever she's doing and perform a heart check by asking her inner self, "What's up? What's the matter? Why so down?" She may come up with a specific instance when someone slighted her. Or maybe it's the anniversary of a tragedy in her life. Or maybe it's the holidays, and her mind is filled with voices of those no longer among the living. Or maybe she's just plain blue for no reason at all.

Whatever the cause of her being down, the remedy is certain: She is to tell her inner woman to hope in God. To wait for Him. Because no matter how she feels today or may feel tomorrow, she will in all certainty "yet praise Him"! There's no doubt about it. So, after allowing herself one quick moan, she can turn her "phaser" to "expectation of praise," and squeeze the trigger. Before she knows it, praises will be bubbling up from her heart and come streaming through her lips, turning her frown upside down.

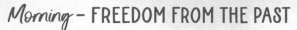

Morning – FREEDOM FROM THE PAST

*[Christ] gave himself for us to redeem us from all wickedness and to purify
for himself a people that are his very own, eager to do what is good.*
TITUS 2:14 NIV

Jim listened to the preacher's call to be saved. As much as his soul cried out, Jim felt too dirty. There were too many terrible things in his past. He wasn't good enough for God, he thought. Finally, the pastor told Jim that God would wash him clean. "Though your sins are as scarlet, they will be as white as snow" (Isaiah 1:18 NASB).

Today, Jim is a deacon and a member of the Gideons. He counsels others who carry similar shame, recounting how God redeemed his life.

Satan uses our mistakes to whisper condemnation: "Look at what you've done! You're not fit for God." But Romans 8:1 (NLT) says, "Now there is no condemnation for those who belong to Christ Jesus."

God redeems your sinful life to use it for His kingdom. Your imperfect past is what gives you compassion for others who struggle. Your teen abortion can help you at crisis pregnancy centers. Your failed marriage can give you a ministry to blended families.

Second Corinthians 1:4 (NLT) says, "He comforts us in all our troubles so that we can comfort others. When they are troubled, we will be able to give them the same comfort God has given us." No past is too terrible. No sin is too great to be used by the redeeming God.

Evening – SIN NO MORE

*He. . .said to them, "He who is without sin among you, let him be the first to throw a
stone at her." . . . When they heard it, they began to go out one by one. . .and He was
left alone, and the woman, where she was, in the center of the court. Straightening up,
Jesus said to her, "Woman, where are they? Did no one condemn you?" She said, "No one,
Lord." And Jesus said, "I do not condemn you, either. Go. From now on sin no more."*
JOHN 8:7, 9–11 NASB

This beautiful passage illustrates Jesus' countercultural treatment of women and His treatment of sinners. The male leaders of the time forcefully brought this adulterous woman into court to degradingly use her as a tool to catch Jesus in a wrong statement. They then planned to brutally stone her. Imagine the fear this woman must have been experiencing, surrounded by a crowd of onlookers in front of a notable teacher of the law.

Instead of condemning her, Jesus poignantly pointed out the sin and hypocrisy of the supposedly pious people who had dragged her to Him. He put this woman, who was worthless in the eyes of the culture, on a level playing field with the leaders of the society. He didn't condone the sin, but rather condemned all sin and loved this broken, scared sinner. He then told her to go and sin no more. This woman, standing alone with Jesus, faced not her condemner, but her Savior.

Christ came not to condemn, but to save. As His daughter, confess your sin; then go and sin no more.

DAY 42

Morning – LINKING HEARTS WITH GOD

"You will receive power when the Holy Spirit comes on you;
and you will be my witnesses. . .to the ends of the earth."
ACTS 1:8 NIV

God knows our hearts. He knows what we need to make it through a day. So in His kindness, He gave us a gift in the form of the Holy Spirit. As a counselor, a comforter, and a friend, the Holy Spirit acts as our inner compass. He upholds us when times are hard and helps us hear God's directions. When the path of obedience grows dark, the Spirit floods it with light. What revelation! He lives within us. Therefore, our prayers are lifted to the Father, to the very throne of God. Whatever petitions we have, we may rest assured they are heard.

We can rejoice in the fact that God cared enough to bless our lives with the Spirit to direct our paths. God loves the praises of His people, and these praises revive the Spirit within you. If you are weary or burdened, allow the Holy Spirit to minister to you. Seek the Holy Spirit and His wisdom, and ask Him to revive and refresh your inner man. Place your hope in God and trust the Spirit's guidance, and He will never let you down.

Evening – WHAT IS HARD?

Good understanding gains favor, but the way of the unfaithful is hard.
PROVERBS 13:15 NKJV

A heart open to understanding indeed gains favor; people will trust and seek her out for comfort and advice. Having an understanding heart is not easy. Why then does Solomon write that the way of the unfaithful is hard? It seems much easier to fall into unfaithfulness, to not bother with trying to understand the hurt or joy of others. On the outset it may seem like less work, but the outcome is bitter.

Faithful followers of God throughout the Bible, especially the psalmists and the prophets, reach a point where they see the wicked prosper while the faithful struggle. They question God's judgment, but they ultimately realize that the prosperity of the wicked is fleeting and that it often comes at the expense of others. While it is hard to remain faithful in this broken world—to read God's Word, to pray, to meet regularly with believers, and to love sacrificially—the path of the unfaithful offers no hope. It is hard: a brutal and self-inflicted separation from the one they were created to be with. We need spiritual eyes to see the consequences as deadly hard. For a growing spiritual awareness and for a heart good at understanding, we also need patience. "Patience, hard thing!" exclaims Gerard Manley Hopkins. But we have a patient Father, who in His "delicious kindness" gives us all we need.

Morning – THE PERFECT AUDIENCE

Listen to my words, Lord, consider my lament. Hear my cry for help,
my King and my God, for to you I pray. In the morning, Lord, you hear my
voice; in the morning I lay my requests before you and wait expectantly.
PSALM 5:1–3 NIV

Greta felt the tug of a small hand on her pant leg.

"Mommy," her toddler, Justin, cried, trying to get her attention.

Her hands were full, putting together peanut butter and jelly sandwiches.

Her oldest daughter gave a shout from the living room, "Mom, the last good strap on my backpack just busted!"

If only I could give each child my undivided attention, she thought. Half an hour later, she shut the door behind her school-age children. "Mommy," Justin called again, "you're not a very good listener." He was right. She leaned down to him. "I'm ready to listen now," she said.

Sometimes it's hard to be the perfect audience for everyone who needs our attention. Thankfully, God is never too busy. He is the perfect audience. He may not reply in your time frame, but He promises to be there every time.

Evening – YOU'VE GOT GOD'S ATTENTION

I will bless the Lord who guides me; even at night my heart instructs me. I know
the Lord is always with me. I will not be shaken, for he is right beside me.
PSALM 16:7–8 NLT

Phone calls, text messages, children shouting your name from down the hall—they can all interrupt and completely end a conversation with someone. Worse yet, once you've regrouped from the distraction, you find that the person you were talking to wasn't even listening in the first place.

Have you ever been in a crowd desperately trying to get someone's attention? Maybe you were telling someone something very important, while they looked over you to see who else was in the room. It can make you feel worthless.

Your heavenly Father would never do that. He loves you and values every moment you are willing to give to Him. You are His focus. His eyes are constantly on you; His ears are tuned to your every word. He's seen every tear you've cried and celebrated every joy of your heart with you.

Even when you feel most alone, you can trust that He is there. He is your constant audience. The more time you spend with Him, the more you will realize that He has a lot to share with you. If you return the favor by giving Him your attention, He will lead you, guide you, and show you things that you'd never discover on your own. He wants to share your life today.

Morning – WAIT EXPECTANTLY

*Listen to my voice in the morning, Lord. Each morning
I bring my requests to you and wait expectantly.*
PSALM 5:3 NLT

Why would the psalmist say he waits *expectantly* upon praying to the Lord each morning? Perhaps it is because he had seen God answer prayers time and time again! When we develop a habit of prayer, of seeking God and presenting Him with our deepest needs, we also learn to expect Him to answer. When we pray, God listens. He shows up. He never fails to hear His children.

Think about a baby who cries out in the night. The baby learns to expect a parent to come and lift him out of the crib to provide comfort, food, or a dry diaper. Babies in orphanages often stop crying. No one comes when they cry. There is no use. The expectation for rescue and provision wanes. Your heavenly Father is eager and ready to meet with you when you come before Him in prayer. The Bible tells us that His eyes are always roaming across the earth, searching for those who are after His own heart. When you lift your requests to the Sovereign God, rest assured that He is ready to answer. Wait expectantly!

Evening – ANSWER ME!

*Answer me when I call to you, my righteous God. Give me relief
from my distress; have mercy on me and hear my prayer.*
PSALM 4:1 NIV

Have you ever felt like God wasn't listening? We've all felt that from time to time. David felt it when he slept in a cold, hard cave night after night while being pursued by Saul's men. He felt it when his son Absalom turned against him. Time and again in his life, David felt abandoned by God. And yet, David was called a man after God's own heart.

No matter our maturity level, there will be times when we feel abandoned by God. There will be times when our faith wavers and our fortitude wanes. That's okay. It's normal.

But David didn't give up. He kept crying out to God, kept falling to his knees in worship, kept storming God's presence with his pleas. David knew God wouldn't hide His face for long, for he knew what we might sometimes forget: God is love. He loves us without condition and without limit. And He is never far from those He loves.

No matter how distant God may seem, we need to keep talking to Him. Keep praying. Keep pouring out our hearts. We can know, as David knew, that God will answer in His time.

Morning – MY MORNING PRAYER

*Let me hear Your lovingkindness in the morning; for I trust in You;
teach me the way in which I should walk; for to You I lift up my soul.*
PSALM 143:8 NASB

Do mornings excite or depress you? "Good morning, Lord!" or "Good Lord, it's morning!" When David wrote Psalm 143, he probably dreaded the sun coming up because that meant his enemies could continue pursuing him and persecuting his soul. "The enemy. . .has crushed my life to the ground" (v. 3). "My spirit is overwhelmed within me; my heart is appalled" (v. 4).

What did David do when he didn't know which way to turn? He turned to the Lord. He stayed in prayer contact with God and meditated on God's faithfulness and righteousness (v. 1), God's past work in his life (v. 5), and His loyal love (vv. 8, 12). He also took refuge in God (v. 9) and continued serving Him (v. 12).

No matter what our day holds, we can face it confidently by practicing verse 8. Let's look for God's loving-kindness and keep trusting Him no matter what. Ask Him to teach and lead us in the way He wants us to go. We have the privilege of offering up our souls (thoughts, emotions, and will) to Him anew each morning. Have a good day.

Evening – RENEWED STRENGTH

*But those who hope in the LORD will renew their strength. They will soar on wings
like eagles; they will run and not grow weary, they will walk and not be faint.*
ISAIAH 40:31 NIV

Several times throughout scripture, the Lord had the writers use the eagle as a comparison to His people. Moses, speaking to the children of Israel just before his death, draws a beautiful picture of the eagle caring for her young. He then compares it to the Lord's leading in our lives. "He found him in a desert land and in the wasteland, a howling wilderness; He encircled him, He instructed him, He kept him as the apple of His eye. As an eagle stirs up its nest, hovers over its young, spreading out its wings, taking them up, carrying them on its wings, so the LORD alone led him, and there was no foreign god with him" (Deuteronomy 32:10–12 NKJV).

Isaiah carries that metaphor a bit further in Isaiah 40. Women seem to be most involved in nurturing their children, and as a result we tire easily. Starting in verse 27 in the Isaiah passage, Isaiah wonders how God's people can say that God is too busy or tired to care for His people. Instead he turns it around and says that even young men and children get tired. Only those who hope in the Lord will He carry on His wings, renewing their strength.

DAY 46

Morning – UNFAILING LOVE

*I will instruct you and teach you in the way you should go; I will counsel
you with my loving eye on you. . . . Many are the woes of the wicked,
but the LORD's unfailing love surrounds the one who trusts in him.*

PSALM 32:8, 10 NIV

How awesome and amazing that the God of all creation wants to instruct us and counsel us personally! He loves each of us individually as if there were only one of us to love. He's watching over us and protecting us. Doesn't that make you want to tell the world about God's unfailing love?

God's love surrounds us always—if we trust in Him. Have you put your complete trust in the Lord? If not, open your heart to Him and ask Him to become the Lord of your life. Jesus is standing at the door of your heart, ready to come in when you respond (Revelation 3:20). Or maybe you've already accepted Christ as your Savior, but you're not really sure if He can be trusted. Know that He has been faithful to His children through all generations and that He is working out every circumstance in your life for your own good (Romans 8:28).

Evening – LOVE'S CURRENT

*The grace of our Lord was poured out on me abundantly,
along with the faith and love that are in Christ Jesus.*

1 TIMOTHY 1:14 NIV

Giving a gift to a loved one often gives us great pleasure. We shop in anticipation of the recipient's excitement in our purchases. When we love that person, our joy can be even greater. So it is with God's love for us. He gave us His Son: a pure and perfect gift, because He loves us in vast measure.

No matter what our attitude may be toward God, we can never forget His precious gift of Jesus Christ. Even if we reflect despair or anger, He loves us. Scripture states grace and love are given abundantly, which means bountifully, plenteously, generously. How can we miss God's love when He is so gracious?

The famous theologian Charles Spurgeon put it this way: "Our God never ceases to shine upon his children with beams of love. Like a river, his lovingkindness is always flowing, with a fullness inexhaustible as his own nature."

This day, rise with the expectation of God's great grace and love. Let your life reflect that love and feel His pleasure. Plunge into the river of His love and feel Him carry you on its current. Relax in His arms in the knowledge that He cares for you.

Morning – MOST SATISFIED

Oh, the depth of the riches both of the wisdom and knowledge of God!
How unsearchable are His judgments and His ways past finding out! "For
who has known the mind of the LORD? Or who has become His counselor?"
"Or who has first given to Him and it shall be repaid to him?" For of Him and
through Him and to Him are all things, to whom be glory forever. Amen.
ROMANS 11:33–36 NKJV

We know that no one has lent God anything, nor has anyone given God advice. We were made in His image, but He is nothing like us and we are nothing like Him.

Everything, from the bright spring breeze to a newborn's laugh, was created by Him. God does not depend on anyone or anything. He is completely self-sufficient. It is because He doesn't rely on anyone that He can love perfectly. How often do we seek man's acceptance over God's acceptance? If we are honest with ourselves, we do this daily. How often are our motives tainted with manipulation because we want to please or be pleased?

God is impervious to manipulation; it is not in His character. He will never tweak His ways to get us to like or accept Him. His complete independency means we can trust His love. He withholds things for our good; He grants things for our good. But don't miss the pinnacle part of Paul's message, "to whom be glory forever." Everything you do as a child of God is for His glory, and everything God does is for His glory. We are most satisfied when God is most glorified.

Evening – TO KNOW HIM IS TO TRUST HIM

Those who know your name trust in you, for you,
O LORD, do not abandon those who search for you.
PSALM 9:10 NLT

Names often reveal the character of a person. This is true in biblical times, especially when it comes to the names of God. A study of His names often brings a deeper awareness of God and who He is. Isaiah, in predicting the birth of Christ, listed several of His names: "For a child is born to us, a son is given to us. The government will rest on his shoulders. And he will be called: Wonderful Counselor, Mighty God, Everlasting Father, Prince of Peace" (Isaiah 9:6 NLT).

In other places He is referred to as Lord Jehovah, Almighty God, Shepherd, Priest, King of kings, and Lord of lords. He is the God who Sees, the Righteous One, Master, Redeemer, the All-Sufficient One. Each name describes a little different attribute or includes the many sides of His character. All are perfectly true about Him.

A study of the names of God, Jesus, and the Holy Spirit not only gives us a deeper insight into the nuances of who He is, but it also strengthens our ability to trust Him implicitly with every detail of our lives. He has promised to reveal Himself to those who truly seek Him out, who truly desire to "know Him and the power of His resurrection and the fellowship of His sufferings, being conformed to His death" (Philippians 3:10 NASB).

DAY 48

Morning – GET UP AND TRY AGAIN

But may the God of all grace, who called us to His eternal glory by Christ Jesus,
after you have suffered a while, perfect, establish, strengthen, and settle you.
1 Peter 5:10 NKJV

Have you ever fallen down in your Christian walk? It doesn't mean you are no longer a Christian, but you stumbled over something in your path that caused you to lose your footing. Perhaps you didn't see the obstacle in time. It's painful to fall, and sometimes it's hard to get up and continue on. While you're lying on the ground spiritually, Satan uses this opportunity to taunt you and accuse you. "You're not really a Christian. If you were, you wouldn't have fallen. You wouldn't have made a mistake. God doesn't need people like you. He's tired of fooling with you. Why don't you just give up?"

Sound familiar? Not only does it sound familiar, but if you're not careful, you will begin to believe it. The shame and remorse you feel because of your shortcoming only add to the lie Satan has just whispered in your ear. Don't listen to any more of his lies. God is a God of grace. The key is to stand up from the place where you have fallen and allow God to restore you, strengthen you, and establish you. He is faithful to His people.

Evening – SECOND CHANCES

"I, even I, am he who blots out your transgressions,
for my own sake, and remembers your sins no more."
Isaiah 43:25 NIV

How many of us have hung our heads low, knowing we really messed up? Wishing we could redo that homework assignment, take back the unkind words that leaped from our mouths without thinking, or even pull back that email message right after we clicked Send. We've all done something we wished we could undo. Often, we think we have failed not only ourselves but also God.

In fact, the Bible is full of people that God used despite their errors. Moses had an anger problem. David was lustful. Jacob was deceptive. The wonderful thing about our faith is that we serve a God of second chances. Not only is He willing, He wants us to confess our sins so He can forgive us. Sing praises for the wonderful blessing of starting over!

Morning – SURRENDERING TO LOVE

Jesus replied, "Anyone who loves me will obey my teaching. My Father will love them, and we will come to them and make our home with them."
JOHN 14:23 NIV

Author and speaker Mary DeMuth has been abused, foreclosed, abandoned, and betrayed—but it was just enough to bring her to a place of surrender, piece by precious piece.

In that surrender, she found the freedom of giving everything to God. In her book *Everything*, Mary writes, "There is always another risk God asks us to take, always another adventure around the corner. But if we stay in the 'good old days,' we won't take the risk or live the adventure today."

What are you afraid of? Who are you afraid of? What is holding you back from serving God with every fiber of your being? Risk trusting Him. Risk believing Him.

The world is dying from lack of God's love; but we are too afraid to reach out, afraid of what it will cost us. We wonder what sacrifices we'll have to make, when He already made the biggest sacrifice.

God is love. And if we love Him, we will obey Him, no matter the cost. Remember, whatever He requires of you, He is big enough to get you through it. Dare to take Him at His word. . .to live fully. . .to obey wholeheartedly.

Evening – STAYING CLOSE

"Be strong and courageous. Do not be afraid; do not be discouraged, for the LORD your God will be with you wherever you go."
JOSHUA 1:9 NIV

It's easy to tell others not to worry. It's easy to remind our friends that God is with them and He's got everything under control. And it's easy to remind ourselves of that when everything's going smoothly.

But when life sails us into rough waters, our natural instinct is to be afraid. We worry and fret. We cry out, not knowing how we will pay the bills or how we will face the cancer or how we will deal with whatever stormy waves crash around us. When life is scary, we get scared.

And believe it or not, that's a good thing. Because when we are afraid, when we are overwhelmed, when we realize that our circumstances are bigger than we are, that's when we're in the perfect place for God to pour out His comfort and assurance on us.

He never leaves us, but sometimes when life is good, we get distracted by other things and don't enjoy His presence as we should. When we feel afraid, we are drawn back to our heavenly Father's arms. And right in His arms is exactly where He wants us to be.

Morning – "HOARDER HOSPITALIZED! COLLAPSED IN WHEELCHAIR WHILE SHOPPING GARAGE SALES!"

Better what the eye sees than the roving of the appetite.
This too is meaningless, a chasing after the wind.
ECCLESIASTES 6:9 NIV

Does this headline warn that garage sales may be hazardous to your health?

No. Nellie's daughter, Ellen, simply reported the where, how, and why of her mother's condition. The sickly woman scarcely wrinkled the flannel hospital sheet that covered her, but her possessions at home—saved for decades—bulged from every cranny.

With Nellie in the hospital and destined to go to an assisted living facility, Ellen attacked one bathroom cupboard with heavy-duty contractor bags. She threw out outdated medicines and creams, broken combs and frayed toothbrushes.

King Solomon, whose wisdom and net worth wowed the world, penned these words of caution about the futility of wanting more.

Heeding this caution isn't easy when the world promotes the grandest vacation, newest car, and best kitchen ever.

Instead, Jesus urged us to focus on building treasures on earth that won't rust, rot, or be stolen. What could be of such great value? Jesus Himself modeled these treasures: when He fed the crowds that followed Him, meeting the needs of those who were hungry, sick, disabled, discouraged. He showed love and kindness, as well as forgiveness and acceptance.

These are all things we can do when we see a need in others.

Hoarding earthly goods leads to trash—not treasure. But taking action to follow Jesus' lifestyle of genuine care for others leads to a priceless investment. And God smiles.

Evening – HOLY BOWL

In that day "HOLINESS TO THE LORD" shall be engraved on the bells of the
horses. The pots in the LORD's house shall be like the bowls before the altar.
Yes, every pot in Jerusalem and Judah shall be holiness to the LORD of hosts.
Everyone who sacrifices shall come and take them and cook in them. In that day
there shall no longer be a Canaanite in the house of the LORD of hosts.
ZECHARIAH 14:20–21 NKJV

If we are honest with ourselves, we don't think of things in terms of "holy" and "unholy." Holiness is a concept that is uncomfortable for most of us. What is holy? We know that God is "holy, holy, holy" and He calls us to be holy. The prophet Zechariah sheds some light on what is holy. Holy is anything consecrated or dedicated to the Lord and for His glory. The high priest used to wear a plaque that had HOLINESS TO THE LORD engraved on it.

Use what you have for God's glory. It doesn't matter if you are a janitor, lawyer, mother, teacher, or brain surgeon. Your skills and gifts are from the Lord and for the Lord.

Morning – HOLY, WHOLLY

But just as he who called you is holy, so be holy in all you do;
for it is written: "Be holy, because I am holy."
1 PETER 1:15–16 NIV

Holiness is one of the most difficult concepts to grasp about God because it is so foreign to us. He is unable to sin, set apart in glorious light. However, we can easily understand why Isaiah fell on his face when he beheld the Lord, feeling his sinfulness weighing heavily upon him (Isaiah 6:5).

Just as the angel cleansed Isaiah's lips, Christ made us His righteous, holy people (1 Peter 2:9). Because Christ has given us His holiness, we don't have to earn it ourselves. For Christians, pursuing holiness isn't fulfilling a set of rules in order to be accepted before God. Instead, it is a heart-deep desire to model our lives after our Savior's perfect example.

Though we are holy in Christ, we still struggle with sin in this life. Where is the Holy Spirit convicting you to practice holiness? Do you have trouble being kind in your words, spoken or unspoken? Are your thoughts filled with peace and thankfulness, or do you struggle with envy? Does the way you treat others honor Christ, especially folks who disagree with you or are different from you?

Don't be discouraged by how you fall short. Our Savior rewards His children who pursue holiness; He will give you grace to learn to practice His ways faithfully.

Evening – STONES OF WORTH

For no one can lay any foundation other than the one we already have—Jesus Christ. Anyone who builds on that foundation may use a variety of materials— gold, silver, jewels, wood, hay, or straw. But on the judgment day, fire will reveal what kind of work each builder has done. The fire will show if a person's work has any value. If the work survives, that builder will receive a reward.
1 CORINTHIANS 3:11–14 NLT

Diamonds and crystal are valuable pieces of rock. But look at precious stones from another viewpoint. Under the inspiration of the Holy Spirit, Paul wrote to the Corinthian church about the materials they were using to build their lives. Of course, Christ is the undisputed foundation of all who claim to follow Him. He is secure, faithful, and everlasting. No life built on Him need fear that the foundation will collapse. It is solid in any and every season. But what is built on top of the foundation has to do with our everyday choices. If we are honoring God and building for eternity, we are using high-priced materials that will last. But if we are focusing on this temporal world, we are throwing together a shack of plywood and thatch, a house that will crumble and dissolve. And the fire of judgment will reveal who really does belong to Him. So today, no matter the month of your birthday, choose the costly materials that will shine for eternity.

DAY 52

Morning – PATIENCE AND PERSISTENCE— THEY DO A BODY GOOD

*Never be lacking in zeal, but keep your spiritual fervor, serving the
Lord. Be joyful in hope, patient in affliction, faithful in prayer.*
ROMANS 12:11–12 NIV

Marnie's eyelids were drooping toward the end of class, even though it was just 5 p.m. She had worked from 6:00 a.m. to 2:00 p.m., rushed home to eat, then traveled to her college classes.

Her professor dismissed class and touched Marnie's arm. "The dean of students wants to see you right away."

Marnie saw the dean studying her college schedule.

"I see that you are taking twenty-one class hours this semester. And you're working full time as well, is that right?"

"Yes."

"We don't advise our students to take more than eighteen credit hours. So we're asking you to drop a couple of classes—for your own good."

"I have straight A's in all my classes. I'm working and paying for college as I go. Just which classes do you think I should drop?"

His mouth snapped shut. "Never mind. Good job!"

Marnie became the only sibling of five to attend college. With the same zeal that she applied to school, she sought God's way for her life while helping those in need.

Paul urges us to persist in our quest for God, following His commands for handling situations and relationships. The path may seem as difficult as Marnie's struggle with full-time work and school. But at graduation, God is waiting there with the words, "Well done, good and faithful servant!" (Matthew 25:23 NIV).

Evening – JUST BE PRESENT

*Then they sat on the ground with him for seven days and seven nights.
No one said a word to him, because they saw how great his suffering was.*
JOB 2:13 NIV

Edna saw a friend rush out of worship on Sunday morning. After the service, she learned that her friend had been called to the hospital by her family. Her husband had been taken by ambulance from his nursing home. Edna asked Pastor Anita if there was anything she could do to help.

Pastor Anita said, "At this point the only thing to do is support the family and pray." Since the pastor had a family dinner to attend, Edna agreed to go and represent the church.

She called ahead and offered to bring food from a drive-through. After picking up their requests, Edna went to the hospital. She asked the family if she could stay and pray for them. They welcomed her presence. Edna sat out of the way and prayed for the Lord's will to be done as He guided the medical professionals and this troubled family.

When Pastor Anita arrived hours later, Edna excused herself and left after sharing hugs.

Like Job's friends, Edna went to sympathize and offer comfort. She accomplished the goal by quietly and patiently sitting with this family. Like Edna, often during emotionally difficult times we give comfort just by our presence. Words aren't required.

Morning – TEMPTED WITHOUT SIN

*Then Jesus was led up by the Spirit into
the wilderness to be tempted by the devil.*
MATTHEW 4:1 NKJV

Christ, being fully God and fully man, could (1) as a man be tempted and (2) as God resist all temptation. But Christ didn't merely refuse to act on Satan's terms and lures; He had no inward desire or inclination to sin, since these in themselves are sin (see Matthew 5:22, 28). We follow a Shepherd who went His entire life without sin. Just because He was fully God does not mean He did not struggle with hunger, pain, or sorrow. We serve a Lord who entered into our humanity and can empathize with us. When we wish to discuss a certain matter—health issues, parenting, relocating our lives—we don't seek sympathy; we wish to hear wisdom and encouragement from someone who has been there. We seek empathy. Our Savior has tread this earth, defeated death and sin. We don't serve an oblivious Lord. Our Lord knows the intricacies of our hearts.

Evening – PRAY FOR HIS WILL

*For this reason, since the day we heard about you, we have not stopped
praying for you. We continually ask God to fill you with the knowledge of
his will through all the wisdom and understanding that the Spirit gives.*
COLOSSIANS 1:9 NIV

Catherine didn't normally worry about her children. They had received a solid Christian foundation and as adults had wisely chosen paths suited to them. Then Cindy brought Seth home. Cindy had always been a self-starter with high personal goals. Cindy with Seth was another story. He appeared to manipulate her.

Catherine had always prayed for supportive Christian spouses for her children. Now Catherine became unyielding in her prayers for Cindy to find the husband God planned for her. Neither Catherine nor her husband felt Seth was that man.

Cindy and Seth dated for six years while finishing college and beginning careers. They were discussing marriage when Seth ended their relationship. Cindy took time off work and came home to lick her wounds.

Catherine listened sympathetically to Cindy's anguish while privately celebrating the relationship's end. Catherine believed the Lord was working in Cindy's life. The following week when Seth called to get back together, Cindy said no.

Two years later, Catherine was lighting a wedding candle for Cindy's marriage to Isaac. Catherine believed her unyielding prayers—for God to lead Cindy to the husband He intended—had been answered. Only through His grace could Cindy have walked away from Seth's controlling ways and found Isaac.

DAY 54

Morning – AN HONORABLE LIFE

*There was a man named Jabez who was more honorable than any of
his brothers. His mother named him Jabez because his birth had been
so painful. He was the one who prayed to the God of Israel, "Oh, that you
would bless me and expand my territory! Please be with me in all that I do,
and keep me from all trouble and pain!" And God granted him his request.*

1 CHRONICLES 4:9–10 NLT

This passage is all that 1 Chronicles has to say about Jabez. He was an honorable man, and God granted him his request. God blessed him, expanded his territory, was with him in all he did, and kept him from trouble and pain. Isn't that amazing?

We can always appreciate the reminder that God hears the honorable. As the psalms show, He doesn't do the same for the wicked. "To the pure you show yourself pure, but to the crooked you show yourself shrewd. You rescue the humble, but you humiliate the proud" (Psalm 18:26–27 NLT). It's important for us to notice that it was because of his good character and respect for the Lord that God noticed and heard Jabez.

We are not asked to be perfect! We are simply asked to live a pure life and to honor the Lord in all we do.

Evening – ETERNAL LIFE NOW

*I am come that they might have life,
and that they might have it more abundantly.*

JOHN 10:10 KJV

Jesus invited people to receive Him as their life. This means future eternal life, which is for real and forever, but also "abundant life" now. He wants to permeate a believer's present consciousness—all our decisions and goals, spending habits, opinions, and use of time. We must realize that our old self has died and Christ is our new life (see Colossians 3:3–4; Galatians 2:20).

Romans 5–8 tells us how to live as Christians, not how to become a Christian, which is the theme of chapters 3–4. The word *believe* occurs twenty-nine times in Romans 3:1–5:2 to show that God's righteousness comes through faith (the Greek word for *believing*). Then the words *live/life* show up twenty-five times in chapters 5–8, where Christians are to experience the resurrection-life (abundant, eternal life now) by resisting sin and pleasing God. Romans 8 does not contrast believers with unbelievers. It speaks of believers who either live according to the flesh (sinful nature) or according to the Spirit (vv. 4, 12–13). What makes the difference? Our minds (vv. 5–7).

Seeing Romans this way may be a new concept, but eternal life is not only our future destination; it should be our present mindset of fellowshipping with Christ daily so we seek His pleasure, not our own. Pleasing Him is the best life.

Morning – THE STRENGTH OF MY HEART

Create in me a pure heart, O God,
and renew a steadfast spirit within me.
PSALM 51:10 NIV

Like most women, you probably pay close attention to your health. Perhaps you guard what you eat to keep your cholesterol down or you head to the gym to burn off excess calories. Maybe you hyperfocus on your clothing size or your BMI. Why? To ensure heart health, of course! Many women eat right, work out at the gym, count calories and carbs, and go for annual check-ups, all in the hope of staying on top of things. Kudos to these health-conscious women! How ironic, then, that so many fail to stay on top of their spiritual heart health. If twenty-first-century women need anything at all, it's a healthy heart. Make a commitment today to keep your spiritual arteries open. No blockages! Let nothing hinder your time with God.

Evening – LEADERSHIP

When he had finished washing their feet, he put on his clothes and returned to his place. "Do you understand what I have done for you?" he asked them. "You call me 'Teacher' and 'Lord,' and rightly so, for that is what I am. Now that I, your Lord and Teacher, have washed your feet, you also should wash one another's feet."
JOHN 13:12–14 NIV

Oh, how we love leading others. . .mostly. There are days when we, as women, lose our way. We push out ahead of others, insisting they should follow us. We look at the end goal without paying much attention to those we're dragging along behind us. We don't see how weary or beaten down they are. We simply want to accomplish what we set out to accomplish. . .at any cost. Today, take a close look at those who are following you. Make sure they're in good shape, spiritually and emotionally. If they're not, focus on their needs, their health, their desires, their goodwill. You will reach your goals that much sooner if everyone on the team is in tip-top shape!

DAY 56

Morning – WHAT DO I NEED?

What is causing the quarrels and fights among you? Don't they come from the evil desires at war within you? You want what you don't have, so you scheme and kill to get it. You are jealous of what others have, but you can't get it, so you fight and wage war to take it away from them. Yet you don't have what you want because you don't ask God for it.
JAMES 4:1–2 NLT

You have probably never schemed to kill anyone, and it's doubtful you have ever declared war. But fighting and quarreling are probably a little more familiar to you. And whether metaphorically or literally, we all have schemed to get what we want, have felt jealous of what others have, and have even waged war against God because of our evil desires.

It has been said that jealousy is wanting what others have, while envy is wanting what others have to be taken away from them. When we focus on the things we don't have, we become bitter and quarrelsome. We may start feeling sorry for ourselves, comparing ourselves to others and wishing we could have what they have. But our energy is focused in the wrong place. Whatever it is you want, ask God. He may not always give you what you ask for, but He will always give you what you need.

Evening – THE COMPARISON TRAP

But let each one examine his own work, and then he will have rejoicing in himself alone, and not in another. For each one shall bear his own load.
GALATIANS 6:4–5 NKJV

In John 21, the apostle John records a conversation Jesus had with Peter shortly after His resurrection. Jesus prepared a breakfast for His disciples after a night of fishing. Then Jesus invited Peter to go for a walk. Just days before, Peter had denied knowing Jesus. Now, three times Jesus asked Peter if the fisherman-turned-disciple loved Him. By asking this question, Jesus not only let Peter know that he was forgiven for his lapse of faith, but also He let Peter know that God still had a purpose and plan for Peter. He also spoke of how Peter would eventually die for His gospel.

Peter, maybe a little embarrassed by all the attention he was getting, looked over his shoulder and saw John following them. Peter asked the Lord, "What about him? How will he die?" Peter fell into the comparison trap.

Jesus answered, "What does it matter to you what I have planned for another? Live your life according to My plan. That's all you need to be concerned about."

And that's all Jesus still requires of His followers. God has a unique plan and purpose for each one, equipping them as they keep their eyes on Him and follow Him daily.

Morning – REDEMPTION STORIES

Let the redeemed of the LORD tell their story.
PSALM 107:2 NIV

For just about as long as the entertainment industry has been around (or longer), redemption stories have been the basis for popular movies and novels and plays. Everyone loves to follow the story of the bad guy turned knight in shining armor, the down-on-his-luck everyman who receives big blessings, the orphan in rags who gains a family and great riches all at once.

If you are a follower of Christ, there's a good chance you've had to exchange something for the path to eternal life. You've had to let something go or give something up. Or perhaps you've been changed in some significant way. No one encounters Jesus Christ and comes away exactly the same.

Let these words encourage you today to tell your story. If you have not told it before, start now. Pick a few small details to share, or give the whole general outline. Tell a loved one. Tell a coworker. Tell your pastor. Tell a friend. Tell a stranger on the subway. Tell anyone who will listen.

You never know how your story might impact someone else. You will never know the strength and love and hope you have to give until you open your mouth and let your truth out.

Everyone loves a redemption story. Why not give them yours?

Evening – THE OLD, OLD STORY

I have inherited Your testimonies forever, for they are the joy of my heart.
PSALM 119:111 NASB

Aren't family stories the best? No family reunion would be complete without their telling. For the hundredth time, Grandma tells of the day she and Grandpa met, Grandpa tells what it was like to storm the gates of Normandy, and everyone laughs about the day when Susie sold the neighbor's dog for a quarter. These family stories provide us with a sense of connection and identity. They link us with family members who died before we were born and give us common ground. In a sense, we inherit the stories of our families. We don't have to experience the event to relish the details as if we were there.

And so it is with the testimony of God. No, we weren't there when He parted the Red Sea and carried the Israelites out of captivity. We weren't with Moses when he received the Ten Commandments, nor were we with young David when he killed the giant. But as God's children, we have inherited these testimonies. These stories are a part of our legacy and give us a common connection with believers throughout the centuries—our brothers and sisters in Christ. Relish the stories of God; they are the joy of your heart.

DAY 58

Morning – HUMILIATING MOMENTS AS RAW CLAY

All the paths of the Lord are lovingkindness and truth
to those who keep His covenant and His testimonies.
Psalm 25:10 nasb

Did you know that God wants to use even our humiliating experiences to transform our character?

In *The Message*, the psalmist says, "I learned God-worship when my pride was shattered" (51:16). The Creator is an artist. If He can't redeem our worst moments, there will be a lot of material that goes unused. God wants to take our failures and lovingly, like a potter sculpts raw clay, mold them into something beautiful.

As our sin-bearer, Jesus endured one of the most painful, visible humiliations the world has ever seen. And yet—through His death, eternal life became available to us. And as human beings with many faults, we will experience visible and painful humiliations, either through our own sins, others' poor choices, or our foolish decisions. But whatever the cause of our embarrassment, when we surrender to God, He can turn it into a tool for our transformation.

Beth Moore, in her Bible study *Breaking Free*, writes, "Let God have your failures. Surrender to Him your. . .most humiliating defeats. God and God alone can use them to make you twice the warrior you ever dreamed you'd be."

Evening – A HUMBLE PRAYER

Then King David went in and sat before the Lord; and he said: "Who am I,
O Lord God? And what is my house, that You have brought me this far?"
2 Samuel 7:18 nkjv

A rather obnoxious man stood in line at an airport, getting angry at the slow-moving queue. Finally, he shoved his way to the front counter, demanding to be waited on.

"I'm sorry, sir," the attendant said, "but you'll have to wait your turn."

Incensed, the man demanded, "Young lady, do you know who I am?"

The woman calmly picked up the microphone and announced, "Ladies and gentlemen, there is a man at the front counter who doesn't know who he is. If anyone can identify him, will you please step to the front of the line and help us out?"

Contrast this man's boastful self-image with David's humility. He asked God: "Who am I, that you would bless my family like this?"

David's prayer exemplifies the respect we should have in approaching God. A proper relationship with God changes a person's attitude from *Do you know who I am?* to *Lord, thank You for knowing who I am.* The first question focuses on us; the second focuses on God's perfection, omnipotence, and graciousness at allowing us to be in His holy presence.

Morning – CONSIDER THE SOURCE

The heart of the discerning acquires knowledge,
for the ears of the wise seek it out.
PROVERBS 18:15 NIV

Joy asked her eight-year-old daughter why she had tried to climb the tree that she fell from. Lily looked up from the cast on her broken arm and tearfully admitted that the neighbor boy had told her to climb the tree, so she thought it would be okay. Joy explained to Lily the importance of considering the source of information before making a decision. Although the neighbor boy was two years older, Lily would have been wise to double-check with an adult. Lily was suffering the consequences of being gullible.

Like Lily, we need to consider the source of information. In the current age of twenty-four-hour news coverage, the same story is reported over and over. It's easy to believe that it must be true when we hear or read a story repeatedly. However, we need to listen with care to what is actually said. People can stretch or omit parts of the truth to sensationalize or distort a story. Discerning listeners use their minds and available resources to verify information before they accept its truth. At a minimum, an internet search engine can be used for research.

We don't need to doubt the word of God; we need to doubt the words of man. We need to take time to consider the source of information and wisely seek its confirmation.

Evening – THE SPIRIT OF TRUTH

"If you love me, keep my commands. And I will ask the Father, and he will
give you another advocate to help you and be with you forever—the Spirit of
truth. The world cannot accept him, because it neither sees him nor knows
him. But you know him, for he lives with you and will be in you."
JOHN 14:15–17 NIV

Turn the other cheek. Love your enemies. Do good to those who hurt you. Give generously. Don't be anxious. Store up treasures in heaven. In the Sermon on the Mount (Matthew 5–6), Jesus presents a perspective on living that must have confused many of His listeners.

For those who don't know or recognize the Holy Spirit, Jesus' teachings don't make any sense. They are countercultural and go against the grain of natural instinct. When Christians are able to forgive those who have hurt them, give generously, or refuse to follow the latest trends and fashions, the world gets confused. To those who don't have the Holy Spirit, these seemingly extraordinary actions must seem unreal, impossible even. Knowing the Holy Spirit makes all the difference. When the Holy Spirit lives in us, we can finally see truth. We have the advocacy and the help we need to follow Jesus' commands—and they make all the sense in the world.

Morning – GOING AGAINST THE FLOW

Whoever claims to live in him must live as Jesus did.
1 JOHN 2:6 NIV

In 2011 NBC News aired a story about an unemployed man who was mining for gold and diamonds on a busy sidewalk outside a handful of prominent Manhattan jewelry stores. The news showed him peering into a crack in the sidewalk while holding a magnifying glass and a tiny broom.

The report stated that some people who walked into the jewelry store later emerged with tiny pieces of lost gold and diamonds, which had fallen off clothes and rings, attached to their shoes. These tiny treasures were then deposited in the sidewalk cracks.

This ingenious man saw what others couldn't see.

When God has called you to do something for Him, you may see what others can't. God will give you a plan for the future. He will call you to a particular task, and others won't be able to see—or envision—what you see. And because they can't see what you see, they may think you are unwise or uninformed, which means you will have to go against the flow.

Jesus' walk was characterized by obedience to His Father even when others didn't agree. He went against the flow. Will you follow His lead?

Evening – WHICHEVER HAND YOU USE

He has made everything beautiful in its time.
ECCLESIASTES 3:11 NKJV

They've been called lefties or southpaws and probably a few other names. They have been forced to adapt to a right-handed world in the way they write, use scissors, play sports, etc., yet they are more likely to be geniuses.

Left-handers make up about 10 percent of the population. And while it is good to be sensitive to the specific issues faced by others, perhaps we can use left-handedness to emphasize something else that is true for all of us.

The Bible tells us that each human being is uniquely precious to God. And He endows us with the traits we need to fulfill His purpose for our lives. Left-handedness is one of those gifts. In Judges 20:16, scripture records the existence of an elite group of warriors in the tribe of Benjamin. These seven hundred men were all left-handed, and "each of them could sling a rock and hit a target within a hairsbreadth without missing" (Judges 20:16 NLT). These guys used their differentness as an advantage.

You may not be left-handed, but there is something about you that is different from others around you. Give that to God and let Him develop it into something special He can use to strengthen you and bless others.

Morning – CLEANING THE PANTRY OF YOUR SOUL

*Brethren, I count not myself to have apprehended: but this one thing I do,
forgetting those things which are behind, and reaching forth unto those things
which are before, I press toward the mark for the prize of the high calling of God
in Christ Jesus. Let us therefore, as many as be perfect, be thus minded: and if
in any thing ye be otherwise minded, God shall reveal even this unto you.*

PHILIPPIANS 3:13–15 KJV

Businessman and minister John G. Lake once said, "Beloved, if any unholiness exists in the nature, it is not there by the consent of the Spirit of God. If unholiness is in your life, it is because your soul is giving consent to it, and you are retaining it. Let it go. Cast it out and let God have His way in your life."

As you grow in Christ, you will find that old thinking has to go to make room for the new understanding of God's desires and plans for your life. It's cleaning the pantry of your soul. Old mindsets and habits are like junk food or packages with expired dates. As you throw out the old, you find the new thoughts and habits bring renewed life and strength in Christ.

Evening – FEELING DISAPPOINTED?

*Though the fig tree does not bud and there are no grapes on the vines, though the olive
crop fails and the fields produce no food, though there are no sheep in the pen and no
cattle in the stalls, yet I will rejoice in the LORD, I will be joyful in God my Savior.*

HABAKKUK 3:17–18 NIV

One of my best friends can always tell when her kids have been in the kitchen after school because there are little fingerprints on the refrigerator. How can you tell that the enemy of your soul has been at work? You can see his fingerprints of disappointment which lead to discouragement, then depression, and finally defeat. According to author Vicki Kraft, the best time to stop the slippery slope to negative emotions is when feelings of disappointment come knocking. The solution? Praise God.

Praise Him that He is at work. Praise Him that He hasn't left you. Praise Him for what He has done. Praise Him for what He is going to do. Praise Him in song. Praise Him with a shout. Like the psalmists did, don't ignore your disappointment, but don't wallow in it in unbelief, either, by lifting your burden to God without throwing in a healthy dose of thanksgiving.

DAY 62

Morning – CLOTHED

She is clothed with strength and dignity; she can laugh at the days to come.
PROVERBS 31:25 NIV

You, as a daughter of the Most High, are clothed with strength and dignity. In those moments when you feel particularly vulnerable and naked, just remember—you are clothed with the strength that God gives you and with the dignity of being His image bearer.

Many things and people in this life can belittle and degrade you. But no matter what the circumstance, you are valued because you are one of God's children. Just like a child who looks so much like his father that it's obvious they're family, you bear your heavenly Father's image. You clearly belong to Him and are loved by Him as part of His family. The value and dignity that God places on you are more significant than whatever the society or anyone else tells you your value is.

Even when you feel totally beaten down and think there is no way you can continue, all you need to do is ask for God's strength. He will clothe you in it to cover up all your vulnerability and brokenness.

No wonder the woman in this verse could laugh at the future. She knew that in God she had limitless strength and a dignity that no one could take away. Nothing in her future, or yours, could change that.

Evening – PROMISES

*Let us hold fast the confession of our hope
without wavering, for He who promised is faithful.*
HEBREWS 10:23 NASB

In this life, you can have endurance and hope because your God is faithful to keep His promises. The Christian life would be hopeless if God were not faithful and trustworthy. But He will absolutely keep His promises. You can (and do) bet your life on that.

God has promised to complete and perfect the good work He has started in you (Philippians 1:6). He will never leave you or forsake you (Hebrews 13:5). He has promised that He will wipe away every tear from your eyes and that in heaven there will no longer be any mourning or crying or pain (Revelation 21:4). He will never allow you to be separated from His love (Romans 8:38–39). He promises that He will come again and that you will be with Him forever (1 Thessalonians 4:16–17). He assures you that no one can take you from His hand (John 10:29).

These are just some of the promises God has made. These aren't just nice sentiments. These are things that God will, without question, bring to pass. He does not break His promises—He will do what He has said He will do. You can put your hope in these promises, knowing that you won't be disappointed.

Morning – BE FILLED WITH JOY

*Now the God of hope fill you with all joy and peace in believing,
that ye may abound in hope, through the power of the Holy Ghost.*
ROMANS 15:13 KJV

Are you fighting a battle that seems futile? Have you lost hope of seeing a resolution? Take heart, you're not alone. Paul, the writer of today's verse, knew about battles, persecution, and rejection. He spent a lot of time writing his messages of hope while in jail. You may not be in a physical jail, but Satan may have you bound in a spiritual prison. It's time to break out of jail and be the victorious Christian you want to be. "How can I do that?" you ask. Look at what Paul wrote:

1. We serve a God of hope. Trust Him to supply you with hope to make it during dark days.
2. God is your source. Rely on Him to fill you with joy and give you peace in the time of trouble.
3. Believe that God is who He says He is, that He has made a way for you through His Son, Jesus.
4. Allow the Holy Ghost to empower you to abound in hope. We are often powerless to conquer our problems, but God's Spirit can arise within us to make us overcomers.

Push the darkness away. God is on your side. Allow Him to work for you.

Evening – EXPECT THE UNEXPECTED

*Then, leaving her water jar, the woman went back to the town and said to the people,
"Come, see a man who told me everything I ever did. Could this be the Messiah?"*
JOHN 4:28–29 NIV

In this story of the woman at the well, Jesus did the unthinkable by talking to a woman, which was not something men did in that time if they were not related to the woman. And He wasn't talking to just any woman but to a woman of ill repute—a fact the woman herself pointed out.

When she took up her jar to get water at the town well, timed to avoid the respectable women who drew water earlier, she had no idea how one conversation would change her life. It is easy to get comfortable in our routines and not look for the unexpected in our walk with Jesus. Like the woman at the well, we come to Him for one thing and get so much more.

Just as Jesus told the woman to leave her past behind and move forward, He wants us to move into the future He has for us, to move beyond just asking for one thing, and to change our thinking into serving Him and telling others about Him.

DAY 64

Morning – KEEPING GOOD SECRETS

*"Be careful not to practice your righteousness in front of others to be seen
by them. If you do, you will have no reward from your Father in heaven."*
MATTHEW 6:1 NIV

"I insist on knowing who is responsible for this!" the general store's owner, Clara, demanded. When she talked, even the ancient rafters of her establishment trembled. You would have thought her outburst was caused by a broken window, a noticeable amount of goods shoplifted, or a burglary at the store.

Instead, she held a decorated paper bag filled with homemade cookies, child-made window decorations sparkly with glue and glitter, a comb, a small bag of pistachios, and a card.

Her employee, Robbie, offered timidly, "There were some little kids tiptoeing around town not long ago. They had a bunch of bags."

In a town so small, secrets were hard to keep. "So it must be that kids' church group. Well," she said, her tone softening, "that was a nice thing to do for me."

Though Clara was not in need of cookies—she was in emotional need—she needed to know that God loves even her.

Jesus added to the concept of giving in secret by explaining that if we are giving to the needy, we are not to make it a public show. Giving to the poor and making payments of tithe were often accompanied by trumpets. But such actions were for show only. The donors felt no compassion or kindness toward the poor.

Jesus cares what we think when we give. Why are we doing it? For God or for us?

Evening – THE GIFT OF PRAYER

*First of all, then, I urge that entreaties and prayers, petitions and thanksgivings, be made
on behalf of all men. . . . This is good and acceptable in the sight of God our Savior.*
1 TIMOTHY 2:1, 3 NASB

There is such joy in giving gifts. Seeing the delight on someone's face to receive something unexpected is exciting. Perhaps the absolute greatest gift one person can give to another doesn't come in a box. It can't be wrapped or presented formally, but instead it is the words spoken to God for someone—the gift of prayer.

When we pray for others, we ask God to intervene and to make Himself known to them. We can pray for God's plan and purpose in their lives. We can ask God to bless them or protect them. You can share with them that you are praying for them or do it privately without their knowledge. Who would God have you give the gift of prayer to today?

Morning – THE DEEP END

*I would have lost heart, unless I had believed that I would
see the goodness of the Lord in the land of the living.
Wait on the Lord; be of good courage, and He shall
strengthen your heart; wait, I say, on the Lord!*
PSALM 27:13–14 NKJV

A woman is often caught off guard when grief crashes upon her with the loss of a deeply loved one. In those times, she can look to God, her major consolation, her refuge, her true and steady rock. For His Word has an amazing power to reach out, to heal, to catch her heart—and breath.

The words of Psalm 27:13–14 contain such power. They are an amazing balm to help heal a woman's heart torn by loss. For her, they serve as a reminder that good times will one day come again. That God is working in this life, on this earth, among these people. That the pain *will* subside, and then God can begin the healing.

Her part? To not give in to despair. To remain strong and brave. That doesn't mean not shedding a tear, for there will be plenty. But to know, deep down, where deep calls to deep, that she is not alone. That Jesus, sitting right beside her, is also weeping. And that one day, she and her loved one will both rise again. That one day, she will bear a lighter heart and the beginning of a smile.

Evening – WE HAVE HOPE IN CHRIST

*And if our hope in Christ is only for this life,
we are more to be pitied than anyone in the world.*
1 CORINTHIANS 15:19 NLT

Karen's heart was broken at the unexpected loss of her husband. Ken had been the focus of her world and they had shared a close relationship. She kept wringing her hands and asking, "What am I going to do?" With her husband gone, Karen felt she had nothing to live for. She loved her children and grandchildren and spent time with them, but they couldn't fill the void left by Ken's absence. She was without hope, a woman to be pitied.

Losing anyone we love can be a devastating experience, but as Christians, we know there is still life in Christ. Our families are important to us, but Christ must be the main focus of our lives. He has promised us eternal life if we're faithful to Him and endure until the end.

If our hope is built on our life here on earth, we will be miserable when trouble strikes. We will have nothing to stand on. An old hymn says, "On Christ the solid rock I stand, all other ground is sinking sand." Life as we know it here will someday pass away, but eternal life in Christ gives us hope for the future. "My hope is built on nothing less than Jesus' blood and righteousness."

DAY 66

Morning – LESSONS FROM THE PAST

"While I was fainting away, I remembered the Lord."
JONAH 2:7 NASB

Corrie Ten Boom once said, "Memories are not the key to the past. They are the key to the future."

This year **may** have been filled with beautiful nostalgia, or you may have come face-to-face with tragedy. Don't block out the bad memories and avoid the pain; rather, make an assessment of where you are. Consider the devastation of your dreams and seek the parts of you that are still alive.

Just as the farmer's land must be turned over and fertilized to make ready for a new crop, God is using each event in your life to make your heart ready to bear spiritual fruit.

Give thanks for all the blessings—and for suffering. Pray and believe in faith for what God has planned in your future.

For those who have hurt you, consider how you may return a blessing for Christ's sake. For those who have abused their power, pray for them. For those you have offended, seek the best way to make peace and find forgiveness.

Romans 8:28 (NLT) says, "God causes everything to work together for the good of those who love God and are called according to his purpose for them."

When we reflect on our lives, it isn't for the sake of self-pity or shame but to exercise our faith. You will be amazed as you watch God unfold His promises.

Evening – THANK YOU, LORD

I will praise the Lord at all times. I will constantly speak his praises.
PSALM 34:1 NLT

While imprisoned, the apostle Paul gave thanks to God, even singing His praises, and it resulted in the salvation of the jailers. What a great lesson for every Christian—when you feel least like giving thanks, that's precisely when you should!

What is your response when you find yourself trapped in traffic, late for a meeting, frustrated in your plans, sick in bed, hurting emotionally, overwhelmed with work, lonely, tired, or confused? Our human nature teaches us we should gripe and fret. Yet scripture says we should give thanks. Only when we surrender our lives to Him and His control is this possible.

Learn to thank Him. Thank Him for being your help in time of trouble. Thank Him for His great wisdom and power. And thank Him for causing every situation in your life to work together for your good.

Giving thanks may not change your circumstances significantly, but it will change you. You'll feel yourself focusing on God—His goodness, kindness, and grace—rather than your own anger, pride, sickness, or inconvenience. Maybe that's why it's such fertile soil for miracles. The biblical commentator Matthew Henry stated it well: "Thanksgiving is good, but thanks-living is better."

Morning – FULLY EQUIPPED

His divine power has given us everything we need for a godly life through our knowledge of him who called us by his own glory and goodness. Through these he has given us his very great and precious promises, so that through them you may participate in the divine nature, having escaped the corruption in the world caused by evil desires.
2 PETER 1:3–4 NIV

As Christians, we are fully equipped to live a godly life on earth. We don't have to live in a state of constant confusion. We don't have to stress about what to do or how to live. God has given us everything we need to be able to follow Him daily.

Second Corinthians 1:21–22 (NIV) tells us that "he anointed us, set his seal of ownership on us, and put his Spirit in our hearts as a deposit, guaranteeing what is to come." When we accept Christ as our Savior and Lord of our life, God gives us *His Spirit*! He places *His very own Spirit* in *our* hearts! Isn't that amazing? Take some time to fully reflect on that!

John 15:26 (NKJV) calls the Holy Spirit our "Helper." We are never alone. God's Spirit is right there with us as we make decisions, as we go about our day, as we face trials, and as we enjoy His blessings. We have a constant helper everywhere we go!

Evening – LOOK WHO IS CHEERING YOU ON!

Therefore, since we are surrounded by such a huge crowd of witnesses to the life of faith, let us strip off every weight that slows us down, especially the sin that so easily trips us up. And let us run with endurance the race God has set before us.
HEBREWS 12:1 NLT

Meagan's boss let her know he needed her to make phone calls to inform customers of a delay in shipping of items they had ordered. The company needed her to fill the gap since a wave of the flu had left them extremely short-handed. He knew this would be difficult for Meagan but encouraged her to step outside her comfort zone.

Numbers? She got. People—not so much! Meagan felt a wave of nausea pass into the pit of her stomach. She took a deep breath and tried to press through it. She bowed her head and asked God for strength.

Perhaps there are things that you have to do that are outside your comfort zone. Remember that you have a crowd of faithful witnesses cheering you on. His strength is perfect to get you through.

Morning – THE MOMENT YOU PRAYED

*"As soon as you began to pray, a word went out, which I have
come to tell you, for you are highly esteemed. Therefore,
consider the word and understand the vision."*
DANIEL 9:23 NIV

Megan had been challenged by a sermon on financial stewardship one Sunday. She and her husband had been setting aside some tithe money for a return mission trip to Poland, but it didn't look like they would be able to go. She began praying right away about what to do with the money and quickly felt nudged to give a large portion of it to the church building project where they had hoped to return for the short-term mission.

That afternoon she told her husband what she was praying over. Right away he felt good about the idea and suggested the same amount she had thought to give. That evening she emailed the pastor and his wife in Poland to let them know what they were going to send.

The pastor's wife shared that their church body in Poland had been praying specifically for God to move hearts to give to their building project. Megan asked what time the Poland church service was and discovered that it was the exact time that she and her husband were talking about what to give.

Evening – PRAY ABOUT EVERYTHING

The LORD directs the steps of the godly. He delights in every detail of their lives.
PSALM 37:23 NLT

When Jennifer passed her six-year-old daughter's bedroom one morning, she saw the little girl kneeling by her bed praying. Jennifer decided not to interrupt her, but she was curious. Bedtime prayers were routine in their household, and she had never seen her daughter kneel and pray in the morning. Later, Jennifer asked Marissa why she had prayed.

"Did I do something wrong?" Marissa wondered.

"No, honey!" Jennifer said. "I just wondered what you were praying about."

"My tooth," said Marissa. "I told God that my tooth is getting loose, and I'd rather have it come out at home than at school."

The Bible says that the Lord delights in every detail of His children's lives. And no matter how old a believer is, they are and always will be God's child.

Adult prayers don't have to be well ordered and formal. God loves hearing His children's voices, and no detail is too little or dull to pray about. Tell God that you hope the coffeehouse will have your favorite pumpkin-spice latte on their menu. Ask Him to give you patience as you wait in line. Thank Him for how wonderful that coffee tastes! Get into the habit of talking with Him all day long, because He loves you and delights in all facets of your life.

Morning – GOD MAKES US BEAUTIFUL

For the LORD takes pleasure in his people;
he will beautify the humble with salvation.
PSALM 149:4 NKJV

Standing in front of a magazine rack can be depressing if you believe everything on the front covers. Women in skimpy clothes with long, flowing locks and perfect figures adorn most periodicals. The article titles are just as daunting: "How to Have the Body of Your Dreams in 30 Days," "What Men Really Want in a Woman," and "Lose 10 Pounds in a Week." Their information on how to be beautiful and be the perfect woman tempts a lot of women into buying the latest issue, thinking it will solve their problems.

The world's definition of beauty is a far cry from God's. We were created in His image, made in His likeness. There's nothing wrong with trying to lose weight, buying a new dress, or getting our hair cut. We all want to look and feel our best—but not by the world's standard. Trying to measure up to others leads to disappointment and low self-esteem.

As God's children, we are made beautiful through Him. It's not a physical beauty like the world lauds. It's an inner loveliness that comes through knowing Christ. We take on a beauty the world can't understand or achieve. To those who know us and love us, we are beautiful women because of God's Spirit within us, radiating a beauty beyond human imagination.

Evening – GOD SEES YOUR BEAUTY ALWAYS

For you created my inmost being; you knit me together in my mother's
womb. I praise you because I am fearfully and wonderfully made.
PSALM 139:13–14 NIV

As Brenda prepared for work, she noticed cars and people crowding her neighbors' lawn. They were having a large yard sale.

"How much for the oak dresser?" she asked Marlene, indicating the neglected piece pushed up against the house.

Her neighbor glanced at the tall antique dresser with a beveled mirror that had been stored for years. She cringed at the broken drawer pulls and the lumpy black finish. Besides noticeable kid scratches, one gleeful grandchild had left a permanent marker scribble on the top.

"Sorry. It's in terrible condition. Five bucks."

Brenda saw instead the graceful lines. She visualized new glass drawer pulls set in a glowing chestnut finish. Beauty was locked inside the vintage piece.

Weeks later, after much stripping, sanding, patching, and staining, Brenda finished the antique dresser. Marlene stopped by. Her neighbor was astonished. "I should have asked you for more." And Brenda just smiled.

Just as Brenda invested time, skill, and patience to bring out the dresser's best, God too sees our potential and brings out the best. His sanding and finish work take away any ugliness and create a glow that all can see and that no cosmetic makeover can give.

DAY 70

Morning – HOPE TO THE FULL

Now may the God of hope fill you with all joy and peace in believing,
that you may abound in hope by the power of the Holy Spirit.
ROMANS 15:13 NKJV

Paul wrote this prayer in the context of explaining his ministry to non-Jewish Christians who could now believe that Jesus came for them as well. Throughout his letter to the Romans, Paul writes of the relationship between Jewish and Gentile Christians, encouraging them to work together since both groups clung to the hope that the Messiah brings. This is hope in a God who has a plan filled with love for creation, hope that He will bring things together in blessing for His followers, and final hope in His return to bring His children in forever-union with their Maker.

Paul knew that at times belief in these truths could wane and they needed to hope. What is most beautiful about the prayer is that Paul did not ask his readers to try to foster and maintain hope on their own, but rather that they would look to God, the source of hope. In sticking to and living out our faith, God fills us with hope (He helps us with the sticking and living out part also). Joy and peace in what we believe allows us, with the help of the Spirit, to live hope filled no matter the circumstance. And we abound, living fully, in the faith that things will turn out all right in the end.

Evening – FORGIVENESS

But Esau ran to meet Jacob and embraced him; he threw his
arms around his neck and kissed him. And they wept.
GENESIS 33:4 NIV

Jacob cheated Esau out of his birthright and the father's blessing reserved for the eldest son. Jacob's act changed both their lives forever. Esau hated Jacob for his deception and betrayal. His anger ran so deep that he planned to kill Jacob and would have had Jacob not fled for his life. Jacob stayed away for twenty years and then started for home even though he feared Esau. What a surprise when Esau ran to meet him and threw his arms around Jacob. He had forgiven Jacob even though his betrayal had been a cruel one.

Forgiveness isn't always easy. Sometimes the hurt is deep and the pain lingers for a long time. The other person seems to get on with her life while you suffer. Esau could have hung on to his anger and killed Jacob when he saw him coming. Instead, he took the first step and ran to meet Jacob, forgiving him. We too can take the first step toward forgiveness. In doing so, we let go of the pain we've been carrying. We find freedom for ourselves and offer the same to the one who hurt us. Is there someone you need to forgive today? Take the first step toward reconciliation. God will give you the strength to go the full distance.

Morning – THE HARD WORK OF HUMILITY

So, as those who have been chosen of God, holy and beloved, put on a
heart of compassion, kindness, humility, gentleness and patience.
COLOSSIANS 3:12 NASB

Miranda spent her life in the shadow of her older sister. For many years, teachers compared her to Megan, asking, "I hope you're going to be as smart as her!" It discouraged and frustrated Miranda.

She chose a different college and career from Megan in order to get away from hurtful comments and unrealistic expectations. She also struggled with resentment and anger toward her sister, who had done nothing wrong. One weekend, however, at a discipleship conference for young singles, Miranda heard a sermon about humility which convicted and challenged her.

"Have you been overlooked and underappreciated?" the preacher asked. "Perhaps instead of bemoaning that fact, you could consider that in some small way, you've been identifying with Christ. He gave up heaven and all its rewards to come to earth as a tiny, human baby. Our own humiliations and lack of accolades can't really compare."

Humility is about surrender, the preacher continued, to the Lord's plan and ways. It's also about being gentle and kind with others who mistreat us and about our perspective as servants of the Most High God. Miranda prayed as tears fell from her face: *Forgive me for letting my exasperation cloud my relationship with Megan. Thank You for a chance to see it all differently.*

Evening – THE REASON MANY RELATIONSHIPS FAIL

"There is no one righteous, not even one."
ROMANS 3:10 NIV

When someone fails to love the way God desires, they may not have recognized this great flaw in their character because it was hidden behind blame as they made copious mental notes about the shortcomings of their beloved. And these shortcomings have led the lover to believe they cannot love their beloved because it's impossible. *If only she wasn't so insensitive. . . If only he was more complimentary. . . If only she took better care of herself. . . If only he was more supportive. . .then I could love.*

This way of thinking is unwise. Another's flaws—and even sin—may stretch or test our love and even make us feel like it's impossible to love. But another's imperfections are never justification for why we can't love, because love is a choice when the emotions of love fail us. Anything less is not genuine love but only self-service. Certainly, in extenuating circumstances we may not be able to maintain a relationship with someone, but we can always love them with the agape love of Christ, which has their best interest in mind.

When the imperfections of those closest to us do their good work to make us more like Jesus, they will drive us to our knees in supplication: *Lord, please help me to be less selfish! Teach me how to love!* But when we don't allow others' imperfections to illuminate our selfishness, inflexibility, and pride, their flaws can even become the reason we justify our ungodly actions, and this is a great tragedy.

Morning – DON'T STOP PRAYING

The effective, fervent prayer of a righteous man avails much.
JAMES 5:16 NKJV

Augustine's mother, Monica, was a devout Christian, but her son was an undisciplined child. Even despite Monica's constant warnings to stay away from fornication, Augustine found himself father to a son and a member of a cult.

Years later, she begged him not to travel to Rome, but despite her advice, he went. She was able to persuade him to listen to the bishop. The words of the sermon lingered as he sat in a nearby garden. A child's song, "Take Up and Read," drew him to the Bible, and Saint Augustine was converted that moment.

Monica could have given up on her wayward son. But she was never willing to accept Augustine as he was in his state of godlessness. She kept praying until she got results.

Jesus tells us to pray relentlessly, like a man who knocks on his neighbor's door in the middle of the night for bread. He said, "Ask and it will be given to you; seek and you will find; knock and the door will be opened to you. For everyone who asks receives; the one who seeks finds; and to the one who knocks, the door will be opened" (Luke 11:9–10 NIV).

Don't give up on your prayers. The answer is closer than you know.

Evening – ENIGMAS

Then Simeon blessed them and said to Mary, his mother. . .
"A sword will pierce your own soul too."
LUKE 2:34–35 NIV

Parenting can be arduous. We mothers would rather die than see our children suffer, especially undeservedly. If they get into trouble with the law, we grieve for them. We may not understand their choices and pursuits. Some mothers even have to bury a child. Although Mary raised a son who never sinned, His life and death caused her to suffer all these hurts. She, along with the disciples, could not understand how Messiah could be rejected or that God could die.

The two Emmaus disciples said, "We had hoped that he was the one who was going to redeem Israel" (Luke 24:21 NIV). He still was. But before He could rule the world as King, He had to atone for the world's sins. The cross before the crown. Grief preceded glory. We may understand this about Jesus, yet we stumble over other enigmas: how God seems to ignore worldwide suffering. That violence and unjust killings abound. What about our sincere prayers that go unanswered?

We must accept that God is inscrutable. Our minds cannot comprehend His ways. Mary was "blessed above all women" and yet pierced in her soul. Remember that the sword-pierced wounds we experience on earth will one day be completely cured. In God's methodology, what we suffer on earth yields glory in eternity (see 2 Corinthians 4:17–18; Romans 8:17–18; 1 Peter 1:6–8). God compensates our losses by giving us more of Himself.

Morning – DRAW NEAR WITH CONFIDENCE

Therefore let us draw near with confidence to the throne of grace,
so that we may receive mercy and find grace to help in time of need.
HEBREWS 4:16 NASB

In this verse you are told that you can approach God's throne with confidence. Why do you approach the throne? So that you can receive mercy and find grace to help in time of need. Why would you need to receive mercy? Those who need mercy are those who have done something wrong, those who are not in right standing with whomever they are asking mercy from. Inevitably you come before the throne of God with the baggage of your sin. And yet you are told to come with confidence before the throne of a holy God who hates sin. You don't need to be perfect or have your act together to come before God with confidence. You only need to be covered in Christ's blood. This confidence with which you approach God's throne is not a self-confidence, but a God-confidence. It's a confidence that assures you that God is for you, that He loves you, and that He sees Christ in you. Your standing before God depends completely on His view of you and not on your own merit. And He sees you as His beloved child. So go boldly to the foot of His throne, knowing that you will receive mercy and grace.

Evening – G.R.A.C.E.

And of His fullness we have all received, and grace for grace.
JOHN 1:16 NKJV

Perhaps you've seen the acronym for G.R.A.C.E. (God's Riches at Christ's Expense). What does that mean to us, His daughters? We face all sorts of challenges and sometimes feel depleted. Dry. In those moments, all of God's riches (peace, joy, longsuffering, favor, help) are ours. What did we do to deserve them? Nothing. That's the point of grace: someone else paid the price so that we could receive God's gifts for free.

Take a good look at today's scripture. God promises not only to give grace and truth, but one gift after another. Picture yourself as a little girl at your daddy's knee. Now picture him giving you not one gift. . .not two. . .but one on top of the other, on top of the other. He overwhelms you with his beautifully wrapped gifts, topped off with ribbons and bows. Talk about blowing your socks off!

God does the same thing when He "gifts" us with things we don't deserve: forgiveness, comfort, satisfaction, provision. What a generous God we serve!

DAY 74

Morning – LOVE AND MARRIAGE

Submit to one another out of reverence for Christ.
EPHESIANS 5:21 NIV

Young couples often approach marriage thinking that their love will survive anything. Then when the first trial tests their faith and endurance, their love crumbles.

Author and aviator Antoine de Saint-Exupéry wrote, "Love does not consist in gazing at each other but in looking outward together in the same direction." Such is the goal of a couple committed to Christ.

Admit it: marriage is work. Yet God unites two people for a common purpose—to lift one up when the other falls, to give instead of receive, to exercise the art of compromise and understanding. On the other hand, a loveless marriage is one based on self-absorption or selfishness on the part of one or both individuals.

The love that once attracted us to our spouse isn't the love that sustains our marriage. Rather, God's love prevails in the lives of the couple who choose to, in mutual submission, place Christ first.

The above scripture indicates that submission applies to both men and women, yet Paul goes on to exhort women to submit to their husbands—for as a woman submits or respects her husband, he, in turn, loves his wife (Ephesians 5:22–28).

The result? A man and woman united in faith, traveling in the same direction.

Evening – ENJOY YOUR ROLE

The head of every man is Christ, and the head of the woman is man, and the head of Christ is God.
1 CORINTHIANS 11:3 NIV

In the 1960s, American society began to commend "doing your own thing." People called it freedom because it broke established limits. While segregation boundaries needed to be eliminated, society's moral values did not. The book of Judges portrays the downward spiral that results from everyone doing what is right in their own eyes. Being a law unto ourselves will never work in society, in schools, in churches, or in families. Why are companies called organizations? Because things run properly when order is followed.

The Bible tells us to submit to government authorities (Romans 13:1–7), to spiritual leaders in our local churches (Hebrews 13:17), and to our husbands (Ephesians 5:22–24). One of the results of being filled with the Spirit is submitting to one another (Ephesians 5:18–21). The Greek word for "submitting" does not mean being controlled by another, but placing oneself under someone's authority. Will our leaders and husbands always be right? No, but they are responsible, before God, for us. The husband's role is to lead lovingly; the wife's role is to follow respectfully. This in no way implies inferiority. In God's eyes, all men and women are equal in importance and value, but we all have different responsibilities. Everyone's role is necessary for harmonious function.

Morning – THE MEASURE OF YOUR FAITH

Go thy way; and as thou hast believed, so be it done unto thee.
MATTHEW 8:13 KJV

The centurion humbly approached Jesus in this one and only biblical account wherein a master came to Christ, pleading for Him to heal his servant.

Jesus must have recognized the soldier's compassion, for He responded immediately, saying He would go to the man's home and heal the boy. But the man humbled himself even more, telling the Christ that he, the centurion, was not worthy to have Jesus come to his home—and finally admitting all Christ needed to do was "speak the word only, and my servant shall be healed" (v. 8).

Hearing this, Jesus actually "marvelled" (v. 10), remarking He had not found such great faith in all of Israel! And in the same hour in which He said, "Go thy way; and as thou hast believed, so it be done unto thee," the centurion's servant was healed.

Might every woman have this measure of the centurion's faith. May she bring not only her own child, but all children before Jesus, humbly pleading with Christ to heal them of mind, body, spirit, and soul. And then go her way, *knowing* that it *will be done* for her just as she believed!

Evening – A TOUCH OF FAITH

*Jesus turning and seeing her said, "Daughter, take courage;
your faith has made you well." At once the woman was made well.*
MATTHEW 9:22 NASB

There once was a woman who'd been hemorrhaging for twelve years. She sought help from a myriad of physicians and spent all that she had, but her issue of blood was worse than ever before. Then one day she heard a healer named Jesus was coming to town. Although she was considered the lowest of the low, someone who shouldn't even be out in public, she decided to make her way through the crowd and reach out to this man. Risking all she had left, she came up behind Him and touched his garment, for she kept saying to herself, "If I can just touch his robe, I will be healed" (Mark 5:28 NLT). Instantly her bleeding stopped. But the story doesn't end there. Jesus immediately felt power flowing out of Him and demanded, "Who touched me?" (Mark 5:31 NLT). Shaking with fear, the woman confessed it had been her. Jesus responded with tenderness and encouragement, "Daughter, your faith has made you well. Go in peace. Your suffering is over" (Mark 5:34 NLT).

What issue have you needed Jesus' help with? What desperately bold exchange between your soul and Jesus have you kept secret? What story can you share with others to remind them of His power and tenderness, to give them a touch of faith?

DAY 76

Morning – WAITING FOR THE STORM TO PASS

*You do not know what will happen tomorrow. For what is your life? It is even
a vapor that appears for a little time and then vanishes away. Instead you
ought to say, "If the Lord wills, we shall live and do this or that."*
JAMES 4:14–15 NKJV

Summer monsoon season in Tucson, Arizona, can bring a haboob—a violent, desert dust storm. Dust forms a high wall with winds up to thirty miles per hour. The storm can last up to three hours. People respond differently to the storms. Some drivers try to press through with extremely low visibility. Others wait it out.

One individual, Dex, shared with a friend, "When Ann and I got caught in the haboob last night, instead of trying to press on through it, we decided to enjoy it. We stopped, went to a movie, ate dinner out, and made it home before 10 p.m."

The storms of life are always going to come. The next time you see a storm on the horizon, follow Dex and Ann's example and choose to have a little fun while you are waiting for the storm to pass!

Evening – GRACE ACCEPTED

*But because of his great love for us, God, who is rich in mercy,
made us alive with Christ even when we were dead in
transgressions—it is by grace you have been saved.*
EPHESIANS 2:4–5 NIV

Have you ever been wrongly accused of something or completely misunderstood? Have the words of your accusers struck your heart, making you feel like you have to make it right somehow, but no amount of reasoning with them seems to help?

If anyone understands this situation, it's Christ Himself. Wrongly accused. Misunderstood. Yet He offered unfathomable grace at all times and still offers it today.

This reminds us that we are to aim to offer this same grace to our accusers and those who misunderstand us. We will be misunderstood when we try to obey and follow God in a culture that runs quite contrary in many ways. Our job is to first accept God's grace and then offer it up to others as lovingly as we can. Like Christ.

Morning – FAULT WITH FAITH IN WISDOM

That your faith should not be in the wisdom of men but in the power of God.
1 CORINTHIANS 2:5 NKJV

There is great danger in putting faith in wisdom—the wrong kind of wisdom, that is, or in worldly knowledge falsely claiming to be wisdom. The most damaging teachings of the modern era have reified skepticism and doubt. It is faith in intellectual doubt that has corrupted the definition of wisdom and lessened the power of God in the eyes of society. The teachers of such "wisdom" are the ones Paul warns Timothy about: they are always learning and never able to come to the knowledge of the truth (see 2 Timothy 3:7). Paul may have referred to the religious leaders of his day, an accusation often made by later Christians against the Jewish Talmudic or rabbinic tradition.

Joseph Rabinowitz, the father of the modern Messianic Jewish movement, initially embraced enlightenment rationalism against his Hassidic background but, by God's grace, came to know the truth and wisdom of God's plan in Jesus as Messiah for both Jews and Gentiles. He found the wisdom that is from above. This wisdom is pure, a source of peace, gentle, willing to yield, merciful, and produces good fruit, without partiality or hypocrisy (see James 3:17). Such wisdom can only be brought about by the power of God, and in this we can place our faith.

Evening – WISE LIKE JESUS

But the wisdom that comes from heaven is first of all pure; then peace-loving, considerate, submissive, full of mercy and good fruit, impartial and sincere.
JAMES 3:17 NIV

Who has wisdom? Look at the fruit of her life. From this verse, we know a wise woman chooses to pursue peace in her community—she forgives someone who hurt her instead of writing him off. She is considerate; she sees others with God's eyes—worthy of her love because they are loved by their Creator, no matter what they have done or left undone. She submits her hurts to her Father, learning from Him how to show mercy as He does. Sincerity blossoms throughout her words and deeds.

If this description of a wise woman leaves you thinking, *That's not me!*, don't worry, you certainly aren't alone. Wisdom is a gift from God, born from a desire to follow His Word out of love for Him. Our own efforts can only conjure up an imperfect wisdom and love for others because our natural state is selfish. Humanity lost its capacity to love purely when Adam and Eve disobeyed God in the Garden.

Thankfully, Jesus changes our hearts when we trust in Him so we can be wise as He is wise. With the Holy Spirit's help, we can grow more like Jesus each day. May His wisdom and love deepen in us and spill over to others!

Morning – ON SOLID ROCK

"Therefore everyone who hears these words of mine and puts them into practice is like a wise man who built his house on the rock. The rain came down, the streams rose, and the winds blew and beat against that house; yet it did not fall, because it had its foundation on the rock."
MATTHEW 7:24–25 NIV

In the Sonoran Desert that spills into Mexico thrives the ironwood tree. Though it is of little use commercially, the tree is an essential hub of plant and animal life. Just as God does, the ironwood tree nourishes and protects every living thing in its heavy shade.

Because of the ironwood's deep roots, the tree stands firm through floods and winds—just like God. He is the same today and always. Ironwoods also enrich the soil by infusing it with nitrogen like God's rich nourishment in our lives. The tree changes the harsh land around it so that living things can thrive. God changes lives for the better. The ironwood lives long and remains hardy. God has been with us since the beginning (John 1:1–2) and will carry us through to the end (Philippians 1:6).

As you build a foundation in your life, look to God's words. They provide a foundation of solid rock: words that survive all storms, words that grow us, guide us, protect us, and provide for our flourishing.

God's Word even outlasts the ironwood tree.

Evening – IT'S ALIVE!

But if you look carefully into the perfect law that sets you free, and if you do what it says. . .God will bless you for doing it.
JAMES 1:25 NLT

Reading God's Word has many benefits. First, the Bible reveals God's heart like a "love letter," nurturing our fellowship with Him. His love is not a mere feeling—it's a fact that gives us confidence to keep trusting Him. Therefore, as we grow in our knowledge about God, we love Him more.

Second, the Bible explains how to live God's way. When we obey God, we will avoid sinful habits, along with the guilt and regrets they cause.

Third, God's Word has power to transform us. Mysteriously, it is "alive and powerful" (Hebrews 4:12; 1 Peter 1:23) and works effectively in us (1 Thessalonians 2:13). Jesus said, "Blessed are all who hear the word of God and put it into practice" (Luke 11:28 NLT).

Want to field-test this? What is currently your greatest need or concern? Find verses that deal with that issue and write them out. Choose one to memorize. Every time that problem pesters you, wield your sword (quote your verse) and ask God for help. Romans 10:13 promises that when we call on the name of the Lord, we will be delivered (saved or rescued).

In a few weeks you will find the problem or temptation diminishing. When we keep responding to the seed of God's Word and using it in our lives, it grows and bears fruit even when we don't realize it.

Morning – A PROMISED HEALING

Behold, I will bring to it health and healing, and I will heal them;
and I will reveal to them an abundance of peace and truth.
JEREMIAH 33:6 NASB

Are you longing to be healed of an affliction? Mary Magdalene suffered with seven demons before Jesus touched her and restored her to life. Scripture doesn't tell us much about how, when, or where Jesus healed Mary. It does tell us that Mary, along with several other women, provided for and supported Jesus so that He could do what God had called Him to do. After Jesus healed her, she became one of His most ardent followers.

This woman, who had been tormented by Satan himself, became a walking testimony of the power of the Light to dispel darkness: "The light shines in the darkness, and the darkness has not overcome it" (John 1:5 NIV).

Whether or not God chooses to cure you here on earth, one day He *will* restore you to total health. In heaven, our bodies will be perfect and no diseases will be allowed to touch us. We will live in peace and prosperity.

Such a promise should make us rejoice. Jesus will strengthen us for this life, whatever it may hold, and will one day turn on the light that will make the darkness scatter for all time. Hallelujah!

Evening – BIOPSIES AND BRAVERY

"For the life of every living thing is in his hand, and the breath of every human being."
JOB 12:10 NLT

What about biopsies? Have you had one? If not, chances are good that you will before your life is over. There seems to be a point in all our lives when the doctors can't diagnose from the outside but have to extract a little piece of the inside of us to look at. This gives them more accurate information about whatever is growing or not growing inside of us. And that's a good thing. If something inside has gone rogue, we surely want the medical team to find out.

But still it's a difficult thing to endure the procedure and then wait for the results. In the interim, all sorts of fears play out in the mind. But why should a Christian be frightened about medical tests? Aren't we supposed to want to go to heaven? Why shouldn't we be happy about whatever report the doctor brings back?

The answer is that God implants the desire to live deep within us and He doesn't take that out when we receive Him as Savior. A biopsy reminds us that there may not be a tomorrow for us to enjoy with friends and family. But biopsies also remind us that God is in control and can see every detail of our bodies from the inside out. Whatever the doctor finds will be news that has already passed heaven's copy room.

DAY 80

Morning – DRUNKARD'S PATH QUILT PATTERN

*Bear with each other and forgive one another if any of you has
a grievance against someone. . . . And over all these virtues put
on love, which binds them all together in perfect unity.*
COLOSSIANS 3:13–14 NIV

"Oh, look!" Danielle commented as she leaned over her classmate's work. "You're going to make a baby's blanket with *that pattern* in the middle?"

The church-sponsored quilting class was using creativity, scraps, and quilt squares already made to provide gift quilts for new mothers at the local hospital.

"Yep!" novice quilter Linda quipped. "Any mom would be thrilled to have such a special gift from a stranger!"

"I don't think so," Danielle continued. "I remember this pattern is called 'The Drunkard's Path.' It means that there is a drunkard in the house. It's like a curse!"

Linda was so upset, she left the class early. Later, she went online and learned that the pattern she'd made into a quilt was not "The Drunkard's Path." But then, Danielle tended to be in crisis mode at all times—with everyone.

By the next class, Linda had finished the quilt. She also had studied Colossians 3, which advises us to clothe ourselves with compassion, kindness, humility, gentleness, patience. . .and especially love. What a stretch with Danielle!

When Linda arrived, Danielle was complimenting another quilter, "Your machine quilted this! Congratulations on learning how to do it!" The lady knew how to encourage—not just criticize. It was a start.

As Linda adjusted her vision, she saw many things to love about Danielle.

Evening – SHARPENING YOUR IRON

As iron sharpens iron, so one person sharpens another.
PROVERBS 27:17 NIV

God never designed us to travel this journey of life alone. We need community. The book of Hebrews says we need to spur each other on to good works. We also need each other for accountability.

God uses other people to grow our character. Other people stretch us and challenge us. They point out our blind spots. They may make us uncomfortable at times.

Sometimes our churches are too big for us to develop true community, which is best done in smaller groups. Serving at church through various ministries or getting involved in a small group or Sunday school class is a good way to find community. Not every group will be a good fit, but don't give up. Pray and ask God to show you where you belong.

In a community group, you can deepen your knowledge of worship and the Bible. You can reach out to your broader community and serve as a group. You can support each other with prayer and share each other's burdens. God will use these people to bring you closer to Him.

Morning – GOD'S MERCY IN OUR NEED

For the wages of sin is death, but the gift
of God is eternal life in Christ Jesus our Lord.
ROMANS 6:23 NKJV

As soon as Marci got into her car, she began sobbing. She put her head on the steering wheel and cried until she couldn't cry anymore. "Lord, help!" she managed to whisper as the tears subsided.

A few minutes earlier, during a follow-up visit after her annual gynecological exam, Marci's doctor had revealed disturbing news. Several possibilities existed for the things going on in her body; none of them were good.

As a single woman with no family living nearby, Marci felt panic as she thought of the next few weeks. Doctors' visits, tests, and all sorts of treatments would eat up her time. When would she work? How would she pay her bills? She had no idea.

Suddenly, her phone rang. It was her prayer partner and best friend, Shellie. "Hello?" Marci said.

"Are you okay? I felt really strongly that I should call," her friend said. Marci gasped and then told Shellie everything.

"You're going to be fine," Shellie said. "Our Bible study class will bring meals, and I can help you drive to appointments. And God is going to carry you when you can't carry on." Marci's tears fell again as she murmured her thanks to Shellie. It was good to not be alone—and it was so kind of God to remind her of that at just the right moment.

Evening – ENCOURAGEMENT DURING DIFFICULT ASSIGNMENTS

Then they answered Joshua, "Whatever you have commanded us we will do,
and wherever you send us we will go. Just as we fully obeyed Moses, so we
will obey you. Only may the LORD your God be with you as he was with Moses.
Whoever rebels against your word and does not obey it, whatever you may
command them, will be put to death. Only be strong and courageous!"
JOSHUA 1:16–18 NIV

God gives us difficult assignments just as He did with Joshua. We *know* God will bless us if we're faithful, but we don't always *feel* it. Often the job seems bigger than our capabilities, and we get discouraged. But God wants us to *know* and *feel* He is responsible for the outcome. We just need to be faithful to act.

As with Joshua, God brings people into our lives to encourage us. The men in today's verses encourage Joshua in four ways: they assure him of their allegiance and willingness to help, they pray for him, they take their own responsibilities seriously, and they offer Joshua words of encouragement he has heard before.

Our assignment is for our benefit and to benefit those around us. While we need to be obedient to do the next right step, we also need to encourage others around us. How can you use one of those four ways to encourage someone else?

Morning – NEIGHBORLY LOVE

*"Do not seek revenge or bear a grudge against anyone among
your people, but love your neighbor as yourself. I am the Lord."*
LEVITICUS 19:18 NIV

Sophie kept to herself, tended her garden, and complained whenever she could. If a child's ball came over her fence, she kept it. If someone stopped to admire her flowers, she rapped on her front window and signaled for them to move on. She even called the police when the laughing at her next-door neighbor's baby shower annoyed her. Yes, Sophie was a difficult neighbor, and everyone stayed away.

One day, the flowers in Sophie's garden looked wilted. The grass had grown tall. Her neighbors felt that something was wrong, but should they get involved? They drew straws to decide who would check on Sophie.

Elaine Keller got the short straw. She knocked on Sophie's door, and the old woman answered, leaning on crutches, her right foot in a cast.

"We were worried," Elaine said. "We want to help you."

"No need," said Sophie.

"But we *want* to!" Elaine protested, and before long she was watering Sophie's flowers, and her husband was cutting the grass.

Sophie never did warm up to her neighbors, but they learned to accept her just as she was—the way that God accepts us. Some people are hard to love; yet that is exactly what God commands of us—in all circumstances to love our neighbors.

Evening – LOVING THE UNLOVABLE

*"You have heard the law that says, 'Love your neighbor' and hate your enemy.
But I say, love your enemies! Pray for those who persecute you! In that
way, you will be acting as true children of your Father in heaven."*
MATTHEW 5:43–45 NLT

Most of us have family members or people in our lives who are difficult to love. Those people that we would rather not run into in the store, so we dart down another aisle hoping they'll check out before we do. You may have one person in your life like that, or many. Difficult people may surround us at every turn. But it's important not to go out of your way to avoid those people. Sometimes running into a difficult person can actually be a "divine appointment!" Maybe you're the only person they'll see all week who wears a smile on her face.

When you happen upon a difficult person whom you'd rather not talk to, take the time to pray for your attitude and then pray for that person. Greet her with a smile and look her in the eye. There is no reason to fear difficult people if you trust in God. He will show you what to do and say as you listen to His promptings (Luke 12:12).

Morning – EXCITEMENT

Because Your lovingkindness is better than life, my lips shall praise You. Thus I will bless You while I live; I will lift up my hands in Your name. My soul shall be satisfied as with [fat and rich food], and my mouth shall praise You with joyful lips. When I remember You on my bed, I meditate on You in the night watches. Because You have been my help, therefore in the shadow of Your wings I will rejoice.
PSALM 63:3–7 NKJV

Sister Motea was a good example of what Jesus says to the church of Smyrna in the book of Revelation. She was poor by the world's standards—a village mother in southern Romania—but spiritually rich in her love of Christ. Loved ones fondly remember Sister Motea's joy in being together with the church family, not wanting to miss any occasion for fellowship. She joined along on youth trips, feeling just as young and desirous to be a part of the kingdom work. Her children grew up in this environment of excitement for the Lord. Of course, they didn't see mom tagging along all the time as much fun, so they would occasionally try to sneak off without her. For one particular church trip, Sister Motea slept in the car to make sure they took her along. Here was a woman whose age did not deter her. She yearned to share the joy that satisfied her soul.

Evening – THE REWARD OF FAITH

"So on that day Moses swore to me, 'The land on which your feet have walked will be your inheritance and that of your children forever, because you have followed the LORD my God wholeheartedly.' "
JOSHUA 14:9 NIV

If we look back on the story of Caleb in Numbers 13 and 14, we see that his heart overflowed with confidence in God. If God said Israel was supposed to get the land, then it didn't matter who was living there; the Israelites would defeat them. Caleb believed that God would do what He said He would do. He was enthusiastically optimistic.

The Anakites, the giants Caleb and Joshua originally spied over forty years earlier, still controlled the land Caleb was to inherit. And he was eighty-five years old. But he was not ready for retirement. He had followed God wholeheartedly, the key to his effectiveness. He was filled with the presence and the power of God. He had pursued God like a hunter closing the gap on his prey. Caleb still welcomed a challenge. Caleb believed God still had work for him to do and would give him the strength to remove the giants from his land.

Ultimately, this is God's story, not Caleb's. Caleb just applied the principle of sowing and reaping, and God showed up like He said He would. Like Caleb, we can rely on God's strength and power to work through us even if we have physical and mental limitations.

DAY 84

Morning – THE WARRIOR SINGS

"The Lord your God is with you, the Mighty Warrior who saves.
He will take great delight in you; in his love he will no longer
rebuke you, but will rejoice over you with singing."
ZEPHANIAH 3:17 NIV

What kind of picture does this verse create in your mind? The Lord is a mighty warrior who leads the armies of angels. Yet He is with us. One of Jesus' names is Immanuel, literally the "with us God." And He takes delight in us. He doesn't rebuke us. He rejoices over us with singing.

This verse from Zephaniah is like a sampler of God's attributes. Look them over again. How does each of these characteristics show up in your relationship with Him? What attribute do you need to know more about? Which do you struggle with?

We sing worship songs to God, but have you thought about His joy over you being so great He bursts out into song? Or maybe He sings you a sweet lullaby like a parent does to a small child. Next time you sing a worship song, think about what kind of song God would sing about you. Let that fuel your worship of Him and deepen your relationship with the one who loves you so greatly.

Evening – MUSIC TO HIS EARS

Speaking to one another with psalms, hymns, and songs from
the Spirit. Sing and make music from your heart to the Lord.
EPHESIANS 5:19 NIV

One of the most powerful moments in the Christian life may turn out to be at a supper table with fellow believers or conversations around a fire. Uplifting and encouraging one another can also happen when we sing. Today many churches resound with praise music that fills the congregation with enthusiasm. These songs should not be directed to those around us but in our hearts to the Lord. Spiritual fullness comes to expression in joyful fellowship, in song and thanksgiving.

King David crawled in caves and crevasses hiding from his enemies, yet he found time to pen many praise songs to the King of kings. Despite his circumstances, he knew God was in control. Paul sang in the dank darkness of a dungeon cell, praising his Creator even though life looked bleak. God's grace was extended to these men as they praised in their suffering.

How much more should we make a melody to the Lord when we are free to move about, to worship, to sing. God wants to hear music from our hearts, not arias with perfect notes. So we will lift up our voices and join in the praise to our Creator and Lord. Harmonious, harsh, or hoarse, He's filtering our melodies with His love.

Morning – REMEMBER LOT'S WIFE

*One of the angels ordered, "Run for your lives! And don't look back or
stop anywhere in the valley! Escape to the mountains, or you will be
swept away!". . . But Lot's wife looked back as she was following
behind him, and she turned into a pillar of salt.*
GENESIS 19:17, 26 NLT

Betsy sat at her kitchen table, reminiscing about the past, wishing she could go back. For the future before her was unknown territory. And she wasn't sure she had the strength to deal with it.

We all think about the people, places, and things we have loved and left behind. But God doesn't want us to become like Lot's wife, so focused on the past that we miss what He's doing in the present. He wants our hearts fixed on His love and strength, our eyes focused on the road before us.

Jesus said, "Remember Lot's wife. Whoever seeks to save his life will lose it, and whoever loses his life will preserve it" (Luke 17:32–33 NKJV). Mrs. Lot is a blatant example of what happens when we try to save our lives. We're stopped in our spiritual tracks. But when we don't look back, when we stop clinging to what was, we end up saving our lives!

Where are your heart and eyes? Take stock now, find a way to let go, and grab hold of all God is doing on the road before you.

Evening – LOVE AND ASSURANCE

*Little children, let us not love with word or with tongue, but in deed and truth. We will
know by this that we are of the truth, and will assure our heart before Him in whatever
our heart condemns us; for God is greater than our heart and knows all things.*
1 JOHN 3:18–20 NASB

These verses start out with an admonition—you ought to show your love in what you do. Love is not well expressed by superficial, noncommittal statements. Rather, a true, earnest love will drive you to action. Think about those around you to whom you can express love, not just by telling them, but by showing your love to them in your deeds. Don't allow laziness or excuses to keep you from reaching out to those who need love.

These verses end with a wonderful assurance for those of us who struggle with guilt and fear. When you are in Christ, be encouraged that nothing can take away your salvation. Your heart may condemn you when you fall into the same pattern of sin again or when you fail to do what you promised yourself and God you would do. But be encouraged—you are not in charge of your standing before God. God is. He is greater than any guilt-ridden and self-abasing heart. Once you are one of His children, you will always have that status. He knows all things, including the fact that your name is written, irrevocably, in the book of life.

DAY 86

Morning – ONLY ONE GOD

*But for us, there is one God, the Father, by whom all things were created,
and for whom we live. And there is one Lord, Jesus Christ, through
whom all things were created, and through whom we live.*
1 Corinthians 8:6 nlt

A coworker told Sue she had decided there were many ways to God. Sue knew the Bible teaches there is only one God and one way to Him. She liked and admired the woman who had spoken to her, but she was thankful she knew what God's Word says. Many voices express themselves in our world, each believing they know the right way, each wanting to convert others to their way of thinking. It's important to know the truth and to listen to the right voice.

The voices may be saying, "If you want to fit in, you need to change," "You must be more tolerant," or "That isn't politically correct." Some of these voices may sound good and we may be tempted to agree. Be careful that your good intentions don't set a trap for you. The voice of error can sound pretty good sometimes.

As Christians, we need to follow God's voice even when it makes us look politically incorrect. We can do this only by reading and knowing God's Word. Only then can we know the difference between the voice of truth and the voice of error. There is only one God, and we must know Him intimately to be able to distinguish between the voices.

Evening – THE GUARANTEE OF FINDING HIM

"You will seek me and find me when you seek me with all your heart."
Jeremiah 29:13 niv

In this verse, God reveals that He doesn't hide where He can't be found but invites us to look for Him and find Him. In the original Old Testament Hebrew, the word *seek* specifically involves seeking God through prayer and worship. Contrary to what some people say, God isn't found by following a long list of legalistic rules and religious regulations. Instead, He's found in sincerity of heart by focusing on nurturing your relationship with Him.

There are few guarantees in life, but this scripture provides one: when you seek God with all your heart, you will find Him. There's no wondering if you'll find Him, if you'll be able to make your way to Him, or if you will be allowed to find Him. There's no question. He will show Himself to you when you genuinely search for Him through prayer and worship.

In *The Case for Faith,* journalist Lee Strobel interviews Peter Kreeft, a world-class philosopher, who makes the following statement: "The Bible says, 'Seek and you shall find.' It doesn't say that everybody will find him; it doesn't say nobody will find him. Some will find him. Who? Those who seek."

Morning – GOD IS NOT A "PRIORITY"

Whatever you do or say, do it as a representative of the Lord Jesus.
COLOSSIANS 3:17 NLT

If most Christians listed their priorities, they would probably put God at the top, followed by family and friends and then other significant areas, but is that really where God belongs—at the top of a list to be compartmentalized and checked off?

Our relationship with God shouldn't be treated as a priority but rather as the essence of everything. God should be the center of marriage, parenting, business practices, thought life, television viewing—everything.

Acts 17:28 (NKJV) says, "For in Him we live and move and have our being." Even something as mundane as meal time should be done for God's glory (1 Corinthians 10:31).

When the patriarch Jacob awoke from his dream about angels descending on a ladder, he declared, "Surely the LORD is in this place, and I did not know it" (Genesis 28:16 NKJV). A. W. Tozer commented, "Jacob had never been for one small division of a moment outside of the circle of that all-pervading Presence. But he knew it not. That was his trouble, and it is ours. Men do not know God is here. What a difference it would make if they knew."

God's presence is with you when you buy groceries, drive your car, put your children to sleep. What are you doing to honor Him through these mundane tasks? The time for God is not first thing each morning; it's every minute of every day.

Evening – THE BATTLE BELONGS TO THE LORD

The commander of the LORD's army replied, "Take off your sandals,
for the place where you are standing is holy." And Joshua did so.
JOSHUA 5:15 NIV

Joshua has some big sandals to fill. Moses is gone and now Joshua is in charge of the nation of Israel. Surrounded by enemies, the tiny nation has its first battle for the Promised Land coming up. And even though he's seen God work in miraculous ways, Joshua must be at least a little afraid.

And then he hears the same message his predecessor Moses did. "Take off your sandals. You're on holy ground."

Moses heard it coming from a burning bush. Joshua hears it from the commander of the Lord's army. If he wasn't scared before, he certainly is now. But ultimately this messenger and his message give comfort to Joshua. He has been anointed to be Israel's leader in the same way Moses had been. The battle isn't Joshua's to win or lose. He just needs to be faithful. The battle is God's. And He's already won it. Joshua just needs to follow orders.

We can have the same comfort that Joshua had. Whatever battle or challenge we may be facing, we don't face it alone. God is with us every step of the way. He will never leave us or forsake us.

DAY 88

Morning – A CHOICE

Yet I will exult in the Lord, I will rejoice in the God of my salvation.
The Lord God is my strength, and He has made my feet like
hinds' feet, and makes me walk on my high places.
HABAKKUK 3:18–19 NASB

Many days, life seems like an uphill battle, where we are fighting against the current, working hard to maintain our equilibrium. Exhausted from the battle, we often throw up our hands in disgust and want to quit. That's when we should realize we have a choice. We can choose to surrender our burdens to the Lord!

What would happen if we followed the advice of the psalmist and turned a cartwheel of joy in our hearts—regardless of the circumstances—then leaned and trusted in His rule to prevail? Think of the happiness and peace that could be ours with a total surrender to God's care.

It's a decision to count on God's rule to triumph. And we must realize His Word, His rule, never fails. Never. Then we must want to stand on that Word. Taking a giant step, armed with scriptures and praise and joy, we can surmount any obstacle put before us, running like a deer, climbing the tall mountains. With God at our side, it's possible to be king of the mountain.

Evening – PRESS ON TO KNOW HIM

"Let us press on to know him. He will respond to us as surely
as the arrival of dawn or the coming of rains in early spring."
HOSEA 6:3 NLT

Monica stood in the church entrance hall, determined to regain control of herself. Stepping into the building had triggered tears—lots of them. As the congregation inside the worship center sang, Monica took deep breaths and wiped her eyes.

Suddenly, Sharon, the congregation's ministry to women coordinator, rounded the corner. "Monica?" she asked. "What's wrong?" Sharon steered Monica toward a bench.

Monica struggled to put words to her emotions. "I just feel like God's not listening to my prayers."

"I feel like that sometimes," Sharon replied.

"You do?" Monica said. As a new believer, she didn't know veteran Christians had doubts.

"Sure!" Sharon said, patting Monica's knee. "Just tell Him about it, even if you feel like your prayers are hitting the ceiling. He already knows how you're feeling anyway."

Monica smiled shyly. "I guess I could do that," she said. "Will it get better?"

"Sure it will," Sharon said. "God is faithful. I don't know how long you'll have to wait, but I do know that He is right here with us. Want me to pray for us?"

"Yes, please," Monica said. "I'd love it."

Morning – GOD'S GRACE IN WEAKNESS

*"My grace is all you need. My power works best in weakness." So now
I am glad to boast about my weaknesses, so that the power of Christ
can work through me. That's why I take pleasure in my weaknesses,
and in the insults, hardships, persecutions, and troubles that I
suffer for Christ. For when I am weak, then I am strong.*
2 CORINTHIANS 12:9–10 NLT

The apostle Paul had many amazing experiences over the years after his conversion, and he saw God bring him through many experiences, each designed to draw him ever closer to his goal to be like Christ. One such experience was getting to visit heaven, whether in the Spirit or out of the Spirit—either in reality or in a vision—he didn't know. But in order to keep Paul humble, the Lord sent a "thorn in the flesh."

Scripture doesn't say exactly what that "thorn" was, but it caused Paul enough pain and trouble that he asked the Lord to take it away, not once but three times. Finally God told him, "My grace is all you need. My power works best in weakness." In other words, "No. All you need is My grace to help you cope with this thorn. For in your weakness you are forced to depend on Me for strength to get you through and still be able to proclaim My gospel. Others can see Me in you, when your 'thorn' should keep you from doing anything at all."

Evening – CONTENT IN CHRIST'S STRENGTH

*I have learned how to be content with whatever I have. . . .
I can do everything through Christ, who gives me strength.*
PHILIPPIANS 4:11, 13 NLT

Sometimes Paul seems like a giant of a man, way above everyone else on the spiritual scale. Granted, it is a manmade scale, certainly not one God uses.

Paul wrote his letter to the Philippian church from a prison in Rome. Prisons in the ancient world were nothing compared to those in our country today. In chapter one, we learn that Paul was guarded day and night by the emperor's own elite guards—the praetorians. Because Paul never backed down from sharing the gospel with whoever crossed his path, many among the guards believed in Christ and then carried the gospel into Nero's palace. Because of this unique opportunity to spread the gospel, Paul rejoiced.

In the latter part of the letter, he declared that the gift the Philippians sent him was welcomed with rejoicing. But even without it he could rejoice because he had learned to be content in whatever situation and condition he found himself. So how was Paul able to do this when so many of God's people today never learn his secret? Before Paul ended the paragraph, he told us: "I can do everything through Christ, who gives me strength." Paul couldn't generate contentment in all situations, but Christ in him could. The same "secret" enables God's people to do the same nearly two thousand years later.

DAY 90

Morning – GOD'S LOVE

For I am convinced that neither death, nor life, nor angels, nor principalities,
nor things present, nor things to come, nor powers, nor height, nor depth,
nor any other created thing, will be able to separate us from
the love of God, which is in Christ Jesus our Lord.
ROMANS 8:38–39 NASB

In this life we often feel we need to work for love. Love can grow stale or be lost altogether or given to another. The promise of love can be used as a weapon against us. But in this verse, an eternal, genuine love is promised you. This promise can be trusted because the love of God has been secured through the sacrifice and death of Christ. This is no promise made on a whim or as a manipulation but one made in blood by the perfect Lamb.

No natural or supernatural power can separate you from God's love. Nothing that is currently happening in your life will separate you from God's love. No matter how scary or uncertain the future seems, it will not separate you from God's love. No height of success or depth of depression and despair will separate you from God's love. Nothing that this life and those in it can throw at you and nothing that you do will separate you from God's love. Not even death, which separates us from everything else we know, will separate you from God's love.

Therefore, go forward in peace and boldness, knowing that you are eternally secure and eternally loved.

Evening – HIS LOVE NEVER QUITS

"Oh, give thanks to the LORD, for He is good! For His mercy endures forever.
And say, "Save us, O God of our salvation; gather us together, and deliver us
from the Gentiles, to give thanks to Your holy name, to triumph in Your praise."
Blessed be the LORD God of Israel from everlasting to everlasting!
1 CHRONICLES 16:34–36 NKJV

God's Word tells us in Psalm 139 that we can never escape the presence of God. He is with us always, no matter where we go or what we do. His love never quits on us. First John 4:10 (NIV) says, "This is love: not that we loved God, but that he loved us and sent his Son as an atoning sacrifice for our sins." God doesn't love us because we did a lot of good things for Him. He doesn't love us because of our last names or because of the jobs we do. He can't love us any more or any less than He already does. He loves us simply because He is our Father and our Creator. In fact, He gave up His very life to show you how much.

You may have had a parent, friend, or spouse abandon you at some point in your life. God won't do that. You may feel alone and fearful. God won't leave you. You may feel sad and crushed. God says He is close to the brokenhearted and saves those who are crushed in Spirit (see Psalm 34:18).

Morning – LIKE GLUE

Surely your goodness and love will follow me all the days of my life.
PSALM 23:6 NIV

Sometimes it's scary to look out into the great unknown. As we stand on the threshold of a new year, we don't know what to expect. Will good things be in store, or do terrible things await?

We don't have the ability to see the future. But we do know one thing for certain. As long as we remain close to our Father, His goodness and love will stay close to us. No matter where we go, no matter where our circumstances may force us, His love and goodness will follow us.

Even when we wander away from His perfect plan for us, He is only a breath away. He promised in Romans 8 that nothing will ever separate us from that love. When life is good, He is there. When life is hard, His love and goodness are right there. Nothing—no sickness or disease, no foul circumstance, no financial difficulty will remove His love from us. It sticks like glue.

The challenge lies in finding His presence in tough situations. Sometimes we may have to look a little closer or search some odd places. But these things will never change: He is there. He loves us. He is good. And He will never leave us.

Evening – GOD'S PROMISES

"God is not human, that he should lie, not a human being, that he should change his mind. Does he speak and then not act? Does he promise and not fulfill?"
NUMBERS 23:19 NIV

Our opinions of God are often shaped by our experiences with people. When we've been hurt, we see God as hurtful. When people lie to us, we subconsciously think of God as a liar. After all, if humans are created in His image, it only stands to reason that God would be like the people in our lives. Right?

Well, no. Yes, we were created in God's image. But we humans are a fallen, broken race. We're sinful. God is without sin.

Humans lie. God doesn't.

Humans go back on their word. God doesn't.

Humans can be mean and hurtful. God is love, and He only acts in love.

God promised good things to those who love Him, those who live and act according to His will. That doesn't mean others won't hurt us or that we won't experience the effects of living in a sin-infested world. But where there's pain, we have a healer. Where there's brokenness, we have a comforter. And where we feel alone, we know we have a friend.

And one day we'll experience the perfect fulfillment of all His promises without the burdens of this world to weigh us down.

Now that's something to look forward to.

Morning – HANG IN THERE

*Let perseverance finish its work so that you may
be mature and complete, not lacking anything.*
JAMES 1:4 NIV

Perseverance can't be rushed. The only way to develop perseverance is to endure pressure over a long period of time. A weight lifter must gradually add more weight if he wants to build up his muscles. A runner must run farther and farther, pushing past what is comfortable. If these athletes want to grow and improve, they must persevere through pressure over time.

The same is true for our faith. If we want to grow as Christians, we have to endure pressure. God allows difficult things into our lives to help build our strength and endurance. Just as the athlete who gives up at the first sign of hardship will never improve at her sport, the Christian who abandons her faith during times of distress will never reach maturity.

No one ever said the Christian life was an easy one. In fact, Christ told us we'd endure hardships of many kinds. But He also said not to get discouraged. When we stick it out and follow Him no matter what, we will become mature and complete, perfectly fulfilling God's plan for our lives.

Evening – NEVER QUIT

*Let us not become weary in doing good, for at the
proper time we will reap a harvest if we do not give up.*
GALATIANS 6:9 NIV

"They've broken my spirit," the elderly woman said as she assessed her damaged garden. Slashed cucumber vines and mutilated vegetables littered the once fruitful plot of land across the street from her home, alongside abandoned railroad tracks. Night vandals had ruined Mrs. Conner's labor of love.

For years she planted, cultivated, and watered her garden, laboriously hauling buckets of water across the street to provide vegetables for needy families. Although well into her eighties, she took pride and pleasure in her work.

As she cleared her vandalized garden of debris, she muttered, "I spent over one hundred dollars on the garden this year, and for what?" Then God spoke, *"Don't quit. If you quit, they've won."*

Are unexpected circumstances breaking your heart and spirit? Are vandals destroying your life's garden? The Bible teaches us to persevere at the exact time the voice within screams, "Give up!"

Difficulties can destroy and sabotage the fruits of our labor, but they cannot rob us of our faith and the power of prayer. Pray for the ones who hurt you; pray for strength and courage, and God will restore your garden in due course.

Mrs. Conner did, and she's still gardening today.

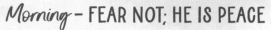

Morning – FEAR NOT; HE IS PEACE

*"You will keep him in perfect peace, whose mind
is stayed on You, because he trusts in You."*
ISAIAH 26:3 NKJV

What are you afraid of? Spiders, darkness, cancer, being alone? All of the above?

Every human being has fears. Maybe you've seen the slogan going around back in the 1990s that said "No Fear." It was plastered on T-shirts and bumper stickers and soft drink cups. But it seems that their confidence was slightly misplaced; the company filed for Chapter 11 bankruptcy in 2011. They did have a reason to fear after all.

Most of us are smarter than to deny that we have any fears. Bravery has been defined not as a lack of fear but as action in spite of fear. Anyone who has worn a uniform that put her on the front lines of battle whether in the jungle, desert, or city streets understands this principle.

But Jesus promised us more help than simply bluffing our way through the things that frighten us. He gave us the promise of peace. In John 14:27 (KJV), He said, "My peace I give unto you." This heavenly peace keeps our hearts and minds and gives us the strength to do things we never thought we could.

As we leave childhood behind and enter the multifaceted world of adulthood, our fears increase in proportion to our understanding of the world and the things that can go wrong. But the peace that He gives also multiplies to more than fit whatever need we have. And Satan has no fiery dart that can penetrate it.

Evening – BOLDLY WE COME

*God's free gift leads to our being made right with God,
even though we are guilty of many sins.*
ROMANS 5:16 NLT

Why do you think it is that as a general population of people, we often assume that God is out to get us? We tend to jump immediately to the notion that God is angry with us and ready to bring down the hammer. We become afraid to go to church or read the Bible—thinking that as soon as we enter the building or crack the cover, we will drown in waves of guilt and condemnation.

We even become too afraid to pray.

This must be one of the devil's most effective schemes—to convince us to fear talking with God—when talking with God is what will ultimately transform us from the inside out. Indeed, prayer is what we were created for. We were created for a relationship with Him—the entire Bible is the story of our being restored to that relationship.

The next time you are afraid to pray, refuse the fear. Know in confidence that, unlike the devil, you are covered by the blood of the Lamb and can enter freely into His presence. You can enter freely because He chose to open the way to you.

Morning – I SHALL RETURN

And the Lord replied, "A faithful, sensible servant is one to whom the master can give the responsibility of managing his other household servants and feeding them. If the master returns and finds that the servant has done a good job, there will be a reward. I tell you the truth, the master will put that servant in charge of all he owns."
LUKE 12:42–44 NLT

General Douglas MacArthur was a military adviser to the Philippine government just before World War II broke out. After the Japanese bombed Pearl Harbor and their invasion of the Philippines seemed imminent, MacArthur escaped at the last possible moment and narrowly missed being spotted by the Japanese. He sent word back to the Philippine people: "I shall return."

Two years later he waded into the water on the shores of the Philippines and said, "People of the Philippines, I have returned." MacArthur made this promise so the people of the Philippines wouldn't think he was abandoning them to the Japanese troops. He wanted them to have hope. And he kept his promise.

In a much greater way, Jesus told His disciples that He would return. He wants us to keep our hope in Him and to be prepared. He expects us to be good stewards or caretakers of the time, talents, and resources He's entrusted to us. When He returns, we will give Him an accounting of what we did with what He gave us.

Evening – PRAY FOR HIS RETURN

The end of all things is near. Therefore be alert and of sober mind so that you may pray.
1 PETER 4:7 NIV

World peace is an ever-present concern and likely one that God's people take to Him in prayer. It seems overwhelming to pray for something that appears impossible, but when Christians pray for peace, they pray knowing that Jesus will fulfill His promise of coming back. How long will it take for Him to return? No human knows. In the meantime, Christians persistently pray for His return and try to live peacefully in a chaotic world.

Around A.D. 600, Jerusalem fell to the Babylonians. The Jews were exiled to Babylonia and held captive for seventy years. God told the prophet Jeremiah to tell His people to settle there and live normally. He said they should seek peace in the place in which they lived until He came back to get them (Jeremiah 29:4–7).

Today's Christians are similar to those Jews. They live normally in an evil world seeking peace on earth while holding on to the promise of Jesus' return.

Paul wrote, "Brothers and sisters, whatever is true, whatever is noble, whatever is right, whatever is pure, whatever is lovely, whatever is admirable. . .think about such things. . . . And the God of peace will be with you" (Philippians 4:8–9 NIV).

May God's peace be with you today and every day until Jesus comes.

Morning – TRUST THE LORD WITH YOUR PROBLEMS

Cast your cares on the LORD and he will sustain you;
he will never let the righteous be shaken.
PSALM 55:22 NIV

Dawn has her fair share of problems. With an elderly father, husband, four children and their spouses, and ten grandchildren, there is always something going wrong. She tries to be a prayer warrior for her family. However, even as she hands the Lord today's problems, she knows that some of them will follow into tomorrow. In addition to the problems that carry over, Dawn knows that tomorrow will also bring new problems.

Dawn knows her faith is the lifeline that sustains her. Dawn needs daily spiritual energy just as her body needs energy from food. She needs both types of energy to face life's problems. Without adequate energy, Dawn's ability to cope would shrivel and her emotions would become raw. Dawn could literally be drawn into a downward spiral. Without God, life could be overwhelming.

The only healthy way Dawn has found to face her problems is with God's help. She casts her cares on the Lord. After letting go, Dawn trusts that God will be with her family as each challenge is faced.

Although God never promised life would be easy, He did promise to sustain us.

Evening – HE IS MORE THAN ABLE

Now all glory to God, who is able, through his mighty power at work within us,
to accomplish infinitely more than we might ask or think. Glory to him in the
church and in Christ Jesus through all generations forever and ever! Amen.
EPHESIANS 3:20–21 NLT

Did you ever hear the saying "The more you know, the more it is you know you don't know"? It's true. Whether it's bees or poetry or chemistry or space, the more we learn about a subject, the more we discover how much more there is to know. But while there is ultimately an end to man's knowledge of earthly things, it's impossible to even begin to grasp how big God is. We don't know even a fraction of His power. Our minds are just not capable of fully comprehending His ability, His character, and His love for us.

When we think of God, we tend to think about His abilities relative to our own. We don't even consider doing great things for Him, because we can't fathom how it could happen. Could you be unknowingly limiting God? Whether or not we recognize it, His mighty power, the Holy Spirit, is at work within us, doing more than we can imagine. Avail yourself of this power—let Him do through you things that you can't even begin to comprehend.

DAY 96

Morning – MAKING GOOD DECISIONS

Trust in the LORD with all your heart, and lean not on your own understanding;
in all your ways acknowledge Him, and He shall direct your paths. Do not
. be wise in your own eyes; fear the LORD and depart from evil.
PROVERBS 3:5–7 NKJV

Everyone goes through tough times, and having to make important decisions during those dark days only adds to the pain and frustration. Marilyn wanted to do the right thing in regard to a failing relationship, but she worried she would make a mistake she'd regret. She went to an older Christian friend for advice. He listened and talked with her, but in the end, he said, "You need to make a decision, but only you can do it. No one can make it for you."

Marilyn knew her friend was right. She began praying earnestly about the situation, relying on God for wisdom and courage. Some days were still hard and she didn't know which direction to take, but she continued to trust God and wait for His help. When the resolution came, Marilyn knew God had intervened and worked things out for the best.

When we learn to trust the Lord and not our own limited understanding, He will direct our paths. The secret is to trust Him with all our hearts and acknowledge Him. God is personal for each of us. He wants to be included in our decisions and our daily lives. No matter what we face, He knows how to resolve it. Whatever you need, trust Him.

Evening – GOD HAS A PLAN

"For I know the plans I have for you," declares the LORD, "plans to prosper
you and not to harm you, plans to give you hope and a future."
JEREMIAH 29:11 NIV

Bill and Sue decided to sell their home and move to a smaller city. They agreed they would not get in a hurry. They wanted God's will for their future home. Sue prayed about the things she wanted in their new home—an older home with wood floors and moldings, room to create a home office, and space for her book collection.

They met with a real estate agent, but neither Sue nor Bill felt God leading them to buy any of the properties they viewed. Two years passed as they continued watching the market for a house. They hoped for a quick sell of their home, but no one showed any interest for months; then a young couple made an offer. About the same time, Bill and Sue found two houses they liked but after an inspection learned the first one had too many problems. They made an offer on their second choice. After they closed and moved in, Sue was walking through the home one day when she stopped in the middle of a room and looked around. Everything she had asked God for was in the home they had purchased. Peace settled over her as she realized God had known the location of the right house and when it would become available and had directed them according to His plan.

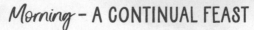

Morning – A CONTINUAL FEAST

The cheerful heart has a continual feast.
PROVERBS 15:15 NIV

Ellen left lunch with a friend in a foul mood, which lasted through afternoon errands, dinner preparation, and kitchen cleanup. Finally, the truth dawned on her: she felt terrible because her friend, who never seemed happy, had complained through their entire lunch.

Ellen vowed to back off on weekly lunches with her friend, instead keeping their communication to short phone calls or texts. *I can pray for her*, she thought. *But I don't have to spend a lot of time with her.*

Our choice of companions has much to do with our outlook. Negativity and positivity are both contagious. The writer of Proverbs says that a cheerful heart has a continual feast. So it's safe to assume that a grumpy heart will feel hungry and lacking instead of full.

While God calls us to minister to those who are hurting, we can do so with discernment. Next time someone complains, ask them to pray with you about their concerns. Tell them a story of how you overcame negativity or repaired a relationship. You could help turn their day around, and you won't feel like you've been beaten up afterward.

Evening – IT ONLY TAKES A MOMENT

Jesus wept.
JOHN 11:35 NASB

In the words of Barnaby from *Hello, Dolly!*: "It only takes a moment to be loved your whole life long." Americans are intrigued by the idea of love at first sight, but there is another kind of love that can happen in a moment that is deeper than romance.

Susan was having trouble finding a friend's grave site when an older woman at the cemetery helped her locate it. On the way out, Susan saw the woman standing at her son's grave and brought her some leftover flowers. As Susan explained, tears welled up in the woman's eyes. Soon they were crying in each other's arms. "I probably won't ever see her again," Susan said, "but I think about her a lot. It's not often you share a fragile moment like that with a stranger."

Romans 12:15 (NASB) says, "Rejoice with those who rejoice, and weep with those who weep." You never know when you are going to be called by God to reach out to a stranger. You never know when a soft word or a kind act of compassion will touch someone's life forever.

Jesus experienced this kind of empathy from Simeon, a stranger in the crowd, who literally felt Jesus' pain when he was summoned to carry the cross for a while. Like Simeon, may every Christian be prepared at any time to bear another's burden and relieve their suffering if only for a little while.

Morning – A NEW HEART

*"I will give you a new heart and put a new spirit within you;
I will take the heart of stone out of your flesh and give you a
heart of flesh. I will put My Spirit within you and cause you to
walk in My statutes, and you will keep My judgments and do them."*
EZEKIEL 36:26–27 NKJV

Sue accompanied her husband, Bill, to a follow-up appointment with the cardiologist following a heart procedure a few months earlier. The nurse checked his blood pressure and took an EKG; then the doctor came in for a visit. After talking with them for a few minutes, he said, "Everything looks great, perfect in fact. It doesn't mean the AFib won't come back, but let's continue with the medication you're taking. It's good for your heart and will help protect you." They left the doctor's office feeling good about Bill's condition.

Before we met Christ, each of us had serious heart problems. In short, we needed a heart transplant. Our heart was sinful, self-centered, and full of carnal desires. God saw our need and provided the necessary operation. He promised us a new heart and a new spirit. He removed the heart of stone and gave us a heart of flesh, one that would respond to His touch. He placed His Spirit within us to teach us to follow His statutes. As we do, He will give us the good report we need to hear from the great physician who performed the surgery.

Evening – FULL REDEMPTION AND LOVE

*Israel, put your hope in the LORD, for with the LORD is
unfailing love and with him is full redemption.*
PSALM 130:7 NIV

Jesus offers each of us full redemption: complete freedom from sin because of His great love for us. God doesn't want us to carry around our list of sins, being burdened by our past mistakes. He wants us to have a clear conscience, a joy-filled life!

The Bible tells us that God removes our sins as far as the east is from the west (Psalm 103:12) and that He remembers our sin no more (Isaiah 43:25; Hebrews 8:12). It's so important to confess your sins to the Lord as soon as you feel convicted and then turn from them and move in a right direction. There is no reason to hang your head in shame over sins of the past.

Turning from sin is tough. Especially when it has become a bad habit. Find an accountability partner to pray for you and check in with you about your struggles, but don't allow the devil to speak lies into your life. You have full redemption through Jesus Christ!

Morning – WHEN YOU ARE TEMPTED

No temptation has overtaken you except what is common to mankind. And God is faithful; he will not let you be tempted beyond what you can bear. But when you are tempted, he will also provide a way out so that you can endure it.
1 Corinthians 10:13 niv

Have you ever felt that temptation was just too great? Have you given in to it? You are not alone. It is not easy to resist temptation. Satan, the prince of darkness, is always seeking to devour God's children. He knows your personal weaknesses and uses them against you. The good news is that there is always a way out when you are tempted to sin. Every temptation that you have ever faced or will face in the future has been experienced by others. No temptation is new. Satan just recycles the same juicy bait and uses it again and again, generation after generation. Staying in God's Word and praying daily will help you to resist temptation. Being part of a Christian community will help with this also. As you bring down your walls and allow other believers to get close to you, they can pray for you and hold you accountable. Remember that no matter what temptations you are facing today, the payoff will be far greater if you resist than if you give in. Jesus stands ready to help you escape if only you will reach out and take His hand.

Evening – RUNNING THE RACE

Wherefore seeing we also are compassed about with so great a cloud of witnesses, let us lay aside every weight, and the sin which doth so easily beset us, and let us run with patience the race that is set before us, looking unto Jesus the author and finisher of our faith.
Hebrews 12:1–2 kjv

The Christian life is a race. It must be run with endurance. It requires training and discipline. It is about putting one foot in front of the other, sometimes quickly, sometimes slowly, but always, always moving forward. When a runner stumbles in a 5K or marathon, what does he do? Does he just sit down right then and there and call it quits? If the race is not run with perfection, does he just throw in the towel? Of course not! Likewise, as you are running the race, when you get sidetracked or distracted, when you fall to temptation or take your eyes off the goal, ask Jesus to get you back on track. An old hymn puts it like this: "Turn your eyes upon Jesus. Look full in His wonderful face. And the things of earth will grow strangely dim, in the light of His glory and grace!" Look to Christ, the author and finisher of your faith. He will run right alongside you, encouraging you every step of the way.

DAY 100

Morning – PEACE WITHIN

A heart at peace gives life to the body, but envy rots the bones.
PROVERBS 14:30 NIV

Valerie carried a chip on her shoulder. Born to an unwed teen mother, she grew up knowing money was always in short supply. Valerie acted out her anger issues, causing school performance problems and brushes with law enforcement. Valerie had it in for the goody-two-shoes girls from wealthy families. She escalated her pranks until she was caught stealing.

During her interview with the high school disciplinary officer, Valerie said that it wasn't fair that her victim had so many more opportunities because she was born into money. She told the officer that it made her sick to be in class with the lucky goody-two-shoes girl.

"Valerie," the officer said, "you aren't using that term correctly." She went on to describe the old British fable titled "Goody Two-shoes." Goody Two-shoes was the nickname for a poor orphan girl who had but one shoe. She bubbles with happiness when a rich gentleman gives her a pair of shoes. The girl grows up to become a teacher and marry a wealthy man. The officer told Valerie that the story showed how heredity didn't need to limit her destiny. If Valerie chose to be grateful for what she had and worked to make the best of her life, the officer believed she would find peace and contentment. If Valerie let herself envy others for the advantages she thought they had, her future would likely be bleak.

Evening – ALREADY LOVED

Behold, what manner of love the Father hath bestowed
upon us, that we should be called the sons of God.
1 JOHN 3:1 KJV

Sheila struggled with feelings of resentment when she heard about fellow authors' successes. Years of late-night toil had led to one book and a weekly newspaper column. But low sales figures on her book and repeated rejections left her discouraged. She prayed for contentment, realizing that her problems were small compared to the rest of the world.

One day, Sheila was playing a computer game with her toddler. On the desk was a copy of her first book. Jenny looked at the illustration of a frazzled mom on the cover and said, "Is that you?"

"No, sweetie," Sheila said, "but Mommy's name is on the cover. See here—it says, 'by Sheila Masters.'"

"Oh!" Jenny said, grinning, "I *love* Sheila Masters!"

Sheila blinked back tears. As she hugged her child, she thanked God for such a simple reminder that whether or not she ever reached the bestselling list, she was already loved—by her family, but more important, by the Father who had given her a gift with words.

Morning – CALLED TO BE STORYTELLERS

*I will sing of the LORD's great love forever; with my mouth I will
make your faithfulness known through all generations.*
PSALM 89:1 NIV

In addition to being prayers and praise songs, some of the psalms also retell portions of Israel's history. The Israelites would sing them together to praise the past deeds of their deliverer (e.g., Psalm 136). Today's worship songs don't list what He's done for us specifically like the Israelites' songs did, but we should definitely follow their example of remembrance.

Christians often use the word *testimony* to name the story of how they accepted Jesus as their Savior. Salvation is a great proof of God's love, but His work doesn't stop there. He daily fills our lives with His provision, nearness, and loving patience. When we recognize what He has done for us, we can be storytellers of His faithfulness, like the psalmist. We gather strength for the challenges ahead when we recall the victories He granted in the past, and our ongoing testimonies of His faithfulness display His love to those who don't know Him personally.

When you feel troubled, tell yourself *your* stories of His faithfulness. When did you feel His comfort when you called on Him for help? When has He provided for your needs beyond expectation? Just as He did then, your unchanging God will never stop caring for you.

Evening – RECYCLING

*Blessed be the God and Father of our Lord Jesus Christ, the Father
of mercies and God of all comfort, who comforts us in all our affliction
so that we will be able to comfort those who are in any affliction with
the comfort with which we ourselves are comforted by God.*
2 CORINTHIANS 1:3–4 NASB

Have you ever considered how much use the Lord can make out of the garbage of our lives? As Christians, we can take the good and bad events we've experienced and use them to witness to others of the goodness of God. When we've walked a path and struggled with a problem, and God has seen us through to the other side, we need to reach out to a brother or sister. Ambassador Clare Boothe Luce once stated, "There are no hopeless situations; there are only people who have grown hopeless about them." That's when we might offer encouragement.

God weaves a life tapestry for each of us; when we focus on the knotted thread, we don't see any beauty. However, a fellow believer can show us his tapestry made from similar knots, and we see the picture. How precious of the Lord to allow us to share with one another. Never underestimate the power of your testimony.

Morning – SIMPLE YET POWERFUL WORDS

*Humble yourselves, therefore, under God's
mighty hand, that he may lift you up in due time.*
1 PETER 5:6 NIV

How can a person talk and talk and talk and yet when it comes time to speak words that have great importance, they are speechless? Two of those weighty words are "I'm sorry."

Without those words—and the sincerity of spirit backing them up—marriages fail, friendships break apart, family members suffer, working relationships become strained, and the church loses its ability to minister to people.

So why do we become tongue-tied on those simple words? Because it is easy to justify our position on any matter. Easy to take our own side in an argument. You name it, and we can find a way to point to someone else as the villain in any given circumstance. We must be the heroes, after all. We know our Bibles. We sit in the same pew every Sunday. We can spot sin in someone else's life faster than you can say, "Judgment Day!" But the truth is, sometimes even as Christians, we choose to play the villain in our life story. We forget kindness. We turn our head on justice. We forget the most important scriptures on love.

We need to take a deep look in the mirror, spiritually speaking, asking the Lord to show us if we are at fault and to give us the courage to make things right with others—to say the simple yet powerful words that can change a heart, a life.

Evening – MAKING ALLOWANCES

*Always be humble and gentle. Be patient with each other,
making allowance for each other's faults because of your love.*
EPHESIANS 4:2 NLT

This verse contains such a simple, forgotten truth, doesn't it? God wants us to be holy. He wants us to be righteous and good and godly. But He knows we'll never get it exactly right until we're made perfect in His presence.

Until then, we all have our faults. Numerous faults, if we're honest with ourselves. And God doesn't want us standing around, whispering and pointing self-righteous fingers of condemnation. God is the only one who is allowed to wear the judge's robe. The only one.

And He doesn't condemn us. Instead, He pours His love and acceptance into our lives, with a gentle admonition to "go and sin no more" (John 8:11 NLT). In other words, "It's okay. You messed up, but it's been taken care of. The price has been paid. I still love you. Just try not to do it again."

Why do we find it so hard to extend grace to others when so much grace has been shown to us? As we go through each day, let's make it a point to live out this verse. Let's be humble, gentle, and patient, making allowances for the faults of others because of God's love.

Morning – TRUTH THAT IS IN PLAIN SIGHT

"Then you will know the truth, and the truth will set you free."
JOHN 8:32 NIV

In the original Greek language, the word for truth in John 8:32 means that it's truth that is in plain sight; it's obvious. It's truth that is right before your eyes.

When I read this, I thought, *Wait a minute! Truth that is right before your eyes? We hardly feel like truth is right before our eyes! It seems like it's hidden and so very difficult to apprehend. Why is this?* As I mulled this over, the thought that immediately came to mind is that our hearts are often so unbelieving.

God tells us who He is; we doubt it. He confesses His love for us in scripture; we ignore it. He tells us how to live; we do things our own way. And so, it is with us like it was with the disciples when Jesus asked them, "Do you not yet see or understand? Do you have a hardened heart?" We see but we don't see. We hear but we don't listen. We know it but we don't understand. All of this means that we miss the truth that is right in front of our eyes; we remain bound when we could be set free. It's not the person who just intellectually knows the truth who is set free; it's the person who knows and believes that is set free.

Evening – THE WORKERS ARE FEW

The Spirit who lives in you is greater than the spirit who lives in the world.
1 JOHN 4:4 NLT

Bailey was excited about her salvation. She told her Christian friend, "Now the real work begins." But her friend replied, "No, the work was done on the cross. You just have to learn to rely on that."

Satan has done a fantastic job of paralyzing Christians with this lie: "I'm not good enough." Satan is called "the accuser of [the] brethren" (Revelation 12:10 KJV), and his most powerful tool is to continually and persuasively remind you of your shortcomings.

So many Christians avoid serving the church because they feel inadequate, uneducated, and unworthy. Jesus said, "The harvest is plentiful but the workers are few" (Matthew 9:37 NIV).

The truth is we are no longer enslaved to sin. Through the Holy Spirit, we have the power to overcome and carry on. Romans 8:37 (NIV) says, "We are more than conquerors through him who loved us." The Holy Spirit is always full of grace for the believer. Every conviction is for growth, sharpening, and disciplining, never guilt and shame.

Satan is right about one thing—we're not good enough; we fail over and over. But here is the difference: our confidence is in Christ, not ourselves. And He has set us free!

Morning – DON'T WASTE YOUR TALENTS

"His master replied, 'Well done, good and faithful servant! You have been faithful with a few things; I will put you in charge of many things. Come and share your master's happiness!' "
MATTHEW 25:23 NIV

Imagine inheriting a fortune and then burying the money in the backyard. You don't want to make a mistake in spending it, so you hide it. Most of us would agree this kind of thinking is ridiculous. We would spend the money, either putting it to good use or just for our pleasure.

The verse above is near the end of the parable of the talents. This servant used the talents the master had given him to create more talents. In biblical times a talent was a measure of weight used for precious metals. It was often used as money.

The spiritual gifts or "talents" God has given us are precious. Yet like a bar of gold sitting in a bank vault, they do no good unless they are used. Every believer receives spiritual gifts or "talents" after receiving Christ. The purpose of these gifts is to build up the body of Christ.

When it comes to our spiritual gifts, many of us still have them buried in the backyard. We don't think we're good enough yet or we're afraid of making a mistake. But notice the servant didn't get judged on how well he did. Just on whether or not he used his talents.

Evening – JOY IN SERVING

Now John also was baptizing at Aenon near Salim, because there was plenty of water, and people were coming and being baptized.
JOHN 3:23 NIV

John the Baptist was single-mindedly focused on what God had told him to do. He went to a place that had the two things he needed to fulfill his mission: water and people wanting to be baptized.

Sometimes we make serving God more complicated than it needs to be. We don't need to wait for conditions to be right or to have more knowledge or experience or resources. We can serve right now where God has us. He will grow us into what He needs us to be.

John had joy because he was doing what he was supposed to be doing. He knew his mission had a season. He was preparing to let someone else, Jesus, take over. It was not about John. It was about God. Mothers with small children can relate to this. The ministry of raising children is just for a season, as we prepare them to be responsible adults. The goal is to work ourselves out of a job.

What talents and interests do you have? What resources has God given you? How can you use what you have right now to serve Him? Be open to see what God brings your way. Serve God and find your joy.

Morning – PRAYING THE MIND OF CHRIST

*We demolish arguments and every pretension that sets itself
up against the knowledge of God, and we take captive
every thought to make it obedient to Christ.*
2 CORINTHIANS 10:5 NIV

As Christ-followers, we are learning to become like Him in our thoughts, words, and deeds. Part of becoming Christlike is also in mastering our minds. Sometimes it is hard to pray because other thoughts interfere with our ability to listen closely to what God is saying. This is a favorite trick of Satan's. . .getting us to think about our to-do list instead of what God is trying to tell us.

By reading and praying scripture and using positive statements in our prayers that claim what God has already said He will do for us, the mind of Christ is being activated in us. By taking captive every thought, we learn to know what thought is of God, what belongs to us, and what is of the enemy. Recognize, take captive, and bind up the thoughts that are of the enemy, and throw them out! The more we commune with God, fellowship with Him, and learn from Him, the more we cultivate the mind of Christ.

Evening – FIX YOUR THOUGHTS ON TRUTH

*And now, dear brothers and sisters, one final thing. Fix your thoughts on
what is true, and honorable, and right, and pure, and lovely, and admirable.
Think about things that are excellent and worthy of praise.*
PHILIPPIANS 4:8 NLT

In a world loaded with mixed messages and immorality of every kind, it becomes increasingly difficult to have pure thoughts and clear minds. What can a believer do to keep her mind set on Christ? Replace the negative message with a positive message from God's Word.

Think about the negative messages that you struggle with the most. Maybe you struggle with some of these: You're not thin enough. You're not spiritual enough. You've made a lot of mistakes, etc.

Dig through the scriptures and find truth from God's Word to combat the false message that you're struggling with. Write the passages down and memorize them. Here are a few to get you started:

- God looks at my heart, not my outward appearance. (1 Samuel 16:7)
- I am free in Christ. (1 Corinthians 1:30)
- I am a new creation. My old self is gone! (2 Corinthians 5:17)

The next time you feel negativity and false messages slip into your thinking, fix your thoughts on what you know to be true. Pray for the Lord to replace the doubts and negativity with His words of truth.

DAY 106

Morning – LET GOD REIGN!

Oh, how great are God's riches and wisdom and knowledge! How impossible it is for us to understand his decisions and his ways! For who can know the LORD's thoughts? Who knows enough to give him advice? And who has given him so much that he needs to pay it back? For everything comes from him and exists by his power and is intended for his glory. All glory to him forever! Amen.

ROMANS 11:33–36 NLT

It's easy for us to believe that we carry the world on our shoulders. We tend to believe, though we may not admit it, that we alone make the world turn. We convince ourselves that worry, finances, or power will put us in control. But in truth God is the one who controls all.

What a blessed peace awaits us! As you go about your day, rest in the assurance that God, not you, is in control. God understands every feeling you experience, and He can comfort you. God knows the best steps for you to take in life, and He is willing to guide you. He is above all and knows all, yet He is not out of reach.

Set your eyes firmly on the Lord, and He will care for you.

Evening – MY HELP COMES FROM ABOVE

Commit everything you do to the LORD. Trust him, and he will help you. He will make your innocence radiate like the dawn, and the justice of your cause will shine like the noonday sun.

PSALM 37:5–6 NLT

Have you ever been on a quest to find the right doctor to cure a particular ill? Maybe you go to your primary care physician and he sends you to a specialist. Perhaps that specialist sends you to a subspecialist. At every step along the way, you groan and say, "I just want someone who can help me!" Aren't you glad to hear that you have a straight shot to your heavenly Father? You don't need a referral. You don't need to wait in line. And He's got the solution to any problem you might be facing. You won't need a second opinion because He'll have things fixed up before you make it that far. Run to Him. Trust Him. He will give you all the help you need.

Morning – STRENGTH IN THE LORD

The Lord is my light and my salvation—whom shall I fear?
The Lord is the stronghold of my life—of whom shall I be afraid?
PSALM 27:1 NIV

Even when it seems that everything is piling up around you, Christ is there for you. Take heart! He is your stronghold, a very present help right in the midst of your trial. Regardless of what comes against you in this life, you have the Lord on your side. He is your light in the darkness and your salvation from eternal separation from God. You have nothing to fear.

At times, this world can be a tough, unfair, lonely place. Since the fall of man in the garden, things have not been as God originally intended. The Bible assures us that we will face trials in this life, but it also exclaims that we are more than conquerors through Christ who is in us! When you find yourself up against a tribulation that seems insurmountable, *look up.* Christ is there. He goes before you, stands with you, and is backing you up in your time of need. You may lose everyone and everything else in this life, but nothing has the power to separate you from the love of Christ. Nothing.

Evening – REJOICING!

Always be full of joy in the Lord. I say it again—rejoice!
PHILIPPIANS 4:4 NLT

Have you ever watched a toddler laugh? It's amazing, isn't it? Those adorable giggles are contagious. Before long you can't help but join in, your laughter filling the room. After all, nothing compares to the sheer joy of an innocent child. It bubbles up from the deepest, God-given place, completely unhindered by concerns, worries, or distractions. How many times do we become so burdened by life's complexities that we forget to rejoice? What would it feel like to let those giggles rise to the surface, even on the worst days? What's that you say? You have nothing to feel joyful about? Look at those flowers blooming in the field! (Beauty!) Check out the food in your pantry. (Provision!) Glance into a grandchild's eyes or a coworker's heart. There's plenty of fodder for a joy-filled life. All we have to do is turn our focus from the pain to the glimpses of heaven right in front of us. Today, may your eyes be opened to many joy-filled moments.

Morning – THE ALABASTER BOX

*As she stood behind him at his feet weeping, she began to wet
his feet with her tears. Then she wiped them with her hair,
kissed them and poured perfume on them.*
LUKE 7:38 NIV

The story of Mary and her alabaster box of high-priced perfume is a familiar one. Historically, this kind of perfume was given to a woman by her parents as a dowry. It was to be used on her wedding night, to be poured out on her husband's feet in an act of submission. So when Mary poured out this costly substance onto Jesus' feet, it was a statement of her complete love, devotion, submission, and obedience. She offered Him all of herself.

Many who witnessed the outpouring of this expensive perfume were angered because it could have been sold for a lot of money and used to fund ministry. They missed the point of her extravagant love. She did not take cheap perfume but some of the most expensive ever made. And she didn't use just a few drops but emptied the container! Mary is a wonderful example for us—to love completely, being humbled at the feet of her Savior, and to offer her complete self. How beautiful and generous! May we be as well!

Evening – GIVING OUT OF NEED

*"Give, and you will receive. Your gift will return to you in full—pressed down,
shaken together to make room for more, running over, and poured into your
lap. The amount you give will determine the amount you get back."*
LUKE 6:38 NLT

As usual, Jesus saw things from a different perspective. He was in the temple, watching people bring their gifts. Instead of honoring the Pharisees, with all their pomp and circumstance, Jesus points out a poor widow. "Truly I tell you," He said, "this poor widow has put in more than all the others. All these people gave their gifts out of their wealth; but she out of her poverty put in all she had to live on" (Luke 21:3–4 NIV).

While the rich gave out of their abundance, the widow gave out of her need. It's not difficult to give when we are sure all our needs are met. We just scrape a little off the top and leave it in the offering plate. Giving out of our poverty is a profound act of faith. When we lay our all on the altar, God promises to multiply it beyond our wildest imagination. What are you holding back from the Lord today? Give. God cannot wait to multiply your efforts.

Morning – MOTHER'S DANCE

The Spirit of the Sovereign Lord is upon me, for the Lord has anointed me to bring good news to the poor. He has sent me to comfort the brokenhearted.
ISAIAH 61:1 NLT

Adam's mother passed away two years before his wedding, a wedding that came just a year or so after he declared to his brothers that he would be the last to marry. This was the sort of thing he didn't mind being wrong about. But then, God had brought some pretty amazing changes to his life, why was he surprised?

The wedding was a wonderful day for everyone present, but Adam and Kayla's families were especially blessed. His brothers toasted to a woman their mother would be proud that Adam had chosen. When it came time for the traditional groom's dance with his mother, guests watched as Kayla's mother, Deb, stepped out onto the floor and danced with her new son-in-law.

This alone would seem sweet enough, but add to it the loss of the bride's sister and only sibling years ago—Linette would be in her early twenties now. Guests who didn't know their stories wondered why some eyes welled up and spilled over. Why some looked away and swallowed hard, and yet others smiled broadly with joy.

This mother's dance with the groom was a beautiful picture of God's love for us, how He provides comfort and joy in this life until we are joined with loved ones in eternity.

Evening – GEMS OF WISDOM

*"Do you hear what these children are saying?" they asked him.
"Yes," replied Jesus, "have you never read, 'From the lips of children and infants you, Lord, have called forth your praise'?"*
MATTHEW 21:16 NIV

Nicole stood at her father's grave. It had been a year since the Lord had taken him home. Although the official cause of death was leukemia, Nicole knew her father had left this world to be with his heavenly Father.

"Dad, I miss you every day. You would be surprised at how many times I hear your words in my mind, or maybe I hear them with my heart. Your rambunctious granddaughter frequently reminds me that you live in our hearts. As you would have said, 'out of the mouths of babes oft times come *gems*.'"

For Nicole, *gems* had oft come from her father's mouth. The advice he most frequently gave was *measure twice and cut once*. Although that *gem* was a carpentry saying, her dad had applied it to making careful decisions. And he had been right. When Nicole took the time to check things twice before taking action, she made better decisions and had fewer regrets.

"Dad, I'm proud to be your daughter. Although I didn't always appreciate your *gems* of wisdom when you shared them with me, now each is a treasure. And Dad you live on each time I pass along one of your *gems* to my daughter."

DAY 110

Morning – PRACTICING GRATITUDE

Everywhere and in every way, most excellent Felix,
we acknowledge this with profound gratitude.
Acts 24:3 niv

"Jean didn't even acknowledge my gift," Dani told her husband. "At the very least, an email would have been nice. Do people even write thank-you notes anymore?"

"I usually text people," Paul admitted.

"You tell people thanks, though. That's good!" Dani replied.

The couple talked for a few minutes about how they could encourage gratitude in their two young children. They decided on a few actions. First, they would buy fill-in-the-blank notes at the local stationery store. Second, Dani would sit down with her two little ones and show them how to write a thank-you letter. Third, the family would verbally share about that particular day's blessings at the table every time they gathered for dinner.

After a few months, Dani acknowledged (gratefully!) that she and Paul had begun the long process of teaching her children to be thankful to God—and to the people in their lives who spent time and/or money on them.

How can you express gratitude to someone today? Send a friend a social media message, thanking them for a kind word; write a note to someone who gives of their time (Bible teacher, committee member, volunteer); call a staff member at your church and tell them "thanks" for all they do; email a relative and praise them for a stellar quality or an act of selfless service.

Evening – LET YOUR THANKFULNESS SHOW

In everything give thanks; for this is God's will for you in Christ Jesus.
1 Thessalonians 5:18 nasb

You were probably taught from a young age to say "Thank you" when someone does something for you. Being thankful doesn't seem like a big deal. But in this verse, Paul asserts that being thankful is God's will for you. All of a sudden, thankfulness sounds like an essential part of our walk with God.

Those who are in Christ have abundant reason to be thankful. You were owned by and enslaved to the horrible master of sin. You were bought from him with a price that could never be repaid— the blood of a flawless Lamb. And not only were you rescued from a life of separation from God, but you were adopted into His family. You have been lavished with grace and love. The Lord has provided for you, brought you into a relationship with Him, and promised you an eternity with Him. He did all this, not because you could do something for Him, but just because He decided to place His love on you. It makes perfect sense that Paul would say your life should be characterized by thankfulness.

In a world where people exhibit an increasing sense of entitlement and self-centeredness, think of how much a thankful spirit will stand out to those around you. Everyone *is* entitled—to death and an eternity away from God. Be thankful, for God's will for you is infinitely better than anything you could deserve.

Morning – A MATTER OF LIFE OR DEATH

*For if you live according to the flesh, you will die; but if by the
Spirit you put to death the misdeeds of the body, you will live.*
ROMANS 8:13 NIV

A diabetic is dependent upon insulin. A cancer diagnosis demands medical treatment. For the blind, a cane or a seeing-eye dog is essential. These are matters of life or death.

The Bible teaches of another such matter. It is an ongoing war within the believer that simply must be won by the right side! It is spiritual life versus spiritual death.

The Holy Spirit indwells believers in Christ. Jesus Himself taught His followers about this third part of the Trinity before He ascended into heaven. He promised that a helper would come. This helper, the Holy Spirit, came when Jesus went away. The Spirit convicts us of sin. The Spirit, sometimes referred to as our counselor, also guides us in truth.

If you are a Christian, the Holy Spirit is your personal power source. The strength to do what is right is within you if you choose to live by the Spirit and not by the flesh. You will be tempted to follow voices that tell you to do as you please or that "it's okay if it feels right." You will experience anger and other emotions that can lead you astray in life. But if you pay attention, your Helper, the Holy Spirit, will reveal the Father's ways. It is a matter of life or death. Which will you choose?

Evening – A WOMAN REBORN

*"No one can enter the kingdom of God unless they are born of water and
the Spirit. Flesh gives birth to flesh, but the Spirit gives birth to spirit.
You should not be surprised at my saying, 'You must be born again.'"*
JOHN 3:5–7 NIV

If you are a believer in Jesus Christ, the old excuses will no longer work. The idea that you can't lose weight, give up smoking, stop drinking, stop frowning, etc., because you were "born this way" no longer applies. When you accepted Jesus, He gave you a new life. A new Spirit that now resides within you has gifted you a divine and heavenly existence.

God once breathed life into you when you were born physically, but now you have been reborn spiritually, brought to life by the breath of the Holy Spirit. You are a new creation (see 2 Corinthians 5:17). Your aims and nature are different, your heart more tender. So erase the thought, *I was born that way*, that keeps playing in your mind. And replace it with God's truth: *I am a new creation in Christ, a daughter of God. With my Father, anything is possible because I can do all things through my Brother who strengthens me.* It's the new improved you, a woman reborn, now a sister of all, courtesy of heaven above.

Morning – THE POWER OF PRAYER

Confess your sins to each other and pray for each other so that you may be healed. The earnest prayer of a righteous person has great power and produces wonderful results.
JAMES 5:16 NLT

There is power in prayer. Do you question this at times? There are many times in scripture when the fervent prayer of a believer actually changes God's mind! In James we read that the earnest prayer of a righteous person has great power and produces great results. You may be thinking that you are not righteous. Have you given your heart to Jesus? If you have accepted Him as your Savior, you have taken on the *righteousness* of Christ. Certainly you are not perfect. In your humanity, you still sin and fall short. But God sees you through a Jesus lens! And so, your prayers reach the ears of your heavenly Father.

Pray often. Pray earnestly. Pray without ceasing. Pray about everything. Prayer changes things. Look at Jesus' example of prayer during His time on earth. He went away to quiet places such as gardens to pray. He prayed in solitude. He prayed with all His heart. If anyone was busy, it was the Messiah! But Jesus always made time to pray. We ought to follow His example. Prayer changes things.

Evening – PRAY PERSISTENTLY

Rejoice always, pray continually, give thanks in all circumstances; for this is God's will for you in Christ Jesus.
1 THESSALONIANS 5:16–18 NIV

The Gospel of Luke tells about a widow who had an ongoing dispute with an enemy. The woman was stubborn and determined to win, and she refused to give up her dispute until a judge ruled in her favor. Many times she went to the judge demanding, "Give me justice!"

This judge didn't care about God or people, and he certainly didn't care if the woman got justice, but he *did* care about himself. The widow was driving him crazy! So, to make her go away, he ruled in her favor.

Jesus used this story to teach His followers about persistent prayer. He said, "Learn a lesson from this unjust judge. Even he rendered a just decision in the end. So don't you think God will surely give justice to his chosen people who cry out to him day and night?" (Luke 18:6–7 NLT)

When evil stalks Christians, they cry out, "Lord, deliver us!" Sometimes it feels like God is far away. But the widow's story reminds believers to be persistent in prayer and remain faithful that God will answer them. When Christians pray, it shows not only their faith in God but also their trust in His faithfulness toward them. In His time, the Lord will come and bring justice to His people.

Morning – MORE THAN A PIECE OF FRUIT

Thank you for making me so wonderfully complex!
Your workmanship is marvelous—how well I know it.
PSALM 139:14 NLT

You know about the fruit analogies for body shapes, right? Are you an apple or a pear? Do you know the advantages and drawbacks of your type? What about the health risks? Did you know that "apples" tend toward heart disease and "pears" lean more toward hormonally fed cancers? What if you're not a truly defined apple or pear but more of a squash or a string bean? Is there honestly anything more degrading than comparing ourselves to fruits and vegetables?

A woman is much more intricately designed than a piece of fruit. And the basic shape of our bodies is something over which we have no control; genetics handles that. We do have a say in what we eat and how we dress and whether we put much effort into exercise and upkeep. But who among us has not failed in these areas at some time or other?

Women were designed by God to be beautiful. And He likes variety. If we're speaking about the plant world, think about the many species of flowers around the globe. They come in every imaginable shape and color and petal dimension. And each of them has its own unique glory. Maybe we should be more like the flowers—stay connected to the source of our being, accept the sunshine and rain, and reflect His glory in how we grow.

Evening – TRUE BEAUTY

Charm is deceptive, and beauty does not last; but a
woman who fears the LORD will be greatly praised.
PROVERBS 31:30 NLT

Have you ever pondered the word *reflection*? When you stare at your reflection in the mirror, do you see your flaws or your beauty? Do you stare at your eyes or the wrinkles around them? Do you notice the intricacies of your mouth? Unless they're in putting-on-makeup mode, most women just take a quick glance in the looking glass before running out the door. Satisfied that the reflection meets expectation, a woman moves on. Oh, how God longs for His girls to see a different kind of beauty than the exterior. May your next glance in the mirror reveal a pure heart, generous hands, an uplifting mouth. When you fear/honor the Lord, your interior beauty will add all the sparkle and shine you need to an already lovely exterior.

Morning – FORGIVING THOSE WHO'VE WRONGED US

He who covers a transgression seeks love, but he who repeats a matter separates friends.
PROVERBS 17:9 NKJV

Shannon tossed and turned, unable to sleep. Finally she got up, padded into the living room, and sat down on the couch.

"Okay, God," she said, "I know I need to deal with this. I just don't know how."

Several months prior, Shannon's best friend, Amy, had stopped talking to her. Shannon tried asking Amy what was wrong, to no avail. It was as if a switch had been flipped. Amy wouldn't even look at her when they were both in the same room. The worst part? Amy had begun spreading vicious lies about her former BFF. Shannon felt baffled, angry, and hurt.

"How can I forgive her, Lord? I don't know what I did or why she's being so ugly to me—and I won't be getting an apology, since she won't even talk to me!" Tears ran down Shannon's face and her shoulders shook. She covered her face in her hands.

Then a voice whispered to her heart, "Give it to Me. Let Me deal with Amy. I died so you could be free of sin."

Shannon sighed. *Yes*, she thought. *I want to be free. I will lay this at Your feet, Jesus. I will forgive.*

Evening – ALL-PURPOSE CLEANER

Then Peter. . .asked, "Lord, how often should I forgive someone who sins against me? Seven times?" "No, not seven times," Jesus replied, "but seventy times seven!"
MATTHEW 18:21–22 NLT

Feelings of resentment, anger, jealousy, and revenge—all can be cleansed away by one solution. Forgiving those who offend us. When Jesus told Peter to forgive 490 times, He meant an unlimited amount. Forgive as often as it takes. It's not easy, but it works. Here's how:

1. Ask God for help. Forgiveness is a spiritual matter, requiring God's power and enablement.
2. Read God's words about forgiveness: Matthew 6:12–15; Mark 11:25–26; Ephesians 4:32; Colossians 3:13.
3. Read God's words about the evils of vengeance: Romans 12:17–21; 1 Peter 3:8–12.
4. Verbalize forgiveness. Tell God, "I forgive [the offender] for [the offense]. Ask God to forgive the offender too.
5. Every time an offense comes to mind, do step 4 again to win this spiritual battle. You will find it crossing your mind less often, and your negative emotions will decline.
6. Enjoy the fact that you did the right thing. You obeyed God.

Some people find it helpful to write down the offenses and then burn the paper. Even though we cannot forget what happened, that's okay. When it shoves back into our thinking, we must substitute this thought instead—*I have forgiven this person because I am a sinner too, and God has graciously forgiven me.*

Morning – PRIDE VS. HUMILITY

A man's pride shall bring him low:
but honour shall uphold the humble in spirit.
PROVERBS 29:23 KJV

A great leader is known by his or her character. It is perhaps the things that one doesn't take part in that sets him or her apart. Great leaders are not prideful or boastful. They don't consider their accomplishments to be things they have done "in and of themselves," but they recognize the hand of God on their lives. Great leaders know that it takes a team to reach a goal. A great CEO treats the lowest man on the totem pole with as much dignity as he treats an equal. A great school principal knows that the teachers, assistants, bus drivers, and cafeteria workers make a huge impact on the students and the climate of the school. No one likes a bragger. It gets old hearing anyone go on and on about themselves. The Bible is filled with the teaching that the low shall be made higher and the proud will be brought to destruction. A paraphrase of this verse as found in The Message goes like this: "Pride lands you flat on your face; humility prepares you for honors." Take note of the areas of your own life where pride may sneak in and destroy. Replace pride with humility. Others will notice. You will not go unrewarded when you seek to be humble in spirit.

Evening – WHO IS IT FOR?

"Say to all the people of the land, and to the priests: 'When you fasted and mourned in
the fifth and seventh months during those seventy years, did you really fast for Me—
for Me? When you eat and when you drink, do you not eat and drink for yourselves?' "
ZECHARIAH 7:5–6 NKJV

We severely kid ourselves if we think and act as though God cannot see or know our motives. But don't we live most of our lives in a concealed manner? What areas of your life do you withhold from the Lord, either intentionally or subconsciously? For most of us it's "mundane" things, such as our job, weight/self-image, chores, getting the car fixed, the morning rush to school or church. There are so many small areas in our lives that we don't offer to Christ either because we don't want to or don't see the need to. This is where we sin.

When we see something as being too menial for the Lord to concern Himself with, we take ownership and add it to our domain—a domain that becomes the "kingdom of self." Whether it is a long process or quick transition, our selfish and prideful hearts begin to harden. We begin to see ourselves as the authority in these small areas.

Ask the Lord to reveal where you rely on yourself and hold your opinion higher than His command. It is in these small and mundane areas that we build a stronger relationship with the Lord. If we can't trust Him in the small things, our faith will not stand when the waves get larger and storms prevail.

DAY 116

Morning – ONLY LOVE REMAINS

Hatred stirreth up strifes: but love covereth all sins.
PROVERBS 10:12 KJV

Marla had a beautiful childhood. She grew up in a home of consistent discipline and love, but she always felt like something was missing. She was captivated by the wonderful stories people shared of how bad their lives were—and how God miraculously intervened. She began to believe she didn't have a story—a *good* story—and she needed to get one.

At nineteen years old, she stepped away from those who loved her, and the enemy opened his mouth and swallowed her up. Years later she found herself using drugs, selling drugs, homeless or with a gang at times, and eventually in jail for possession. She had a story now—what would her parents say? Could God really love her again?

Peter and Greta visited their daughter in jail and discovered she was ready to turn her life around. Marla confessed her sins to God and to her parents, served her time in jail, and came home. She thought it would be different—that her parents would resent her for what she'd done, but consistently they loved her. They showed her the true picture of God's forgiveness. They allowed the past to be the past—and only love remained.

Evening – JONAH'S PRAYER

*"When my life was ebbing away, I remembered you,
LORD, and my prayer rose to you, to your holy temple."*
JONAH 2:7 NIV

Jonah ran from God. He knew where God had directed him to go, but he refused. He thought he knew better than God. He trusted in his own ways over God's. Where did it get him? He ended up in the belly of a great fish for three days. This was not a punishment but rather a forced retreat! Jonah needed time to think and pray. He came to the end of himself and remembered his Sovereign God. He describes the depths to which he was cast. This was not just physical but emotional as well. Jonah had been in a deep struggle between God's call and his own will.

In verse 6 of his great prayer from the belly of the fish, we read these words: "But you, LORD my God, brought my life up from the pit." When Jonah reached a point of desperation, he realized that God was his only hope. Have you been there? Not in the belly of a great fish, but in a place where you are made keenly aware that it is time to turn back to God? God loves His children and always stands ready to receive us when we need a second chance.

Morning – INDESCRIBABLE GRACE

*I would like to learn just one thing from you: Did you receive the
Spirit by the works of the law, or by believing what you heard?*
GALATIANS 3:2 NIV

Kristi accepted Christ at the age of twelve, but she spent her teenage years living in fear of "messing up" and not pleasing God. Perhaps her fear stemmed from a controlling mother, or maybe she misunderstood what her preacher taught. Whatever the reason, Kristi exhausted herself by trying too hard. She focused on what she didn't do, at the expense of peace and contentment in Christ.

Finally, during college, a mentor explained that she was trying to earn what was already hers. This mentor began walking Kristi through the scriptures and explaining to Kristi that God sees His children as righteous and holy because of Jesus' sacrifice on the cross. The concept of grace, once a dim, distant concept to Kristi, exploded in her mind and heart. Suddenly, she was filled with an unexplainable joy.

Ever since her second awakening, Kristi has been on a mission to spread the message of grace. She parents with purpose and loves her friends well, because she accepts God's approval of her through His Son. Even her non-Christian friends have noticed the difference—for which Kristi gives God all the glory.

Evening – LOVE AND MERCY

*"Therefore, I tell you, her many sins have been forgiven—as her great
love has shown. But whoever has been forgiven little loves little."*
LUKE 7:47 NIV

The woman in this verse recognized who Jesus was and washed His feet with her perfume. The Bible says that she lived a sinful life but that her faith in Christ saved her. She, who was guilty of much, was forgiven much. She experienced amazing grace and undeserved mercy. She loved Jesus and did what she could to worship Him.

Have you ever received a speeding ticket? Then you most likely deserved it. But have you ever deserved a speeding ticket and the officer let you off the hook? What a huge relief! That's mercy. The Bible tells us that the punishment for sin is death, but the gift of God is eternal life (Romans 6:23). The sinful woman didn't deserve mercy, and neither do we. But through Christ, we have been forgiven much.

God's Word says that if you've been given much, much is expected (Luke 12:48). This applies to many situations. Have you been given love and mercy? Yes, indeed! Then you're expected to show love and mercy in return.

DAY 118

Morning – FALLING OUT OF LOVE

And so we know and rely on the love God has for us. God is love.
Whoever lives in love lives in God, and God in them.
1 JOHN 4:16 NIV

"Mom," Zola said, "Ken and I are getting a divorce."

Her mother sat silently at the kitchen table letting the words slowly sink in. Divorce was against everything she believed in. "Why?" she asked.

"No *one* reason," Zola answered. "We just fell out of love."

It happens often—life gets in the way, hearts fall out of love. Human love fails, and people get divorced.

In Malachi 2:16, God says that He hates divorce. He compares it to violence. Those are strong words. But does that mean that God hates divorced people? No. God loves them.

Human relationships are vastly different from God's relationship with humans. Unlike divorce, the God-human relationship cannot fail. God never falls out of love with His people. He can't. He loves not because He feels love but because He *is* love.

When couples grow apart, they should be encouraged to work through their difficulties and try to salvage their marriage. But when all else fails, God does not. He loves them through their brokenheartedness and helps them to move on: "For I know the plans I have for you," declares the LORD, "plans to prosper you and not to harm you, plans to give you hope and a future" (Jeremiah 29:11 NIV).

Evening – LOVE GONE COLD

Sin will be rampant everywhere, and the love of many will grow cold.
MATTHEW 24:12 NLT

In a messed-up world that continually gives us advice contrary to what the Bible says, love and relationships get messed up too. When people become inconvenienced by their marriages and relationships, the common response today is to run. They stop showing love for each other and allow a cold heart to settle in.

God wants us to honor our commitments, and in doing so, we honor Him. Relationships take a lot of work. Marriage is a constant process of serving your spouse, trusting and forgiving each other daily. Friendships take patience and understanding. Families need lots of love and grace.

When you allow love to grow cold in your relationships, you turn from God's will in your life. Our primary purpose on earth is to love the Lord and love others (Matthew 22:37–39). Even when it's tough or uncomfortable. Remember that love is a choice.

So when you feel love growing cold, pray for God's love to shine in your heart and warm up your relationships.

Morning – CHOOSING FAITH

Be still in the presence of the Lord, and wait patiently for him to act. Don't worry about evil people who prosper or fret about their wicked schemes. Stop being angry! Turn from your rage! Do not lose your temper—it only leads to harm. For the wicked will be destroyed, but those who trust in the Lord will possess the land.

PSALM 37:7–9 NLT

Our faith is tested when life doesn't go the way we expect it to, when people who aren't following God prosper, and we seem to be an afterthought. At times we even go so far as to blame God for the things that are going wrong.

Even though it seems like the wicked are prospering and we are sitting on the sidelines, our daily grind is not in vain. Each day we are faithful is another seed planted. It may take time for it to grow, but grow it will. There will be a harvest.

Faith sees the facts but trusts God anyway. Faith is forcing yourself to worry no longer but to pray in earnest and leave the situation in His hands. Faith is choosing to trust and rest in His plan, rather than fret about what could happen. We must choose faith even when we don't feel it. It is through choosing faith that we please God. Choose faith, and see what He will do.

Evening – THE DEFINITION OF FAITH

Now faith is confidence in what we hope for and assurance about what we do not see. . . . And without faith it is impossible to please God, because anyone who comes to him must believe that he exists and that he rewards those who earnestly seek him.

HEBREWS 11:1, 6 NIV

Eyes of faith help us see the spiritual gifts God gives us. Faith allows us to see things normally unseen. Throughout the Old Testament, there are stories of people whose faith in God demonstrates what faith in action looks like: Abel sacrificed to God with a heart of worship, Enoch started following God in his later years, Elisha saw angel armies, and Noah built an ark in a land without rain.

In whom or what do you place your faith? God's character and His promises are faithful. Faith is the pathway to our relationship with God. We have faith to please God, to earnestly seek Him and believe in His reward, even when we can't see it with earthly eyes. We need to cultivate our eyes of faith, knowing that most of our reward for a faithful life will not be found in this life but in the next.

How do you grow your faith? Start with obedience. Worship, walk by faith, and share your journey with others. Faith will follow your obedience. Ask God to help you exercise your eyes of faith so you can see Him working. If you can't see Him, ask Him to reveal Himself to you.

Morning – THE HIGHER ROAD

"In this world you will have trouble. But take heart! I have overcome the world."
JOHN 16:33 NIV

During World War II, the Nazis imprisoned author Dr. Victor Frankl. As the Gestapo stripped him and cut away his wedding band, Frankl thought, *You can take away my wife, my children, and strip me of my clothes and freedom, but there is one thing you cannot take—my freedom to choose how I react to whatever happens to me.*

John 16:33 acknowledges that Jesus overcame the world on our behalf, so we are fully equipped to do the same.

It's difficult to trust God against all odds when problems slash us like a paper shredder. Yet it is during those times that God gives us a clear choice: choose faith or break under the harsh realities of life.

Dr. Frankl had learned somewhere in his life's journey to take the higher road. He knew that faith and how we react to people or problems is a choice, not a feeling. We can respond in the flesh or submit to the Holy Spirit whatever happens to us. Often that means asking for forgiveness though you've done nothing wrong, encouraging someone despite their negative attitude, or extending a hand and risking rejection.

Mature believers know that hardships are a part of life, but Jesus has paved the pathway to overcome. And although taking "the higher road" is less traveled, it's worth the trek.

Evening – HURT HAPPENS—LOVE ANYWAY

"I have loved you even as the Father has loved me. Remain in my love."
JOHN 15:9 NLT

Do you ever feel like Jesus overcame life's challenges more easily than you because He was God? It's important to realize that Jesus lived His life as a man—empowered just as you are today as a believer. He relied on His relationship with God and the Holy Spirit working in Him to do all that He did. He too was human. He suffered pain, hurt, and disappointment just as you do.

Imagine His feelings when brothers, sisters, aunts, uncles, and cousins refused to believe He was the Messiah or discounted His words of truth because He was family. How painful it must have been to have those closest to Him reject Him. Jesus knew that Judas would betray Him and Peter would deny Him. Jesus must have felt that hurt deeply—and yet He loved them anyway. In the face of the cross, He asked God to forgive those who put Him there.

When faced with pain or disappointment, it's easier to become angry, defend yourself, or even sever the relationship. The same Spirit that empowered Jesus to live His faith can empower you. When hurt happens—choose to love anyway!

Morning – THE WORD FOR EVERY DAY

As for God, his way is perfect; the word of the LORD is tried:
he is a buckler to all them that trust in him.
2 SAMUEL 22:31 KJV

A few years ago, Jenna followed the advice of a mentor and began praying for God to give her one special word for the year. Two years ago, He impressed upon Jenna the word *refuge*, and it was perfect, because her family moved and experienced a lot of stress during the next year. It comforted her over those hectic and emotionally draining months to meditate on *refuge*.

Last December, God led her to ruminate on the word *delight* for the year. And what an interesting—and yes, delightful—few months it was. Over and over, He brought the word to her attention, sometimes in surprising places. Often, meditation on delight turned to prayer, as Jenna praised and thanked God for His provision and peace.

God's Word is such an incredible gift, one that goes hand in hand with prayer. It's amazing, really, that the Creator of the universe gave us the scriptures as His personal Word to us. When we're faithful to pick up the Word, He is faithful to use it to encourage us. Reading and praying through scripture is one of the keys to finding and keeping our sanity, peace, and joy.

Evening – USE IT OR LOSE IT

"Therefore consider carefully how you listen."
LUKE 8:18 NIV

Doing God's Word, not merely hearing it, was one of Jesus' repeated themes. His parable of the sower illustrated four different responses we can have whenever the seed of the Word of God hits our thinking. With a hard heart, we will have no response and the truth will disappear as if *stolen*. A rocky heart *starves* the seed, not allowing it to take root. If our heart is cluttered with weeds of worldly cares, the seed gets *strangled*. But with a positive response to truth, we *sustain* it and let it change us, producing fruit in our lives.

Jesus concluded by saying that the more truth we learn and practice, the more God will reveal. But if we stop using what we learn, we will lose even what we thought we had (Matthew 13:12; Mark 4:24–25; Luke 8:18). If we do nothing with the seed, it can do nothing for us.

This principle reminds me to evaluate what I do with truth from God. When I read His Word or hear a sermon, do I respond to Him obediently? Does it correct my behavior, shape my worldview, and get all the way to my fingers and feet? Like panning for gold, the more I seek, the more I will discover. James 1:25 says that continuing in God's Word—not forgetting what we hear, but doing it—makes us blessed in what we do.

DAY 122

Morning – WHERE WE FIND OUR WORTH

Don't be selfish; don't try to impress others. Be humble, thinking of others as better than yourselves. Don't look out only for your own interests, but take an interest in others, too.
PHILIPPIANS 2:3–4 NLT

It's not abnormal to want to be recognized, adored, or even famous. People do crazy things to get their five minutes of fame. To be treasured and loved is one of our deepest desires as human beings, so it's not surprising to see people who will do anything they can to fulfill this longing.

What is abnormal is finding a woman who—instead of qualifying herself—edifies, encourages, and celebrates others. A woman who, throughout a conversation, may never once bring up her own accomplishments, but who goes home in full confidence of who she is and has lost nothing from never being the topic of conversation. If anything, she is more full of life and purpose because she was able to give another what we all so desperately need: love and acceptance.

Put others first. That is a very real way we can give honor to the Lord. Make it your goal to put yourself aside and listen to a friend. Encourage them in every area you can, and simply love on them.

Evening – THANK YOU

I have not stopped giving thanks for you,
remembering you in my prayers.
EPHESIANS 1:16 NIV

After Japan attacked Pearl Harbor, President Franklin Roosevelt issued an order proclaiming much of the US Pacific Coast as a military area and excluding people of Japanese ancestry from living there. In 1942, more than one hundred thousand Japanese were forced to relocate to "war relocation camps." Among them was the Honda family who lived near Los Angeles.

Young Rose Honda, a seventh grader, had to leave the school she loved, a place where she excelled both academically and socially. Relocation affected not only Rose but also her school friends and teachers. They kept in touch through letters.

Today, the Manzanar National Historic Site marks the location of one of the camps. On exhibit there is a letter from Rose's school written to the family. It thanks them for all the gracious things they did and credits them for building up a fine spirit among Japanese students who were forced to relocate. The letter goes on to praise Rose and to encourage her toward coming back soon.

A sincere letter expressing gratitude is one way for Christians to encourage one another. Paul often wrote letters when he was in prison, and he relied on his friends' letters for support.

Written words last—so write a letter today. Tell someone thank you. Encourage them with your words.

Morning – TRUE FRIENDSHIP

Rejoice with those who rejoice; mourn with those who mourn.
ROMANS 12:15 NIV

True Christian friendship has this verse stamped all over it. Do you have a friend who truly finds joy in your successes? When you are on top of the world, this person is genuinely happy for you. When you are sad, you have seen tears come to her eyes. This is not a friendship found every day. It is rare and to be treasured.

As believers in Christ, we have this high call on our lives. Pray that you might truly celebrate with others, not secretly wishing you were the one receiving the blessing. On the other hand, know that at times sorrow and loss are so deep that a hug and an "I love you" will mean the world. Lots of words are not needed in such times. To mourn with the mourner is the greatest gift you can give. Just to show up, to extend help, to show love.

If you have such a friend, you no doubt cherish her. Make it your aim to live out Romans 12:15 in small ways this week. Stand and cheer when others are victorious. Stand close by and be ready to comfort them when they experience disappointment or loss.

Evening – A FRIEND WHO STICKS CLOSER THAN A BROTHER

Now it came about when he had finished speaking to Saul,
that the soul of Jonathan was knit to the soul of David,
and Jonathan loved him as himself.
1 SAMUEL 18:1 NASB

The relationship between David and Jonathan was like that of brothers. Proverbs 18:24 (NIV) says it this way: "One who has unreliable friends soon comes to ruin, but there is a friend who sticks closer than a brother." Everyone hits a rough patch now and then. This world is not our home. As believers, we are aliens here. One day we will truly be at home in heaven with the Lord. Until then, it is important that we stand strong with one another through the ups and downs of life. Consider the depth of Jonathan's love for David.

Jonathan, the son of King Saul, protected David from death when Saul grew jealous of David. He created a secret way of getting the message to David that he indeed needed to flee the kingdom. The two hated to part, but it was their only option. In the end, the Bible tells us it was David who wept the hardest when he had to leave Jonathan. No doubt, David recognized the value of his true friend who stuck closer than a brother. Do you have a friend in need? Life gets busy. Don't ever be too busy to help your friends, to be there for them as Jonathan was for David.

Morning – FOR LOVE'S SAKE

*"For I was hungry and you gave Me food; I was thirsty and
you gave Me drink; I was a stranger and you took Me in."*
MATTHEW 25:35 NKJV

Marie was a regular at her neighborhood coffee shop. The past several chilly spring mornings, she had noticed a homeless man sitting in the courtyard a few feet outside the coffee shop. This morning she walked up to him and sat down next to him. "Hi!" she started. "I noticed you seem to like this courtyard as much as I do." She extended her hand and said, "My name is Marie; what's yours?"

"I'm Jack," he replied after a pause. "Most people act like I'm invisible, so I was a little startled when you spoke to me."

"Well, Jack," Marie said, "I'm going in to get a cup of coffee. Would you like a hot cup of coffee this morning?"

Jack nodded his head and smiled.

God is love, and He desires for you to extend His love to others. It's easy to let the homeless, the less fortunate, or the unlovely remain invisible. When you take time to smile at a stranger or acknowledge someone's presence with a hello, you are demonstrating kindness and extending the heart of God to that person.

Evening – CHOOSE LOVE

*Therefore I urge you, brethren, by the mercies of God, to present your bodies a living and
holy sacrifice, acceptable to God, which is your spiritual service of worship. And do not
be conformed to this world, but be transformed by the renewing of your mind, so that
you may prove what the will of God is, that which is good and acceptable and perfect.*
ROMANS 12:1–2 NASB

Only through the power of Christ at work within us can we choose to love when we don't feel like it. He changes us from the inside and gives us a new way of thinking.

First Peter 4:8 (NLT) says, "Most important of all, continue to show deep love for each other, for love covers a multitude of sins." This verse tells us to keep choosing love. No matter what. Choose love.

Love is a choice, and your attitude is a choice. Our emotions and feelings often get the better of us. If you are facing a challenge or a difficult person and you don't feel like choosing to love, ask God to transform your heart and mind. Ask Him to go before you and to help you choose a loving and right attitude.

Morning – AGING WELL

So refuse to worry, and keep your body healthy. But remember
that youth, with a whole life before you, is meaningless.
ECCLESIASTES 11:10 NLT

Our society is youth-obsessed. As soon as movie stars get past a certain age, they're offered fewer roles. Websites post pictures of "past their prime" actors' sagging, wrinkled frames. Even magazines touting the benefits of becoming seasoned often airbrush and edit photos of their subjects.

Why are we reluctant to celebrate aging? It is a natural process, and the alternative isn't good. Perhaps we are uncomfortable with one day being less useful, dependent on our loved ones, or feeble in body and mind. Maybe we're afraid of death. Heaven seems far away at times.

However, God takes a different view of getting older. In Leviticus 19:32 (NIV), the scriptures say, "Stand up in the presence of the aged, show respect for the elderly and revere your God." Job 12:12 (NIV) says, "Is not wisdom found among the aged? Does not long life bring understanding?"

Look for godly women in your church or community who have aged well. Ask them how they feel about getting older. You'll probably discover they love the age they are and wouldn't trade their hard-won wisdom for all the anti-wrinkle cream in the world. As Audrey Hepburn once said, "And the beauty of a woman, with passing years only grows!"

Evening – WISDOM THROUGH A CHILD'S EYES

Choose my instruction instead of silver, knowledge rather than choice gold, for wisdom
is more precious than rubies, and nothing you desire can compare with her.
PROVERBS 8:10–11 NIV

Although Linda didn't have children of her own, she had taught Sunday school for many years. Linda knew she had learned more from her students than they had learned from her. Recently, though, she had decided a younger teacher might be better for her rambunctious class.

Sunday morning Linda added pieces to her felt board as she taught the story of the angel who appeared to Moses from within a bush that was on fire but didn't burn up. After completing the story, Linda asked her class what they had learned.

June blurted out, "Miss Linda, I learned that God talked through the angel."

Holly added, "I learned that Moses had faith that God would save the Israelites from the bad Egyptians."

Wanting to encourage her reluctant boys, Linda asked if they had any thoughts. She smiled and nodded at Kenneth when he glanced at her. "Um, Miss Linda, you're kind of like that angel. You're old and you tell us about God. You're like the bush on fire too. For some reason, God doesn't want you to burn up."

Renewal flowed through Linda's teaching spirit. She knew the Lord spoke to her through Kenneth. She heard God tell her to continue sharing His lessons as a Sunday school teacher.

DAY 126

Morning – RAISE THE ROOF

Oh come, let us sing to the Lord! Let us shout joyfully to the
Rock of our salvation. Let us come before His presence with
thanksgiving; let us shout joyfully to Him with psalms.
PSALM 95:1–2 NKJV

In the 1600s, lyricist Johann Schütz penned these words in his song "Sing Praise to God Who Reigns Above": "Thus all my toilsome way along, I sing aloud Thy praises, that earth may hear the grateful song my voice unwearied raises. Be joyful in the Lord, my heart, both soul and body bear your part: To God all praise and glory."

What a wonderful exhortation for us today. Toilsome way? Weary? Sing! Be joyful in your heart! Not many had it rougher than King David, who curled up in caves to hide from his enemies, or Paul in a dark dungeon cell, yet they still praised God despite the circumstances. And our God extended His grace to them as they acclaimed Him in their suffering.

The Lord wants to hear our shouts of joy and see us march into the courtyard rejoicing. He hears our faltering songs and turns them into a symphony for His ears. So lift up your voices and join in the praise to our Creator and Lord. Let's lift the rafters and allow Him to filter our offerings of joy with His love.

Evening – A JOYFUL NOISE

Sing aloud unto God our strength:
make a joyful noise unto the God of Jacob.
PSALM 81:1 KJV

Aren't you glad the Bible commands us to "make a joyful noise unto the Lord" instead of saying something like "Sing like an angel"? Many are born with amazing vocal abilities. They wow us with their choir productions and their amazing solo performances. But some of the rest of us are lucky to croak out a word or two in the right key.

God doesn't care about your vocal abilities. He longs to hear a song of praise rise up out of your heart, even if it's sung in three or four keys. Think about that for a moment. He's listening as millions of believers sing out—in every language, every key, every pitch. And it doesn't bother Him one bit because He's not listening to the technique, He's listening to the heart.

Still not convinced? Read the book of Psalms from start to finish. It will stir up a song in your heart, and before long your toes will be tapping and your heart bursting. Why? Because you were created to praise Him. So, don't worry about what others will think. Make a joyful noise!

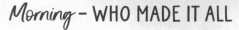

Morning – WHO MADE IT ALL

Children of God without fault in the midst of a crooked and perverse generation, among whom you shine as lights in the world.
PHILIPPIANS 2:15 NKJV

When you really get to talking with fellow students or coworkers, it is astonishing to discover how unbiblical ideas about the origins of the earth have taken deep root in our society.

Now, it is very important to be focused on showing Christ's love rather than correcting every wrong idea held by others, yet drawing attention to the fact of God's creative work is actually very significant. Evolution is a complicated theory, but at its core is an unwillingness to acknowledge the sovereignty and authority of a Creator. Those who do not want to be subject to Him simply deny that He even exists and find another way to explain this world with its genetic complexities and majestic wonders. Charles Darwin and others after him do not embrace the fact that humanity came into existence because of a loving God who gave us breath and free will and an eternal destiny. They cannot, for it would cause their entire structure of thought to tumble. And today, there are generations of people who simply accept what they have been told. But we know the truth and are called to give witness to it. Not in a strident and rude manner but in a confident and peaceable way. This is the way we shine as lights, illuminating the truth.

Evening – A CREATIVE GOD

In the beginning God created the heavens and the earth.
GENESIS 1:1 NIV

Did you realize that you are made (designed, created) in the image of a very creative God? It's true! He breathed life into you, after all. It stands to reason that some of His creativity would have spilled over into you, His daughter.

The same God who created the heavens and the earth—who decided a giraffe's neck should be several feet long and a penguin should waddle around in tuxedo-like attire—designed you, inside and out! And He gifted you with a variety of gifts and abilities, all of which can be used to His glory.

So, what creative gifts reside inside of you? Have you given them a stir lately? Maybe it's time to ask God which gifts are most useable for this season of your life. He's creative enough to stir the ones that can be used to reach others. He will bring them to the surface and prepare you to use them—much like He did during Creation—to bring beauty out of dark places.

So, brace yourself! Your very creative God has big things planned for you!

DAY 128

Morning – UNFAILING LOVE

Let your unfailing love surround us, Lord, for our hope is in you alone.
Psalm 33:22 nlt

We hope that our sports team will win the big game and that Starbucks will bring back its hazelnut macchiato. We also hope that our jobs will continue to fulfill us and pay our bills and that God will answer a heartfelt prayer with a long-awaited yes.

Whatever we're hoping for, it's easy to think that God doesn't care about the details of our lives. However, just as a parent cares about everything that happens to her child, so God longs to share every part of our day. Why not talk to Him about all our needs and desires?

As we sip our morning coffee, we can jot down thanks for morning blessings such as flavored creamers and hot water for our shower. While we do our jobs, we can regularly bring our concerns (and coworkers) before God's throne. We could keep scriptures scribbled on Post-it notes in our cubicle—or on our desk—to remind us to think with God's thoughts throughout the day, instead of falling back on worldly patterns. When we lay our head on the pillow at night, we can voice the answered prayers that grace our lives, drifting off to sleep in gratitude at God's unfailing love.

Those small, simple actions add up to a day filled with hope and gratitude. . .and those days add up to a life well-lived.

Evening – GOD IS IN THE DETAILS

Give all your worries and cares to God, for he cares about you.
1 Peter 5:7 nlt

Do you ever wonder if God cares about the details of your life?

Take a look at nature. God is definitely a God of details. Notice the various patterns, shapes, and sizes of animals. Their life cycles. The noises they make. Their natural defenses. Details!

Have you wandered through the woods? Towering trees. Their scents. The cool refreshment their shade provides. The different types of leaves, and the tiny, life-bearing veins that run through them. How intricate!

What about the weather? It is filled with details from the hand of your God. The Creator sends raindrops—sometimes gentle and kind, other times harsh and pelting. He warms us with the sun, cools us with breezes, and yes—it is true—He fashions each snowflake, each unique, no two alike! The same way He designs His children!

Do you wonder if God cares about that struggle you are facing at work or the argument you had with a loved one? Is He aware of your desire to find that special someone or the difficulty you find in loving your spouse? He cares. Tell Him your concerns. He is not too busy to listen to the details. He wants to show Himself real and alive to you in such a way that you know it must be Him. The details of your life are not *little* to God. If they matter to you, they matter to God.

Morning – JUST IN TIME

Therefore let us draw near with confidence to the throne of grace,
so that we may receive mercy and find grace to help in time of need.
HEBREWS 4:16 NASB

As believers, our lives become exciting when we wait on God to direct our paths, because He knows what is best for us at any given moment. His plans and agenda are never wrong. We just need to practice living on His schedule and spending time in prayer. But that's easier said than done! Often we are chomping at the bit, and it's hard to wait.

Once we fully realize He knows best and turn our lives over to the Spirit for direction, we can allow God to be in charge of our calendar; His timing is what is paramount.

When chomping at the bit for a job offer or for a proposal, His timing might seem slow. "Hurry up, God!" we groan. But when we learn to patiently wait on His promises, we will see the plans He has for us are more than we dared hope—or dream. God promises to answer us; and it never fails to be just in time.

Evening – THE FINAL RESULTS

I have planted, Apollos watered; but God gave the increase.
1 CORINTHIANS 3:6 KJV

Sometimes, as women, we work until we're ready to drop, and it seems as though it doesn't make a difference. We teach classes, sing on the praise team, and attend prayer services, but we don't see any results for all our hard work. We attend the women's group, visit the sick, and cook for all the church functions, but no one seems to notice how hard we work.

The problem is expecting something to happen immediately when the final result is in God's hands. We don't have the ability or power to save anyone or change lives. Relax. You're in good company. Paul said he had planted. He meant that he had done his part by planting the seed of the gospel in people's hearts. Then Apollos came behind him preaching and teaching, watering the seed that Paul had planted. From that point on, they had to wait for God to do His part. He is the only one who can cause those seeds to take root and grow. Too often we try to do God's work for Him. We want to see results right away, but it could be months or even years before we see the result of the seed we've helped to plant. Our job is to continue planting or watering whether we see any results or not and allow God to bring forth the harvest.

Morning – THE PERFECT REDEEMER

*"Who are you?" he asked. "I am your servant Ruth," she replied. "Spread the
corner of your covering over me, for you are my family redeemer."*
RUTH 3:9 NLT

Ruth was a woman of faith. After suffering the loss of her husband, she could have wallowed in grief and misery. Instead, she chose to follow her mother-in-law, Naomi, to a place where she knew no one in order to honor her late husband (and, perhaps, the God he had introduced her to).

Ruth was also a woman of action. She worked hard to glean in the fields, toiling with intention and consistency. The owner of the fields, Boaz, noticed her work ethic and was impressed. Later, Ruth followed Naomi's advice and found Boaz at night while he was sleeping. Because he was a relative of hers and a man of integrity, he agreed to spread his covering over her as her "family redeemer." This meant he promised to marry and take care of Ruth (and Naomi).

Ruth's story has much to teach us. Just as Ruth moved on from grief to action, we can ask for God's help to move past our own losses and not get stuck in bitterness or anger. With His help, we can honor others and not wallow in self-pity or destructive habits. Also, as His strength and forgiveness cover our weaknesses and failures, we can find peace and joy. He is the perfect Redeemer who takes care of us so we don't have to worry about providing for ourselves.

Evening – NOT FLYING SOLO

*For we are God's handiwork, created in Christ Jesus to do
good works, which God prepared in advance for us to do.*
EPHESIANS 2:10 NIV

Sometimes when we think about doing "God's work," self-doubt can get the better of us. We tell ourselves that we aren't smart or skilled enough; we remember all our skipped prayer times and say, "The Lord wouldn't want to use me since I've been ignoring Him. Besides, my work probably isn't worth that much anyway in the big picture, *if* I don't completely mess up."

In Ephesians 2, Paul emphasizes that we weren't saved because of anything we had to offer, but we received God's gift of salvation through faith. He made us anew in Christ "to do good works" (v. 10); we can't brag about deserving salvation, and we can't brag about our good works being our big idea either! God planned them for us ahead of time to fit in with His perfect plan.

We may fear that our errors will "ruin" what God has going on. Consider that the work itself is a gift—the all-powerful Creator chooses to use us—ordinary believers—to accomplish mighty things. Throughout the Bible, we read stories of unremarkable people doing amazing things for the Lord because they trusted in His strength to do them. If God has work for us, we can have confidence that He will equip us for the job, no matter the challenges ahead.

Morning – O THE DEEP, DEEP LOVE OF JESUS

*I pray that out of his glorious riches he may strengthen you with
power through his Spirit in your inner being, so that Christ may dwell
in your hearts through faith. And I pray that you, being rooted and
established in love, may have power, together with all the Lord's holy people,
to grasp how wide and long and high and deep is the love of Christ.*

EPHESIANS 3:16–18 NIV

The apostle Paul encouraged the people in Ephesus with his words in an effort to explain how far-reaching God's love was. Immeasurable. Unfathomable.

In the late 1800s, the lyricist Samuel Trevor Francis entertained the idea of ending his own life. In the midst of despair, he felt God reach out to him, and he wrote a stirring hymn echoing Paul's words. "O the deep, deep love of Jesus, vast, unmeasured, boundless, free! Rolling as a mighty ocean in its fullness over me! Underneath me, all around me, is the current of Thy love, leading onward, leading homeward to Thy glorious rest above!"

What an amazing picture. That He should care for us in such a way is almost incomprehensible. Despite our shortcomings, our sin, He loves us. It takes a measure of faith to believe in His love. When we feel a nagging thought of unworthiness, of being unlovable, trust in the Word and sing a new song. For His love is deep and wide.

Evening – THE POWER OF GOD'S LOVE

*And above all things have fervent love for one another,
for "love will cover a multitude of sins."*

1 PETER 4:8 NKJV

Let's face it—we're human. As Christians, we endeavor to follow the teachings of Christ but fall short. Periodically our actions take the course of a runaway train. Maybe a brother tested your patience and your intolerance of his behavior ignited you to lash out in anger. Perhaps a sister in Christ took the credit publicly for some good work you did in private and you seethe. Or maybe someone falsely accused you and you retaliated.

Every believer is flawed, and too often we fail miserably. Peter—endowed with a few flaws of his own—admonished the Church to love one another intensely. He, above all, had learned the power of repentance and forgiveness, having denied Christ three times after the Roman soldiers apprehended Jesus. Yet Peter was one of the first to see Jesus after His resurrection, and it was Peter who first reached Jesus on the Sea of Galilee. There, the Lord commissioned Peter to feed His sheep. After Jesus' ascension, Peter—the spokesman of the apostles—preached the sermon that resulted in the conversion of approximately three thousand souls (Acts 2:14–41).

Christ's love forgives and disregards the offenses of others. His love covers a multitude of sins. That's the power of God's love at work. Love resurrects, forgives, restores, and commissions us to reach others for the kingdom.

Morning – I AM

*God said to Moses, "I AM WHO I AM. This is what you
are to say to the Israelites: 'I AM has sent me to you.'"*
EXODUS 3:14 NIV

The words "I am" ring out in the present tense. These words are used some seven hundred times in the Bible to describe God and Jesus. When Moses was on the mount and asked God who He was, a voice thundered, "I Am." In the New Testament, Jesus said of Himself, "I am the bread of life; I am the light of the world; I am the Good Shepherd; I am the way; I am the resurrection." Present tense. Words of hope and life. I Am.

Who is God to you today? Is He in the present tense? Living, loving, presiding over your life? Is the Lord of lords "I Was" or "I've Never Been" to you? Have you experienced the hope that comes from an everlasting "I Am" Father? One who walks by you daily and will never let go? "I Am with you always."

We are surprised when we struggle in the world, yet hesitate to turn to our very Creator. He has the answers, and He will fill you with hope. Reach for Him today. Don't be uncertain. Know Him. For He is, after all, I Am.

Evening – GOD IS GOOD

*Praise the LORD, for the LORD is good;
sing praises to His name, for it is pleasant.*
PSALM 135:3 NKJV

We hear it in church. We say it to others. We want to believe it. God is good. All the time.

The Bible says it, so we know it is true. Jesus lived it so we could see it in living color. But sometimes, when life yanks hard and pulls the rug out from under us, we begin to doubt. And that is probably a normal human temptation. Though we know that good parents discipline their children and sometimes allow them to learn "the hard way," we expect God, our heavenly Father, to do it differently.

So we need reminders. And He put them in our world everywhere we turn, at unexpected junctions and in the most ordinary places. Warm sunshine, brilliant flowers, rainbows after storms, newborn babies, friendships, families, food, air to breathe, pets, church dinners, sunrises, sunsets, beaches, forests, prairies, mountains, the moon and stars at night, and puffy clouds in the day. All around us are hints that God is good and that His works are beautiful and life-giving.

When disease or tragedy or hardship enters our lives, we can rest assured that God is not the author of these destructive things and that someday He will cleanse this globe of its misery and set everything right. Until then, He has given us His strength, His hope, and His promise. That is enough to keep us going.

Morning – WATCH WHERE YOU'RE GOING

Your word is a lamp for my feet, a light on my path.
PSALM 119:105 NIV

Vickie had her mind on her husband who was in the hospital and didn't notice the concrete parking space barrier. She hung the toe of her shoe on it. Without warning, she fell forward, landing on her left knee. She stood and examined her wounds. Her hand was scraped and her knee hurt, but nothing life threatening. She went on to the hospital to visit Sonny even though she could tell her knee was swollen. Later, the evidence of her fall showed in ugly black and blue bruises. She placed ice on her knee and kept it elevated as much as possible. The injury wasn't serious, just painful.

Sometimes we hang our toe on obstacles in our Christian walk. We may stumble around spiritually and even fall sometimes, but we don't have to remain on the ground. We can pick ourselves up and begin walking again. It may be painful at first, and we may even sustain a few scrapes and bruises and feel swollen from our fall, but God offers us healing. All we have to do is reach for His Word. God has given us a lamp through His Word, which shines light on our path as we walk day by day. Turn on the lamp by reading your Bible daily.

Evening – GRITTIN' IT OUT

It is God who arms me with strength, and makes my way perfect.
PSALM 18:32 NKJV

Do you know what grit is? Have you thought much about it?

Grit is that tough and tenacious quality that gets us through the difficult times. And though the circumstances and challenges differ, women in every generation have used it aplenty.

Think of the grit of the women on the *Mayflower* who endured seasickness and squalor and privation to help birth a nation. How about the women who traveled west on wagon trains and put up with dust and hardship and often left their china on the mountainsides and their children buried under the wagon ruts? Then there are the women who came through the Great Depression and tried to steady their men who had no income and no hope, and the women who sent their sons off to fight the Great War and watched them return debilitated by mustard gas and shell shock. We could also talk about the women in the 1940s who waved goodbye to sweethearts and husbands and then marched off to war plants to fight for freedom on the home front. These great generations knew a lot about grit and the God from whom such stern strength comes.

These women stepped up to the task to which they were called. May we commit to doing the same when the day to show our grit comes. And may we rest in the strength that never fails.

Morning – STAND STILL

And Moses said unto the people, Fear ye not, stand still, and see
the salvation of the LORD, which he will shew to you to day. . . .
The LORD shall fight for you, and ye shall hold your peace.
EXODUS 14:13–14 KJV

The children of Israel enjoyed a triumphant exodus from Egypt, but danger soon overtook them. They had only journeyed a short time when they looked up to see Pharaoh and his army marching toward them. They were afraid and immediately started making accusations against Moses, claiming he had brought them to the wilderness to die. They said they would have been better off staying in Egypt. But Moses encouraged them not to be afraid. They were to stand still. The Lord, their God, would fight for them. They were to hold their peace.

Are you facing an enemy? Do you feel afraid of impending danger? Moses told the people to do four things: fear not, stand still, see the salvation of the Lord, and hold your peace. The children of Israel experienced a great victory that day. God parted the waters of the Red Sea so they could cross over on dry ground, then He allowed that same water to drown the Egyptian army. Moses' advice is good for us also. We can put our trust in God without fear and wait for God to do battle for us. Whatever is coming toward you, God can handle it.

Evening – A STRONG TOWER

The name of the LORD is a strong tower:
the righteous runneth into it, and is safe.
PROVERBS 18:10 KJV

When a young man walked into a convenience store and pointed a gun at Dorothy, she managed to remain composed and do as he asked, but as soon as he left, she fell apart. The full implication of what had happened made her so afraid, she had to quit her job. When Anna's husband experienced a serious heart complication and had to be rushed into surgery, fear overwhelmed her and made it hard to pray. When a neighbor posed a threat to their security, David and Becky moved to a new neighborhood to feel safer.

Everyone has felt fear at one time or another. It may have been hearing a doctor's diagnosis of a terrible disease, being the victim of a crime, or being alone in a strange city, but everyone has been afraid at sometime in their life. Fear can paralyze us and keep us from feeling secure and confident. The name of the Lord is a place of safety for His people. We can't stop bad things from happening to us, but when they do, we can call on His name. He provides a haven of safety for us, both physically and mentally. The next time you feel afraid, run to Jesus. His name is the strong tower you need.

Morning – THE RIGHT ASSURANCE

*And we know that all things work together for good to them that love
God, to them who are the called according to his purpose.*
ROMANS 8:28 KJV

"God won't give me more than I can handle." You hear this phrase a lot. Is it true? Does the Bible say this?

The origin of this phrase is 1 Corinthians 10:13, which is actually dealing with the idea of temptation and says that God "will not allow you to be tempted beyond what you are able, but with the temptation will also make the way of escape, that you may be able to bear it" (NKJV).

Sadly, this verse is used by many who do not know Christ but who find some measure of mental comfort in the idea that, no matter what they are experiencing, even if it is the consequences of sinful choices, God is not allowing them to bear too much. This just isn't so. Proverbs 13:15 (KJV) declares that "the way of transgressors is hard." The crushing consequences of sin will break you and cast you aside.

Only the ones who are following Christ can lay claim to the promise that God will work all things together for good. Those who trust and obey can rest in the assurance that everything (the good and the bad) fits together in the pattern He has laid out for them.

Evening – BIBLE BOOKENDS

*"Look, I am coming soon. . . . I am the Alpha and the Omega,
the First and the Last, the Beginning and the End."*
REVELATION 22:12–13 NLT

God often used literary structure in His Word to call attention to something important. For example, the Bible has "bookends," showing that history (His-story) will go full circle and accomplish His purposes. These bookends are the first two and last two chapters of the Bible.

In Genesis 1–2 the world had perfect environment, no sin or death, and God conversing with His people. Revelation 21–22 portrays a new heaven and earth, again without sin or death and with unhindered fellowship between God and His people. The 1,185 chapters in between contain rebellion against God, people in conflict, evil and violence, tears, pain, and death. However, those chapters also display God's redemptive plan through Jesus, who atoned for our sins, conquered death, and will destroy the works of the devil. He lived a sinless life, experienced the death we deserve, and rose again.

At this time in history, we are in the "between" chapters. Corruption and evil abound. Society grows increasingly godless and amoral. Families are fragmented; relationships are disposable. But Revelation 21–22 will come. Everyone who has accepted the redemption Jesus provided will live with Him forever, because He said, "Let anyone who is thirsty come. Let anyone who desires drink freely from the water of life" (Revelation 22:17 NLT).

Morning – WHEN YOU GIVE YOUR LIFE AWAY

*Which of you, intending to build a tower, sitteth not down first,
and counteth the cost, whether he have sufficient to finish it?*
LUKE 14:28 KJV

Henry David Thoreau once said, "The price of anything is the amount of life you exchange for it." Busy lives often dictate that there is no time for the important things. People say, "Oh, I don't have time for this or that," or, "I wish I had the time. . ." The truth is you make the time for what you value most.

Every person has the same amount of life each day. What matters is how you spend it. It's easy to waste your day doing insignificant things—what many call time wasters—leaving little time for God. The most important things in life are eternal endeavors. Spending time in prayer to God for others. Giving your life to building a relationship with God by reading His Word and growing in faith. Sharing Christ with others and giving them the opportunity to know Him. These are the things that will last.

What are you spending your life on? What are you getting out of what you give yourself to each day?

Evening – JESUS' PERSPECTIVE ON PRIORITIES

*But Martha was distracted with all her preparations; and she came
up to Him and said, "Lord, do You not care that my sister has left
me to do all the serving alone? Then tell her to help me."*
LUKE 10:40 NASB

We often wear busyness as a badge of honor because busyness can equal productivity and usefulness. It's important to ask ourselves, however, whether busyness takes away from—or adds to—our faith journey.

When Jesus dined in the home of Mary and Martha, Martha prepared the meal for her special guest, while Mary (in a highly unusual move for a woman during biblical times) sat at Jesus' feet, listening to His teaching. Martha understandably felt frustrated that Mary wasn't helping her, and she asked Jesus to rebuke her sister. However, Jesus told Martha that Mary had chosen the "better part." The Bible doesn't say what Martha replied or how she felt. Perhaps she felt relieved.

Picture yourself receiving a text that an important person was coming to your house. You might scurry around, tidying the bathroom and plumping the couch cushions. If your guest said, "Sit down. Relax! I don't want you to make a fuss over me. I just want to be with you," you would feel grateful. . .peaceful. . .and treasured.

Today, as you plan your to-do list, prioritize time to sit and reflect on God's Word. Instead of rushing around to accomplish things you feel *should* be done, ask God what He wants you to do. You might be relieved.

Morning – OUR TRUE ENEMIES

*"I am not referring to all of you; I know those I have chosen.
But this is to fulfill this passage of Scripture: 'He who
shared my bread has turned against me.'"*
JOHN 13:18 NIV

Jesus knows when He chooses His disciples that Judas will betray Him. That was the way God's plan of salvation would come about. And yet, until this point, Jesus never treats Judas in any way that would indicate He knew of Judas's impending betrayal. In fact, Jesus sharing His bread with Judas in this way shows honor. Jesus treats Judas with much more grace and love than we could imagine. For over three years, Jesus treats Judas like the other disciples.

But what Judas meant for evil was part of God's plan. Is it possible Christ loved Judas because He knew Judas was crucial to the redemption plan?

Ultimately, only God knows our true enemies. He reveals them to us when we need to know. Everything God does has a purpose, usually a far bigger one than we can see. Even when we are determined to do wrong, God loves us with an unfathomable love.

Is there something in your life you need to look at with new eyes, with the perspective that somehow God can use It for good and for His glory?

Evening – OBEY AND SERVE WITH YOUR HEART

*And now, Israel, what does the LORD your God ask of you but to fear
the LORD your God, to walk in obedience to him, to love him, to serve
the LORD your God with all your heart and with all your soul.*
DEUTERONOMY 10:12 NIV

One morning Bonnie felt compelled to share muffins with her neighbor, Richard. As a widow, Bonnie wasn't comfortable taking her freshly baked muffins to the divorced man. She didn't want a neighborly gesture to be mistaken for a romantic interest.

When she still felt the need at 3:00 p.m., Bonnie gave in and walked to Richard's with a plate of muffins. She left Richard's, glad she had obeyed her heart. It seemed like he appreciated her neighborly visit even more than her gift.

As Bonnie walked home, she greeted Marge, an elderly neighbor out for exercise. Moments after they passed, Bonnie heard a loud thud. Turning, she saw that Marge had fallen and had been knocked unconscious when her head hit the pavement. As she hurried to Marge's side, Bonnie called 911. Before finishing the call, Richard had joined her with a blanket. While Bonnie stayed with Marge, Richard went to get Marge's husband.

As Bonnie watched for the ambulance with Marge, she realized the reason she had felt compelled to take muffins to Richard. The Lord needed both her and Richard to be together at this time to help Marge.

DAY 138

Morning – A LISTENING FRIEND

The purposes of a person's heart are deep waters,
but one who has insight draws them out.
PROVERBS 20:5 NIV

Diane was faced with a tough decision. She had been offered her dream job, but it involved a salary cut and a cross-country move. Her current job paid the bills, but she was not happy. She longed for change but craved security. She called her friend Lisa, who met her for coffee. As Diane talked about her dilemma, Lisa merely listened and asked questions. How would you feel if you didn't take the job? What if the move doesn't work out and you have regrets? Before long, Diane had made her decision. Ironically, Lisa didn't offer a word of advice, but Diane found herself extremely grateful to her good friend for helping her sort things out.

When friends come to us with problems, it's easy to give advice. We immediately think of what we would do in the situation and offer a quick solution. But this proverb offers wise words about listening. Most people can find the answers to their own problems, especially through the eyes of a friend who listens well and asks good questions. Insight is about asking the right questions, not offering up solutions. One of the best ways we can love others is to listen, draw them out, and support them as they come up with their own solutions.

Evening – WISE WOMAN

Then a wise woman cried out from the city, "Hear, hear! Please say to Joab,
'Come nearby, that I may speak with you.'". . . I am among the peaceable and
faithful in Israel. You seek to destroy a city and a mother in Israel."
2 SAMUEL 20:16, 19 NKJV

In the midst of a siege on a city, the Lord sent an unlikely messenger to the commander of King David's army. A wise and courageous woman speaks into the chaos and preserves the city. She is Christ's calm in the storm, bringing reason into a tumultuous time.

We are called to be the calm in a storm. The only reason this woman could possibly speak with Joab amid the battle is through God's wisdom, power, and protection. She lays out the matter at hand before Joab and shows him his folly. She speaks the truth with grace and humility.

The same wisdom, power, and protection the Lord gave this wise woman He offers to you. In times of crisis, speaking and thinking rationally are difficult feats, but anchor your trust in the one and only unchanging God.

This woman did not demand; she did not provoke or diminish. She questioned Joab and asked for understanding. Our God is a God of understanding and wisdom, and though there are times He will not reveal the reason or purpose of an event, we must trust and rest in His unshakable character.

Morning – REMAIN IN HIS LOVE

*"As the Father has loved me, so have I loved you. Now remain in
my love. If you keep my commands, you will remain in my love,
just as I have kept my Father's commands and remain in his love."*
JOHN 15:9–10 NIV

Remaining in Christ's love is the only way to bear fruit that will last. John 15 gives us a beautiful picture of what bearing fruit means. What kind of fruit are we talking about here? The kind of fruit that makes a difference for Christ. The fruits of the Spirit are love, joy, peace, patience, kindness, goodness, faithfulness, gentleness, and self-control (Galatians 5:22–23). These are the fruits that honor God and come from a life that is growing in Him.

The Bible says that if we remain in God's love, we will bear much fruit. So how do we remain in His love? John 15:10 tells us the answer: "If you keep my commands, you will remain in my love." We can have complete joy and bear all kinds of spiritual fruit if we follow God's Word and live a life that pleases Him.

Just as a branch that has been cut off from the vine can do nothing, we can do nothing that matters if we aren't connected to the vine.

Evening – CONTINUE IN HIS LOVE

"As the Father loved Me, I also have loved you; abide in My love."
JOHN 15:9 NKJV

What does it mean to "continue" or "remain" in Christ's love? Since His love is perfect and was shown in the flesh, remaining in His love means staying connected to the person of Jesus Christ through the priceless gift of His Spirit.

Throughout your day, ask God to give you creative ways to stay connected to Jesus. Here are a few examples:

- When you get up and walk to the coffeepot to turn it on, pray that God will pour His love into You so that you can pour it into others.
- During your shower, ask God to cleanse you of your sins.
- As you put on your makeup or brush your hair, meditate on His beauty and goodness. Ask Him to make you aware of the beauty He gives through creation and other people throughout the day.
- As you eat meals, praise God for the food He gives us in His Word. Take time to meditate on scripture, even if it's just for a few moments, as you eat. If you eat with others, pray for opportunities to talk about Him.

DAY 140

Morning – SCORING AN INHERITANCE

*An inheritance that can never perish, spoil or fade. This inheritance is kept
in heaven for you, who through faith are shielded by God's power until the
coming of the salvation that is ready to be revealed in the last time.*
1 Peter 1:4–5 niv

Sarah's best friend was helped out of a financial hole just in the nick of time by an unexpected family inheritance.

While Sarah was happy for her friend, she began feeling sorry for herself at the same time. After all, what was wrong with her that she had no inheritance and probably never would? On the contrary, if there were an inheritance coming from her family, it would be their debt, but thankfully that couldn't really happen. A piece of furniture or two, that was all there appeared to be.

Sarah made sacrifices to pay down her mortgage faster and save some money. Meanwhile, her best friend paid off her entire house and credit card debt while making plans to pay cash for a barn they were going to have built.

It was a monumental task for Sarah not to be incredibly jealous. She struggled with it all until God showed her in the Word the inheritance she did have coming, and this one would last forever!

Evening – A BIGGER BATTLE

*For though we live in the world, we do not wage war as the world
does. The weapons we fight with are not the weapons of the world.
On the contrary, they have divine power to demolish strongholds.*
2 Corinthians 10:3–4 niv

One of Janice's acquaintances was talking badly about her. It seemed that the only motivation behind the unkind words was jealousy. Nonetheless, Janice felt upset when she heard the things that were being said. She searched herself for something offensive she might have said or done and hadn't realized, but she could think of nothing.

After talking with a trusted friend who also knew the person speaking badly of her, Janice's friend stated clearly, "It's not you."

Janice couldn't help think how the enemy had twisted something to achieve this. Some bit of information was received wrongly, or a thought was planted. Any number of things could have been contorted by the enemy who loves to destroy.

Rather than make Janice bitter, this experience helped her consider how often any of us may be unknowingly influenced by the enemy. Most importantly, she renewed her commitment to being more spiritually alert. What the enemy meant for evil, God once again used for good!

Morning – FIVE MINUTES OF GLORY

*And whatever you do in word or deed, do all in the name of the
Lord Jesus, giving thanks to God the Father through Him.*
COLOSSIANS 3:17 NKJV

A local writers' group gives members a chance to share with the rest of the group their writing successes. They call this time "five minutes of glory." The author is allowed to stand in front of the group for five minutes to share what they've published recently. They are allowed to hold up a copy of the published work and share any information about the piece that they'd like. This five minutes is intended as a means of encouragement for those seeking publication or just beginning to write. It is not meant as a bragging session.

Sometimes as Christians, we forget to share "five minutes of glory" with others by telling them what God has done for us personally. We should never take credit for the blessings that come our way or do good deeds with the purpose of impressing others. Our time of sharing with others should give God full credit and serve as encouragement for others who may need a good word.

The next time God does something for you—either a blessing from Him or an ability He has given you to accomplish a task—share "five minutes of glory" with someone else. Just be sure all the glory goes to God.

Evening – THE WORLD IS WATCHING

*How great is the goodness you have stored up for those who
fear you. You lavish it on those who come to you for protection,
blessing them before the watching world.*
PSALM 31:19 NLT

We humans have a tendency to focus on what we don't have. We lament not having enough money or time. We become frustrated with our physical limitations and fret about things not turning out the way we wanted them to. We're even good at whining about these things. But remember, the world is watching. You may not think much of a whine here and there, but others are watching to see how we respond to this God whom we say is so loving and good.

One of the ways God demonstrates His love to a hurting world is to lavish His love upon His children. When we whine and complain about little things, we diminish God's blessing to us before a watching world. It's important for us to respond appropriately to all of God's blessings and to demonstrate how deeply our heavenly Father loves us.

DAY 142

Morning – DON'T STUMBLE OVER YOUR PRIDE

Pride goes before destruction, a haughty spirit before a fall.
PROVERBS 16:18 NIV

When we praise a child, we often express our pride in them. The excitement of seeing a toddler do new activities is often accompanied by little claps, big smiles, and joyous comments like "I'm so proud of you." We encourage children to be proud of their accomplishments and to build on their successes. Since God cautions us about the failure that can follow pride, should we encourage it in children?

Secondary education now utilizes group projects that don't focus on building competitive pride. Based on one completed project, each group member receives the same grade. Students learn the value of teamwork and the success that comes from working together. The group project encourages each student to value the output from the team as much as their individual contribution.

News reporters love to reveal the problems that follow celebrities who become overly prideful. When they become too focused on themselves and their accomplishments, they often lose those who support and love them. Pride also seems to stand in the way of good sense and the ability to heed warnings of danger. Without prudent caution, people make poor choices that lead to failures.

The Bible even tells us in 1 Timothy 3:6 that the devil lost his position in heaven due to pride. We certainly don't want to stumble over our pride and share his fate. We need to see our value as part of God's team.

Evening – SPINNING JUST FOR HER

For by the grace given me I say to every one of you: Do not think of yourself more highly than you ought, but rather think of yourself with sober judgment, in accordance with the faith God has distributed to each of you.
ROMANS 12:3 NIV

Miss Ego—let's call her Olivia Braggart—comes into a room looking great, smelling great. Even the air around her has a rosy-colored hue. She knows the world is spinning just for her. And so, Olivia naturally feels she should be the life of the party and even sit at the head table. Why not? But just when she sashays up to the front and sits herself down, the hostess—who is slightly mortified at Olivia's audacity—leans down and whispers that the seat she is now occupying was not meant for her. It is for her honored guest.

Uh-oh.

Olivia does a whole-body blush. She scurries off, breaking a heel, hoping no one saw the social blunder. What could have gone wrong in her thinking? Really, it comes down to one little word, but one big sin.

Pride.

When we place our focus on "me" 24-7, issues are bound to arise. Let us think on God. Let us think of others. As long as we seek the Lord and have the mind of Christ, we won't have to worry about being sent back to the end of the line. With Christ by our side, we will always be just where we need to be.

Morning – LIAR!

"When he speaks a lie, he speaks from his own resources,
for he is a liar and the father of it."
JOHN 8:44 NKJV

No one likes to be lied to. And after awhile, a liar is not believed. We've all heard the story of the little boy who cried wolf one too many times.

But there is one liar to whom we listen over and over. Yeah, you guessed it! Satan, the father of lies.

Why do we perk up our ears when he comes slithering around? Has he ever had anything good to say, anything that was totally truthful or helped us in our walk with Christ? Do we think he has changed in the last thousand years? Is he now trustworthy?

Not on your life. Jesus dealt with his treachery by quoting the Word of God and telling Him to "heel." He could do that because, as the Son of God, He has authority over all things and everyone. We do not have that type of sovereignty, but we do have power in the name of Jesus and in His shed blood. James 4:7 (NKJV) admonishes us to "resist the devil and he will flee from you." He has no lie or ploy that can stand against Christ's authority over him. When we are being attacked, we can be confident that "greater is he that is in [us], than he that is in the world" (1 John 4:4 KJV).

Evening – MY CHILD

After this manner therefore pray ye: Our Father which art in heaven.
MATTHEW 6:9 KJV

The famous theologian Charles Spurgeon said, "[The Lord's] prayer begins where all true prayer must commence, with the spirit of adoption, 'Our Father.' There is no acceptable prayer until we can say, 'I will arise, and go unto my Father.' "

What a beautiful word picture this paints: a child in supplication before his heavenly Father. Not a stranger before an unknown god but a child of the King. Yet it takes faith to receive and believe that picture. Our lives on this earth burden us with negative thought patterns, ripping us from the arms of Jesus into self-condemnation and guilt. To absolve ourselves from this reoccurring problem seems impossible. "No one else has _____." We can fill in the blank with feelings of unworthiness and doubt.

Know this: The enemy loves to divide and destroy by isolating us and making us feel rejected. What a liar he is. We are loved with a great love by the Creator and must allow that thought to permeate our souls. God loves us so much He sent His Son to teach a pattern of prayer. And that pattern begins with the words that give us heart-knowledge: we are His children.

Morning – MOVE THE STONE

"Roll the stone aside," Jesus told them. But Martha, the dead man's sister, protested, "Lord, he has been dead for four days. The smell will be terrible."
JOHN 11:39 NLT

Jesus had been a frequent visitor to Martha's home. Now He has come again to raise her brother from the dead. Though, if you asked Martha, if Jesus had come when they first asked Him to, her brother wouldn't be dead. And now He wants to open up the tomb. Martha doesn't understand any of it.

When Jesus asks for the tomb to be opened, Martha doesn't express amazement that Jesus intends to raise her brother from the dead. Instead, she's worried about the smell.

Aren't we often like that? God tells us to do something, to take a step of faith, to do our part so He can work. Instead of focusing on what God's going to do, we worry about how it's going to affect us.

It's also interesting that Jesus asked for the stone to be moved. If He was about to resurrect a dead body, moving a stone from in front of the tomb was a small thing. But He wanted their participation. He wanted them to put their faith in action. If they believed He was really going to raise a body that had been dead four days, then moving the stone from the tomb was the first step to show their faith.

Evening – INSTANT FEEDBACK

The fear of man brings a snare, but he who trusts in the LORD will be exalted.
PROVERBS 29:25 NASB

Our world is obsessed with instant fame. According to the official YouTube statistics page, the site has over a billion users, almost one-third of all people on the internet. Anyone with an iPhone and a clever catchphrase or touching moment can become an overnight sensation.

Brian Robbins, the owner of the company that created YouTube channels for teens and tweens, told *The New Yorker*, "When you speak to kids, the number one thing they want is to be famous. They don't even know what for."

It's rare to find people who want to do the right thing with no expectations of praise, but that's exactly what Jesus encourages us to do: "Don't do your good deeds publicly, to be admired by others, for you will lose the reward from your Father in heaven. When you give to someone in need, don't do as the hypocrites do—blowing trumpets in the synagogues and streets to call attention to their acts of charity! I tell you the truth, they have received all the reward they will ever get" (Matthew 6:1–2 NLT). He says the same thing about prayer and fasting.

When we perform for men's praises, we miss the rewards from God, which may not come in this life, but heavenly gifts are worth the wait!

Morning – ONLINE ENCOURAGEMENT

And now, dear brothers and sisters, one final thing. Fix your thoughts on what is true, and honorable, and right, and pure, and lovely, and admirable. Think about things that are excellent and worthy of praise.
PHILIPPIANS 4:8 NLT

Negative and impure thoughts cross our minds on a daily basis. Social media and TV don't help either. Even Christian friends jump on the bandwagon and post thoughts and ideas online that make us cringe.

Instead of running away from connecting with people online because you've had enough, make it your goal to be a light in what can be a very dark, negative atmosphere. Encourage good and right thinking. Comment, post, and share God's love with your friends as much as possible.

For the next thirty days, why not plan to post, text, or write at least one encouraging comment every day? Post encouraging scripture; text a friend a note to make her smile; tweet your favorite quote; share sweet stories about your husband and kids on your blog.

Before you grumble or complain about something online, stop and fix your thoughts on what is true, right, and pure. Then see if your comment is still valid.

Evening – WATCH WHAT YOU THINK

Let this mind be in you, which was also in Christ Jesus.
PHILIPPIANS 2:5 KJV

As a young bride, Sue stayed at home while her husband went to work every day. With time on her hands after she finished the housework, Sue began watching soap operas. She enjoyed the stories even though some of the scenes were sexually suggestive and left little to the imagination. Like many other women, Sue didn't realize how addictive this form of entertainment could become, affecting her thoughts even when she wasn't watching the programs.

Women of all ages are faced with images and words on a daily basis that affect their thought processes. In an age saturated with electronic devices, it has become easy to receive and send messages, videos, and photos in mere seconds. It's all too easy to join in with whatever others may be reading, tweeting, or posting.

Paul cautioned his readers to have the mind of Christ—a pure mind that is pleasing to God. When we find ourselves deluged with carnal images, it's time to allow Christ to take control of our thoughts. Satan will steal our minds and hearts if we aren't careful. Ask God to give you the mind of Christ so you can stay pure in an impure world.

DAY 146

Morning – ASK GOD FIRST

The Israelites sampled their provisions but did not inquire of the LORD.
JOSHUA 9:14 NIV

The Gibeonites pretended to be from a distant land to make a treaty with Israel. The Israelites trusted in what they could see and made judgments based on appearances. They did not inquire of God.

Throughout scripture, God begs us to inquire of Him. Often we don't because we think we can handle it. We only go to Him for big things. But in the Gibeonites' case, the data was falsified; Israel was intentionally deceived. God knows all the information about a situation, far more than we ever could.

Even though the Israelites had been deceived, the covenant they made with the Gibeonites was still binding. They were obligated to defend the Gibeonites, even though God had told them to conquer the land.

Asking for God's guidance doesn't mean everything will go the way we expect. But when we ask, the events of our lives do go according to God's plan. Jesus inquired of God before choosing the twelve disciples. Judas was among the twelve. God intentionally allowed Jesus to pick a man who would betray Him so God's plan for our redemption would be accomplished.

Asking God puts the burden on Him to reveal to us His will. In what area of your life have you been handling things on your own? Where do you need to seek God's will?

Evening – HE WILL GIVE YOU THE WORDS

"Alas, Sovereign LORD," I said, "I do not know how to speak; I am too young." But the LORD said to me, "Do not say, 'I am too young.' You must go to everyone I send you to and say whatever I command you."
JEREMIAH 1:6–7 NIV

Marianne was asked to give the message for an upcoming Sunday worship service when the pastor would be on a retreat. At first she hesitated, then nicely said, "No." She remembered mentioning that she wasn't trained in the ministry and really didn't believe she had enough public speaking experience. Somehow, the lay leader didn't hear her. He just said, "Well, I believe you'll have a worthy message."

That evening, as Marianne considered her predicament, she took it to the Lord in prayer. She repeated her reasons for not being capable of preparing and giving the requested sermon. Her devotional reading the following morning was about how God told a young Jeremiah that he would one day be a prophet to nations. Could this be the answer to her prayer? Like Jeremiah responding that he was too young, Marianne had responded by saying she lacked training and experience. Marianne knew that, like Jeremiah, if she trusted the Lord, He would give her the message she needed to deliver.

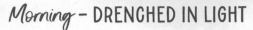

Morning – DRENCHED IN LIGHT

The people walking in darkness have seen a great light; on those
living in the land of deep darkness a light has dawned.
ISAIAH 9:2 NIV

With already two hours more of daylight than the short, dark winter days, Clair felt revived returning from an evening walk. Her front steps, always in the shadows during the winter solstice, were now warm with sunshine. Newly planted petunias reached for the sunlight from their pots, basking in the drench of warmth along with Clair.

Birds chirped from all around as they found building materials for nests and food for their young. A robin fluttered near her as if looking to see if she had anything useful. The fragrance of a blooming tree was brought over by a gentle breeze that made her sigh with happiness.

These were the days she longed for in the thick of waiting for winter to end. She let it melt her for a moment as she sat on the porch step and savored the moment, thanking God for the simple things in this spring day.

Evening – LOOK UP!

Your love, LORD, reaches to the heavens, your faithfulness to the skies.
PSALM 36:5 NIV

In Bible times, people often studied the sky. Looking up at the heavens reminded them of God and His mighty wonders. A rainbow was God's sign to Noah that a flood would never again destroy the earth. God used a myriad of stars to foretell Abraham's abundant family, and a single star heralded Christ's birth.

The theme of the heavens traverses the scriptures from beginning to end. The Bible's first words say: "In the beginning God created the heavens." The psalmist David shows God's greatness in comparison to them: "the heavens declare the glory of God." And in the New Testament, Jesus describes the end times saying, "There will be signs in the sun, moon and stars. . . . At that time [people] will see the Son of Man coming in a cloud with power and great glory."

Some of God's greatest works have happened in the sky.

This immense space that we call "sky" is a reflection of God's infinite love and faithfulness. It reaches far beyond what one can see or imagine, all the way to heaven. Too often jobs, maintaining households, parenting, and other tasks keep us from looking up. So take time today. Look up at the heavens, and thank God for His endless love.

DAY 148

Morning – HE EQUIPS US

Therefore, since we have this ministry, as we
have received mercy, we do not lose heart.
2 CORINTHIANS 4:1 NKJV

Lucy and her husband, Matt, looked at each other and grinned. They had just spent an hour and a half consuming a four-course meal, engaging in deep conversation, and looking into each other's eyes. It was pure gift. . .one that they did not take lightly.

The couple, who had adopted several foster children, often heard phrases such as "We don't know how you can take care of all those kids" or "I could never do what you do!"

Because she heard those comments so often, Lucy now answered the same way every time. "We wouldn't last a week—or a day—without the Lord," she always admitted. "He has called us to this ministry, and He equips us with His energy and strength each day."

Some days were harder than others for the couple, who had no special training. However, some days were simply glorious. They both loved the feeling of being in the center of God's will, out on the edge of their own capabilities. They were also immensely grateful for people who gave them gift cards, babysitting, and opportunities for nights away from their loud, high-maintenance brood.

"Ready to go back home?" Lucy asked Matt as she squeezed his hand.

"Ready," he said.

Evening – FINDING GOD REAL

The fool says in his heart, "There is no God." They are corrupt, and their ways
are vile; there is no one who does good. God looks down from heaven on all
mankind to see if there are any who understand, any who seek God.
PSALM 53:1–2 NIV

"I used to be an atheist. Now, I'm not." The congregation clapped and cheered this young man's story at a baptismal service celebrating several new believers in Christ. One lady shared how lost and empty she had become and how her friends' faith walks drew her to church and then to Christ Himself. Story after story brought hope to life.

One woman and her husband shared how hopeless they had each come to feel. Their marriage was falling apart. Some costly decisions caused him to lose his job. For some time she had been considering divorce, just like those in her family had chosen. She thought she had made up her mind to leave him. That was until some neighbor friends from church came alongside them.

They sought God. He answered. It was a process, of course, this journey of faith, but trusting God with their struggles was life changing. He has been a very real presence in helping them work through things.

Morning – OFFERING OURSELVES TO GOD

Then the people rejoiced, for that they offered willingly, because with perfect heart
they offered willingly to the Lord: and David the king also rejoiced with great joy.
1 Chronicles 29:9 kjv

Diane had felt sad and empty for months, ever since her only child left for college. A single mom with a full-time job, Diane had poured herself into Colton's world with all her non-work time and energy. Soccer games, music concerts, and sleepovers filled her world.

Now, she felt empty, alone. . .and old. She considered getting a dog, but that didn't seem fair to the animal, since she would be gone every day, all day. She took up a hobby, but it didn't satisfy, either. She prayed about what she should do and tried to be patient. Grief, she knew, took time.

One afternoon, she sat in her office taking a coffee break. As she read the day's paper, a new ad for a volunteer opportunity caught her eye. The local crisis pregnancy center advertised a need for mentors to guide young single moms. Suddenly, her heart leapt. She knew that God had led her to read the paper at that moment.

I could pour myself out again, she thought, *and use what I've learned in parenting to help others*. The prospect filled her with joy, and she picked up the phone to call the center.

Evening – A GOD OF COMFORT

Yea, though I walk through the valley of the shadow of death, I will fear
no evil: for thou art with me; thy rod and thy staff they comfort me.
Psalm 23:4 kjv

Loss of any kind is never an easy thing to go through, whether it's the death of a loved one, the loss of a relationship, or a financial mishap. When we lose someone or something, we lose a part of ourselves.

Bill and Sue were stunned when their friendship with another couple ended. The gap left by their friends wasn't easily filled, and they grieved the broken relationship. Victoria lost a good friend to a terrible accident and missed the talks they shared. Some grieve the loss of a job, a home, or a church. No matter what the loss, we can feel overwhelmed by the emptiness and the change it makes in our lives.

If you've been feeling the pain made by changes in your life, read Psalm 23. If anyone knew about loss or change, it was the psalmist David. King Saul wanted to kill him, forcing him to run for his life. He lived in caves, went hungry, and faced betrayal from his family, yet he knew God would restore him. He took comfort in God and His promises. We can do the same. No matter what we are facing, we can count on God to lead us beside still waters and walk with us through the valley of loss.

DAY 150

Morning – CULTIVATING CONTENTMENT

I wait for the LORD, my whole being waits, and in his word I put my hope.
I wait for the Lord more than watchmen wait for the morning,
more than watchmen wait for the morning.
PSALM 130:5–6 NIV

What are you waiting for—a job, a relationship, physical healing, financial provision? Whatever answer to prayer you are longing for, remember that often it's in the waiting that God performs His perfecting work on our character. Joseph waited for many years, serving in Pharaoh's house (even ending up in jail) before God promoted Him. Abraham waited until he was a century old to see the child God had promised to him and Sarah decades before. God was still at work in both men's lives, though His actions and plans were hidden.

Maybe you've waited for God to come through, and so far, He hasn't. The word *advent* means "arrival or coming, especially one which is awaited." Like the silence the people of Israel endured for four hundred years between the last spoken prophetic word and the arrival of the Christ child, perhaps you've endured silence from God for so long that you think He's not there, not listening—or not inclined to come to your rescue.

No matter what you're going through, please know that God is for you, not against you. He aches with you. And He offers us a choice: be chained in fear or changed by grace.

Which will you choose today?

Evening – COMMON DAYS

And so, dear brothers and sisters, I plead with you to give your bodies to God because
of all he has done for you. Let them be a living and holy sacrifice—the kind he will find
acceptable. This is truly the way to worship him. Don't copy the behavior and customs of
this world, but let God transform you into a new person by changing the way you think.
Then you will learn to know God's will for you, which is good and pleasing and perfect.
ROMANS 12:1–2 NLT

Author William Arthur Ward said, "Gratitude can transform common days into Thanksgiving, turn routine jobs into joy, and change ordinary opportunities into blessings." When we live a life of worship, every day can be Thanksgiving! Each task that God gives you to do—even the mundane acts of mopping the floor—can be done as an act of worship to God.

God tells us that He wants us to live a life of everyday worship. He wants to transform us from the inside out. This isn't about trying harder to please God or going to church more and giving more money. It's about letting the Spirit of God lead you in every moment and thanking Him along the way. It's about listening for His still, small voice and following Him no matter what everyone else is doing.

If we let gratitude do its work in our hearts, the common days become holidays! Is every day Thanksgiving in your heart?

Morning – WHEN WORDS FAIL ME

Before a word is on my tongue you, Lord, know it completely.
PSALM 139:4 NIV

Pastor John's message on Sunday morning had been about prayer. After the service, Melissa, a young mother in the congregation, asked the pastor if they could speak privately.

"Pastor," she said, "I can't pray. Your prayers sound so beautiful. But when I pray, I sometimes have no words, and when I do they sound. . .well. . .stupid."

Her pastor smiled reassuringly. "Melissa, God doesn't care how eloquent your words are. He cares about what's in your heart. Without you telling Him, God already knows your thoughts and desires. When you pray, speak to Him as if you're talking with your loving Father."

Sometimes Christians feel so overwhelmed by their needs or by the greatness of God that they simply can't pray. When the words won't come, God helps to create them. Paul says in Romans 8:26 (NLT), "And the Holy Spirit helps us in our weakness. For example, we don't know what God wants us to pray for. But the Holy Spirit prays for us with groanings that cannot be expressed in words."

God hears your prayers even before you pray them. When you don't know what to say and the words won't come, you can simply ask God to help you by praying on your behalf.

Evening – PRAYER CHANGES THINGS

*One day Jesus told his disciples a story to show
that they should always pray and never give up.*
LUKE 18:1 NLT

Have you ever felt like you don't have enough energy to utter one more word to anyone, let alone share your feelings with the Lord? Or maybe you've been asking God for the same thing over and over again, and you feel like He's either not listening or has decided not to answer.

Jesus gives us a picture of how He wants us to pray in Luke 18. The persistent widow wears down the judge with her constant request until he finally gives in. God wants us to come to Him with everything. He has given us an open door to approach His throne with confidence at all times (Hebrews 4:16).

If an uncaring judge finally responded to the widow's constant pleas, how much more will the God who created us and loves us respond to ours? No matter what you are bringing before the Lord, don't give up! Keep talking to Him. The process will change your heart to be more like His. So when you feel all prayed out, remember that God is listening and working on your behalf.

DAY 152

Morning – CLOTHES ARE NOT THE PERSON

*"And why do you worry about clothes? See how the flowers of the
field grow. They do not labor or spin. Yet I tell you that not even
Solomon in all his splendor was dressed like one of these."*
MATTHEW 6:28–29 NIV

Lily feared her teenage daughter placed more value on being accepted by a clique of girls than she did on her values. Kristen had just flopped on the sofa after pleading for *the* famous brand jeans all her friends were wearing. Kristen's drama-queen theatrics centered on needing the right clothes to fit in, to be loved by her friends.

"Kristen, I'd like to ask you a question on a different topic. Do you love your pets?"

"Mom, you know I do!"

"Kristen, as a shelter volunteer you could have picked perfect animals. Doesn't it seem strange that you've adopted a cat with half an ear missing and a three-legged dog?"

"Mom, they're perfect for me. They're as loving as any of the shelter's adorable kittens and puppies. My cat and dog just have their own unique look."

"Kristen, God would be happy with your choice of pets. He wants us to measure worth by looking inward to see the natural beauty of a loving heart. What would God think about your friends who worry more about the clothes you wear than the beautiful person you are?"

With a sigh, Kristen said, "He wouldn't approve."

Evening – DO NOT WORRY

*"Therefore I tell you, do not worry about your life, what you will eat
or drink; or about your body, what you will wear. Is not life
more than food, and the body more than clothes?"*
MATTHEW 6:25 NIV

Suzanne watched her daughter preening. Lucy was making her last mirror check before her prom date arrived. The stylist had achieved a soft up-do for Lucy. With her hair out of the way, the glitter on Lucy's shoulders highlighted her movements. Suzanne might be prejudiced, but she thought the deep green chiffon dress perfectly accented Lucy's figure and complexion.

As Suzanne started telling her daughter how lovely she looked, Lucy interrupted with worries about her appearance. Lucy turned to her mom and said, "I'm too fat. I won't be able to eat dinner without every mouthful showing in this dress." She continued on, fretting that her date wouldn't like how she looked. Lucy was even convinced that her friends would look much nicer than she.

Suzanne put her hands on those lovely glitter-covered shoulders and looked Lucy in the eyes. "Sweetheart, you are the young woman God intended you to be. You are perfect in His sight. You know that you are so much more than how you look. God is interested in the person you are, not the clothes you wear and certainly not what you eat tonight. Put your worries away and have a wonderful time at prom."

Morning – MERCIFUL HEART

"For in the way you judge, you will be judged; and by your standard of measure,
it will be measured to you. . . . You hypocrite, first take the log out of your own eye,
and then you will see clearly to take the speck out of your brother's eye."
MATTHEW 7:2, 5 NASB

"It's been weeks. . ." Natalie told her mother over coffee. "She keeps calling me, texting me, and I haven't responded to her. She just doesn't get it."

"Obviously your friendship is important to Shelley," her mother began, "or she wouldn't keep trying to speak with you. Maybe you need to take a step back."

Natalie fumed. "Mom, she doesn't act like a Christian; even though she says she is one."

Mom hit a nerve. "And your response to her has been Christlike? Honey, we can't have a double standard. When we hold others accountable to reflect Christ and they fail us, we want to judge them. When we fail, we give ourselves a pass. This causes division in the church and confusion for those who do not share the faith.

"Jesus called us to a life of grace and mercy. Shouldn't we also extend that grace to others as He did? Perhaps you should give Shelley the opportunity to share her side of the story."

Natalie nodded. She knew her mother's words were truth.

Evening – GOD IS BIGGER THAN THE WRONG DONE TO YOU

"But if you do not forgive others their sins, your Father will not forgive your sins."
MATTHEW 6:15 NIV

It can be tough to forgive. It presses us to the edge of ourselves where we are forced to acknowledge that God is greater than the wrong that has been done to us. When we choose to forgive, it keeps God's power in perspective.

Someone may stop loving you, insult you, steal from you, or abuse you, but that person will never be able to destroy the love that God has for you or His sovereign rule over all that concerns you. God's redeeming love is bigger than your enemies. This is what Joseph acknowledged after his brothers threw him in a pit and sold him into slavery: "You intended to harm me, but God intended it for good" (Genesis 50:20 NIV).

Think about something someone has done to you that has demanded forgiveness. Do you believe God is bigger than the wrong? Are you convinced His love and His rule are redemptive? If so, let the person who has wronged you off the hook. Stop thinking that he or she has ruined your life and that you will never recover—because God is a redeemer.

DAY 154

Morning – BECAUSE I LOVE YOU

*Whoever spares the rod hates their children, but the one
who loves their children is careful to discipline them.*
PROVERBS 13:24 NIV

Julie saw the five-year-old's frame slump against the wall. Jeremy had been sent to time-out—again. It almost broke Julie's heart when she had to discipline her son. She often wondered if she was doing the right thing, if she had been too harsh or too quick in reacting. One thing she did know, she loved her son deeply and wanted him to grow up to be a responsible, confident person.

God's discipline has the same goals. Discipline administered by a loving forward-looking parent with a goal of helping the child become all that he can become means that He loves us. His purpose for this is so we can share in His holiness. Discipline is never enjoyable, for either the person giving the discipline or the one on the receiving end. But if we look at correction as a sign of His genuine love for us, it will help us to change our behaviors out of love for ourselves and our heavenly Father.

Evening – DISCIPLINE EQUALS LOVE

*"The Lord disciplines the one he loves,
and he chastens everyone he accepts as his son."*
HEBREWS 12:6 NIV

"Mom, it's not fair!" Delia yelled. "I hate you!" The teen stomped up the stairs, ran to her room, and slammed her door—hard.

Delia's mother, Faith, sighed. She knew she was doing the right thing by telling her daughter she couldn't attend an unsupervised party, but it wasn't easy to hear venomous words from the girl who once called her "Mommy."

As she prayed for Delia and herself, Faith felt God remind her that He often felt hated by the ones He birthed too. The truth drove her to her knees. "Lord," Faith prayed quietly, "I'm sorry for the times I've thrown tantrums when you told me no. I believe you always have my best interests at heart."

Love takes many forms, and sometimes it looks like discipline. God disciplines His children in order to get them back on the right track or teach them that His plans are always better than the world's path.

Have you felt the Lord's discipline and taken it as rejection? Remember, He will never leave or forsake us—no matter how we act.

Morning – BEAUTIFULLY IMPERFECT

*Yet I am confident I will see the Lord's goodness
while I am here in the land of the living.*
PSALM 27:13 NLT

Being in process is not pretty. In fact, sometimes it's downright ugly. When life gets too busy and overwhelming, oftentimes we snap. There is only so much our minds can sort through and only so much our tired bodies can handle.

Remember—we must give ourselves grace. We must allow ourselves to be imperfect. Yes, we want to handle every situation with finesse and poise, but sometimes trying to achieve that goal only makes the situation worse. We are exhausted in every way and we cannot handle it the way we want. If we are completely honest, we only show our worst to one, maybe two people we trust. Everyone else gets the dressed-up version and the still-smiling face.

We are imperfect, so let's find some comfort in that. We can accept that we are broken and work from there. A lot of the time we stress ourselves out by trying to be flawless. But when we put that type of obsessive striving aside, we can sort through the pieces with a clear head because we're not hindered by trying to do it "just right." There is freedom in giving ourselves permission to be imperfect.

Evening – NO CONDEMNATION

Therefore there is now no condemnation for those who are in Christ Jesus.
ROMANS 8:1 NASB

There is no condemnation for you who are in Christ Jesus. This means there is no room for guilt or blame in your life. Even when you do things that make you feel like you have failed God, yourself, or others, your standing before God does not change. When you are in Christ, you are clothed in the clean, holy robes of God's Son. When God looks at you, He doesn't see the sins you've committed or the things you haven't done; He sees His holy, blameless Son.

How is this possible? It's possible because Christ died in your place. The sins that would have condemned you in God's holy court were placed on Christ's shoulders and buried with Him. They have no hold over you anymore. So let go of your guilt and regret. Acknowledge that Christ's work on the cross was enough to cleanse and purify you before a holy God. And live in the freedom of the knowledge that no one and nothing can condemn you. Christ has stood in your place so that you can come boldly before the Father in the clean robes that have been washed in the blood of the Lamb. Ask for His forgiveness and claim His forgiveness in your life.

Morning – YOUR HUSBAND IS FIRST YOUR BROTHER

Those who love God must also love their fellow believers.
1 JOHN 4:21 NLT

We hear the word *love* so often in our culture that it has lost the richness it is meant to convey. Jesus said, "By this everyone will know that you are my disciples, if you love one another" (John 13:35 NIV). Yet in the church as a whole, the greatest of all love institutions—marriage—is often lacking the unconditional love to which God calls us.

The care we show for the homeless, mentally handicapped, foster children, cancer survivors is the same love the Bible admonishes us to show our spouses. It is no less a witness of God's unconditional love as the others, perhaps even more.

G. K. Chesterton once wrote, "Love means loving the unlovable—or it is no virtue at all." Perhaps the reason we can love strangers better than spouses is because we aren't faced with a stranger's sins every day. We can give money or a hug or an afternoon and move on. But a wife must live with her husband's financial irresponsibility, workaholism, or critical tongue every single day.

Until we learn to love our spouses with the same unconditional love we proclaim to have for others, we will damage our witness for Christ. In the words of John Piper, "Staying married. . .is not mainly about staying in love. It is about keeping covenant. . .the same kind Jesus made with His bride when He died for her."

Evening – LOVE IS A MANY-SPLENDORED THING

Flee from sexual immorality.
1 CORINTHIANS 6:18 NIV

When Sheila finished yet another sexually graphic romance novel from a popular writer, her husband, Dennis, was dismayed. She whined, "Why can't you be more like that?" Dennis could never measure up.

What was the fictional guy like? He was taller than she was, with thick hair she loved to entwine in her fingers; his touch and kisses scalded her with passion, and without a shirt, he had a six-pack that didn't come from cans in the refrigerator.

But fictional romance is no more real than catalogs for "average women" using size 2 models who had surgery to enhance their measurements.

Paul primarily addressed men when he approached this topic of honoring God with the body—and mind. But women face temptation too. Sexual sin can be crowded out when we allow the Holy Spirit to rule our bodies and thoughts.

Pastor Jimmy Evans, author of *Marriage on the Rock*, discourages women's romance reading because it opens the door for sexual sin.

What is a woman to do? Choose wisely. Honor God and the commitment to one's helpmate. Turn away from temptation from unsuitable media overload.

Appreciate the love of the man scuffing around in a worn bathrobe who cleans up after the baby or the dog, washes dishes, helps around the house, and cares for his wife when she's sick.

Now isn't that better than the fictional version of Mr. Right?

Morning – WOMEN OF FAITH

*When I call to remembrance the genuine faith that is in you,
which dwelt first in your grandmother Lois and your
mother Eunice, and I am persuaded is in you also.*
2 TIMOTHY 1:5 NKJV

When the apostle Paul thought of young Timothy, one thing stood out. Timothy had true faith. He had been raised by his mother and grandmother to love and trust the Lord. Perhaps you come from a long line of Christian women, or maybe you are a first-generation Christ-follower. Either way, these verses have a message for you. We all influence children. Perhaps you have your own children or nieces and nephews. Maybe you spend time with friends' children. Some of you may be grandmothers. Others may work with children either in your career or in a church ministry role. Whatever the situation, you have a great impact on children who look up to you.

It is important to note the trait that stood out was not perfection. It was faith. We cannot be perfect examples for our children. But we can teach them about faith! The way you respond to life's trials speaks the loudest. Children learn about faith when they see it lived out before them. Like Eunice and Lois were wonderful examples for Timothy, may you influence the next generation to place their faith in Christ Jesus.

Evening – THE COURAGE TO SEE GOD AT WORK

*So the king of Jericho sent this message to Rahab:
"Bring out the men who came to you and entered your house,
because they have come to spy out the whole land."*
JOSHUA 2:3 NIV

God had rescued the Israelites from Egypt by dividing the Red Sea. He led the way through the desert as a pillar of cloud by day and a pillar of fire by night. He provided food and water. For forty years, their clothes did not wear out.

The king of Jericho had heard of this big God and His people, who were camped outside his city ready to attack. Rahab, a prostitute, had heard of this God. But her decision was different from the king's. She looked at the same evidence as the king and made a different decision.

She heard that God was a punishing God and a rescuing God. Jericho had been a wicked city and was going to be punished. She hid the spies that came in to scout out the city. She told them she believed in their God and wanted to be rescued along with her family. Her actions flowed from her realization of who God is. Her faith not only gets her mentioned in James and Hebrews, but she also becomes part of the lineage of Christ.

What does your knowledge of who God is lead you to do? How can you step out in faith?.

DAY 158

Morning – THE LIGHT OF HIS WORD

"He has redeemed my soul from going to the pit,
and my life shall see the light."
JOB 33:28 NASB

Natasha hung up the phone in shock. The doctor had just called, confirming her worst nightmare: Natasha's mammogram had come back positive for cancer.

Her mind and heart raced. She shook uncontrollably and broke down in sobs. After several minutes, she took a deep breath and sighed, her energy spent.

What now? she thought. She sat, numb, for several minutes. Natasha knew she needed to call her parents, siblings, and friends, but she wasn't ready to do that yet.

And then a voice in her head whispered, *"Read the Bible."*

Natasha shakily stood up, walked over to her bookshelf, and took out her well-loved and well-worn Bible. She turned hungrily to the Psalms and read several out loud, as if to convince herself of the truth they held. Slowly, her heart rate returned to normal, and her thoughts slowed.

Then, Natasha turned to the book of Job in the Old Testament. This servant of God had suffered terribly, yet he never cursed God. Natasha read several passages, and when she came to Job 33:28, she underlined it.

I will hold on to this verse, she thought. It became her lifeline throughout her ordeal with cancer.

Evening – STAND FIRM!

Cast your cares on the LORD and he will sustain you;
he will never let the righteous be shaken.
PSALM 55:22 NIV

The storm tore through the neighborhood, upending patio furniture and blowing trash cans down the street. After the tempest passed, the residents ventured outside to inspect the damage. Roof shingles were found in some yards. Several large tree branches had narrowly missed damaging vehicles, while some trees were completely uprooted. It was a horrendous and frightening sight, one that was very unsettling to many.

We believers often have horrible storms in our own lives: unemployment, death of a loved one, serious illness, wayward children. He who stands with Christ stands firmly, as if anchored to the ground. Although it seems as if we will be destroyed in these life storms, God will not allow it. To quote the great preacher Charles Spurgeon, "Like pillars, the godly stand immoveable, to the glory of the Great Architect."

Morning – I WAS SORT OF BLIND, BUT NOW I SEE!

"But blessed are your eyes because they see, and your ears because they hear."
MATTHEW 13:16 NIV

Jean, not yet old enough to drive, coached her grandma around on the streets of the city. Most often, they weren't going far. But even short treks could be white-knuckle experiences, such as when Grandma asked, "Jean, is that a tree or a person ahead?"

After they safely passed by the obstacle—a light pole—Jean suggested, "Grandma, I'll go with you to the eye doctor."

The doctor explained, "Mrs. Brown, you have cataracts. The lens of the eye makes things look cloudy as if you were looking through sheer curtains. Yours are like trying to see through three layers of sheer curtains. You won't be able to renew your driver's license without getting both cataracts fixed."

When the doctor removed the patch after her first cataract surgery, Grandma cried, "I can see!" Like her eyesight, her driving vastly improved after that.

When Jesus walked on earth, he healed many from physical blindness. He also recognized those whose spiritual blindness kept them from seeing and hearing the truth of His words. Some decided, in spite of His teachings, that Jesus was a threat to their investments, business, or positions. Jesus applauds those whose spiritual eyesight is 20/20. He spotlighted the disciples, whose hearts and lives were changed because of Jesus. They saw. They heard. They believed.

We have the treasure of God's Word, which gives us clear vision here all the way to heaven.

Evening – OPEN THE BOOK

For everything that was written in the past was written to teach us,
so that through the endurance taught in the Scriptures and the
encouragement they provide we might have hope.
ROMANS 15:4 NIV

"Out with the old and in with the new!" is unfortunately some Christians' philosophy about the Bible. Yet the Old Testament scriptures are vital to every believer. We cannot understand the power of the New Testament until we embrace the teachings, wisdom, and moral laws of God revealed in the Old Testament. After all, the Old Testament points directly to the coming of the Messiah, Jesus, and our salvation.

The apostle Paul reminds us that everything in the Bible was written with purpose—to teach us that through our trials and the encouragement of God's Word, we might have hope.

Life is tough, after all. We get discouraged and, at times, disheartened to the point of such despair it's hard to recover. Yet the Word of God ignites the power of a positive, godly fire within.

Reading *all* of God's Word is paramount. It is the source of hope, peace, encouragement, salvation, and so much more. It moves people to take action while diminishing depression and discouragement. As the writer of Hebrews put it, "For the word of God is alive and active. Sharper than any double-edged sword" (Hebrews 4:12).

Need some encouragement? Open the Book.

DAY 160

Morning – NEW BELIEVERS

Then he said to his disciples, "The harvest is plentiful but the workers are few.
Ask the Lord of the harvest, therefore, to send out workers into his harvest field."
MATTHEW 9:37–38 NIV

The Bible tells about a woman named Lydia who, unlike many women of her time, was a merchant. She sold expensive purple cloth. Lydia worshipped the true God of Israel, but she had not yet become a believer in Christ.

One day, Lydia and others gathered near a river just outside the city of Philippi. It was the Sabbath, and Paul and several of his companions were in town teaching the people about Jesus. They went down by the river and talked with the women there. While Lydia listened to them, God opened her heart to receive the message of Christ. Lydia believed and was baptized. Then she persuaded Paul and his companions to stay at her home for a while. This was the beginning of Lydia's service for the Lord. The Bible suggests that her home became a meeting place for believers.

Encouragement is important to new believers. When Lydia accepted Christ, she was eager to learn more about Him. Paul and his companions agreed to go to her home, where they encouraged her in her faith. Perhaps you know a new believer who could use your encouragement. Think of ways you can help them today.

Evening – PASS IT ON!

After the usual readings from the books of Moses and the prophets,
those in charge of the service sent them this message: "Brothers, if you
have any word of encouragement for the people, come and give it."
ACTS 13:15 NLT

Who doesn't need encouragement? After the reading in the temple, the rulers asked Paul and his companions if they had a word of encouragement to share. Paul immediately stood up and proclaimed how the fulfillment of God's promise came through Jesus; and whoever believed—whether Jew or Gentile—would receive forgiveness and salvation (Acts 13:16–41).

The scriptures state that as Paul and Barnabas left the synagogue, the people invited them to speak again the following Sabbath. And as a result of Paul's testimony, many devout Jews came to Christ. Not only that, on the next Sabbath, nearly the entire town—Jews and Gentiles alike—gathered to hear God's Word (Acts 13:42–44).

Encouragement brings hope. Have you ever received a word from someone that instantly lifted your spirit? Did you receive a bit of good news or something that diminished your negative outlook? Perhaps a particular conversation helped to bring your problems into perspective. Paul passed on encouragement and many benefited. So the next time you're encouraged, pass it on! You may never know how your words or actions benefited someone else.

Morning – LOVING SISTERS

*But Ruth replied, "Don't urge me to leave you or to turn back
from you. Where you go I will go, and where you stay I will stay.
Your people will be my people and your God my God."*
RUTH 1:16 NIV

The story of Ruth and Naomi is inspiring on many levels. It talks of two women from different backgrounds, generations, ethnicity, and even religion. But rather than being obstacles to loving friendship, these differences became invisible. Both women realized that their commitment, friendship, and love for each other surpassed any of their differences. They were a blessing to each other.

Do you have girlfriends who would do almost anything for you? A true friendship is a gift from God. Those relationships provide us with love, companionship, encouragement, loyalty, honesty, understanding, and more! Lasting friendships are essential to living a balanced life.

Evening – A LOVING FRIEND

*A generous person will prosper;
whoever refreshes others will be refreshed.*
PROVERBS 11:25 NIV

Are you convinced that you don't have enough friends—or perhaps your friends aren't meeting your needs? Consider what kind of friend you are. The timeworn axiom "To have a friend, be one" rings with truth.

Good friends listen deeply. We all need someone who can share our load and with whom we can be gut-level honest. This type of friend is invaluable when you feel you can't go one more step.

Good friends also mentor gently and lovingly. Single mom Leticia, 35, has a best friend, Naomi, who's in her seventies. Naomi pushes Leticia to take care of herself and not forget her own needs in the midst of career, kids, and church activities. Maybe there is someone you could nudge into a healthier lifestyle or more active spiritual life.

Finally, good friends forgive freely. They don't judge too harshly or take things extremely personally. Instead, they give friends the benefit of the doubt, knowing that no woman is perfect and sometimes people make mistakes. They are thankful for grace-filled friends and try to forgive as God has forgiven them.

DAY 162

Morning – OPPORTUNITIES TO LOVE

*"If you love those who love you, what credit is that to you?
Even sinners love those who love them."*
Luke 6:32 NIV

On a Jamaican vacation, an American couple admired the beautiful sun-kissed shores and blue skies as they walked to the local marketplace. On the way, a young woman begged, "Lady, I braid your hair; I braid your hair." The American woman said no, but the young woman's advances continued.

Then a towering man with dreadlocked hair approached: "Hey mon, you want some stuff?" The couple knew what that meant and politely told him they were Christians. "Ahhh, you *Krischans*," he said as he backed away.

Unfamiliar surroundings unnerved the couple. Yet God had another plan. Approaching the marketplace, the American woman prayed for God's love for the very people who made her uncomfortable.

Soon others approached the couple: a boy selling handmade yo-yos, a man asking questions, a young single mother. Unlike before, the couple stopped to talk with them. They bought a yo-yo from the boy and handed him a child's Bible tract that was tucked in the bottom of their bag. They shared Christ with him as others gathered to listen. They exchanged addresses with the single mother, and she later came to Christ. As the couple returned to the hotel, the drug pusher sat curbside with his friends. Suddenly he bellowed, "Hey Krischans! Pray for me."

God waited to pour out His love, and the couple nearly missed the opportunity because of their unfounded discomfort. Now that's uncomfortable.

Evening – BE KNOWN FOR LOVE

Dear friends, let us love one another, for love comes from God. Everyone who loves has been born of God and knows God. Whoever does not love does not know God, because God is love.
1 John 4:7–8 NIV

"God is love." It is a verse many remember learning in Sunday school or Vacation Bible School. But what does it mean? God is, by His very nature, love. All that He does is out of a heart overflowing with unconditional love. God's unconditional love surpasses any other that we have ever received or given.

Christians are to be known by our love. Lyrics of a song written many years ago put it this way: "We are one in the Spirit. We are one in the Lord. . . . And they'll know we are Christians by our love." But do they? Do the people within your sphere of influence know that you are a Christian by your love? Or do you blend in with the crowd? Be a vessel of grace and peace. Let love be your trademark, a distinctive sign that you are a believer. You may never know the impact this will have for the kingdom.

What does love look like? It takes all shapes and forms. Some examples might be helping others, going the extra mile, offering words of encouragement, or putting your own ambitions aside in order to put others first.

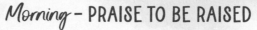

Morning – PRAISE TO BE RAISED

My God, I cry out by day, but you do not answer, by night,
but I find no rest. . . . To you they cried out and were saved;
in you they trusted and were not put to shame.
PSALM 22:2, 5 NIV

Life isn't easy. We've heard many platitudes meant to encourage us. Being a complainer is not attractive. You need to find the silver lining in every cloud. If life gives you lemons, make lemonade. Smile even when it hurts.

Most of us try to begin our day by thanking God for our blessings before we face our challenges. But when we feel despair, is it acceptable to complain or do we need to bury those emotions? The Bible recounts times when people cried out to the Lord, times when they voiced their complaints. In Psalm 22 we're told that Christ poured out His soul to His heavenly Father throughout His sufferings. If we follow Christ's example, we can take our complaints to God in prayer as long as we, like Christ, also acknowledge our love for and trust in God.

If we just complain to others, we won't solve our problems. If we praise God and trust Him to stand with us during our trials, He will raise us up to handle our problems. Maybe we need to replace those old platitudes with this one: Complain and remain, or praise to be raised.

Evening – SING—EVEN IF YOU DON'T FEEL IT

Come, everyone! Clap your hands! Shout to God with joyful praise!
PSALM 47:1 NLT

Nikki noticed Pam wasn't her normal, bubbly self. She watched as her friend walked slowly into the sanctuary and sat down. Normally she was bouncing around, talking to their friends, and sharing stories of what God had done in her life that week. Nikki slid into the seat next to her. "So what's up? Why are you bummed out today? It's not like you."

"It was a horrible week at school; work didn't go well either. It just seemed like everything that could go wrong this week did," Pam confessed. Nikki knew that Pam's husband had been away on business for most of the month as well, and that added pressure.

"Well, you made a good decision by coming to church today," Nikki told her. "The Lord's house is the best place to be when you're bummed out, and the best thing to do is worship!"

Pam hugged her friend and said, "Yes, I am going to sing my heart out."

When worship began, Pam didn't feel anything different, but she sang anyway. Then halfway through the second song, she fully surrendered her emotions to the Lord. Before the pastor came to the platform to share his message, she realized her heart had changed, there was a real smile on her face, and faith started to rise and carry her above her circumstances of the past week.

DAY 164

Morning – LIFTING THE VEIL

*And He will destroy on this mountain the surface of the covering
cast over all people, and the veil that is spread over all nations.*
ISAIAH 25:7 NKJV

When Moses came down from Mount Sinai, his face gleamed with having been in the presence of God. But this shining skin scared the people. So Moses wore a veil in public whenever he received God's commands and delivered them to Israel. Paul mentions how this veil remains over the hearts of the Jewish people who do not see Yeshua ben Yosef (Jesus son of Joseph) as Messiah. The nations outside of Israel also had a veil spread over their minds, but theirs was due to the election of the Jewish nation as the people of God. His covenant with the Jews started through faithful Abraham, and the rest of the world came to know Him through His relationship with the children of Israel. Ultimately, all creation is covered with the veil of sin, and God had to come down Himself to bring us light.

God has lifted the veil. No, He has torn it, destroyed it. He offers a way back to the friendship humans had with Him before the fall into sin. Through Jesus the law was fulfilled and all nations given the truth. He swallowed up death that came with fear and ignorance.

Evening – ROCK OF ESCAPE

*Saul quit chasing David and returned to fight the Philistines. Ever since that time,
the place where David was camped has been called the Rock of Escape.*
1 SAMUEL 23:28 NLT

Hearing that Saul was after him, David fled to a great rock and hid there. Just as Saul was about to capture David, Saul had to give up the chase and return to fight the Philistines. Ever since then, David called his hideout "the Rock of Escape."

Unsure of her footing, longing to find peace and rest, desperate for protection from circumstances, yearning for the silence only God can provide, woman also has an escape: God. "For who is God besides the LORD? And who is the Rock except our God?" (Psalm 18:31 NIV). In Him, as nowhere else, is she safe from pursuers, be they in the form of family or friends, strangers or enemies, thoughts or circumstances, things seen or unseen. Here in her sanctuary she can rest easy, soak up the quiet, gather her forces together, remember the power of the spiritual over the material, and revive herself.

But how does she get to her Rock of Escape? By stilling her mind and approaching God. By trusting in Him alone. By calling out, "My Lord! Save me!" By faithfully camping herself in His presence. By basking in His precious words of peace, comfort, and solace.

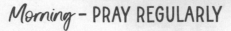

Morning – PRAY REGULARLY

Evening, and morning, and at noon, will I pray,
and cry aloud: and he shall hear my voice.
PSALM 55:17 KJV

Jenn and her mom had a close relationship. Whenever something exciting happened, they emailed or called each other immediately. Throughout the day, they often communicated by texting on their cell phones. If Jenn was having a hard day at work or her mom was facing a medical test, they would encourage each other.

God wants our prayer life to be like Jenn and her mother's relationship. He wants us to call upon Him morning, noon, and night—and many times in between. It may seem like your heavenly Father is far away, but in reality, He is just a prayer away at any given time. He is always eager to help you when you feel your strength is failing. He loves to rejoice over you in your victories, and He will provide a calm in the midst of the storm when you need to be comforted.

Before you run to someone else, run to God. He is your Creator, Redeemer, and friend. He knows you better than anyone else, and He is never too busy to hear your prayers.

Evening – CALL ME

"Call on me in the day of trouble; I will deliver you, and you will honor me."
PSALM 50:15 NIV

"Call me and we'll do lunch."

"Call me and we'll talk more."

"Call if you need anything."

How many times have we said those words or heard them in return? Those two little words, *call me*, which hold such significance, have become so commonplace we barely think about them.

But when God says He wants us to call Him, He means it. He must lean closer, bending His ear, waiting, longing for the sound of His name coming from our lips. He stands ready to deliver us from our troubles or at least carry us through them safely.

David called on God in his troubles. Some of those troubles were of David's own making, while others were out of his control. It's a good thing God doesn't distinguish between the troubles we deserve and those we don't deserve. As far as He's concerned, we're His children. He loves us, and He wants to help us any way He can.

While He doesn't always choose to fix things with a snap of His fingers, we can be assured that He will see us through to the other side of our troubles by a smoother path than we'd travel without Him. He's waiting to help us. All we have to do is call.

Morning – WAITING ON GOD

Let us not become weary in doing good, for at the proper
time we will reap a harvest if we do not give up.
GALATIANS 6:9 NIV

Theologian John Owen wrote, "For the most part we [Christians] live upon successes, not promises—unless we see and feel the print of victories, we will not believe."

The Christian walk is about faith. Hebrews 11:1 (NKJV) describes it as "the substance of things hoped for, the evidence of things not seen." Faith is trusting God to keep His promises, even while we wait.

It's easy to depend on God when all is well, but hard times may cause doubt whether God really is good. However, if you cling to God's promises, you will experience tremendous growth. Grapes don't grow overnight. They slowly ripen, attached to the vine for sustenance. Likewise, Jesus said, "I am the vine; you are the branches. If you remain in me and I in you, you will bear much fruit" (John 15:5 NIV).

In the Old Testament, God called David to the throne, but King Saul refused to abdicate and attempted to kill his successor. David had many opportunities to kill Saul, but spared him because he trusted God. David wrote, "Indeed, none of those who wait for You will be ashamed" (Psalm 25:3 NASB).

No matter what you're facing, sustain yourself in the Word and in prayer. Trust that God will bring you through this season, and don't give up. In God's time, He will deliver you.

Evening – WATCH EXPECTANTLY

But as for me, I will watch expectantly for the LORD; I will
wait for the God of my salvation. My God will hear me.
MICAH 7:7 NASB

In this verse Micah has prayed to God and is now waiting expectantly for what He will do. How often do you pray without really thinking that God hears or cares? Or maybe you think your prayers are just too big (or too small) to matter to Him.

You pray to the sovereign and all-powerful God who loves you. This means you can pray big and often and you can expect God to act. Obviously, we don't know how God will answer a prayer, because His ways are far above our ways. So watch expectantly to see how He will act in ways beyond your imaginings.

Wait for God. Too often we become impatient after we pray, wanting a quick fix or an obvious and direct answer. In this verse we find that Micah was willing to wait for God to answer. While you wait, praise Him for what He is already doing in your life.

Your God will hear you. Be confident in this. God does not turn away from His children. He hears you and desires to give you good things. Next time you pray, be confident that the Most High God is listening.

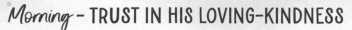

Morning – TRUST IN HIS LOVING-KINDNESS

But I have trusted in Your lovingkindness; my heart shall rejoice in Your salvation. I will sing to the Lord, because He has dealt bountifully with me.
PSALM 13:5–6 NASB

How do you trust in God's loving-kindness? First, you have to believe that He loves you, right now, as you are. Do you really believe that? Or are you still trying to earn God's love by attempting to do enough good things to merit His favor? Or maybe you're convinced that God is merely putting up with you and your daily failures to be perfect. Because you have received Christ, you must believe that God loves you fully, perfectly, and unconditionally, despite what you have or haven't done. Isn't this the kind of love we all long for? So accept it, be humbled by it, and be eternally grateful for it.

Because you know that God *loves* you and is *for* you, you can trust that He will take care of you and work out everything in your life for your good and His glory. It may be hard to comprehend how a certain circumstance could possibly be worked out for good. But the all-powerful, sovereign God is on your side. You can trust fully in His loving-kindness.

So praise God and rejoice in the love He has for you. He loves you and has set you aside as one of His own. There will not be one moment in this life, in death, or in eternity when He will not be with you. He has indeed dealt bountifully with you!

Evening – GOD IS IN THE DETAILS

Nevertheless, each person should live as a believer in whatever situation the Lord has assigned to them, just as God has called them. This is the rule I lay down in all the churches.
1 CORINTHIANS 7:17 NIV

Sometimes we wonder why God puts particular information in the Bible—like the parts of the Old Testament with numbers and dates that don't seem relevant to our lives. What purpose does it serve for us? But its presence in God's inspired Word shows God is in the details, and He loves us in a personal and intimate way. He has called us to the situations we are in, with the people who are around us, for a particular reason.

Other verses expand on this concept:

- Matthew 10:29–31 tells us God has His eye on us individually. He's focused on our needs. He sees us.
- Matthew 6:28–32 says God is well aware of our financial needs. He knows our specific needs and has plans beyond what we can see.
- Romans 14:2–4 tells us God sees our individual weaknesses and struggles. He provides specific ways to help us grow our faith and provides people and situations to help us stand.
- Romans 12:3–6 says we each have different gifts to serve, bless, and help others.

Think about a friend God brought into your life at a particular time when you needed that person or when God provided for your needs in an unexpected way. Focus on how God loves you individually.

DAY 168

Morning – UNEXPLAINABLE LOVE

*No power in the sky above or in the earth below—indeed,
nothing in all creation will ever be able to separate us from
the love of God that is revealed in Christ Jesus our Lord.*
ROMANS 8:39 NLT

Aaron was a hard kid. After fourteen foster homes in seven years, he immediately began his normal routine of "impossible to love" antics, but his newest foster parents didn't react the way all the others had. It seemed no matter what he did, they weren't surprised or shocked. Their words were always soft. And although he had seen hurt sometimes in their eyes, not once had they mentioned calling his caseworker.

After disciplinarian actions and hours of detention at another new school, Aaron was suspended. Expecting to finally see a reaction, Aaron began to pack his things. Mr. Kensington walked into his room and asked, "What are you doing?"

Aaron mumbled, "Packing. I figure now you'll be sending me back."

Mr. Kensington sat down on the bed. "Aaron, we're going to do everything we can to help you succeed."

"Why would you do that?" Aaron snapped.

"Because we love you, and we'll never stop loving you."

Aaron's eyes filled with tears. He knew it was true. Aaron was finally home.

Evening – DIFFERENT KINDS OF LOVE

This is my commandment, that ye love one another, as I have loved you.
JOHN 15:12 KJV

Not all love is the same according to the Greek translation of God's Word. For instance, *philia* is defined as a loyalty and friendship for family members or friends. *Eros* is a passionate, sensual desire. *Storge* is a natural affection shown between parent and child.

The one most familiar comes from the word *agape*, meaning not only general affection but to hold someone in high regard. The New Testament applies agape love in the relationship between Jesus and His disciples. It is one of self-sacrifice and a giving spirit to all, both friend and foe.

Jesus commands us to love our neighbor as we love ourselves (Matthew 22:39). He doesn't say, "Love your neighbor as long as they keep their dogs from barking or if they maintain their yard and stay on their side of the fence." Rather, he commands us to love as He loves us.

That's God's agape love. It's unconditional and powerful. Agape love builds not destroys; it accepts others' imperfections and is tolerant of people who do things differently than we do.

What's your definition of love? Take some time today and exercise God's love in the same manner He loves you, and see what happens!

Morning – GOD AS PARADOX

"Surely I spoke of things I did not understand, things too wonderful for me to know."
JOB 42:3 NIV

Satan challenged God to a kind of duel, with Job as the test case. God let Satan destroy Job's wealth, children, health, and reputation. No wonder Job complained about paradoxes with God (see Job 7:20–21; 9:22–24; 10:3; 30:20–24), so God showed Job paradoxes in nature.

The first was that God spoke out of a storm (Job 38:1; 40:6), yet lightning and wind had caused most of Job's losses. God also presented paradoxes in the animal kingdom. Wild animals cannot be tamed and seem to have no purpose, yet God made them (Job 39:5–12). Likewise, there is no sensible explanation to undeserved suffering except that God wills it, even allowing Satan to cause it in Job's case. The ostrich cannot fly, yet it runs faster than a horse (Job 39:13–18). No one controls Behemoth (Job 40:15–24) or Leviathan (Job 41). If Job cannot explain the natural world that God created, how could he understand the spiritual world or try to "tame" the Creator Himself?

Job realized he should not question God, demand answers, or think he can advise God (Job 42:2–4). God is a paradox—we can know Him, and yet He remains inscrutable and incomprehensible. He is just, because that is His nature, but we cannot prove it. We simply believe it.

Satan's challenge was to see if Job would keep believing God for who He is, apart from the blessings He gives. Job did. Do you?

Evening – HE IS GOOD

"Will you discredit my justice and condemn me just to prove you are right?
Are you as strong as God? Can you thunder with a voice like his?"
JOB 40:8–9 NLT

While God loves us unconditionally and wants to bless and love us, we must remember that He is first and foremost the one and only God. He is the last word—the final judge. Have you spent time reading through the Old Testament? There we see God display His power. We see Him destroy entire people groups. We see Him do some scary stuff that is hard to accept.

Seeing this side of God can strike fear in us—and it should. We should learn to fear God, because as the scripture says, His ways are higher than our ways, His thoughts higher than our thoughts. He will do things we don't understand.

But while He is huge and terrifying and sometimes confusing, we know we can trust Him. As you continue to read through the Bible, you'll also see that He protects, provides for, and unconditionally loves the people who trust Him. Not the people who are perfect, *the people who trust Him.*

> *"Then he isn't safe?" said Lucy.*
> *"Safe?" said Mr. Beaver. "Don't you hear what Mrs. Beaver tells you? Who said anything about being safe? 'Course he isn't safe. But he's good."*
> —C. S. Lewis, *The Lion, the Witch and the Wardrobe*

DAY 170

Morning – KNOWN AND LOVED

*"I am the good shepherd, and I know My own and My
own know Me, even as the Father knows Me and I know
the Father; and I lay down My life for the sheep."*
JOHN 10:14–15 NASB

Do you fear being known and rejected? Do you feel that if someone truly knew you they couldn't possibly love you? In these verses, Christ asserts that He knows you. But He doesn't just know you as a casual acquaintance or even an intimate friend. His knowledge runs deeper than that. He knows you in the same way that He knows the Father. In the Trinity, Christ and the Father are one. So He is saying that He knows you in the same way that He knows Himself. There could not be a deeper or more intimate knowledge. He knows all the things that you hide from everyone else—He knows the temptations, the frustrations, the lost hopes, the rejections, the insecurities, and the deep desires that you may hardly acknowledge to yourself.

Even though Christ knows the darkest and most secret parts of you, He still loves you. He doesn't love you because He can gain something from it. He doesn't love you on a surface, nonchalant level. He *laid down His life* for you. There is no greater love. He knows you better than anyone else does, and yet He loves you with a deeper, purer love than anyone else can give you. You are deeply known and deeply loved.

Evening – A PERSISTENT LOVE

*"O Israel," says the LORD, "if you wanted to return to me, you could.
You could throw away your detestable idols and stray away no more."*
JEREMIAH 4:1 NLT

Reading the Bible can be scary at times, as we see God threaten to destroy entire nations. All throughout Jeremiah, the Lord speaks of the punishment that is about to befall His people. He goes on and on about the destruction that will come to their cities and families. And yet He continually says things like, "If you return to me, I will restore you so you can continue to serve me" (Jeremiah 15:19 NLT).

God's love for us is vast and deep, and He offers more than second chances! Even though some may never decide to choose Him—and He must deal with them as He sees fit—He continually offers us the chance to return to Him. What wonderful news this is for us!

If you are feeling like you are past redemption, take heart! Read through the book of Jeremiah and be reassured that He desires you. Use a highlighter to mark every time He offers redemption. As you do this, you will begin to see that He ultimately desires for you to be with Him.

Morning – MOVING IN GOD'S STRENGTH

*I am full of power by the Spirit of the LORD. . . . In God I have
put my trust; I will not be afraid. . . . I am for peace. . . . My help
comes from the LORD, who made heaven and earth. . . . Because You
have been my help, therefore in the shadow of Your wings I will
rejoice. . . . Now therefore, O God, strengthen my hands.*
MICAH 3:8; PSALM 56:11; 120:7; 121:2; 63:7; NEHEMIAH 6:9 NKJV

At times, when a task lies before us, we begin to doubt our ability. Writers hesitate, their hands hovering above the keyboard. Mothers look at their to-do lists, the words blurring before them as overwhelmed feelings creep in. Businesswomen consider the meeting they will soon be leading, not sure of the words to say. Unfocused, unsure, untethered around the tasks before us, we flounder.

Let God take over. Tap into His power and claim it for yourself. Put all your trust in the God who vanquishes fear, who can help you do all He has called you to do. He's done so in the past, and He will definitely do so in the present. Rejoice in His presence, and allow Him to work through you as your hands begin moving in His strength.

Evening – SECRET DESIRES

*Trust in the LORD, and do good; dwell in the land, and feed on His faithfulness.
Delight yourself also in the LORD, and He shall give you the desires of your heart.
Commit your way to the LORD, trust also in Him, and He shall bring it to pass.*
PSALM 37:3–5 NKJV

Some of us never pursue our deepest desires out of fear of what people will think or fear of failure. But such fears can keep us from living the life we long for. So how do we slay the dream killers? We lean on God and become confident in Him. We do things His way. It is then we find ourselves dwelling in His territory and being fed on His promises. Such faithfulness sustains us in a way worldly fears cannot. And when we take joy in God's presence, allowing Him to be our guide and giving all our secret plans and dreams over to Him, He will give us the desires of our hearts. So put all your faith in God, the dream maker. Bring your desires before Him. Listen for every whisper, every leading He sends your way. Then simply trust as you commit your way to Him, not forcing the issue but confident that in His will, His way, His timing, He'll bring all your dreams into being.

DAY 172

Morning – DON'T SWEAT THE SMALL STUFF

*I consider that our present sufferings are not worth
comparing with the glory that will be revealed in us.*
ROMANS 8:18 NIV

When a woman gives birth, the time she spends in pregnancy and labor can seem like an eternity. She's uncomfortable. She's nauseous. She's swollen. And it all leads up to hours, maybe even days of painful labor and suffering.

But then she holds that beautiful son or daughter in her arms, and the memory of any pain fades so far to the background, it's not even worth considering. The joy of seeing the one she loves face-to-face fills up her heart and mind so completely, it wipes away any shadow of discomfort and suffering. Plus, the years of joy and fulfillment that child brings are much longer than the months of pregnancy or the hours of labor.

That's how heaven will be for us. Life is like pregnancy and labor. This life isn't the completion, it's the preparation! Our years here are just a moment compared to eternity. When life is difficult, don't sweat it. It won't last forever. One day we will leave it all behind to be flooded with His complete, perfect love and acceptance. All the pain of this life will be lost in comparison to the complete peace we'll experience, forever and ever.

Evening – PERFECT PEACE

*You will keep in perfect peace all who trust in you, all whose thoughts are fixed
on you! Trust in the LORD always, for the LORD GOD is the eternal Rock.*
ISAIAH 26:3–4 NLT

Our lives are a series of moments. And that's what our minds get caught up in, the day-to-day minutiae, the little niggling worries, the what-ifs, the how-comes, and the why-fors. But God wants us to have a different perspective, not an in-the-moment viewpoint but an eternal one. Because when we look at the big picture, our day-to-day worries—the ones that get our hearts beating out of control and our thoughts ricocheting around in our heads—are really nothing to be upset about. That takes trust in a power so much higher than ourselves. But when we have that trust, that confidence in the eternal Rock who can never be moved, we are blessed with a peace that blesses us within, keeping us healthy in mind, body, spirit, soul, and heart. Such a calm also blesses those around us, for it's contagious.

So fix your mind on the one who sees and knows so much more than you ever will. Put your confidence in the one who has your name written on the palm of His hand. Practice being in His presence during quiet hours. And then, the moment stress and chaos begin creeping in, call God to mind, and He will surround you with that big-picture, perfect peace.

Morning – EVEN THE LITTLE THINGS

*But be sure to fear the LORD and serve him faithfully with all
your heart; consider what great things he has done for you.*
1 SAMUEL 12:24 NIV

No one likes sweeping dust bunnies out from under the fridge, scrubbing grout, or filing taxes. Sometimes the boss will assign a grueling task, or worse, an extremely tedious one. It's tempting to expend the minimum effort required and get on with the better things in life. This can happen in relationships as well—we manage the minimum amount of closeness and small talk without any real depth or connection.

However, as God's children we are called to a higher standard. Not just to "get things over with," but to do all things to His glory. Practically, this means doing our best in whatever task or goal we pursue, knowing that He is the final inspector of our work, tasks both big and small.

So, should we scurry to scour the oven until the metal squeaks for mercy? No, we don't work out of fear or out of cold duty (though sometimes those are the motives that compel us), but because we desire to please God, knowing how much He loves us. The way we do the "little things" reveals for whom we labor—for us? For our employers, family, or friends? We may benefit from our efforts, but ultimately our work is for our Father.

Evening – WORK AS UNTO GOD

*Work willingly at whatever you do, as though you
were working for the Lord rather than for people.*
COLOSSIANS 3:23 NLT

Whatever you do today, work as if you are working for the Lord rather than for man. What does that mean? For the employee, it means work as if God is your supervisor. He does see and hear everything you do. When you are tempted to slack off, remember that the Bible warns against idleness. When you are tempted to grumble about your boss, remember that God has put you under this person's authority— at least for this time. For the stay-at-home wife or mother, it means that even changing a diaper or washing dishes can be done for the glory of God. This verse has to do with attitude. Are you working in the right spirit? Work is not a bad thing. God created work. God Himself worked in order to create the earth in six days. And on the seventh, He looked at the work of His hands and He rested. Consider your work a blessing. If you are employed, remember today that many are without jobs. If you are able to stay at home with your children and keep your house, keep in mind that many are not able to do so for one reason or another. Whatever you do, work as if you are working for God.

Morning – REVEALING AND HEALING

*"Call to Me, and I will answer you, and show you great and mighty things,
which you do not know. . . . I will bring [them] health and healing; I will
heal them and reveal to them the abundance of peace and truth."*
JEREMIAH 33:3, 6 NKJV

God again beckons His people to put Him to the test. He wants His daughters to call to Him so that He can answer them. He longs to show them great and mighty things. One of these great and mighty things is healing—both physical and spiritual. Part of healing includes an abundant knowledge and experience of God's peace and truth.

In Jeremiah 33 God told the prophet His plans to restore Jerusalem, to bring the people back from captivity in Babylon, and to forgive their rebelliousness. He promised mercy and the coming of a descendent of King David who would be called the Branch of Righteousness and who would rule in joy. Chapter 33 bursts with the beauty of God's grace as it points forward to the great plan of rescue, not just for the Jewish people captured by the Babylonian king Nebuchadnezzar during Jeremiah's time, but to the salvation of creation through Messiah Jesus. God accomplished in Jesus the mightiest of deeds, a plan for redemption that we could never imagine. Through Jesus, God revealed to us, daughters of Eve, peace and truth since He is the Prince of Peace and the way of truth.

Evening – FOR THIS VERY PURPOSE

*"But I have raised you up for this very purpose, that I might show you my
power and that my name might be proclaimed in all the earth."*
EXODUS 9:16 NIV

In 1952, Dr. Virginia Apgar designed and introduced the Apgar Score, an unbiased score of the baby's condition after birth used to evaluate their transition to life outside the womb. A baby's score is calculated by the heart rate, respiratory effort, muscle tone, skin color, and how they respond when a catheter is used in the nose. A low Apgar Score alerts doctors to the need for life-saving intervention for newborns.

Virginia knew she wanted to become a doctor by the time she graduated from high school. The death of her oldest brother from tuberculosis and another brother's chronic childhood illness may have influenced her determination to help others.

Leadership discouraged Dr. Apgar from continuing in her dream to become a surgeon because other women had failed to establish successful careers in the surgical field. Despite this, she pressed to step outside of the social norm by completing her surgical residency in 1937. She was the first woman recognized as a full professor at Columbia University College of Physicians and Surgeons in 1949.

God has given you a purpose and a desire to fulfill your destiny. What is your dream? Trust God today to put His plans in motion.

Morning – THIRSTING FOR MILK

In fact, though by this time you ought to be teachers,
you need someone to teach you the elementary truths of
God's word all over again. You need milk, not solid food!
HEBREWS 5:12 NIV

Lila was a new Christian. She had made the choice to become a Christian as a mature adult and was now eager to learn more through Bible study. She asked the pastor which Sunday school class she should join. When he suggested the women's class, Lila told him she would rather go to something for beginners. The pastor told her the church didn't have a beginners' class. He assured Lila that she would be comfortable in any group.

Lila was skeptical but took the offered text for the women's class. The first Sunday Lila attended, the leader asked everyone to introduce themselves. Of the eight women in the class, three called themselves cradle-to-grave Christians, two had been Christians over twenty years, and three had made their decision over forty years ago.

When it was Lila's turn, she told the ladies that, as a new Christian, she didn't think she had enough background to fit in. The leader laughed as she opened her Bible to Hebrews 5:12. After reading the scripture aloud, she said, "Lila, we are all still growing in our Christian walk. We will never reach a point where we have all of the answers and, being new, you can probably provide insights and ask questions that would never have occurred to us. So let's grow together."

Evening – DEEP ROOTS

"They will be like a tree planted by the water that sends out its roots by
the stream. It does not fear when heat comes; its leaves are always green.
It has no worries in a year of drought and never fails to bear fruit."
JEREMIAH 17:8 NIV

Watering your garden doesn't seem difficult, but did you know you can train a plant to grow incorrectly, just in the way you water it? By pouring water from the hose for only a few moments at each plant, the root systems become very shallow. They start to seek water from the top of the soil, and the roots can easily be burned in the summer sun. By using a soaker hose, the water slowly percolates into the ground, and the plants learn to push their roots deeper into the soil to get water.

Jeremiah talked about a larger plant, a tree. A tree needs deep roots to keep it anchored in the ground, providing stability. The roots synthesize water and minerals for nourishment and then help to store those elements for a later time. Our deep spiritual roots come from reading God's Word, which provides stability, nourishment, and refreshment.

Morning – EVERYDAY WAYS

The heavens are telling of the glory of God; and their
expanse is declaring the work of His hands.
PSALM 19:1 NASB

Another day had come and gone. It wasn't a special day—that Janet knew of anyway. She sat in her backyard and watched the sun set. Glorious shades of orange melded with yellow and bright red, all artfully meshed at the edges with a now navy-blue sky. It was unlike any sunset she had ever seen. *God showing off again*, she mused.

As she thought about it, no two sunsets were ever the same. The sun went down in a slightly different location along the horizon each day at a slightly different time depending on the season. The color variations were never exactly the same, as if an artist had painted it.

But then, a great artist did paint it. Every day. Something new.

Janet thought about how deeply God must love her and each of His children to give us a fresh work of art in the skies every day of our lives. Many duties and burdens may fill our days, and He loves us in the midst of all of it, enough to provide beauty and wonder all along the way.

Evening – THE SIMPLE THINGS

In him our hearts rejoice, for we trust in his holy name.
PSALM 33:21 NIV

Think about the simple pleasures in everyday life—that first sip of coffee in the morning, waking up to realize you still have a few more minutes to sleep, or putting on fresh, warm clothes right out of the dryer on a cold winter morning. Perhaps it's a walk along the beach or a hike up the mountains into the blue skies that give you a simple peace.

God knows all the simple pleasures you enjoy—and He created them for your delight. When the simple things that can come only by His hand fill you with contentment, He is pleased. He takes pleasure in you. You are His delight. Giving you peace, comfort, and a sense of knowing that you belong to Him is a simple thing for Him.

Take a moment today and step away from the busyness of life. Take notice and fully experience some of those things you enjoy most. Then share that special joy with Him.

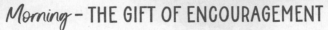

Morning – THE GIFT OF ENCOURAGEMENT

We have different gifts. . . . If it is to encourage, then give encouragement.
ROMANS 12:6, 8 NIV

As a Christian, what is the inward desire of your heart? To witness? To serve? To teach? In the book of Romans, Paul lists the different gifts God gives His children according to His grace. These gifts of grace are inward desires and abilities used to further the kingdom of God. Encouragement is one of those gifts.

Have you ever met someone who seems to have the right thing to say at just the right time? Intuitively, she notices when someone is troubled and proceeds to listen and speak words to uplift and encourage.

Paul spoke of encouraging as a God-given desire to proclaim God's Word in such a way that it touches hearts to move them to receive the gospel. Encouragement is a vital part to witnessing because encouragement is doused with God's love. For the believer, it stimulates our faith to produce a deeper commitment to Christ. It brings hope to the disheartened or defeated soul. It restores hope.

Perhaps you are wondering what "gift" you possess. The Bible promises us that every true believer is endowed with at least one or more spiritual gifts (1 Corinthians 12). How will you know your gift? Ask God, and then follow the desires He places on your heart.

Evening – SHARING JESUS NATURALLY

"But you are my witnesses, O Israel!" says the LORD. "You are my servant.
You have been chosen to know me, believe in me, and understand that I alone
am God. There is no other God—there never has been, and there never will be."
ISAIAH 43:10 NLT

Although Nonette became a Christian at age ten, as a teenager she was shy and afraid of what others thought of her. She became hesitant to talk about Jesus. Once, however, she boldly shared her faith. During a Bible study, Nonette became concerned about a girl in her youth group. Samantha wasn't born again, and Nonette knew God wanted Sam to accept Christ. Nonette decided *she* was the one to help her.

One night after the study, Nonette and a friend cornered Sam. Then Nonette went into the "spiel" she had practiced. But Sam yelled at her and ran away. *I tried too hard,* Nonette realized. *I scared her off.*

It was years before Nonette would verbally witness again. She doesn't know what became of Sam, but after several years of being a non-witness, Nonette realized that she wasn't being obedient to Christ's mandate to share the gospel with the world, and she began to look for opportunities to talk about Jesus kindly and winsomely. When she does, Nonette feels God's presence and His approval—like a father who is proud of his daughter for "just trying."

Morning – WITH ALL YOUR STRENGTH

Let all that I am praise the LORD.
PSALM 146:1 NLT

Christian scholar Larry Taunton launched a national campaign to interview college atheists. He discovered, "Our former church-attending students expressed [positive] feelings for those Christians who unashamedly embraced biblical teaching. [Michael] told us, 'Christianity is something that if you really believed it, it would change your life and you would want to change [the lives] of others. I haven't seen too much of that.' "

It's not enough to love God with a passing "I love you a lot" sentimentalism. Jesus told us to love God "with all your heart and with all your soul and with all your strength and with all your mind" (Luke 10:27 NIV). God wants devotion like David's, who said, "Bless the LORD, O my soul: and all that is within me, bless his holy name" (Psalm 103:1 KJV).

This kind of passion characterized the apostles, missionaries, and evangelists throughout history whose fervent devotion spread like fire and changed the landscape of Christianity. We aren't called just to love God but to love Him with intensity.

As Puritan minister Samuel Ward said, "The fervency of the true zealot is in the spirit, not in show. . .such a man's worth cannot be set forth with the tongues of men and of angels."

Evening – WITH ALL YOUR SOUL

"Be zealous."
REVELATION 3:19 NASB

Tasha's son was saved at youth group and shared the gospel with her. She was so amazed at this news, she couldn't wait to hear more. She eagerly entered the church with great expectation.

The music moved her. The message challenged her. The excitement was all over her face. She looked around at the Christians who sat stoically around her and asked herself, "Am I missing something? Is this how Christians are supposed to act?"

Why is it that Christians have no problem screaming for their favorite football team or dancing at a pop concert, but in the church with the greatest news on earth, the majority of us sit complacent and unmoved?

Jesus said we should worship God with all our heart, soul, mind, and strength (Luke 10:27). But for some reason many have cut out the soul in worship. They will worship God with their minds and mean it with all their hearts. But the emotional expressions that start in the depths of the soul are suppressed.

Every Christian should have the experience of seeing the congregation from the choir loft. The blank stares and emotionless participation are glaring. As Puritan Samuel Ward wrote, "Christian zeal is a spiritual heat wrought in the heart of a man by the Holy Ghost." Perhaps if the fire of zeal were practiced, it would spread and bring revival.

Morning – AN EXTRAVAGANT GOD

Return to the LORD your God, for he is merciful and compassionate,
slow to get angry and filled with unfailing love.
JOEL 2:13 NLT

There are often times when we are exhausted and discouraged and we allow our minds to roam to dark places. Despair and disappointment set in. A woe-is-me attitude prevails within us. How is it possible to rise from the doldrums? How do we continue? We turn our faces toward the Lord God and know He is in control.

Scripture tells of God's mercy and loving-kindness. It speaks out and urges us to come back to God. This doesn't necessarily mean a change of circumstances, but a change of heart. This change is a choice we intentionally make. It's not necessary to be in a church building or a revival when we make this choice. While many changes happen there, ours can be in our closet, our car, or our office. We reach inwardly to the Highest and ask for His mercy. And scripture says He is merciful and full of grace. He hears our prayers.

Focusing on the negative, choosing despair, doesn't bring life. Voluntarily focusing on Jesus will. Praise Him for all your blessings: they are there, look for them. Some might be tiny, others magnificent. But they're all because of our Lord Jesus Christ. He is a most patient God and extravagant in His love.

Evening – FILL YOUR MINDS WITH GOOD

Finally, brethren, whatever things are true, whatever things are noble, whatever
things are just, whatever things are pure, whatever things are lovely, whatever things
are of good report, if there is any virtue and if there is anything praiseworthy—
meditate on these things. The things which you learned and received and
heard and saw in me, these do, and the God of peace will be with you.
PHILIPPIANS 4:8–9 NKJV

Do you categorize yourself as an optimist or a pessimist? Do you look on the bright side of things, or can you always find something negative in every situation?

If you are more of a Debbie Downer, don't lose hope! Even if your mind goes directly to the negative, God can change you. He does this by transforming you and renewing your mind. Ask Him to daily fill your mind with good things: thinking the best about people and circumstances, not the worst. Seek the power of God to take every thought captive and you'll begin to see a change in you! Make a list of scriptures that will renew your mind. Start with these:

"Do not conform to the pattern of this world, but be transformed by the renewing of your mind. Then you will be able to test and approve what God's will is—his good, pleasing and perfect will" (Romans 12:2 NIV).

"We demolish arguments and every pretension that sets itself up against the knowledge of God, and we take captive every thought to make It obedient to Christ" (2 Corinthians 10:5 NIV).

If you are perpetually optimistic, stay the course and pray for the people in your life who have a tendency to bring others down.

DAY 180

Morning – A HEART OF FAITH AND HONOR

"He lifts the poor from the dust and the needy from the garbage dump.
He sets them among princes, placing them in seats of honor. For all
the earth is the Lord's, and he has set the world in order."
1 Samuel 2:8 nlt

This is just a part of the prayer that Hannah, mother of Samuel, prayed as she left her son to live with Eli the priest and serve the Lord all his life. Samuel was her firstborn, a child she desperately prayed to God for, and she fulfilled her promise and left Samuel in the care of Eli.

Have you ever considered how hard it was for her to pray this prayer of praise to God? She finally had a child, but she was committed to her promise to offer him in service to the Lord. She would not be the one to raise him and experience all of his "firsts" in life. And yet she prayed this prayer that does nothing but honor the Lord. Even if there were moments when she wished she hadn't made such a promise, she praised Him. "My heart rejoices in the Lord! The Lord has made me strong" (1 Samuel 2:1 nlt).

We can learn so much from Hannah in the short space she is written about in 1 Samuel. She honored the Lord above all else and trusted His ways. May God give you a heart of courage that honors Him and strengthens you.

Evening – ONLY THROUGH GOD

For by thee I have run through a troop: by my God have I leaped over a wall.
2 Samuel 22:30 kjv

We've all heard stories about people performing seemingly impossible acts of heroism in the face of danger—lifting a car off of someone, carrying an injured person for several miles to reach help. Other stories tell how people survive being stranded in a blizzard or walk away from a terrible accident uninjured. How did they do this? Common sense often plays a big part in survival, but today's scripture tells us where our strength comes from. God enabled the writer of this verse to survive the obstacles he faced.

We may never face the tragedies we read about or see on the news, but we deal with adversity every day. A job loss, a bad medical diagnosis, or a child being bullied at school are only a few of the problems faced by people like us every day. How do we handle it? We can deal with the trouble that comes our way through God and His powerful strength. We may not face a troop or have to jump over a wall, but by our God, we can face a financial crisis, divorce, or disease. Take courage today in knowing that God is here for you and you can leap over that wall of adversity.

Morning – CANS

He is the Maker of heaven and earth, the sea, and everything in them—
he remains faithful forever. He upholds the cause of the oppressed
and gives food to the hungry. The LORD sets prisoners free.
PSALM 146:6–7 NIV

Shelley held on to him as they bobbled on and off the roadside on a moped. They needed groceries, and aluminum cans brought ten cents each. She held the bag as he bent down to grab the cans. At the end of the evening, they went home with twenty dollars' worth. A dear friend was watching their infant son, who they soon packed into the car. The three of them were off to the grocery store to get food to last until payday.

Years later, she would think back to this time and thank God for the provision, even though it seemed so hard. It was such a humbling season in their lives.

Following it though, God brought them to a good job and community where they would stay for decades and raise four sons. They grew in their faith and their freedom In Christ. Yes, God had been faithful, and continued to be.

Evening – GOOD & PLENTY

Then Jesus called his disciples and told them, "I feel sorry for these people.
They have been here with me for three days, and they have nothing left to eat.
I don't want to send them away hungry, or they will faint along the way."
MATTHEW 15:32 NLT

There they were. Four thousand men—not including the women and children. They'd been hanging with Jesus, watching the miracles of healing the mute, the crippled, the lame, and the blind. Now the crowd was hungry. But where, the disciples asked, would they get enough food to feed all these people—especially since they were in the wilderness (no takeout available)? Jesus never answered that question. Instead He asked the disciples what they had on hand. The response: "Seven loaves of bread and a few small fish." Amazingly enough, after Jesus thanked God for that food, broke it into pieces, and gave it to the disciples to distribute, there was enough food for all of those people—plus leftovers!

The point of the story? Jesus will never let any of His people go away hungry. He will always find a way to give His daughters what they need—and more! This limitless God can do anything, anywhere, with anything! He's the Lord of not only good—but plenty!

DAY 182

Morning – GRIEF

" 'He will wipe every tear from their eyes. There will be no more death' or mourning or crying or pain, for the old order of things has passed away."
REVELATION 21:4 NIV

How quick women are to skip past grief. The loss of a loved one. The loss of a relationship. The loss of a job. Women face these things far too often. And how do most respond? They stiffen the upper lip and plow forward, not always taking adequate time to truly mourn what they've lost. One of the hidden dangers of neglecting grief (and yes, you can neglect it) is illness. When women don't take the time to mourn their losses, the physical body pays a price. In fact, emotions pay a price too. If you're not careful, your body will wear down and your emotions crater. And, if you let things go too long, your spiritual life will weaken too. Today, many will need to hear these words: there's nothing wrong with grieving. God doesn't want you to park there too long, but do take the time to mourn. Then, once you're done, God will dry your eyes, lift your chin, and give you courage to face tomorrow.

Evening – SITTING AND SECURE

My salvation and my honor depend on God; he is my mighty rock, my refuge. Trust in him at all times, you people; pour out your hearts to him, for God is our refuge.
PSALM 62:7–8 NIV

Heavy rains blew in under the overhang at a sharp angle. Rae checked the cover over her infant daughter in the carrier on her lap. She peeked in at her cute little face and took in deeply the sweet aroma of her baby's breath. They had just been on their first shopping trip together. Sitting on that red bench outside Hill's department store, she savored the moments as they waited for her husband to pick them up.

Rae could not have known that this was their only shopping trip and that her daughter would stop breathing during that very night. There was no way she could be prepared for the pain that came from losing her and then waiting until eternity to see her again. Rae returned many times to that blessed moment on the red bench and thanked God for it.

Later, for a long time, she didn't want to count her blessings for fear of losing them. After years of wrestling with God, she came to sit securely on life's benches of blessing—never knowing what would come of tomorrow, but trusting God with all of it.

Morning – KICK ENVY TO THE CURB

*But if you harbor bitter envy and selfish ambition in
your hearts, do not boast about it or deny the truth.*
JAMES 3:14 NIV

For several weeks, Mandy noticed herself getting restless and discouraged whenever she logged on to her computer. After talking with her pastor-husband, Ron, she admitted that she felt envious of several of her friends because they had more money than she did. They seemed to be constantly acquiring expensive possessions and traveling to far-off places. Some of her pals were stay-at-home moms like Mandy, but those who worked full-time often posted about awards banquets, business trips, and other (seemingly) glamorous aspects of their jobs.

"Honey, why don't you take a break from social media?" Ron asked. After praying about that suggestion, Mandy decided it was a wise idea. Each morning, instead of immediately powering up her computer and logging on to Facebook, she took out her Bible and read the scriptures. She then spent time praying about her contentment level and asking God to remind her of His many blessings.

Within a few days, Mandy felt more peace in her spirit. She also acknowledged that God had placed her in her current role after she had prayed for years to have children and a family. Ron encouraged her too: "Hon, our life has less frills and more fulfillment."

He's right, she thought. *Sure, I'm not making the big bucks, but I* am *making a big difference in my children's lives by pouring myself into them.*

Evening – WAITING ON GOD

Yet true godliness with contentment is itself great wealth.
1 TIMOTHY 6:6 NLT

If you were raised in the 1960s or '70s, you might remember receiving large, heavy catalogs from Montgomery Ward or Sears and Roebuck in the fall of each year. If you're like many children from those decades, you pored over the catalogs with glee, circling items you wanted (especially in the toy section of the book) for Christmas, birthdays, or other special occasions.

As modern-day women, we tend to see things we never knew we needed when we shop in malls or big box stores. Also, we spend time surfing online and end up pinning wish list items to boards on Pinterest. While there's nothing wrong with dreaming and wishing, there's a fine line between making a wish list and becoming discontent with what God's given us.

How do you know if you've crossed that line? Next time you shop or pin, examine your heart. Ask yourself prayerfully: Am I coveting what others have? Do I feel discouraged by the age or size of my home/car/closet? Have I begun to grumble about what I don't have instead of being thankful for what I already own?

If you find yourself becoming greedy and ungrateful for the blessings God has bestowed, take a time-out from shopping. Instead of looking online for things to buy, make a list of the things God has given you (both large and small). You might find that you don't really "need" anything, after all.

Morning – PRAY EXPECTANTLY

*But when you ask, you must believe and not doubt, because the one
who doubts is like a wave of the sea, blown and tossed by the wind.*
JAMES 1:6 NIV

Do you pray expecting God to answer? George Müller did. Müller was a nineteenth-century evangelist known for his faith in prayer. He studied the Bible and trusted in God's promises. Müller documented fifty thousand answers to prayer, giving credit to his meditation on the scriptures and unbending faith in God. The answers to some of his prayers came in less than twenty-four hours, and others took much persistence and waiting. By faith, Müller trusted God to provide an answer without him asking for anyone's help. He wanted to prove that God is faithful and that He hears when people pray.

George Müller's prayers were rooted in faith. His example suggests that the one who prays must be willing for God to answer in His own time, in His own way, and by His own power. The latter was at the center of Müller's prayers. Instead of trying to find the answer himself, Müller relied on God alone. He opened his heart to God's answer, whatever it was, and he trusted God to answer according to His plan.

Prayer takes faith, persistence, and a willingness to let God have His own way. Try praying daily with that in mind, and expect God to answer.

Evening – HANNAH'S PRAYER

*The eyes of the LORD search the whole earth in order to
strengthen those whose hearts are fully committed to him.*
2 CHRONICLES 16:9 NLT

There are many great prayers in the Bible. There are prayers for wisdom and for unity, prayers of repentance and negotiation with God. Hannah's was an anguished prayer for a child.

Hannah was barren. She prayed before God with a broken heart and promised God that if He gave her a child, she would commit him to the Lord all the days of his life. God heard and answered her prayer. Does God always answer the prayer for a child in this way? No, He doesn't. There are women whom God loves deeply and unconditionally who will not bear a child in this life. But in this case, God granted Hannah a male child whom she named Samuel. She only had Samuel for a short time before she took him to Eli, the priest. Samuel was not an ordinary child. He heard the voice of God at a very young age. He grew up to become a judge and prophet that could not be matched in all of Israel's history.

God is looking for ordinary men and women whose prayers reflect hearts completely committed to Him. He found such commitment in Hannah, and He answered her prayer.

Morning – HOW TO BE A NATURAL BEAUTY

*Your beauty should not come from outward adornment, such as
elaborate hairstyles and the wearing of gold jewelry or fine clothes.
Rather, it should be that of your inner self, the unfading beauty of
a gentle and quiet spirit, which is of great worth in God's sight.*
1 PETER 3:3–4 NIV

Are you one of those people who loves clothes, shoes, jewelry, and current hairstyles? Many of us are! We like looking put together when we go to work or church. Who doesn't feel wonderful when wearing a great outfit we know complements us? Or maybe you're one who hits the gym more than most in pursuit of that perfect swimsuit body?

While there is nothing wrong with wanting to look nice or fit, outward looks will eventually fade. The beauty that will never fade comes from the inside. When we know that the Master Creator made us, we can go into any situation with confidence knowing God wants us the way He made us and that He has a plan for our lives. What adornments are you investing in?

Evening – A PICTURE FROM THE INSIDE

*But the LORD said to Samuel, "Do not look at his appearance or at the height
of his stature, because I have rejected him; for God sees not as man sees,
for man looks at the outward appearance, but the LORD looks at the heart."*
1 SAMUEL 16:7 NASB

Penny sat next to her good friend, Louise, waiting for service to start. "Years ago, people dressed up for church," Louise commented. "When I was a little girl, getting ready for church started on Saturday night. It was quite an ordeal at our house. My mother washed three heads of hair—mine, my younger sister's, and hers. Then she rolled our hair on sponge rollers, and as uncomfortable as it was, we slept all night that way. She set out our church shoes, frilly socks, and dresses the night before."

Penny nodded. "And now it's so casual even some pastors wear jeans on the platform—and that's all right with me! I think it reminds me that people examine us based on our outward appearance, but God isn't concerned with that. His focus is deep within our hearts. We can be dressed up, with every hair in place, and be a total wreck on the inside."

"Been there; done that," Louise replied. "I've pretended to have everything together, but God knew that my heart was full of sin and rebellion. God knew the real me, and I was only deceiving myself."

Morning – FORGIVENESS

*"For if you forgive other people when they sin against you,
your heavenly Father will also forgive you. But if you do not
forgive others their sins, your Father will not forgive your sins."*
MATTHEW 6:14–15 NIV

While checking your email, an invitation from a friend pops up in your inbox. Instead of excitement, a horrible, careless remark she once said about you leaps to mind. Your stomach clenches —the comment hurts as much as it did the moment you first heard it. You've tried to forgive her, but anger still needles your heart.

Forgiveness is much more costly than simply saying the words "I forgive you." Forgiveness means letting go of the right to hold a person's wrongs against them. Instead, you absorb the debt the offender owes you. We can give up our right to demand retribution because we are whole in Christ—forgiveness doesn't diminish us. It is out of His grace that we can offer grace to those who've hurt us. As Jesus' followers, we show our gratitude for His forgiveness toward us when we model His actions.

Often, forgiveness looks more like a process than an event. It's okay if forgiving someone takes a long time. Prayer will help that process; asking sincerely for God to bless those you want to forgive will keep your heart soft and free of bitterness. When hurt comes back to haunt you, throw your pain on Christ—He will help you let go.

Evening – LETTING GO OF THE LIST

*Teaching us that, denying ungodliness and worldly lusts,
we should live soberly, righteously, and godly in the present age.*
TITUS 2:12 NKJV

Molly stood in line at the concession stand, deep in conversation with her friend Katrina when she caught a glimpse of Erica out of the corner of her eye. She stopped talking midsentence as the list under Erica's name began to play. *She was so horrible to you. How can she call herself a Christian? She doesn't act like she should. . . .*

Katrina interrupted. "You're doing it again. Don't you see what's happening? The list is stealing your life. It isn't hurting anyone but you— and my relationship with you."

Molly bit her lip. "You are right. I am judging Erica, saying she doesn't act like a Christian when I'm not being Christlike either."

"I have an idea," Katrina said. "You could write out the list, cross off each offense with a pencil, confess aloud that you forgive the person who hurt you, and then toss that piece of paper in the trash. Just like God let your list go, you've got to let the list you have for each of these people go."

Molly smiled. "I really think I can do that!"

Morning – UP AND AWAY

*Then, because so many people were coming and going that they
did not even have a chance to eat, he said to them, "Come with me
by yourselves to a quiet place and get some rest." So they went
away by themselves in a boat to a solitary place.*
MARK 6:31–32 NIV

Dexter had been playing in the woods near the house for some time now. His mother looked out the window scanning the boyhood terrain with tree forts, a fire ring, and scrap wood. It was hard not to worry when she thought back to the times she had to run out in a hurry to help her injured sons.

Just then she spotted him about twenty feet up in one of the trees, sitting there. A bit panicked, she ran outside. "What are you doing?"

"I'm just reading and relaxing," Dexter said calmly from his comfortable perch.

He had always been an agile climber, and she knew it wouldn't be right to steer him away from the strength and courage that would grow him to manhood, but this was a bit rattling. "I'm okay, Mom." He reassured her, seeing her conflicted face.

Afterward in the house he agreed that he would let her know in the future when he was reading in a tree, and she resolved to do two things. She thanked God that he desired time alone to think and read, even though it was so high up; and she would pray more!

Evening – A MOTHER'S TRUST

Keep me as the apple of Your eye; hide me under the shadow of Your wings.
PSALM 17:8 NKJV

Have you heard of Betty Stam? She and her husband, John, serving as missionaries with the China Inland Mission, did not have time to escape with their infant daughter before the invasion of the Red Army. Their captors plundered their home, seized their money, made them write a ransom letter, and then marched them away to another city, where they were stripped of their outer clothing and the next morning paraded down a city street lined with jeering onlookers. At the place of execution, they were forced to kneel in the dust and then beheaded.

But, walking up Eagle Hill that December day in 1934, Betty was leaving behind, hidden in some blankets, her three-month-old baby, Helen Priscilla. She left her with some diapers, milk powder, and ten dollars. She had no way of knowing that the baby would survive for twenty-four hours all alone and would be found by Chinese Christians and taken to her maternal grandparents in another part of China. What kind of mental anguish must she have endured as she walked away from that room, knowing she would likely never return and wondering what would become of her child? We will never know what she thought or how she prayed. But we mothers of today can trust our children to the same God who watched over little Helen Priscilla. They are in His care, and when we are gone, He will still be there.

Morning – BLESSED REDEEMER

For God so loved the world that he gave his one and only Son,
that whoever believes in him shall not perish but have eternal life.
JOHN 3:16 NIV

Compassion is "sympathetic consciousness of others' distress together with a desire to alleviate it" (Merriam-Webster). Oh, how our God loved us and showed His compassion. He knew we were a sinful people, and we were in peril. Our eternal lives were at stake. And He had a plan. He provided a way for redemption.

Despite the fact we did not deserve His unmerited favor, grace, He gave it to us anyway. He looked down on mankind and desired to bridge the separation between us. He sent His Son, Jesus, to die on the cross for our sins so we might live the resurrected life. Once we've accepted this free gift, we can rejoice!

We were in distress, and God came to the rescue. What a mighty God we serve! And how He loves us. The rescuing Shepherd came for His flock. He bore what we deserved because He had such compassion. True love, which our Father gives, is eternal. He loved us before we loved Him. What an amazing concept He desires us to grasp! Know today your heavenly Father loves you.

Evening – IT'S NOT ABOUT THE DOS AND DON'TS

Who hath saved us, and called us with an holy calling, not according to
our works, but according to his own purpose and grace, which was given
us in Christ Jesus before the world began, but is now made manifest by
the appearing of our Saviour Jesus Christ, who hath abolished death,
and hath brought life and immortality to light through the gospel.
2 TIMOTHY 1:9–10 KJV

More than six hundred Jewish laws are derived from the Ten Commandments that God gave Moses. Before Jesus the Messiah came, they had to follow a list of rules in order to live a life that pleased God and assured them of His continued blessing in their lives.

Jesus came to the earth; gave His life; and defeated death, hell, and the grave so you could choose eternal life. You are not saved because of a list of dos and don'ts you follow. Instead, it's all about surrendering your heart to God. You are His child by His grace. Once forgiven, He doesn't remember your sins.

Our world is moved by conditional love: I will love you if you do this or that. Thankfully, that has no place in your relationship with God. His love is unconditional. You don't have to work from a list for God to accept you. His grace has already made you lovable and acceptable to Him. There is nothing you can do to make God love you any more or any less.

Morning – GOD'S GIFT

*"I tell you, you can pray for anything, and if you believe
that you've received it, it will be yours."*
MARK 11:24 NLT

Notice the words in this verse. It says we're to believe we have received what we pray for. That's past tense. It doesn't take faith to believe our prayers will be answered after what we asked for is in plain sight. Trusting Him for answers before we see them is what the Lord wants.

The Bible tells us that without faith it is impossible to please God (see Hebrews 11:6). That may sound harsh, but scripture also promises that He gives each of us a measure of faith (see Romans 12:3).

If you gave your daughter a present and she left it on a shelf, unopened, you'd be disappointed. It may have been something she really wanted, so you found the perfect gift and wrapped it beautifully, but it is useless just sitting there. It's the same with God's gift of faith. We don't have to struggle with positive thinking or work up enough faith. All we have to do is accept what He has already provided and exercise the faith He gives.

Some people misuse this scripture and pray for foolish things that aren't according to His will. But when we stay close to Him, our desires will line up with His, and we can have complete confidence that we will receive our request.

Evening – BREAKING BARRIERS

*Now the gates of Jericho were securely barred because of
the Israelites. No one went out and no one came in. Then the
LORD said to Joshua, "See, I have delivered Jericho into your
hands, along with its king and its fighting men."*
JOSHUA 6:1–2 NIV

Anastasia started walking with Christ in her twenties. That's when she began praying for her father to know God too. She invited him to church often, and once in a while he joined her at an Easter or Christmas service. In her thirties she still called him Daddy, and she was still praying, but now she had a husband praying with her too; and as the years went along, her children joined in.

This circle of prayer for Daddy and Granddaddy grew and continued. Anastasia would not give up seeking God for her father. When Anastasia was in her fifties, Daddy was a great-granddaddy, and they kept praying. He would still come along to church with them most holidays, though it was getting much more difficult with his cane and hearing impairment.

One year Anastasia's daughter died tragically in a car accident. Anastasia struggled deeply but kept her focus heavenward, where she knew her daughter was. Her father was angry with God but couldn't help but notice the depth of his daughter's faith.

When Daddy was in his eighties, the persistence of the enlarged circle of prayer finally saw its answer, and he came to Christ. Anastasia shared the news with everyone she had ever asked to pray for him. It was a glorious day of rejoicing!

DAY 190

Morning – TRIALS AND WISDOM

*Consider it pure joy, my brothers and sisters, whenever you face trials of many
kinds, because you know that the testing of your faith produces perseverance.
Let perseverance finish its work so that you may be mature and complete,
not lacking anything. If any of you lacks wisdom, you should ask God, who
gives generously to all without finding fault, and it will be given to you.*

JAMES 1:2–5 NIV

Trials and troubles are an everyday part of living here in a fallen world. Pastor and author Max Lucado says, "Lower your expectations of earth. This isn't heaven, so don't expect it to be."

Things won't be easy and simple until we get to heaven. So how can we lift our chins and head into tomorrow without succumbing to discouragement? We remember that God is good. We trust His faithfulness. We ask for His presence and peace during each moment. We pray for wisdom and believe that the God who holds the universe in His hands is working every single trial and triumph together for our good and for His glory.

This verse in James tells us that when we lack wisdom, we should simply ask God for it! We don't have to face our problems alone. We don't have to worry that God will hold our past mistakes against us. Be encouraged that the Lord will give you wisdom generously without finding fault!

Evening – WORKING FOR US

*Even though our outward man is perishing, yet the inward man is being renewed
day by day. For our light affliction, which is but for a moment, is working for
us a far more exceeding and eternal weight of glory, while we do not look
at the things which are seen, but at the things which are not seen.*

2 CORINTHIANS 4:16–18 NKJV

"A moment of pain is worth a lifetime of glory," Pete Zamperini told his brother Louis in the movie *Unbroken*. He wanted Louis to focus on the big picture. If he could endure the physical pain of training and punishing himself as a runner, he could enjoy Olympic glory the rest of his life.

Scripture has a similar idea: a lifetime of affliction is worth an eternity of glory. Not to minimize our trials—they are painful and often progressive because our physical bodies are perishing. But compared to eternity, our troubles are light and momentary. And extremely beneficial. Somehow God allows them to work for us to produce exceeding glory in eternity. The passage tells us to look at the big picture, at the unseen spiritual things. As we focus beyond this life and fellowship with Christ through His Word and prayer every day, we will be renewed on the inside.

A gospel song says, "It will be worth it all when we see Jesus." We Christians can endure suffering in this life knowing it works for us in the next.

Morning – THE NEXT STEP

Your word is a lamp for my feet, a light on my path.
PSALM 119:105 NIV

Change is unsettling. It doesn't matter who we are—old or young, rich or poor, married or single. Change can be exciting, but it also brings with it the unknown. And that can be a little unnerving.

When we face changes, the path ahead often looks dark and twisted. We squint and strain to see down the road, but we just can't see clearly. But we don't always need to see into the distance. We only need to see the step ahead of us. Then another step. Then another step.

When the path ahead is obscure, we can go to God's Word for guidance. His Word will light our way. Oh, it may not tell us exactly what's coming a year from now or even a month from now. But if we depend on Him and follow the guidance He's given us, His Word will act as a road map for the step ahead. It will light the pathway at our feet so we know we're not stepping off a cliff.

When we rely on His Word and follow it consistently, we can trust His goodness. Even when the future is unclear, we can move ahead with confidence, knowing He will lead us to the best place for us, and His goodness and love will stay with us every step of the journey.

Evening – DON'T REFUSE INSTRUCTION

Hear instruction, and be wise, and refuse it not.
PROVERBS 8:33 KJV

Have you ever made the statement "I wish I had listened to what they told me." Most people have either spoken or had that thought at some point in their lives. When we're young and naive, we think we know more than our elders. As we grow and mature, we realize just how smart and wise they were. By then, it's sometimes too late to sit at their feet and learn.

As a young girl, Vickie often heard her grandfather talk about how he rode in a covered wagon and the fact that his grandmother was part Cherokee. He experienced and endured many trials Vickie will never know about. When all that information was available to her, she thought it unnecessary. It was the past; it didn't apply to her life. Now she wishes she had learned more about the events that made her ancestors the hardworking individuals who loved their family and endured much hardship.

God has instruction for His people if they will listen and accept what He has to say. We're no longer children, but we still need instruction even as adults. We need the instruction of God's Word. The writer of today's proverb tells us to be wise and not refuse the instruction given to us. God's instruction means eternal life or eternal damnation. We would be wise to accept His words as our own.

Morning – TEST THE SPIRITS

The naive believes everything,
but the sensible man considers his steps.
PROVERBS 14:15 NASB

Joyce was in the kitchen while her elementary-aged children watched a popular cartoon movie. Joyce was surprised to hear one of the characters say something about existentialism—an atheistic philosophy. *What is this doing in a kid movie?* she wondered. Joyce sat down to investigate and discovered an entire storyline blatantly expressing themes of godlessness and idol worship.

In a world that is increasingly antagonistic toward Christianity, parents can no longer trust the mainstream media to protect the minds and souls of children.

Satan is called "the prince of the power of the air" (Ephesians 2:2 KJV), and his greatest weapons to manipulate the mind are logic, philosophy, doubt, and desensitization.

What beliefs are your children absorbing through the movies and music you allow into your home? First John 4:1 (NKJV) says, "Beloved, do not believe every spirit, but test the spirits, whether they are of God." These spirits can be found in something as simple as a cartoon.

Pay close attention to the message of the entertainment you enjoy. Every plot and lyric has an underlying belief system or worldview that the writer wishes to convey, deeper than just entertainment value. Watch television with your kids and be on guard.

Evening – YOUR DAILY EARFUL

"O LORD, there is none like You, nor is there any God besides You,
according to all that we have heard with our ears."
1 CHRONICLES 17:20 NKJV

What was the first thing your ears heard this morning? After your alarm, that is. What did you listen to while you brushed your teeth, drove to work, made a run to the grocery store, or picked up the kids from an activity? Chances are, you were listening to some form of music while you were completing some of these duties. In fact, according to a 2014 survey conducted by Edison Research, most US citizens listen to about four hours of audio per day.

Four hours is one-sixth of your day. It's a lot of time for mental stimulation or acquiring information or receiving inspiration. What is filling your ears, penetrating your heart, and affecting your mood? Challenge yourself this month to increase the amount of time you spend listening to Christian music and programming. A mind can only take so much of the talk show rants and human-interest stories and catastrophic news, not to mention the detriment of sexually charged dialogue and politically correct but biblically incorrect commentaries. Go through the playlist on your device and examine it through the grid of God's Word. Set your satellite or traditional radio stations to choices that will glorify Christ and edify you. And then watch your attitude take on a new look.

Morning – A WONDERFUL CORD-SHIP

*A person standing alone can be attacked and defeated,
but two can stand back-to-back and conquer. Three are
even better, for a triple-braided cord is not easily broken.*
ECCLESIASTES 4:12 NLT

Alone, a woman may be beaten down spiritually, emotionally, or physically. But when one woman teams up with another, the two have a better chance of standing firm together! Like Ruth who refused to leave Naomi, a woman who pledges herself to a female friend not only pulls up and strengthens herself, but her friend as well. Their fates forged together, they seek to help each other in every manner of ways—building each other up, sharing life experiences, bearing each other's burdens, sharing each other's sorrows, celebrating each other's successes, seeking wisdom in the quest to understand the opposite sex, discussing methods of child rearing, exploring new employment avenues, challenging and comforting one another, and keeping each other firmly footed on the spiritual path.

When two women who are bound in such a friendship add love and fellowship with God to their "cord-ship," they become even stronger. With Christ in the mix, this now "triple-braided cord" will not easily fray.

May all women find a special way to honor their girlfriends, their God, and their special cordship.

Evening – BUILDING FRIENDSHIPS

A friend loves at all times, and a brother is born for a time of adversity.
PROVERBS 17:17 NIV

Today's world isn't designed for friendship. It's too fast paced, with too many demands and too much stress. Oh, we're connected to everyone, all the time, through text messaging and cell phones and Facebook. But as fun as Facebook may seem, it robs us of face-to-face time. We're so distracted with everything at once, we find it hard to focus on one thing, one person at a time.

But friendship demands one-on-one, face-to-face time. And although most of us don't feel we have a lot of time to give, we must! We simply must make friendship and building real flesh-and-blood relationships a priority.

God created us for relationships. And although a well-timed email or text message may lift us up at times, there's simply no replacement for a real, live hug. There's no substitute for a friend sitting beside you in the hospital, holding your hand. And we won't have those things unless we're willing to put aside our high-tech gadgets and invest time in the people around us.

Today, let's make it a point to turn off our cell phones. Let's step away from our computers for a while and have a real conversation with someone. That person may just turn out to be a true friend.

DAY 194

Morning – LOVE FOR ONE ANOTHER

*Now all who believed were together, and had all things
in common, and sold their possessions and goods,
and divided them among all, as anyone had need.*
ACTS 2:44–45 NKJV

Alex and Kay rushed out of their garage to feel the heat of the forty-foot flames hot against their backs. They jumped in their cars and barely escaped the fire that burned their beautiful home and much of Oklahoma in 2012. As they pulled away, all they had were the clothes on their backs. Over the next twenty-four hours, they discovered that hundreds from their small, rural community had lost everything. Immediately, blessings began to pour in, and the people came together to care for one another.

A local church became the hub for relief supplies and encouragement to the displaced. Alex was overwhelmed when friends and family from several church congregations filled his car with food, clothing, and toiletries. One man asked Alex, "What size shoe do you wear?" Alex replied, "A ten." The man bent down, unlaced his work boots, and handed them to Alex. Alex drove home with tears of gratitude and thanks flowing from his heart.

Evening – WITHOUT LOVE

*If I speak in the tongues of men or of angels, but do not have love,
I am only a resounding gong or a clanging cymbal.*
1 CORINTHIANS 13:1 NIV

Without love, all the good deeds in the world are just a bunch of noise! Like resounding gongs or clanging cymbals, the Pharisees of Jesus' day went about their good works. Over and over, they repeated them. They were duties, not desires of the heart. They based everything on ritual rather than relationship. Are there Pharisees among us today? Certainly! Our job as Christ-followers is to show the world the love of God. We do this with open hearts and open arms. We do it in the workplace, in the marketplace, and in our homes. We do it as we come and go; with our children and with other people's children; with our spouses, neighbors, and coworkers. The world desperately needs to see extravagant love in us, love that cannot be explained by any means other than the fact that we walk with the author and Creator of love. Don't go about your good deeds out of guilt or so that someone will notice how nice you are. Do good deeds so that others will notice Jesus in you and glorify your Father who is in heaven. Do good deeds out of love. It will always come back to you tenfold.

Morning – PRAISE HIM WHEN IT HURTS

*Trust in the Lord with all thine heart; and lean not
unto thine own understanding. In all thy ways
acknowledge him, and he shall direct thy paths.*
PROVERBS 3:5–6 KJV

Bridgett and her youngest daughter were alike in many ways. As her daughter became a young adult, though, their relationship sometimes felt like it would break in two. Bridgett's heart ached for the times when her daughter adored her—the times when "Mommy" was the only one who could fix her hurts and dry her tears.

Bridgett had learned that any words she had to say about her daughter's life choices would only widen the gulf between them. So she took her own hurts to her heavenly Father daily and prayed for God's grace and direction for both their lives. "Lord, I trust You to bring about Your purpose and plan for us."

Each time she was tempted to worry about her daughter and the choices she was making, she intentionally praised God for working in her heart. A little more than a year passed and Bridgett began to see change. Her daughter's heart softened, and God-ordained opportunities opened up for her. The mother-daughter relationship improved, and Bridgett knew her prayers were being answered through her decision to praise God through prayer.

Evening – REJOICE!

Rejoice in the Lord always. I will say it again: Rejoice!
PHILIPPIANS 4:4 NIV

Paul wrote these words from prison. Considering his circumstances, it doesn't seem like he had much reason to rejoice. Yet, he knew what many of us forget: when we have the Lord on our side, we always have reason to rejoice.

He didn't say, "Rejoice in your circumstances." He told us to rejoice in the Lord. When we're feeling depressed, anxious, or lost in despair, we can think of our Lord. We can remind ourselves that we are so very loved. We are special to God. He adores us, and in His heart, each of us is irreplaceable.

Perhaps the reason we lose our joy sometimes is because we've let the wrong things be the source of our joy. If our joy is in our finances, our jobs, or our relationships, what happens when those things fall through? Our joy is lost.

But when God is the source of our joy, we will never lose that joy. Circumstances may frustrate us and break our hearts. But God is able to supply all our needs. He is able to restore broken relationships. He can give us a new job or help us to succeed at our current job. Through it all, despite it all, we can rejoice in knowing that we are God's, and He loves us.

Morning – WITH A SONG ON HIS LIPS

*"The Lord your God is with you, the Mighty Warrior
who saves. He will take great delight in you. . . .
[He] will rejoice over you with singing."*
ZEPHANIAH 3:17 NIV

Our relationships with our earthly fathers can greatly affect how we view our heavenly Father. Whether consciously or not, we take the earthly father we can see and try to puzzle out what our heavenly Father is like. Some women had attentive, loving fathers. If only this were the norm! Some fathers were absent, never known to their daughters. Other fathers violated the family's trust through abuse or neglect. Some fathers were caring but distant—emotional connection difficult or nonexistent.

Where our earthly fathers have fallen short, our heavenly Father does all perfectly and to the full. He is full of mercy, full of loving-kindness, absolutely just and right. He brings order where there is disorder, peace instead of confusion. He heals bodies and broken hearts, and He keeps all His promises.

Though the Father rules over the whole universe, He is also close to us. He does not love us at arm's length, His disapproval looming if we misstep. He *sings* and rejoices over His children; He *delights* in that we belong to Him. The love of our great God surpasses all earthly love in its perfection, its sacrifice, its provision, and its salvation. Regardless of our family backgrounds, our Creator perfectly loves and delights in us.

Evening – I.C.E.

*I will praise the Lord, who counsels me; even at night my
heart instructs me. I keep my eyes always on the Lord.
With him at my right hand, I will not be shaken.*
PSALM 16:7–8 NIV

Think about the people in your life whom you have on speed dial. Who do you call first when crisis hits? Many of our phones actually have an I.C.E. programmed at the top of our contact list so that EMTs can have a phone number to call "in case of emergency."

And while having an emergency contact is important and necessary, sometimes we can come to depend on these people more so than God. Especially if our first response to any kind of crisis is to call a best friend, a mentor, or a professional counselor instead of going straight to the Lord. We think that just because our friends have skin on, they'll be able to help us in more tangible ways.

The truth is that God is able to do way more than we could ever ask or imagine (Ephesians 3:20), and He wants us to come to Him with everything first. He will counsel us and set our feet in the right direction.

There is nothing wrong with calling a friend or spiritual mentor and getting godly advice! Oftentimes God uses those very people to help you. The problem arises when we put those people before God.

Morning – ASK HIM

*"Call to me and I will answer you and tell you
great and unsearchable things you do not know."*
JEREMIAH 33:3 NIV

After a long day at work, Sue went home, where more frustration awaited her. Bills needed payment without enough money to pay them all. Another of the cars needed repair. One of the kids was having issues that gave him a bad day too. And on top of it all, she had a spat with her husband.

Sue once again spent some time yelling out to God for answers. "God," she said, "I'm tired of having to come to You for help! Why can't You just be with me all the time to help me?"

There were tears and a pause, and she was taken aback. His still, small voice reminded her that He never leaves her—not ever. Sue realized that she was the one who veered away from Him. After more calling out to God, in a calmer tone this time, she began to see His direction and how she should respond to her challenges.

Evening – THE-GOD-WHO-SEES

*Now the Angel of the LORD found her. . .[and] said to her, "Return to your
mistress, and submit yourself under her hand.". . . Then she called the
name of the LORD who spoke to her, You-Are-the-God-Who-Sees.*
GENESIS 16:7, 9, 13 NKJV

Hagar ran away from her circumstances: Sarai, an abusive mistress. Part of Hagar's trouble had been caused by her own actions. For having become pregnant by Abram, she had begun disrespecting the childless Sarai.

We too sometimes think we can run from our troubles. But when we come to the end of ourselves, God is there, ready to give us the wisdom we need but may not want. He may ask us to go back, telling us how to "be" in our circumstances: submissive, obedient, loving. He had a vision for Hagar that she would be the mother of a son and have many descendants.

Even today, this God-Who-Sees sees you and your situation. He is ready to reveal Himself to you and share His wisdom. He may not remove you from your circumstances, but He will give you the word you need to get through them. Afterward, you'll see your situation in a new light, with a new hope for your future, step by step.

Morning – WITH ALL YOUR STRENGTH

Whatever your hand finds to do, do it with all your might.
ECCLESIASTES 9:10 NIV

"Now we have one day more," said Oxford chaplain Joseph Alleine in 1664. "Let us live well, work hard for souls, lay up much treasure in heaven this day, for we have but a few to live." Little did he know that only four years later, at age thirty-four, his time on earth would end.

Every single moment of life is a gift. We dare not waste one. "To live is Christ," said the apostle Paul (Philippians 1:21 KJV). Our lives were made to reflect God's glory, not just on Sundays or mission trips or during women's Bible study class, but in respecting our husbands and modeling decency and kindness for others. It's in the things we say, do, and think when no one is there to give credit. It's in the times we choose to do the right thing even when it hurts.

Every moment has a purpose for God's kingdom. It's time to be zealous for righteousness in the course of everyday life, and God has promised a treasure trove awaiting us in heaven. The irony is that earthly life will also be filled with treasures—happy marriages, strong children, peace of mind, and joy unspeakable and full of glory.

Evening – A HAPPY HEART

For the despondent, every day brings trouble;
for the happy heart, life is a continual feast.
PROVERBS 15:15 NLT

British comedian, actress, and singer Joyce Grenfell once said, "Happiness is the sublime moment when you get out of your corsets at night." Of course, we no longer wear corsets, but what a wonderful feeling it is to take off those control-top panty hose and brassieres before getting into our pajamas. It's those modest moments of pleasure that make us smile. But they are so easy to overlook. The trick is to search for them each and every day.

Find some moments of pleasure in the smallest of things—the smile on your baby's face (regardless of whether or not it's from gas), the crazy antics of your cat or dog, the sparkle in your husband's eyes, the squirrels frolicking across your lawn. Instead of focusing on the troubles that lie before you, make sure you take time out for all the good things that are happening. And if good things seem far and few between, *make* them happen. Take a bubble bath while reading a good book. Paint your nails. Buy a coloring book and have at it! Play your ukulele. Do something that makes you laugh out loud or smile in utter contentment. Look to have a continual feast in the blessings of God as you serve Him and others with all the gladness in your heart.

Morning – STAYING CLOSE

*There was also a prophet, Anna, the daughter of Penuel, of the tribe
of Asher. She was very old; she had lived with her husband seven years after
her marriage, and then was a widow until she was eighty-four. She never
left the temple but worshiped night and day, fasting and praying. Coming up
to them at that very moment, she gave thanks to God and spoke about the
child to all who were looking forward to the redemption of Jerusalem.*

LUKE 2:36–38 NIV

Talk about commitment. Anna had been widowed since she was a young woman. There's no mention of her having children. Instead of finding another husband, she decided to live out her days serving God.

Anna's years of commitment paid off when she was very old. God made sure that Mary and Joseph brought Jesus to that particular temple so Anna could see Him, hold Him, and declare His presence to all who would listen.

If we want to catch God in His work, in the middle of His most exciting acts, we must stay close to the place He's working. In that day, it was the temple. Today, it might be at church or in the middle of a particular ministry project. But when we put our own schedules and agendas first and disregard God's work, we miss out on His most thrilling exploits.

Like Anna, we should do all we can to serve God and stay close to His work. When we do, we'll witness some amazing feats.

Evening – WHAT'S YOUR "BUT GOD" STORY?

*But God demonstrates his own love for us in this:
While we were still sinners, Christ died for us.*

ROMANS 5:8 NIV

Some people believe God set the world in motion, then stepped back just to watch it spin without intervening in the lives of men. A simple search for the phrase "but God" in scripture shows otherwise. According to Khouse.org, the exact phrase "but God" is used sixty-four times from the Old Testament to the New.

In Genesis 20:3, Abraham gave his wife, Sarai, to Abimelek, but God intervened and came to Abimelek in a dream, telling him that he was as good as a dead man since Sarai was married.

In Genesis 41:16, Joseph couldn't give Pharaoh the interpretations for his dreams, but God could (and did).

In Genesis 45:5, there was a famine, but God sent Joseph ahead of his family through a nasty betrayal to save the lives of many people, including his brothers who had betrayed him.

In Jonah 1:17, Jonah ran from God, but God provided a great fish to swallow Jonah.

In Acts 2:24, Jesus was put to death, but God raised Him from the dead.

How awesome! But God! God was involved in the lives of men and He is still involved now, intervening, guiding, and ruling. What's your "but God" story?

DAY 200

Morning – A WOMAN'S BOLDNESS

Then she said, "Give me a blessing; since you have given me the land of the Negev, give me also springs of water." So he gave her the upper springs and the lower springs.
JOSHUA 15:19 NASB

Most critics have labeled the Bible to be an oppressive book, which has contributed to the marginalization of women throughout the centuries. Those critics never truly read the Bible. Many who called themselves Christians, unfortunately, have twisted parts of scripture and pulled passages out of context to justify their otherwise unbiblical view and treatment of women; but God reveals a beautiful picture of women in His Word. Achsah, the daughter of the faithful warrior Caleb, married the valiant Otniel. This bold woman approached her new husband and urged him to ask her father for a field. Otniel, not only a mighty warrior but also a kind husband and wise judge, seems to have respected his wife. She received land as her dowry but found it to be a dry place. Achsah petitioned Caleb again, but this time she went herself. Caleb knew the justness of her request, and he gave her both the upper and lower springs of water. God includes this brief story of Achsah perhaps because He wants His daughters to be bold. If God calls someone to a special task, He will also mold the hearts of those around her—just like He did with Caleb and Otniel.

Evening – WOMEN TRANSFORMED BY GRACE

Soon afterwards, He began going around from one city and village to another, proclaiming and preaching the kingdom of God. The twelve were with Him, and also some women who had been healed of evil spirits and sicknesses: Mary who was called Magdalene, from whom seven demons had gone out, and Joanna the wife of Chuza, Herod's steward, and Susanna, and many others who were contributing to their support out of their private means.
LUKE 8:1–3 NASB

The scriptural account records that Jesus changed the lives of all who came into contact with Him. Some of these He changed simply by entering their world, and others were changed in more dramatic ways. Of course, Mary, His mother, was the first woman whose life was radically altered by His incarnation. The sisters Mary and Martha knew Him as a frequent guest and friend. Other women contributed to His ministry and daily life through financial support; they followed Him, weeping, as He carried His cross and came with spices to prepare His body that misty third morning.

Then there were the women whose lives He drastically changed—the woman at the well in Samaria, the woman caught in adultery and thrown at His feet, the widow whose son He raised from the dead, and the woman with the bleeding disorder who was made well from touching His robe. As Creator, Jesus understood the inner longings of a woman's heart and offered redemption for hurts and the promise of hope and healing. And He still does today.

Morning – THE WANT FOR WONDER

Praise the LORD God, the God of Israel, who alone does such wonderful things.
PSALM 72:18 NLT

G. K. Chesterton said, "The world will never starve for want of wonders; but only for want of wonder." There are so many wonders in the world—places to see, goals to accomplish, exciting special effects—and yet many of us are still missing "awe."

The church is struggling too. Almost all of us—Christian and non-Christian alike—have grown up with a view of God as loving, accepting, and forgiving, and we have learned to take those attributes for granted. We've lost the wonder of His majesty.

In the early days of the apostles, many Jews repented and were baptized. They devoted themselves to teaching and fellowship, and "a deep sense of awe came over them all" (Acts 2:43 NLT). They were amazed by God!

We can regain our wonderment through reading God's Word. The more we learn about Him and our own condition, the more we can appreciate His love. Proverbs 25:2 (KJV) says, "It is the glory of God to conceal a thing: but the honour of kings is to search out a matter."

Is it time for you to examine the character of God in a fresh way? Pray today that He would open your eyes to His wonderful mysteries.

Evening – THIS IS MY GOD

"The LORD is my strength and my song; he has given me victory. This is my God, and I will praise him—my father's God, and I will exalt him!"
EXODUS 15:2 NLT

In Acts 17, Paul was preaching to the people of Athens who were worshipping a host of gods. He even found an idol they had built to an "unknown god." Paul called out their ignorance and told them the truth about the Living God:

"The God who made the world and everything in it is the Lord of heaven and earth and does not live in temples built by human hands. And he is not served by human hands, as if he needed anything. Rather, he himself gives everyone life and breath and everything else. From one man he made all the nations, that they should inhabit the whole earth; and he marked out their appointed times in history and the boundaries of their lands. God did this so that they would seek him and perhaps reach out for him and find him, though he is not far from any one of us. 'For in him we live and move and have our being.'" (v. 24–28 NIV)

This is our God, and He is worthy of all our praise! He is our strength and our song. He gives us victory through Christ. We are exactly where He has placed us, and He has a great purpose for doing so.

DAY 202

Morning – DON'T GIVE UP!
GOD SEES YOUR POTENTIAL

> *"The Lord does not look at the things people look at. People look
> at the outward appearance, but the Lord looks at the heart."*
> 1 Samuel 16:7 niv

"I'm sorry, miss," the metro newspaper editor began as he addressed one of his journalism students. He couldn't remember her name. "You're just not cut out for the writing life. I can't pass you. Find another field of study."

The college student's eyes misted. "But I was tops in journalism at my junior college."

"You've got straight F's because you're a poor proofreader. That's where good writing starts. Change fields of study."

Miss J.'s heart was on the ground. She graduated in another field. Years later, she enrolled in a non-credit class: magazine writing. Her first story was purchased by a popular slick magazine. Over the decades, hundreds of articles followed, as well as anthologies and an award-winning book.

Miss J. smiled the day she was asked to be a writing workshop leader—in the city where she washed out in journalism. God had seen all along what she could be.

Our Creator sees more of our hearts and potential than anyone on earth. Just as He saw a king in David—while his siblings might have thought of him as only a pesky little brother—God sees the best of what we can be. He believes in us.

When it comes to believing what others believe we can and can't accomplish—trust in God instead and soar without limits!

Evening – INSIGNIFICANT

> *"But you, Bethlehem Ephrathah, though you are small among the
> clans of Judah, out of you will come for me one who will be ruler
> over Israel, whose origins are from of old, from ancient times."*
> Micah 5:2 niv

Funny how we always look to the big, important places for our news. We tune our televisions to Washington, D.C., or the Kremlin or some other such significant spot. But more often than not, the stories that get our attention happen in small towns, even in our own neighborhoods.

The same is true of people. We expect great men and women to graduate from Harvard or Princeton. We expect them to be tall and beautiful and have impressive social connections. We watch with bated breath to see what these qualified youngsters will contribute to our world.

Yet, we're often surprised when truly great men and women come from our own city block or from the local farm up the road. What? A farmer? What can he possibly know?

God loves surprises. He likes to work through seemingly insignificant people. That way, when a truly humble person with truly humble circumstances accomplishes something great for God, He gets the credit. And if He chooses insignificant people from insignificant places, I suppose that means He may choose me. Or you. Any one of us can be great for God, when we recognize the greatness is only from Him and not from ourselves.

Morning – THUNDER ROARS

But everyone who calls on the name of the Lord will be saved.
JOEL 2:32 NLT

Do you ever tremble with fear? Whether it be from dangers without or emotional distress within, fear can paralyze people. It is as though a hand grips us by the throat and we are pinned in place with nowhere to go. Yet the Lord our God has said do not be afraid, He will save us.

The book of Psalms reveals a man who quivers and hides in caves to escape his enemies. Time and again David calls out to the Lord because he has been taught God will calm his fears. The circumstances do not always change, the thunder may still roar, but just like David, we can know our lives are secure in the hands of the Almighty Creator of the universe. He *will* save us. It's a promise.

Today make a list of those things that cause you to quake in your boots. Read the list out loud to the Lord, and ask Him to provide the necessary bravery to overcome each one. Ask Him to see you through the deep waters and to hold you tightly over the mountaintops. For when you call on His name, He hears and answers. Listen closely and remember He saves.

Evening – HIS PRESENCE IN OUR PANIC

"I have no peace, no quietness; I have no rest, but only turmoil."
JOB 3:26 NIV

Felicia's toddler, Noah, lay beside her on the bed. She got up to turn off the light. As soon as she flipped the switch, Felicia got back in bed. Suddenly, he sat up and yelled, "Mommy! Where are you? I can't see you!"

Felicia immediately got up and turned a small light back on. "Mommy's right here," she said soothingly. "I'm not going anywhere." As soon as he could see his mom, Noah quieted down and began to fall asleep.

Similarly, Job cried out to God with questions and confusion after his family, livelihood, and health had been taken from him. God let Job's friends give their (wrong) perspectives on why he was suffering, and then He swept in and silenced all of them with His own questions—and His overwhelming presence.

When we are afraid and anxious, God turns on the light for us, just as Felicia turned on the light for her son. Sometimes the light comes through comforting scriptures. At times, it appears with the touch of a family member. Light often breaks through with a hymn or a worship song that we hear on the radio.

Though we may not understand why we have to suffer, praise God, He never leaves us in the dark for too long. . .and He never, ever leaves us alone.

DAY 204

Morning – MOSES CHOSE
ETERNAL REWARDS

*Choosing rather to suffer affliction with the people of God than to enjoy
the passing pleasures of sin, esteeming the reproach of Christ greater
riches than the treasures in Egypt; for he looked to the reward.*
HEBREWS 11:25–26 NKJV

How could affliction and reproach be a greater goal than ruling a country and owning fabulous wealth? Human thinking would see Moses as accomplishing great things for God by becoming Pharaoh and freeing the Hebrew slaves. But then Moses would get the credit, and no one would witness the power of the one true God. Even though Moses experienced failure, exile, and a forty-year-long wait, God could only use a humble servant. Moses chose to lay up treasure in heaven, even if it meant giving up the fortune he deserved on earth.

This eternal perspective kept Moses from enjoying sin's temporary pleasures. Instead of looking at the benefits of being the son of Pharaoh's daughter (Hebrews 11:24), he focused on spiritual things, choosing "the reproach of Christ" and enduring "as seeing Him who is invisible" (vv. 26–27). Moses lived for eternal, not earthly, rewards.

As Christians, we get to choose our focus and the goals we devote our lives to. While eternal life is a free gift, not a reward, to everyone who believes in Christ, the Bible also teaches that believers will receive rewards in heaven for being "good and faithful servants."

Evening – CITIZENSHIP

*For our citizenship is in heaven, from which also
we eagerly wait for a Savior, the Lord Jesus Christ.*
PHILIPPIANS 3:20 NASB

Your citizenship is in heaven; you are just passing through this world. This is not your home, your country of origin, or your final destination. You were created by God and will one day return home to Him.

If you ever feel like you don't belong here, like the world is too confusing and frightening for you, it's because deep down you know that this is not your home. God has placed you here for a purpose. He has sent you as His ambassador. Strive to do His will and to glorify Him on this earth. Make the most of this pilgrimage you're on. Just as someone from another country loves to talk about and teach others about their home country, so we ought to tell others about heaven and the one who is enthroned there. Always be aware that something better awaits you. That the very city in which God dwells is your home.

Keep your eyes focused on your Savior. Wait for Him with eager anticipation. He will come again and you will be with Him forever. What a beautiful life you have to look forward to. Don't lose sight of it.

Morning – WORKING HARD

*Whatever you do, work at it with all your heart,
as working for the Lord, not for human masters.*
COLOSSIANS 3:23 NIV

Paul encouraged his readers to work hard, with all their hearts. Many of the new converts were enslaved to non-Christian masters. The tension between Christians and non-Christians increased when the non-Christian had the authority to lord it over the Christian.

But the wisdom in this verse applies to us today. We should always work hard, always give our best, even if we don't like our bosses. Ultimately, the quality of work we do reflects on our Father. If we're lazy or if our work is below standard, it has a negative impact on the body of Christ. But when we meet our deadlines and our work exceeds expectations, we give others a positive impression of what it means to be a Christian.

If we want to get ahead in our jobs and we want to help build the kingdom of God, we must have impeccable reputations. One way to build a positive reputation is to be a hard worker. When we do our absolute best at any task, people notice. When we consistently deliver quality products and services, people notice. We honor God and we honor ourselves when we work hard at the tasks we've been given.

Evening – HOPE FOR THE FUTURE

*"For I know the plans I have for you," declares the LORD, "plans to prosper
you and not to harm you, plans to give you hope and a future."*
JEREMIAH 29:11 NIV

Debra was discouraged. She had been so hopeful when she received her college diploma. A year later with only a part-time job, she still needed to live at home to make ends meet.

Although Debra wasn't musically talented, she agreed to help coordinate the children's Christmas production at church. Her reluctance turned to enthusiasm as she was able to lead improvements using her organizational skills.

Debra received positive feedback from people each week. She was happy the Lord was using her talents.

After the *organized* chaos of getting the right costumes on each child, Debra started the dress rehearsal. She was thrilled when everything came together and the children were able to shine.

Then during the cast party, a stern older man asked to talk privately with Debra. She braced herself for criticism. Instead the man asked if she would be interested in interviewing to be his office manager. His daughter had told him, "Debra can organize anything and always keeps a cool head." Debra agreed to the interview.

When she became a volunteer, Debra never dreamed her efforts would become a stepping stone to her future.

Morning – SEEKING ADVICE

The Lord says, "I will guide you along the best pathway for your life.
I will advise you and watch over you. Do not be like a senseless horse
or mule that needs a bit and bridle to keep it under control."
PSALM 32:8–9 NLT

There is a key word in this passage: *advise.* The Lord says He will advise us and watch over us. But what if we don't take the time to ask for His guidance? How many times have we been sidetracked, lost, and confused simply because we never asked for the Lord's advice?

In the hurried lives we live, it's easy to fall into a routine and switch over to autopilot. Our calendars are teeming with activities and deadlines, and all too often we simply enter "survival mode." You could say that we become similar to the mule in this scripture—putting hardly any thought into our days and simply being guided by chaos and distraction.

God has more for us. If we take the time to seek out His counsel, He will advise us. He will guide us along the best pathway for our lives and watch over us. He will give us purpose, and our lives will be filled with adventure and divine encounters.

Evening – CALL UNTO ME

Look to the Lord and his strength; seek his face always.
PSALM 105:4 NIV

A young woman received distressing news from her boss. In a panic, she phoned her mother to ask for guidance; she called her best friend for an opinion; she discussed the matter at lunch with coworkers. But not once did she seek the Lord's face.

Scripture encourages us to pray about everything—to send our cares and petitions heavenward. Why do we persist in running to others instead of Him? David, the psalmist, had no choice but to rely on the Lord as he fled his enemies. The lyrics of the Psalms remind us he was no stranger to loss and fear. Yet he cried unto the Lord. His words in Psalm 105 encourage us to remember what He has done before. Paul sat in the pits, literally, and sang songs of praise. While we might not be in dire straits like those men, we certainly have problems and can read scripture to see how the Lord has worked and have confidence He is near.

Let us work to seek His face always. Know the Lord cares about each detail of your life, and nothing is a secret or a surprise to Him. Reach for the best and expect results. It might require a time of waiting, but His answers are always unsurpassed.

Morning – LOVING FULLY

*Jesus replied: "'Love the Lord your God with all your
heart and with all your soul and with all your mind.'"*
MATTHEW 22:37 NIV

When Jesus commanded His followers to love God with all their hearts, souls, and minds, He meant that loving God fully means putting aside everything that gets in the way of a relationship with Him. Everything. That's no small order in a world filled with distractions.

So how can today's Christians set aside everything to fully love God? The answer is to shift their desire from serving themselves to serving Him. Love requires action, and the Holy Spirit gives believers power to glorify God with everything they do. Praising Him for His provisions is one way to love Him. Doing selfless acts of service for others as if working for Him is another way. So is loving others as He loves us. Studying the Bible and being intimate with God in prayer is the ultimate act of love toward Him. When Christians center their lives on their passion for God, they learn to love Him fully.

Loving God with heart, soul, and mind takes practice. It means thinking of Him all day and working to glorify Him through every thought and action. It means putting aside one's own desires to serve someone greater.

Is it possible to love God more than you love anyone or anything else? You can try. That in itself is an act of love.

Evening – BLESSABLE

*Love the LORD your God and. . .serve him with all your heart and with
all your soul—then I will send rain on your land in its season.*
DEUTERONOMY 11:13–14 NIV

We all want God's blessings. We want it to rain on our crops; we want the sun to shine on our picnics; and we want a gentle breeze to relieve us from summer's scorch. We want job security and bigger paychecks.

Though God allows some blessings to grace every person in the human race, there are some keys to receiving more of God's goodness. If we want God's blessings, we must be blessable.

So how do we become blessable? We must love God. And we must serve Him with all our hearts.

Loving God is the easy part. But the evidence of that love comes through our service to Him, and that's a little harder.

When we love God, we serve Him by loving others. We serve Him by taking the time to mow the widow's lawn or prepare a meal for someone who's ill or provide a coat for someone who's cold. We serve Him by offering a hand of friendship to the friendless or by saying something positive about the victim of gossip.

When we love God and our actions show evidence of that love, we become blessable. That's when God will pour out His goodness on us in ways we could never imagine.

Morning – PROVIDING IT ALL

"For God so loved the world that He gave His only begotten Son, that whoever believes in Him should not perish but have everlasting life."
JOHN 3:16 NKJV

Beginning with Adam, God provided for His loved ones: a ram for Abraham to spare his son, manna for the wandering Jewish people. The Bible resonates with the provisions of a mighty God. And the Word says our God is the same today as He was then. So we know He will provide for our needs. True love reflected by His care for us every day.

His provision is not just for our material needs, but more importantly He extends us unmerited favor, grace, when we least deserve it. He provides us with an all-encompassing love once we accept it. And He seals His promises with the gift of the Holy Spirit making us heirs to the throne. When we realize the depth of care we've received from our heavenly Father, it is breathtaking.

Always a step ahead, He made provision before any need existed. God gave us His all, His best, when He gave us His Son. He provided it all. We serve a glorious and mighty God.

Evening – A DECLARATION OF DEPENDENCE

"Sacrifice thank offerings to God, fulfill your vows to the Most High, and call on me in the day of trouble; I will deliver you, and you will honor me."
PSALM 50:14–15 NIV

Most of us value our relationships, whether they are with family, friends, or coworkers. We like being in relationships with those who offer love, commitment, and trust because we feel valued. Perhaps not so ironically, today's verse reveals that God wants the same things from us. He wants thankful, trusting, and faithful children, people whom He can delight in and who can delight in Him.

As our heavenly Father, He wants to help us, especially in times of trouble. That dependency on Him recognizes that everything we have comes from Him. The practical way to depend on Him comes through an honest, consistent lifestyle of prayer, where we offer ourselves and our needs. Through prayer, we draw near to Him and get to know Him better. In doing that, we'll become the thankful, trusting, and faithful children He desires.

Morning – KEEPING OUR TESTIMONY

*And the Lord was with Joseph, and he was a prosperous man;
and he was in the house of his master the Egyptian. And
his master saw that the Lord was with him.*
GENESIS 39:2–3 KJV

Joseph had been sold to some traveling merchants by his brothers. The travelers carried him to Egypt, where he was sold once again to Potiphar, an officer of Pharaoh. Joseph could have sat down in a corner and felt sorry for himself. He could have said, "I'm in a foreign country where no one knows me. I don't worship like these people. I can't live for God here." But Joseph didn't do any of those things. He proved himself a trustworthy servant, and his master took note of it, making Joseph his overseer. It made no difference that he had been brought to a different place; God was with him.

You may be living in a home or working at a job where you are the only Christian, but no matter where you are, God is able to bless you and direct your life if you allow Him to. No matter what environment you find yourself in, God will be there. Your situation may be painful, you may be fearful, the people around you may abuse you in some way, but like Joseph, God will be with you. Trust Him to take care of you.

Evening – IT DOESN'T TAKE MUCH

*Let your speech always be with grace, seasoned with salt,
that you may know how you ought to answer each one.*
COLOSSIANS 4:6 NKJV

Jay was walking through the grocery store parking lot when he saw a young woman on the verge of tears. He wasn't sure how to help, but he approached her saying, "God sent me over to tell you that He loves you and everything is going to be okay."

That was the message Tiffany needed. Jay was able to comfort her and invite her to church, and eventually she accepted Christ and was baptized.

Sometimes the Holy Spirit is subtle. Jay could have ignored the nagging feeling in his heart and reasoned that someone else would help. But he obeyed. He didn't do anything dramatic or dangerous, nothing to write a movie script about. He simply reached out with the love of Christ.

Peter tells us, "Always be prepared to give an answer to everyone who asks you to give the reason for the hope that you have" (1 Peter 3:15 NIV). Tiffany didn't even know the question to ask, but Jay was ready to give her the answer she didn't know she needed.

Would you be bold enough to intervene? Be obedient to the nudges of the Holy Spirit, and see how He uses you to work little miracles.

DAY 210

Morning – POWERED UP

Now to Him who is able to do far more abundantly beyond all that we ask or think, according to the power that works within us, to Him be the glory in the church and in Christ Jesus to all generations forever and ever. Amen.
EPHESIANS 3:20–21 NASB

One day two blind men yelled out to Jesus. People tried to tell them to be quiet. But the men kept shouting, asking Him to have pity on them. Suddenly Jesus stopped in His tracks, then asked them, "What do you want Me to do for you?" (Matthew 20:32 NASB). The blind men said they wanted to see. And so, God honored that request. But the men got so much more in return. Not only did they obtain their vision, but they were also given the eye-opening opportunity to follow this man of miracles!

God is asking each of His daughters the same question: "What do you want Me to do for you?" He wants her to not let others dissuade her from telling Him exactly what she wants—no matter how impossible or improbable the request may seem. He wants her to be specific, yet also to dream big—for He is a limitless God, ready to do so much more than one woman could ever ask or imagine! He wants her to then begin expecting the unexpected as she continues to travel with Him down the road with a lighter, more joyful step.

Evening – SPEAK TO ME, LORD

"And it shall come to pass afterward that I will pour out My Spirit on all flesh; your sons and your daughters shall prophesy, your old men shall dream dreams, your young men shall see visions."
JOEL 2:28 NKJV

Has God ever given you a dream or vision? Peter quoted this verse from Joel on the day of Pentecost, when God poured out the Holy Spirit on new believers. The prophecy was fulfilled then and continues today.

We need to ask God for wisdom and discernment about supernatural occurrences, but that doesn't mean we should dismiss dreams, visions, and prophecies as poppycock. God speaks to His children in many creative ways. It's thrilling to know He does—tragic if we don't listen.

Maybe we have trouble thinking the Lord would give us a significant dream because we feel unworthy. But after all, today's scripture mentions "all flesh." That sounds pretty all-inclusive. If we don't expect to hear from Him, we won't even pay attention. If we belong to Him, we should have our spiritual ears tuned to hear Him whenever and however He chooses to communicate.

God does what it takes for us to notice—regardless of whether it seems logical. He even spoke through a donkey one time in the Bible (see Numbers 22:28). Hopefully, we won't be that hard of hearing. We should welcome His voice, whether it's through the scriptures, nature, dreams, a pastor, or any other creative means. Listen.

Morning – FINDING JOY

*And now, dear brothers and sisters, one final thing. Fix your thoughts on
what is true, and honorable, and right, and pure, and lovely, and admirable.
Think about things that are excellent and worthy of praise. Keep putting
into practice all you learned and received from me—everything you heard
from me and saw me doing. Then the God of peace will be with you.*
PHILIPPIANS 4:8–9 NLT

Your mind is powerful. The thoughts you choose to dwell on have the power to determine the outcome of your day. They can pave the way for a calm and grateful heart, or set a course for cynicism and disbelief.

There is such a benefit to fixing your thoughts on things that are good, pleasing, and perfect. God was not being legalistic when he said to think on these things. He was giving us sound advice. He was showing us the path to peace. What makes your heart beat a little faster? What brings joy to your heart and a smile to your lips? What makes your eyes crinkle with laughter and your feet step a little lighter? Think about these things.

Life is meant to be enjoyed. Relish the simple things! God made the playful puppies, galloping horses, and singing birds. He enjoys them, and He invites you to enjoy them too.

Evening – THE MIND—SATAN'S BATTLEGROUND

Blessed are those who find wisdom, those who gain understanding.
PROVERBS 3:13 NIV

Charles Stanley said, "The mind is the devil's battleground." Satan has been using mind games to twist the truth since the beginning of time, and nothing has changed.

Have you ever had a thought like this: *John left his clothes all over the floor again! Who does he think I am? His maid? He never has had any respect for me and all the work I do around here. He doesn't love me. He probably never has!*

Suddenly, just because your messy husband left clothes around, in your mind, he has never loved you. In many cases, a few more convincing fallacies like these will add up and eventually lead you to divorce.

Second Corinthians 10:5 (NIV) says, "Take captive every thought to make it obedient to Christ." Satan has the ability to make anything sound like the truth, so capture each thought and test it against scripture. This holds true for what we think of others, ourselves, and God.

Romans 12:2 (NKJV) says, "Do not be conformed to this world, but be transformed by the renewing of your mind." Keep a sharp eye for these trains of logical thought that can take you to the wrong conclusions, and continually study the Word of God so that you may know the truth even when it defies the logic of this world.

Morning – BUILDING TRUST

Trust in the Lord with all your heart and lean not on your own understanding;
in all your ways submit to him, and he will make your paths straight.
PROVERBS 3:5–6 NIV

Many corporations take their executives to leadership training courses to develop better working relationships. Divided into teams, these people have to learn to trust one another. One favorite exercise is on the ropes course. A person is trussed up in a harness, steps off a tall tower, and is flung into a wide-open space, trusting his team members will guide him safely back to the ground. It takes a measure of courage to make yourself participate, but the results are usually exhilarating.

Placing our trust in a loving heavenly Father can sometimes feel like stepping off a precipice. Why? Perhaps it is because we can't see God. Trust is not easily attained. It comes once you have built a record with another over a period of time. It involves letting go and knowing you will be caught.

In order to trust God, we must step out in faith. Challenge yourself to trust God with one detail in your life each day. Build that trust pattern and watch Him work. He will not let you down. He holds you securely in His hand. He is your hope for the future.

Evening – REACH OUT

Now faith is the assurance of things hoped for, the conviction of things not seen.
HEBREWS 11:1 NASB

Driving through the fog is scary and a cause of many accidents. Isn't it wonderful that we don't have to worry about steering our lives through a fog? The God of the universe is our director, and we can have faith that He will steer us clear. Problems may arise, hazards might jump in our pathway, but when we reach our hand to the Lord, He reaches down to us.

Scripture teaches that we are to hope in Him. To have Christ at the center of our lives and to recognize His mighty power is to rely on the tried and true. Generations before us tell of His wondrous care. David was pursued by enemies; he cried unto the Lord. Paul was beaten and imprisoned; he cried unto the Lord. The willingness to wait for God, the eager expectation, was the faith of the men of old.

The word *assurance* literally means "a thing put under. . .a foundation." With this solid foundation, we can hope for the future—those unseen things. A believer looking forward to a union with God is assured that He will be there, waiting to receive him.

Lean into Him. Reach for the heavens, knowing full well He will grasp your hand.

Morning – HE CARES FOR YOU

"You yourselves have seen what I did to Egypt, and how I carried you on eagles' wings and brought you to myself."
EXODUS 19:4 NIV

Often we feel deserted. As though God doesn't hear our prayers. And we wait. When Moses led the children of Israel out of Egypt toward the Promised Land, he did not take them on the shortest route. God directed him to go the distant way, lest the people turn back quickly when things became difficult. God led them by day with a pillar of clouds and by night with a pillar of fire. How clearly He showed Himself to His children! The people placed their hope in an almighty God and followed His lead. When they thirsted, God gave water. When they hungered, He sent manna. No need was unmet.

The amount of food and water needed for the group was unimaginable. But each day, Moses depended upon God. He believed God would care for them.

If God can do this for so many, you can rest assured that He will care for you. He knows your needs before you even ask. Place your hope and trust in Him. He is able. He's proven Himself over and over. Read the scriptures and pray to the one who loves you. His care is infinite. . .and He will never disappoint you.

Evening – OUR DAILY BREAD

"Give us this day our daily bread."
MATTHEW 6:11 NKJV

A young woman gazed out her window as the morning sun just began to touch the snow-covered peaks of the Colorado Rockies. Her thoughts could hardly be collected and organized, and so she just stared and prayed, "Lord, give us today our daily bread." Her husband was in a job where he was criticized daily and treated like dirt. Each day felt like Russian roulette, as they never knew if their cars would get them to work or not. Money was tight. Their grocery budget was minimal. Being new to the area, they had no one to turn to.

"Give us this day our daily bread."

Each day, the Lord answered this prayer. He gave them what they needed, whether it be patience, mental or physical strength, food, or faith. A bill never went unpaid. A stomach never went hungry. A body never went unclothed. The Lord provided all their needs.

Eventually, slowly, their situation began to improve. They were able to buy a new car, she picked up more hours at work, and he found a new job. A community began to form around them. Looking back, she remembers it as one of the best years of her life. It was a year she walked closely, intimately, with her Savior.

Morning – STRENGTH

Then Hannah prayed and said: "My heart rejoices in the Lord; in the Lord my horn is lifted high. My mouth boasts over my enemies, for I delight in your deliverance. There is no one holy like the Lord; there is no one besides you; there is no Rock like our God."
1 Samuel 2:1–2 NIV

Hannah was filled with sorrow because she could not have children; and her husband's other wife taunted her because of this. Even though Hannah was the favorite wife (her name means favored), she still longed to be a mother. So she brought her suffering heart before God in prayer, and God graciously answered. He gave her a son whom she named Samuel and who became one of the greatest judges and prophets of the Old Testament. God did not stop there. He also gave her five other children after Samuel. In the scripture reference above, the word *horn* means strength. Hannah acknowledges that Jehovah God is her strength. In her deepest pain and overwhelming despair, she first turned to God. His answer filled the longing in her heart and drew her to a deeper worship of God. He is the only one who can give strength to overcome the worries of this world. God calls His children to seek deliverance from their burdens only in Him, because any other option is futile and fleeting.

Evening – IT'S WEDDIN' TIME!

"There will be heard once more the sounds of joy and laughter. The joyful voices of bridegrooms and brides will be heard again, along with the joyous songs of people bringing thanksgiving offerings to the Lord. They will sing, 'Give thanks to the Lord of Heaven's Armies, for the Lord is good. His faithful love endures forever!'"
Jeremiah 33:10–11 NLT

White orchids and warm breezes graced the newlyweds smiling broadly as they descended the church steps surrounded by cheers of joy. A gleaming white limo awaited them beyond the blowing bubbles, as light as their spirits this day.

This was wedding number three of the ten that Shelby had been invited to this year. 'Tis the season! It was a privilege to experience so many celebrations with dear friends and family. Yet, for Shelby it was bittersweet. One thing that never failed to pierce her heart was the bride and father dance. For Shelby and her husband, it was a regular reminder that their daughter who died twenty-five years ago would be in the marrying stage of life now. With each wedding, this dance brought contemplative emotion for them.

Thankfully, as the years wear on, they anticipate the dance in eternity that will far exceed anything in this life. Furthermore, we can look forward to the dance of Christ with His bride, us— and it's impossible for us to imagine how glorious this will be.

Morning – GOD'S EMPOWERING GRACE

The boundary lines have fallen for me in pleasant places;
surely I have a delightful inheritance.
PSALM 16:6 NIV

I once met a woman who lamented over a friend's success. "She is receiving promotion after promotion. She is doing in her ministry career what I want to do in mine. I have prayed. I have asked God to help me use my gifts and talents serving Him the same way she is serving Him, but nothing has happened. Any time I try anything, I get shut down. I feel like God has forgotten me and I don't have any value in the body of Christ."

As I spoke with this woman, I thought that the kingdom of God is like a farmer's field and each of us has been given a patch to work and to tend. One person has been given a large patch, another has been allotted a smaller assignment. One person works in a noticeable part of God's field, another in a less visible part—but all assignments are important.

What this woman failed to see is that God's grace—or His unmerited favor—empowers us to do what we need to do. Grace will enable you to accomplish your God-given assignment. But where grace is absent, you won't be able to move that mountain. Therefore, don't waste your precious time envying someone else's accomplishments or worrying about how you are being shortchanged. Know that the Lord has a plan for you to serve Him in a unique way. Rest in this truth.

Evening – JEALOUSY

For you are still controlled by your sinful nature. You are jealous of one
another and quarrel with each other. Doesn't that prove you are controlled
by your sinful nature? Aren't you living like people of the world?
1 CORINTHIANS 3:3 NLT

Jealousy. The green-eyed monster. The great friend robber. The undeniable tool of the enemy, meant to bring division, dissatisfaction, and other negative feelings. Why do women struggle so much with jealousy? Why do they long to have what others have? Whether it's looks, figure, money, husband, job, or position in ministry, each woman is entitled to what God gives her. It's hers and hers alone. God elevates and provides in His time and His way. It's not for us to decide or even comment on (though it's hard to keep our mouths shut when we're convinced God got it wrong). There's never a time when jealousy is okay. Never. No finger-pointing. No "Why do good things always happen to her and not to me?" No "I don't get it, Lord. Why did You make her so pretty and me so ugly?" Nope. None of that. Each to his—er, her—own. Now, while it's on your mind, speak to that green-eyed monster and watch him disappear!

Morning – TALK TO YOUR BEST FRIEND

God is faithful, who has called you into
fellowship with his Son, Jesus Christ our Lord.
1 Corinthians 1:9 niv

When do you pray? How often do you call on God? Where do you talk to Him?

Just as we converse with our spouse or best friend about what's happening in our lives, the Lord expects and anticipates conversations with us too.

Yes, He knows all about us, but He desires our fellowship one-on-one. Jesus chose twelve disciples with whom to fellowship, teach, and carry His gospel to every nation. They lived and ate with Jesus; they knew Him personally; they were His best friends. In the same manner, God gives us the divine privilege to know Him on a personal level through our relationship with Christ.

When, where, or how we talk to God is of little importance to the Savior. We can converse with the Lord while driving down the street, walking through the park, or standing at the kitchen sink. We can ask for His help in the seemingly insignificant or in bigger decisions. Our concerns are His concerns too, and He desires for us to share our heartfelt thoughts with Him.

Fellowshipping with God is talking to our best friend, knowing He understands and provides help and wisdom along life's journey. It's demonstrating our faith and trust in the one who knows us better than anyone.

Evening – WHEN GOD'S PEOPLE PRAY

Pray for the peace of Jerusalem: "May those who love you be secure."
Psalm 122:6 niv

When it comes to making a difference in this world, sometimes it's easy to feel helpless. Wars are being fought on the other side of the world. People are starving, suffering, hurting. As much as we'd like to help, there's not much we can do, right?

Except, there is something we can do. It's the most powerful thing anyone can do—we can pray. God, in all His power, has invited us to come alongside Him. He's asked us to join Him in His work by praying for each other.

For centuries, God's people have been treated unfairly and unjustly. Yet we've survived when other groups haven't. The reason we've survived when so many have sought to silence us is because we have something our enemies don't have. We have the power of God behind us.

When we pray, we call upon every resource available to us as the children of God. We call upon His strength, His compassion, His ferocity, His mercy, His love, and His justice. We have the ability to extend God's reach to the other side of our town or the other side of the world, all because we pray.

Morning – HIS LIKENESS

As for me, I will behold thy face in righteousness:
I shall be satisfied, when I awake, with thy likeness.
PSALM 17:15 KJV

Throughout the ages women were given an ideal image of womanhood, which society encouraged them to emulate. The ideal woman constantly changed, as is seen through the history of fashion, women's rights, and changing social and cultural traditions. One of the wonderful things about God is that He never changes; neither does Christ as the only example of what it means to be the perfect human. Society today, both Eastern and Western, places much of a woman's value in her appearance: clothes, makeup, and body type. It is easy for a woman to make idols out of these things. However, a Christian woman should bear the image of Jesus. If she loves Jesus with her whole heart, she will seek to please Him; He is the only person who has already poured out more love on her than any earthly man ever will or can give her. The holy and pure characteristics of Jesus are the only things that produce satisfaction: his joy, peace, patience, goodness, love, faithfulness, etc. So, when women allow the Holy Spirit to work in them these characteristics, they will have true beauty, not the fleeting beauty and popularity of the world.

Evening – BIBLICAL ENCOURAGEMENT FOR WOMEN

Don't be concerned about the outward beauty of fancy hairstyles, expensive jewelry, or beautiful clothes. You should clothe yourselves instead with the beauty that comes from within, the unfading beauty of a gentle and quiet spirit, which is so precious to God.
1 PETER 3:3–4 NLT

The world encourages women to dress provocatively, to invest in expensive products and styles, all to make them "better." This is not how God judges a woman's heart. God is concerned with what is on the inside. He listens to how you respond to others and watches the facial expressions you choose to exhibit. He sees your heart. Certainly it is fun to buy a new outfit or spend some time and effort accessorizing. There is nothing wrong with this in and of itself. Where the trouble comes is when the world's messages drown out God's call on your life. The Lord desires that you clothe yourself with a gentle and quiet spirit. He declares this as unfading beauty, the inner beauty of the heart. Focus on this and no one will even notice whether your jewelry shines. Your face will be radiant with the joy of the Lord and your heart will overflow with grace and peace.

Morning – FORGIVING OTHERS

As far as the east is from the west,
so far has he removed our transgressions from us.
PSALM 103:12 NIV

Forgiveness. The word rolls off the tongue much more easily than it penetrates the heart. When someone has wronged you, it is natural to feel hurt. It is not easy to forgive a person who has wounded you. Forgiveness is no small thing. It is a tall order. The greater the offense, the harder you may find it to forgive. The model prayer that Jesus taught His followers includes this line: "Forgive us our trespasses as we forgive those who trespass against us." What was Jesus saying here? He was reminding us to emulate our Father's ability to forgive. Have we not all sinned and fallen short of the glory of God? Certainly! But our heavenly Father forgives us. He removes the dark stain of sin and says He will speak of it no more. It is gone. As far as the east is from the west. That is a long way! God does not keep bringing up your past sins. If you have asked Him to forgive you, He has. Pray for your heavenly Father to reveal to you just how much He loves you. As you experience His love and forgiveness, you will want to forgive others—regardless of the depth of the hurt they have caused in your life.

Evening – PRAYING FOR FORGIVENESS

Who can understand his errors? Cleanse me from secret faults. Keep back Your
servant also from presumptuous sins; let them not have dominion over me.
Then I shall be blameless, and I shall be innocent of great transgression.
PSALM 19:12–13 NKJV

Sin is part of our lives in a fallen world. It would be impossible to know all of our errors. The psalmist's prayer here is one worth emulating. He asks for forgiveness for his known sins and also for those committed unconsciously. Who knows how many times per day we offend God without even being aware of the offense? We have sinned in the past. We will sin in the future. And we have sinned even this very day, if only in our thought lives. And so we come before a Holy God, through Christ, who makes a way for us to enter into His presence. We come and we lay it down. We ask to be forgiven for that which we did on purpose and that which we did not. The psalmist prays that presumptuous sins would not have dominion over him. The Message calls them "stupid sins." The New International Version refers to these sins as "willful." The apostle Paul warned against taking advantage of grace. The Christian should be constantly on guard against sin because sin breaks God's heart.

Morning – MOTHER: A CHILD'S FIRST TEACHER

She speaks with wisdom, and faithful instruction is on her tongue.
PROVERBS 31:26 NIV

Once inside the century-old candlelit church, two women tiptoed down the wide aisle between wooden pews. One visitor whispered, "You can really feel the presence of God in this church."

"I think so too," her friend agreed. "And look at this—Mary, mother of Jesus, teaching her young son about God!"

It was like no other statue either had seen in any church. The marble statue of Mary glowed in the candlelight as she pointed to scriptures from which she was teaching the boy Jesus—perhaps ten years old.

Whether or not the artist's rendition is accurate for the culture of the time, the message is clear: teaching godly values and a righteous lifestyle begins at home. A mother is a child's first teacher. What a responsibility!

Today's mother has to handle many things at once. Most work, keep up the house and family, pay bills, plan and prepare meals, and spend time with their husbands—if married.

Sometimes it may seem that the least of all her jobs to squeeze in is to spend time nurturing her children. But God doesn't think of it as a small job at all.

Godly women who guide and mentor their children—or grandchildren—leave a godly legacy, influencing generations to come.

Through our love and teaching, God's words become real ones to live by.

Evening – THE GIFT OF LISTENING

*My dear brothers and sisters: You must all be quick
to listen, slow to speak, and slow to get angry.*
JAMES 1:19 NLT

When Ginger lost her job, it became a huge blessing for her and for her family. Financially, she was concerned as each month doors remained closed to opportunities for employment. But in the middle of a financial challenge, she discovered what she'd been missing each day with her children.

Now that her schedule was clearly flexible, she scheduled her job interviews and other errands around the boys' school drop-off and pick-up times. The first afternoon she picked up her third grader, she discovered he was full to overflowing with the details of his day. He shared things on the ride home about his day, what he hoped and even imagined. Once he arrived home, his desire to talk turned off and he went on about his afternoon. The same seemed to be true for her seventh grader. Time in the car became a wonderful exchange with each of her boys.

When she had the opportunity to go back to work full time or work two part-time jobs from home, she kept the flexible schedule so she could continue the afternoon conversations in the car with her sons. She was careful to really listen and hear their hearts.

Give your children your undivided attention sometime during the day.

DAY 220

Morning – HELP MY UNBELIEF!

*"What do you mean, 'If I can'?" Jesus asked. "Anything is possible
if a person believes." The father instantly cried out, "I do
believe, but help me overcome my unbelief!"*
MARK 9:23–24 NLT

This story in the New Testament tells of a man who brought his demon-possessed son to Jesus for healing. First he asked the disciples to drive out the demon, but they could not. Then he said to Jesus, "But if you can do anything, take pity on us and help us."

The man had his focus on his problem instead of on Christ. He was thinking about how long his son had been possessed and the great damage that had been done. He wasn't convinced that Jesus could do anything about it. But Jesus corrected the man and showed him that anything is possible through Christ.

Are you facing hard times right now? Does your faith feel a little weak? When you are tempted to let your problems get the better of you and you feel that your faith isn't strong enough to overcome, pray for God to change your thinking from doubt to firm faith in Christ. And remember, when you are weak, He is strong!

Evening – ASK IN FAITH

*But he must ask in faith without any doubting, for the one who
doubts is like the surf of the sea, driven and tossed by the wind.*
JAMES 1:6 NASB

What does it mean to ask God for something *in faith?* Does it mean we believe that He *can* grant our requests? That He *will* grant our requests? Exactly what is required to prove our faith?

These are difficult questions. Many who have prayed for healed bodies and healed relationships have received exactly that, this side of heaven. Others who have prayed for the same things, believing only God could bring healing, haven't received the answers they wanted.

There is no secret ingredient that makes all our longings come to fruition. The secret ingredient, if there is one, is faith that God is who He says He is. It's faith that God is good and will use our circumstances to bring about His purpose and high calling in our lives and in the world.

When we don't get the answers we want from God, it's okay to feel disappointed. He understands. But we must never doubt His goodness or His motives. We must stand firm in our belief that God's love for us will never change.

Morning – LOVE IN THE DARK

*This I recall to my mind, therefore I have hope. The LORD's
lovingkindnesses indeed never cease, for His compassions never fail.
They are new every morning; great is Your faithfulness.*
LAMENTATIONS 3:21–23 NASB

This is a familiar and beautiful passage. The Lord will always show you loving-kindness. He will never cease to have compassion on you. He is forever faithful. And yet, if you are going through a time when God's love seems farther away than it's ever been, you may think these sentiments are only for those who are experiencing good things in their lives.

Though these verses are familiar, they are almost always taken out of context. These verses are a small island of hope in an otherwise desolate chapter. The author of these verses is suffering deeply. He is greatly afflicted and nearly without hope. But even in the deepest pit of despair, he has the experience to back up his claims that God's love has never ceased from his life. When you go through a dark period in your life, be encouraged by the testimony of this fellow child of God. God is not a fair-weather God who abandons you when the going gets rough. His love will find you and carry you through the darkest and most soul-wrenching of trials. You can have the same faith and unwavering confidence in His compassion that you have in the fact that the sun will rise in the morning. There is hope even in the darkest place.

Evening – UNDESERVED SUFFERING

Rise up, be our help, and redeem us for the sake of Your lovingkindness.
PSALM 44:26 NASB

God's loyal love is based on His character, not on our conduct. He doesn't always reward our righteousness in this life, and at times He inexplicably seems to mistreat us despite our faithfulness. He gives victory and allows defeat, but He is merciful. Psalm 44 expresses this well.

Attributed to the Sons of Korah, Psalm 44 has a literary structure that forms a step pyramid (ziggurat). Ten lines (verses 1–8) comprise the bottom step and recount God's *past deliverance* of Israel. The next step up has eight lines (verses 9–16) describing their *present defeat* and disgrace. Then six lines (verses 17–22) present the *people's defense*: they had done nothing wrong. The last four lines (verses 23–26) express their *perplexing dilemma*: God seems to be asleep, hidden, and forgetful.

What is the answer? The psalm gives no solution. The answer is—God does not have to give answers. We can ask God for deliverance, but it's up to Him. His discipline process often chastises our sin, but mostly it trains our character.

The structure of the psalm draws the reader's attention upward to the point at the top of the pyramid. In Hebrew, the last word of the psalm is "loving-kindness." We must trust God's loyal love despite what we are going through. Our circumstances can never negate His faithfulness.

Morning – FIXED AND FOCUSED

I trusted in, relied on, and was confident in You,
O Lord; I said, You are my God.
PSALM 31:14 AMPC

Trusting God might sometimes seem attainable. Other times, not so much. Factoring in things like your background, upbringing, childhood, and the relationships you have experienced throughout life, trust might be a very difficult thing to do.

If trusting God seems like it's nearly impossible, you might be tempted to put your faith and hope into things and people. This is because they might seem able to provide a quick fix or instant gratification. Yet the paradox is that as you abide in Jesus, all you need is to trust Him with things and people.

In Psalm 31, David petitions for God to shower His grace and mercy on him for help and protection in regard to his enemies. He cries out to God in desperation for the challenges in this life, looking for—and expecting—God to fight for him.

Can you relate to David's pleas when you consider the stories and struggles both you and your fellow brothers and sisters face? No matter what's happening, know that God is able. Have mustard seed faith to trust in, rely on, and be confident in His faithfulness, and He will lead you to victory.

Evening – THE HAND OF GOD

"For I am the LORD your God who takes hold of your right
hand and says to you, Do not fear; I will help you."
ISAIAH 41:13 NIV

If there is a scripture you need to have handy in times of trouble, this is it! Post it on your fridge; write it on a sticky note to tack up in your car; commit it to memory so that the Spirit of God can bring it to mind when you need to hear it most.

Psalm 139 tells us that God created us and knows everything about us. He knows when we sit and when we get up, and He knows every word that's on our tongue before we speak it. Psalm 139:7–10 tells us that no matter where we go, His hand will guide us and hold us.

Heading to the emergency room? Repeat Isaiah 41:13 and remember that God is holding your hand. Afraid of the future? Stop worrying and trust the God who loves you and has great plans for you. Facing a problem that you cannot possibly bear? Take hold of God's mighty hand and believe that He will help you.

Morning – ACCEPTABLE WORDS

Let the words of my mouth, and the meditation of my heart,
be acceptable in thy sight, O Lord, my strength, and my redeemer.
PSALM 19:14 KJV

When Jean wondered why Sally hadn't greeted some of the other members coming into the church, Sally jokingly said, "That's not my job." Later, during the service, her words came back to her and she felt ashamed that she had said it even in a humorous light. After the service, she went to Jean and asked if she had taken her seriously. Jean said no, but Sue felt that God hadn't been pleased with what she had said.

As Christians, we should be careful of the words we speak and what we meditate on. Matthew 12:34 (KJV) teaches us that "out of the abundance of the heart the mouth speaketh." If our hearts are clean, it helps keep our words acceptable. We never know when someone might take something we say the wrong way. There will always be those who take things wrong on purpose, but being aware of our words can keep us out of trouble. But even more importantly, our words should be pleasing to God. When our speech pleases Him, we won't be as likely to offend others. Proverbs 10:19 (NIV) teaches us that "the prudent hold their tongues." If we ask Him, God will help us to hold our tongues and speak those words that please Him and are not offensive to others.

Evening – ENCOURAGING THOSE AROUND YOU

Pleasant words are like a honeycomb,
sweetness to the soul and health to the bones.
PROVERBS 16:24 NKJV

Are you an encourager? Are your words pleasant and cheerful when you enter a room? Do you find yourself talking mostly about yourself, or do you focus on the other person in the conversation? The tongue is a powerful thing. Words can encourage or discourage, build up or tear down. As you go throughout your day today, seek to be one whose words are healing to the body and sweet to the mind as the writer of Proverbs describes. If you are in the workplace, take time to greet your coworkers with a genuine *"Good morning."* Be sure to truly listen for an answer when you use the phrase *"How are you?"* rather than moving on as if your question were rhetorical. You will find that while kind words encourage the person that receives them, speaking them to others will also bless you. You will feel good knowing that you have lifted someone's spirits or shared in their sorrow. You will begin to focus on others rather than going on and on about your own problems or plans. It has been said that conversation is an art. Hone your conversation skills this week. Speak words of encouragement, words of life that remind the hearer he or she is special to you, and more importantly, to God.

Morning – LIVING IN HARMONY

Live in harmony with each other. Don't be too proud to enjoy the company of ordinary people. And don't think you know it all! Never pay back evil with more evil. Do things in such a way that everyone can see you are honorable. Do all that you can to live in peace with everyone.
ROMANS 12:16–18 NLT

Picture yourself at the symphony. The musicians file in, one by one, as the audience members take their seats. Before long a violinist begins to warm up. Then a clarinet player. Then another musician, followed by another. After a minute or so, you want to stick your fingers in your ears. There's no rhyme or reason to what they're playing. It's a cacophony, dissonant and painful to the ears. This is what life is like when you're out of harmony with those around you. You're like an individual instrument playing madly in a different key than the person next to you. God loves for you to live in harmony with those around you. Maybe it's time to step back, wait for the conductor's cue, then link arms with your family, friends, and coworkers to play the most beautiful tune of your life.

Evening – FRIENDSHIP

*There are "friends" who destroy each other,
but a real friend sticks closer than a brother.*
PROVERBS 18:24 NLT

Remember when you were a kid, how you put glue on your palms and let it dry? You waited until it hardened to peel it away, then grinned at the masterpiece it created. You could see every crease, every wrinkle, every joint. In some ways, a great friendship is like that. A friend who sticks closer than a great brother is, indeed, a masterpiece. She has your imprint on her heart, every tiny detail exposed. . .and yet she loves you anyway. She knows the good, the bad, and the ugly, and she chooses to adore you despite all that. She knows what makes you tick and understands your heart, your motivation. She's got your back when the enemy rears his head, but she's also the first to give godly guidance when you've lost your way. Want her to stick like glue for years to come? Just return the favor. Be the kind of friend you want to have.

Morning – SINCERE LOVE

Love must be sincere. Hate what is evil; cling to what is good.
ROMANS 12:9 NIV

The words *I love you* come easily for some people; for others, those words are withheld and only shared sparingly. As important as those three little words are, they're not nearly as important as the actions behind the words.

Sincere love clings to what is good. Sincere love always protects. It is always patient and kind. It always seeks to bring honor to others. Sincere love always builds up and never tears down.

Some families tell each other they love each other frequently. Yet they gossip and slander and backbite. They seek to dishonor one another at every opportunity. They harm each other's spirits and break each other's hearts. Their words of love aren't sincere.

Others speak the words less frequently, but their actions show kindness and love. The words they do speak bring honor; they build one another up and find ways of showing their love through action.

The words *I love you* are important; we need to hear them. But they ring shallow when they're not backed up with sincere, loving motives and actions. Let's work to show sincere love—backed by actions—to the people God has placed in our lives.

Evening – SEW IN LOVE

Do not merely look out for your own personal interests,
but also for the interests of others.
PHILIPPIANS 2:4 NASB

"Who sews anymore?" Karen said while sipping coffee with her Bible study group. "It makes me sad. My mother used to sew everything for us kids, and I sewed for my kids until it wasn't 'cool' anymore."

"I miss sewing too," said another woman.

"So do I," said a third.

As the women continued to talk, they decided to organize a one-day sewing event at their church. Participants made shorts and shirts for a missionary to distribute to children in Africa. A shared interest in sewing turned into a selfless act of love.

Each day, God provides opportunities for His people to love one another in random ways. A woman in Oklahoma whose mother had been in a nursing home continued to volunteer there after her mother died. A former teacher in Texas offered free after-school tutoring. A lady who loved gardening helped seniors with theirs.

Acts of love don't need to be complex. Jesus said, "If you give even a cup of cold water to one of the least of my followers, you will surely be rewarded." Often, the simplest acts have the most lasting effects. Sometimes, the greatest reward is seeing a simple act of love bring about extraordinary results.

How can you share God's love today?

Morning – WHY PRAISE GOD?

Though he slay me, yet will I trust in him.
JOB 13:15 KJV

One woman asked an honest question: "How can I praise God when everything in my life is falling apart?" Who hasn't pondered that question in moments of defeat, despair, or grief?

In the book of Acts, Paul and Silas, under Roman law, were publicly stripped and severely beaten for their faith. Afterward, they were jailed. Yet with bloody backs and shackled feet, they sat in a dirty cell undefeated. Rather than question God's intentions or apparent lack of protection, the scriptures state that around midnight, "Paul and Silas were praying and singing hymns to God" (Acts 16:25 NIV).

The power of prayer and praise resulted in complete deliverance. The prison doors flew open, and their chains fell off. What's more, the jailer and his family accepted Christ, and these ardent believers were able to witness to other inmates.

It's difficult to praise God when problems press in harder than a crowd exiting a burning building. But that's the time to praise Him the most. We wait for our circumstances to change, while God desires to change us despite them. Praise coupled with prayer in our darkest moments is what moves the mighty hand of God to work in our hearts and lives.

How can we pray and praise God when everything goes wrong? The bigger question might be: How can we not?

Evening – TRADING COMPLAINTS FOR PRAISE

Praise the LORD, for the LORD is good;
sing praises to His name, for it is pleasant.
PSALM 135:3 NKJV

No one likes a complainer. But most of us like to complain. Just being able to grouse about something seems to make us feel better, or at least vindicated in our irritation. Yet Philippians 2:14 (NKJV) tells us to "do all things without complaining."

This is a hard one for me. When things bother me, I talk, and when something isn't right in my day, my natural inclination is to comment on it. And that leads, sometimes, to more negative observations.

God knows that we become what we focus on. He desires that we be people of praise. Remember the Hebrews in the wilderness and how they complained and murmured every time something went wrong? Eventually, it affected their faith and they did not believe they could defeat the giants in Canaan, and God let them wander around for forty years until they were all dead. No doubt, many of them saw their sin, but it was too late to change the consequences.

The antidote for complaining is praising. Praise is the language of Christians. When we are praising, we are focusing not on ourselves but on Christ and His glory. And of course, this is where we find the most happiness.

Morning – A WOMAN'S FAITH

Then Jesus said to her, "Woman, you have great faith! Your request is granted." And her daughter was healed at that moment.
MATTHEW 15:28 NIV

This Canaanite woman has a demon-possessed daughter. She and her daughter are descendants of the people Joshua and Israel drove out of the Promised Land due to their sin.

Jesus' treatment of this woman is puzzling at first. He begins by ignoring her pleas. But she keeps following Him and His disciples. Then when He does talk to her, He seems to imply that she is a dog and doesn't deserve His attention.

But Jesus is doing something much bigger here. In treating her the way that any Jewish man would, He is giving her an opportunity to express her faith in Him, something her heritage has denied her. Her determination proves the strength of her faith.

He is delighted to grant her request. He commends her faith, and He uses the same term of endearment, *woman*, that He used with His mother at the wedding where He turned water into wine. Jesus is proving to her that heritage doesn't determine her relationship with God; her faith does.

He invites you as His daughter to come to Him and relate to Him in a personal and loving way. Let Him show you how much He loves and values you.

Evening – HOW GOD LOVES HIS DAUGHTERS

"Why should our father's name disappear from his clan because he had no son? Give us property among our father's relatives."
NUMBERS 27:4 NIV

The Promised Land of Israel was to be divided among the twelve tribes of Jacob. One of his descendants, Zelophehad, only had daughters, no sons. At that time, women were not allowed to inherit. But his five daughters went to Moses and asked for the land that would have belonged to their father.

Moses is so shocked by their request that, instead of making a ruling himself or consulting with his leaders, he takes their request to God to ask what to do. The culture perpetuated the lie that God didn't care about women. God acted in a countercultural manner and granted the women their request.

This story also shows that our spiritual inheritance is not determined by our earthly parents. The women admitted their father had died in his sin of unbelief, but God did not hold that sin against them. He provided the inheritance and blessings their earthly father could not.

These women demonstrated their faith in God's Word by asking for their share of the land *before* any of it had even been conquered. After God led Israel to conquer the land, they reminded Joshua of their inheritance.

God is passionately concerned about the unique challenges of being a woman in this world. He wants us to come to Him and ask Him for blessings. He is the perfect Father.

Morning – YOUR GREATEST DELIGHT

His delight is in the law of the LORD,
and in His law he meditates day and night.
PSALM 1:2 NKJV

What are your heart's desires? To be happy? To find purpose? To be loved? There is a way to satisfy those longings without fail. Psalm 37:4 (NASB) says, "Delight yourself in the LORD; and He will give you the desires of your heart."

Many Christians expect God to provide their desires, but they don't want to delight in Him. They treat their relationship with God as a duty, a desperate plea for help, a religious luck-charm, a daily dependence, but a delight? That requires far too much time and energy.

A relationship without delight is like a marriage with no passion or friendship. Yes, you can perform the duties of married life, but it will become a prison. Nehemiah 8:10 (NASB) says, "Do not be grieved [by the words of the Law], for the joy of the LORD is your strength." We should love and serve God, not to avoid His wrath, but rather out of gratitude and awe.

When you live this way, you will find the delights of your heart, just as Albert Schweitzer wrote: "Your life is something opaque, not transparent, as long as you look at it in ordinary human ways. But if you hold it up against the light of God's goodness, it shines and turns transparent, radiant, and bright. And then you ask yourself in amazement: Is this really my own life I see before me?"

Evening – DESIRE GOD

Whom have I in heaven but You? And besides You, I desire nothing on earth. My flesh
and my heart may fail, but God is the strength of my heart and my portion forever.
PSALM 73:25–26 NASB

Do you ever look forward to meeting God in heaven? He is waiting for you there to welcome you home once your pilgrimage on earth is done. You can look forward to that extraordinary meeting. But God is not a distant being who is looking down on you from the sky, aloof and unreachable until the next life. He is present and active in your life now and offers you a relationship with Him. The psalmist who wrote these verses says that apart from God, there is *nothing* on earth that he desires. What an amazing perspective and remarkable passion. Do you have that same desire for God—believing that nothing on this earth could please you if it is devoid of Him? God will be your focus and all-consuming passion in heaven, so start on the trail of eternity now by putting Him first in your life and committing to spend time with Him and in His Word.

Even when your heart, body, and emotions fail you, God is your strength and will be for eternity. He is the only one in whom you can have a rock-solid faith and who will never fail you even through death.

Morning – THE EXPECTANT

Therefore the LORD will wait, that He may be gracious to you;
and therefore He will be exalted, that He may have mercy on you.
For the LORD is a God of justice; blessed are all those who wait for Him.
ISAIAH 30:18 NKJV

God is looking for women to bless. He's waiting for His daughters to look up and seek His face, to spend some quality time with Him. But some women are staring at their path, their thoughts miles away from heavenly happenings. Carefully they walk, heedless of God's direction, their eyes glued to the ground so they don't trip up. Their ears are plugged into a smartphone, so they cannot hear God's whispered, "Pssssssssssssst! Look up! Look up here!" And in the evening, when they should be more receptive to His call, they turn on the TV. Once tuned in, they become tuned out—spiritually and physically.

To break the cycle, women of today need to stop and look around for God. To yearn for His presence and all that comes with it—His victory, favor, love, peace, joy, and friendship. To live a life certain of the knowledge that with their eyes on, ears open to, and heart centered on Jesus, they can *expect* to be blessed.

Evening – THE INSISTENT WOMAN

But she came and began to bow down before Him, saying, "Lord, help me!"
. . . Then Jesus said to her, "O woman, your faith is great; it shall be done
for you as you wish." And her daughter was healed at once.
MATTHEW 15:25, 28 NASB

This Canaanite woman is a wonderful example of perseverance in the midst of discouragement. After she made her first urgent plea to Christ, for Him to heal her possessed daughter, He did not answer. As if that weren't bad enough, the disciples begged Jesus to send her away. In response, He gave the disciples the reason He was ignoring her: she was not an Israelite. Yet the Canaanite woman continued, now upon her knees, worshiping, crying, praying, pleading. When Jesus again refused, her woman's logic served her well, as she gave Him a reason why He should grant her request (see Matthew 15:26–27). As a result, not only was the insistent woman's request granted, but Jesus commended her for her great faith—and her daughter was healed at that moment.

How insistent is God's daughter today? How much discouragement will she ignore? How far will she go to intercede with God for the ones she loves—no matter who they are, no matter if they are saved or unsaved? How ready is she to get down on humbled knee? How great is her faith?

Morning – DUST

*Just as a father has compassion on his children, so the
Lord has compassion on those who fear Him. For He Himself
knows our frame; He is mindful that we are but dust.*
PSALM 103:13–14 NASB

Do you ever feel weak or inconsequential? Or like the slightest wind of difficulty could just blow you away? These verses tell you that you are but dust and that God is aware of that. That doesn't sound very encouraging, does it? But when you think about it, great strength can be gleaned from this truth.

The Lord knows your frame. He knows that at times you are prone to weakness and worry and lack the strength to continue. So if you are harboring guilt that you have not lived up to some heavenly standard that you feel God has placed on you, release that guilt. He is mindful of what you are capable of and doesn't ask that you be some kind of superwoman. This is not an excuse for complacency or laziness, but an encouragement that your efforts are recognized and smiled on by God.

Even though you are but a speck of dust in the history of the universe, God has compassion on you and knows you as a father knows his child. How stunning! It doesn't matter that you sometimes feel weak and inconsequential—the Most High God knows and loves you. In that truth resides all the strength and value you need.

Evening – BE OF GOOD CHEER

*But the Lord said to Samuel, "Do not consider his appearance or his height,
for I have rejected him. The Lord does not look at the things people look at.
People look at the outward appearance, but the Lord looks at the heart."*
1 SAMUEL 16:7 NIV

Many are waiting to hear from others that they are valuable. They go from group to group until they settle on the highest bidder. No matter how badly this group mistreats them, they think, *This is what I am worth.* But that's not truth. Only God knows your potential. Only God knows the hidden talents He has placed within you. Only God knows His plan for you. Only God knows your heart. Other people will always sell you short!

God told the prophet Samuel to pick out the new king of Israel, for God had revealed he would come from that lineage. God looked over the ones who arrived and asked Jesse if he had another. God was after someone whose heart was turned toward Him. When the youngest, least likely boy arrived, the Lord said, "Rise and anoint him; this is the one" (1 Samuel 16:12 NIV).

David became the king of Israel because he listened to God and poured out his heart to Him. God chose David because God looked at David's heart. And He liked what He saw. Today, turn your heart toward God so He will be pleased.

Morning – WONDERFUL YOU

*For you created my inmost being; you knit me together
in my mother's womb. I praise you because I am fearfully and
wonderfully made; your works are wonderful, I know that full well.*
PSALM 139:13–14 NIV

Many of us look at ourselves and find something we want to change:
"I wish I had Julie's figure. I hate my hips."
"I love Marcia's curly hair. Mine is so straight and hard to manage."
"Maybe I will color my hair auburn. Brown looks mousy."
And yet, many of the very things we may not like are what make us unique. The psalmist says that we are fearfully and wonderfully made. That means that we are made in such a way to produce reverence and inspire awe. Our bodies are complicated and wondrous in the way they work and heal.

By looking at ourselves the way God looks at us, we can see that our differences are reason to praise Him and acknowledge that it is right to honor, love, and be grateful for all of His creation, including us. Even though we may not understand why He gave us the physical attributes that He did, we can praise Him since we know He took great love and pleasure in creating us.

Evening – THE DEFINITION OF LOVE

*Love is patient and kind. Love is not jealous or boastful or proud or rude. It does not
demand its own way. It is not irritable, and it keeps no record of being wronged. It does
not rejoice about injustice but rejoices whenever the truth wins out. Love never gives
up, never loses faith, is always hopeful, and endures through every circumstance.*
1 CORINTHIANS 13:4–7 NLT

The refined, pristine, perfect definition of love is. . .well, let's explore. The above scripture gives us a bird's-eye view of what love truly embraces: patience and kindness and lack of pride, jealousy, or rudeness. Love isn't demanding nor is it irritable, and it keeps no record of wrongdoing. It rejoices in the truth and never quits or loses faith!

What Christian exemplifies all of those attributes all of the time? None. Now read today's verse again and substitute the word *love* with *God*. Ready? Next, read the verse as if God were talking to you, personally. He never gives up on you, never loses faith in you; and His love never fails. Most of all, despite your imperfections and failures, He continues to love you.

C. S. Lewis said, "He loved us not because we were lovable, but because He is love." What is the true definition of love? God.

DAY 232

Morning – LIFE COACH

And he will be called Wonderful Counselor.
ISAIAH 9:6 NIV

There's a new title for an old profession: life coach. The phrase was first used in 1986 and refers to an advisor who helps people set and reach goals, deal with problems, and make decisions. Professionals can be trained and receive a certification to be a life coach.

While this is a worthy, fulfilling profession, we need to remember we already have a life coach. God sends His Holy Spirit to anyone who asks, and He guides us. He gives us wisdom. He shows us the best way to live.

The problem is, many of us don't want to listen to His counsel. We want what we want. We want to live the way we think is best, the way that seems easiest or most comfortable for us right here, right now. But God is more concerned with the big picture than our current circumstances. Oh, He will guide us through today, but if we listen to Him carefully and follow His direction, we will end up on the best path for eternity.

Our wonderful counselor isn't in it for the paycheck or to build a résumé. He loves us and only wants what is best for us. When we are confused about which way to go, which decision to make, we can go to our life coach. We can trust that He will always lead us in the right direction.

Evening – THE PRICE OF SIN

The LORD said to Joshua, "Do not be afraid of them; I have given them into your hand. Not one of them will be able to withstand you."
JOSHUA 10:8 NIV

Joshua is following the book of the Law, just as God had instructed him, in taking the Promised Land. God is driving out Israel's enemies because of their wickedness, not because of Israel's righteousness. Israel is just the vehicle God uses to provide punishment to nations who refused to repent of their sin and turn to Him. Sin leads to death.

These nations were given a chance to make peace with God. Rahab did. The Gibeonites did, even though it was through deception. Anyone who wants peace with God gets it.

In the Garden of Eden, Adam and Eve were cursed because of their sin. But Christ's death—something that is normally considered failure—overturns Adam and Eve's rebellion and becomes the ultimate means of victory over death and sin. He paid the price for us, and we receive the blessing instead of the punishment.

Jesus' obedience and holiness were the only things that could take away the curse of our sin. God raised Him and made His enemies a footstool for His feet, just as He did for Joshua. Joshua's conquering of the Promised Land was a physical and temporary representation of what Christ does to sin on a universal and permanent basis. God did not abandon us to the brutality of our sin. Peace with God is possible because of Christ.

Morning – I DID IT MY WAY

*Those who trust in themselves are fools,
but those who walk in wisdom are kept safe.*
PROVERBS 28:26 NIV

People tend to think of themselves as intelligent beings—full of insight and understanding, especially if they have acquired academic degrees and accolades. They like to think they can make it on their own. That they are a powerhouse of strength and a font of sound judgment. That they can breeze through life fueled by their own wit and wisdom. People love to say, "I did it my way."

But this kind of thinking is folly and anything but wise.

We do need assistance. We need counsel from godly men and women, and most of all we need help from the ultimate guide—whose name is Jesus.

How have you chosen to live your life? Do you tread lightly, knowing you are fallible and fallen and in need of the Lord's daily guidance? Or do you bulldoze forward no matter what, confident that you'll make it in your own understanding? Proverbs 3:6 (NKJV) instructs, "In all your ways acknowledge Him, and He shall direct your paths." What a promise. What relief!

In the end, that is the essence of true wisdom—to say, "I did it God's way."

Evening – FREEDOM IN OBEDIENCE

*I run in the path of your commands,
for you have broadened my understanding.*
PSALM 119:32 NIV

The psalmist has a curious saying here. *I'm earnestly following Your rules, because You've set me free.* Wait a sec. Rules equal restriction, confinement, and unhappiness, right? A sinful attitude views rules as a nuisance or "necessary evil." Our orderly and perfect God set down His law to show us that, first, He is holy and we are not, and second, the rules are there for our benefit and protection so we can lovingly and rightly interact with Him and our fellow human beings.

It may be strange to consider, but God's rules do make us free, but we only view them as life-giving and glorious after we trust in Christ. He changes our hearts to want to do what is right instead of chasing after our selfish, ultimately destructive desires (Jeremiah 17:9). Even with a changed heart, we still have a lot to learn. The Holy Spirit through the Word teaches us how to see the beauty of God's commands, and we grow in our delight in Him.

I'm free to be a rule-follower? We don't lose our individuality when we submit to the Lord. Rather, we become more how humanity was created to be in the beginning—in unbroken fellowship with the Father, loving Him and displaying His marvelous ways to a watching world.

Morning – DO NOT FEAR

"Do not fear, for I am with you; do not anxiously look about you,
for I am your God. I will strengthen you, surely I will help you,
surely I will uphold you with My righteous right hand."
ISAIAH 41:10 NASB

Fear can seep into our lives so easily. We fear the unknowns of the future. We fear we didn't handle a certain situation as well as we should have. We fear we are too inadequate, or too busy, or too unmotivated to handle the things being thrown at us in the present.

But in this verse, God tells you not to fear. This isn't just an idle, "Don't worry, you'll be okay" kind of statement. In fact, He *commands* you not to fear. How can He be so confident that you are completely safe so that He can command you not to fear? Because He is with you. The God who created, sustains, and governs this entire world is with you. With that perspective, what is there to fear?

Stop looking anxiously around you at all the burdens, worries, and fears of your life. Instead, focus on your God. He promises to strengthen and help you. Nothing in this world is so overwhelming that you cannot overcome it with the almighty God's strength. And even when you feel that you have fallen with no strength to get up, He promises to hold you up with His hand.

Evening – 20/20, 20/20 VISION

So he answered, "Do not fear, for those who are with us are more than those who
are with them." And Elisha prayed, and said, "LORD, I pray, open his eyes that
he may see." Then the LORD opened the eyes of the young man, and he saw. And
behold, the mountain was full of horses and chariots of fire all around Elisha.
2 KINGS 6:16–17 NKJV

One morning Elisha and his servant were surrounded by an enemy army with its horses and chariots. Having seen the odds against them, his servant man, who apparently only had earthly vision, freaked out, asking Elisha, "What will we do?"

The prophet seems rather calm with his reply of "Don't worry. Our army is bigger than theirs." But then he prayed that God would open the servant's eyes so that he could see how well protected he and the prophet were. So God honored Elisha's request—and the scales from the servant's spiritual eyes fell away, revealing a mountain full of charioted cavalry.

When women of the Way open their eyes of faith, the shadows of this world shrink away and fear abates. The more they understand the absolute and awesome power of their God, the better their 20/20, 20/20 vision and the less terror this world holds for them. And with the fading of the darkness of worry, dread, and anxiety comes the Son's brilliant light of peace, faith, and serenity.

Morning – AN EXCLUSIVE PLACE

*But now they desire a better, that is, a heavenly country. Therefore God is
not ashamed to be called their God, for He has prepared a city for them.*
HEBREWS 11:16 NKJV

There are many old songs about heaven that speak of it being a city. Those songwriters of yesteryear used phrases like "the pearly white city," "the city built foursquare," and "the city that never knows night." The Bible tells us that heaven is a city, a place built for God's children and populated with saints from all the ages.

Have you realized that those who make it to that city never say the word *goodbye*? There are no endings there. There are no deaths or partings or moving vans. Existence there will be an ongoing, joyous present. Think about the joy of arriving home for Christmas or coming to a family reunion, that moment when you walk in the front door to warm hugs and happy cries of welcome—that's the delight of every moment of eternity. Isn't it a comfort to know that we have this place waiting for us when this life is over?

Heaven is prepared for those who are in relationship with God. The only way to get there is by accepting the sacrifice of Jesus Christ's work on the cross. Salvation is an inclusive invitation to an exclusive place. Have you made plans to go?

Evening – A GLIMPSE OF HEAVEN

*" 'He will wipe every tear from their eyes. There will be no more death' or
mourning or crying or pain, for the old order of things has passed away."*
REVELATION 21:4 NIV

When the Israelites were preparing to cross into the Promised Land, they celebrated Passover. They had not been in the land long enough to cultivate it and create a rich harvest, but what they did eat they ate in anticipation of what God had promised them.

It is the same with heaven. Our time on earth is small and faded compared to the glory of heaven. While we are working through our difficulties here, we anticipate heaven, like the Israelites did the Promised Land.

Heaven will be a place of beauty. There will be no death, pain, fear, or impurity. God's creation will exist in the full glory He originally intended, not the wrecked-by-sin version we live in now. No sinfulness will mar it.

Relationships will deepen and expand and be deeply fulfilling without our sinfulness creating barriers between us and others. Rewards, restoration, and comfort are awaiting us. God will make it all up to us—all the loss, pain, and sorrow we experience in this world.

God gives us glimpses of heaven now to encourage us on our journey. He knows we can't see the whole picture, and He condescends to our frail humanity to give us what we need for the journey.

Morning – GET INTO THE MOVIE FREE?
DREAM ON

My son, do not despise the LORD's discipline, and do not resent his rebuke,
because the LORD disciplines those he loves, as a father the son he delights in.
PROVERBS 3:11–12 NIV

"Dad, will you please let us kids go to the show on Saturday? It's only three bottle caps apiece. We can get into the movie free! You have pop machines in your gas station. You throw away lots of bottle caps each day. Dad, please!" Maggie's face was hopeful.

Her father met her look squarely and replied, "No, honey. If you and your brother and sister want to go to the show bad enough, you can work for it. We have chores here, and our neighbors need help too."

"But Dad. . . ," Maggie began.

"Maggie, it's important for each one of you to do your part—by working to earn your way. No free pass."

Maggie's dad was successful in teaching his children by firmly saying "No" when needed. Dad's discipline guided them to responsible adulthood, just as God's "No" stands firm as He guides us along a responsible Christian walk.

When God provided manna daily for the Israelites who fled to the desert, the food was raw. They picked it, pounded it, and then baked it into cakes.

Their food in Egypt had included garlic, leeks, fish, and grains of the fertile Nile Valley, but even there, people worked to eat. The severe desert conditions honed God's people into sojourners of strength as they trusted Him daily for His provision.

Evening – GODLY WORKERS

We hear that some of you are living idle lives, refusing to work and meddling in
other people's business. We command such people and urge them in the name
of the Lord Jesus Christ to settle down and work to earn their own living. As for
the rest of you, dear brothers and sisters, never get tired of doing good.
2 THESSALONIANS 3:11–13 NLT

God wants His children to be active, to be earning their daily bread. When hands are busy with their own business, they are less likely to delve into someone else's. In other words, working keeps people out of trouble. Yet, there is another type of danger that may crop up in the life of a worker—that of making work her all in all, with no room to spare for helping others, including those in her own family.

Yes, it's important for a woman to help earn the bread—either by working outside or inside of the home. But it's even more important to be doing that work in love. To be blessing the lives of others in the midst of the working day. To be working for God—not wealth.

Laboring for the Lord instead of working for wealth, recognition, and power will keep women energized and able to meet whatever challenges come before them.

Morning – RENEW YOUR STRENGTH

Yet those who wait for the LORD will gain new strength;
they will mount up with wings like eagles, they will run
and not get tired, they will walk and not become weary.
ISAIAH 40:31 NASB

Andrew Murray was a South African writer, teacher, and Christian pastor in the late 1900s who captured the heart of prayer with these words about Jesus: "While others still slept, He went away to pray and to renew His strength in communion with His Father. He had need of this, otherwise He would not have been ready for the new day. The holy work of delivering souls demands constant renewal through fellowship with God."

Each day you give a part of yourself to that day—spiritually, emotionally, physically, financially, and socially. Within each of those areas of life, you need to refuel. Spiritually, the only way to recharge is a renewal that comes from God. Waiting for a fresh outpouring of His life-giving Spirit brings a newness and a fresh perspective on all the other areas of your life. Give your best each day by drawing on the strength of your heavenly Father and spending time with Him.

Evening – SEEK GOD

"I love all who love me. Those who search will surely find me."
PROVERBS 8:17 NLT

Did you ever play hide-and-seek as a child? Sometimes it was easy to find your sibling or friend. A foot sticking out from behind the couch or chair was a dead giveaway! Other times, a playmate may have selected a better hiding place. He was harder to find. You searched high and low. You looked behind doors and beneath beds. You lifted quilts and moved aside piles of pillows. But you didn't give up. Not until you found him!

Scripture tells us that God loves those who love Him and that if we search for Him, we will surely find Him. One translation of the Bible says it this way: "Those who seek me early and diligently shall find me."

Seek God in all things and in all ways. Search for Him in each moment of every day you are blessed to walk on this earth. He is found easily in His creation and in His Word. He is with you. Just look for Him. He wants to be found!

DAY 238

Morning – THE CROWN OF LIFE

Blessed is the man who endures temptation; for when
he has been approved, he will receive the crown of life
which the Lord has promised to those who love Him.
JAMES 1:12 NKJV

Stephen is known as the first Christian martyr. Stoned to death for preaching Christ unashamedly, as he entered heaven, he saw Jesus standing at the right hand of God. Stephen stood up for Jesus, and Jesus stood up to welcome him home to heaven! Stephen endured a great trial. He paid a high price—his life. Stephen received the crown of life that day as he entered into the glory of heaven. In fact, did you know that his name means "crown"?

As you face temptations and trials in your life, be encouraged. Realize that Christ-followers through the ages have endured persecution. The temptations you face have been struggles for believers for centuries. The good news is that the Bible tells us God will always provide a way out when we are tempted. Look for that way! Cling to that Christian support system when you are tempted to stray from God. Make necessary changes that will help you to defeat Satan's desire that you succumb to his traps. One day you, like Stephen, will receive the crown of life!

Evening – A WAY OUT

The temptations in your life are no different from what others experience. And
God is faithful. He will not allow the temptation to be more than you can stand.
When you are tempted, he will show you a way out so that you can endure.
1 CORINTHIANS 10:13 NLT

Is there a hang-up in your life that is hard to get over or get rid of? Temptation comes in all shapes and sizes, so what might be tempting to you isn't a problem for someone else. The opposite is also true. The comforting thing is that everyone has been there. We all make mistakes, and whatever is tempting you, you can bet that it has also tripped up many others too.

It's so easy to get discouraged when we mess up. Especially when we mess up in the same area over and over again. Christopher Columbus said this: "I am a most noteworthy sinner, but I have cried out to the Lord for grace and mercy, and they have covered me completely. I have found the sweetest consolation since I made it my whole purpose to enjoy His marvelous presence."

Here's the encouraging thing: whenever you face temptation, God promises to provide a way out. Look for it! In every moment that you are tempted, look for it! Pay attention to the interruptions that occur during temptation and grasp hold of them. They may just be "divine appointments" there to lead the way out!

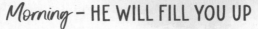

Morning – HE WILL FILL YOU UP

I am the Lord your God, who brought you up out
of Egypt. Open wide your mouth and I will fill it.
PSALM 81:10 NIV

Beth didn't understand why her best friend, Nicole, got up each Sunday for Bible study and church. As an adult, Beth felt free to make her choice to skip the organized religion thing.

Life was good. Beth and Nicole had jobs at the same bank. Beth's car was almost paid for and she had just purchased her first home. Then came the announcement that their bank had been bought by a larger one with a branch down the street. Beth and Nicole would lose their jobs when their location closed.

Beth railed to Nicole about how unfair it was that they were being eliminated. She feared she might lose her house. Nicole let Beth vent her financial worries until she started to blame God.

Nicole told Beth that God would never forsake them. He wanted to help them with their problems and fill their souls with His blessings. Nicole encouraged Beth to attend church with her on Sunday and open herself to the Lord's blessings.

The following day Beth said, "Nicole, I've been so foolish. I thought I could handle things without attending church. I want what you have. I want to feel the peace that comes from knowing my happiness is found in my relationship with God and not in my earthly possessions."

Evening – LOVING IN SPITE OF

Live in harmony with one another. Do not be proud, but be willing to associate
with people of low position. Do not be conceited. Do not repay anyone
evil for evil. Be careful to do what is right in the eyes of everyone. If it is
possible, as far as it depends on you, live at peace with everyone.
ROMANS 12:16–18 NIV

Jason didn't know what bothered him more about Matt, the grizzly looking army veteran: the fact that Matt obviously hadn't bathed recently or his vile, angry attitude. What Jason did know was that this man needed help. His house was almost literally falling down around him; he didn't have a car; and he wasn't eating well.

Jason kept trying to befriend Matt. Most people wouldn't have bothered. But Jason saw Matt as someone who really needed to experience God's love and continued to minister to him, although often it was extremely difficult. Eventually, Jason's persistence paid off. Matt dedicated his life to Christ.

DAY 240

Morning – THE RIGHT TOOLS FOR THE JOB

By his divine power, God has given us everything we need for living a godly
life. We have received all of this by coming to know him, the one who called
us to himself by means of his marvelous glory and excellence.
2 Peter 1:3 nlt

Have you ever tried to hang a picture without a hammer? Or make a dress without a sewing machine? Or bake a pie without an oven? Trying to do a job without the right tools can be difficult, inefficient, and even impossible. Having the right tools for the job can mean the difference between frustration and success.

As we journey through the Christian life, we may feel frustration. We may feel like we lack the patience to deal with a difficult spouse, or the forgiveness to let go of anger toward someone who has hurt us. We may become tired and discouraged, lacking the energy to continue the Lord's work. But the Bible promises us that God has already given us everything we need. From time to time the tools we need may not seem readily available, but we can hold tight to the truth that His divine power has made them available to us. The more we come to know Him, the more we realize our calling. We can be assured that He will equip us with everything we need to do His work.

Evening – THE RELUCTANT SERVANT

He will also keep you firm to the end, so that you will be blameless.
1 Corinthians 1:8 niv

In *The Hobbit*, Gandalf invites Bilbo Baggins on an adventure of a lifetime, but Bilbo responds, "We are plain and quiet folk and have no use for adventures. Nasty, disturbing, uncomfortable things! Make you late for dinner! I can't think of what anybody sees in them."

That's the way many of us treat the call of God. He promises to guide us and provide the power to overcome, but we would rather stay undisturbed.

Moses and Jonah were both examples of men who were reluctant to accept God's call. Moses was insecure—slow of speech and unassertive. Jonah was simply rebellious. Yet both men eventually fulfilled God's purposes. . .because God wanted them to. Neither Moses nor Jonah was eager, but after kicking and screaming, God finally used them to save the Jews and the Ninevites.

Philippians 1:6 (nkjv) says, "He who has begun a good work in you will complete it." God does the work, and for some amazing beautiful reason, He wants to include us!

No matter how incompetent we feel, we can rest assured that God will not let us fail. He will provide us with everything we need to accomplish His perfect plans.

Morning – REAP IN JOY!

*Remember this: Whoever sows sparingly will also reap sparingly,
and whoever sows generously will also reap generously.*
2 CORINTHIANS 9:6 NIV

The list of requirements for the executive assistant job included more than technical expertise. "Care enough to greet visitors with a warm welcome and a million-dollar smile. Be sure that a friendly attitude radiates from your office setting. Demonstrate your caring attitude by maximizing efficiency and minimizing mistakes when dealing with coworkers." Although the job description was for a support staff position, most of it was just as applicable for the CEO as the storeroom clerk.

All of us want to feel appreciated, and we like to deal with a friendly person. Have you ever worked with a person who seemed to have a perpetually bad attitude? You probably didn't feel particularly encouraged after an encounter with this coworker. Yes, sometimes things go wrong, but your attitude in the thick of it is determined by your expectations. If you expect things to turn out well, you'll generally have a positive mental attitude. Treat everyone with genuine kindness, courtesy, and respect, and that is what will be reflected back to you.

Evening – THE CHOICE TO BE CHEERFUL

A cheerful look brings joy to the heart; good news makes for good health.
PROVERBS 15:30 NLT

"So how are you feeling now?" Jolene asked her grown son on the phone. He seemed to be gasping for breath.

He sniffled as he answered, "I just got back from a three-mile run. I feel just okay, not good."

"Have you been taking the vitamin shakes I sent you?"

"Sometimes."

"What did the doctor say?"

"He ruled out everything big. But he doesn't know what's wrong, either. He said to go to a specialist."

"Did you?"

"It's impossible to get an appointment here. Not yet."

"Are you getting enough sleep?"

"I can't remember. But I'm still sick."

"A positive attitude helps," his mother chirped. "Live longer, better, and have more fun. Look at the good! I do!"

"Mom, I know how to take care of myself! I've been eating vegetables and good stuff! I exercise! You think that Pollyanna stuff cures everything. Well, it doesn't. I'm still sick!"

Jolene smiled, realizing her son was well enough to run and sass his mother. He would recover—even without a great attitude.

King Solomon, inspired by God, penned this divine wisdom over three thousand years ago. Researchers today know that a positive attitude affects both the length and the quality of one's life. Attitude plays a big role in winning over disease. Attitude is also a choice.

When faced with challenges, choose to stand up straight and smile. Feel the blessings in a positive attitude.

Morning – MAKE PRAISE

"Do not be afraid! Don't be discouraged by this mighty army, for the battle is not yours, but God's. . . . But you will not even need to fight. Take your positions; then stand still and watch the LORD's victory. He is with you."
2 CHRONICLES 20:15, 17 NLT

When an army of troubles comes up against you, you have two choices. You can run and hide in fear or you can take courage, standing still and strong in your faith and God's power, and watch what He does.

That's what King Jehoshaphat did. When told that three mighty armies were coming to attack him, he, a king, got down on his knees and prayed to God. He recognized the weakness of himself and his kingdom, telling God, "We are powerless against this mighty army that is about to attack us. We do not know what to do, but we are looking to you for help" (v. 12). Knowing God would hear his prayer, he pleaded for guidance—and got it. Filled with faith and courage, he instructed his singers to "walk ahead of the army, singing to the LORD and praising him" (v. 21). The result? The armies attacked and killed each other. All that was left for Jehoshaphat's people was to pick up the plunder.

Got an army of troubles coming at you and your family (aka queendom)? Take heart, make praise, "and you will succeed" (v. 20)!

Evening – TRIPLE POWER

The Spirit of God, who raised Jesus from the dead, lives in you. And just as God raised Christ Jesus from the dead, he will give life to your mortal bodies by this same Spirit living within you. . . . And because we are his children, God has sent the Spirit of his Son into our hearts, prompting us to call out, "Abba, Father."
ROMANS 8:11; GALATIANS 4:6 NLT

Timid and shy? We needn't be.

God, the giver of all things, sent us both His Son, Jesus, and the Holy Spirit. Meanwhile, Jesus, who paved the way for us to reach God, acts as our mediator. At the same time, the Holy Spirit helps us to pray, discern right from wrong, and understand God's Word.

This three-in-one power resides in each and every one of us, steering us to love God, ourselves, and others. When we live that life of love, we're surrounded by a screen of protection that shields us from evil.

So, daughter of God, what need do you have to be afraid? You've a mighty triple power within, enabling you to say, "Though a mighty army surrounds me, my heart will not be afraid. Even if I am attacked, I will remain confident" (Psalm 27:3 NLT).

So go now into the months ahead in love, knowing that with God, Jesus, and the Holy Spirit living and breathing within you, you have the courage to do all you have been called to do.

Morning – SUCH AS I HAVE

*Then Peter said, "Silver and gold I do not have, but what I do have I
give you: In the name of Jesus Christ of Nazareth, rise up and walk."*
ACTS 3:6 NKJV

Have you ever been asked to fill a position for which you felt unqualified? Your first thought is to say no. Surely there is someone better qualified than you for the job. Satan doesn't make your decision any easier. He whispers negative thoughts into your ears. "You can't do that; you're not good at it." "Everyone's looking at you and thinking what a bad job you're doing." "You're making a mess of this. Let someone else do it." All of his thoughts are lies, of course. Maybe you aren't as experienced as the last person who had the job, but you're the one God chose. You may not have the abilities or talents of others, but you have something God can use.

When Peter and John approached the lame man at the gate of the temple, Peter didn't hesitate to tell him they didn't have any silver or gold for him. But he had something the man could use. He said, "What I do have I give you." God is looking for those who are willing to give what they do have. He knew before He called you what you could do, and He also has the ability to qualify you to do whatsoever He requires. Give God whatever You have and allow Him to use it.

Evening – GOOD GIFTS

*And when they were come into the house, they saw the young child with Mary
his mother, and fell down, and worshipped him: and when they had opened their
treasures, they presented unto him gifts; gold, and frankincense and myrrh.*
MATTHEW 2:11 KJV

The wise men gave expensive gifts to Jesus—rare treasures, fitting for a king. The gifts themselves didn't really matter, though. The important thing was that they realized the value of the one who received the gifts. They wanted to give their best because He was worthy of the best.

We may not be able to give large amounts of money or expensive gifts to God. But since He's God, He doesn't really need our treasures. More than anything, He wants us to recognize Him as God. He wants our gifts to Him to be the best we can give, because that shows we understand who He is. He wants our offerings to Him to be an outpouring of our love for Him and our worship of Him.

Whether we give Him our time, our talents, or a portion of our money, God is pleased when those gifts come from a pure heart. And when we offer our lives to Him—every aspect—He smiles. He accepts our gifts, humble as they may be, when He knows we offer them out of sincere worship of the one true God.

DAY 244

Morning – DEALING WITH DEPRESSION

"My grace is all you need. My power works best in weakness."
2 CORINTHIANS 12:9 NLT

A grief response to loss feels a lot like depression. Having been widowed twice, Elisabeth Elliot knew that feeling well. A poem that helped her is called "Do the Next Thing." We may feel like we can't go to work or carry out our responsibilities, but we should do them anyhow. There is power in obeying. Before God parted the Jordan River, the priests had to step into the water (Joshua 3). God gives strength when we take the first step. He has promised to exchange His power for our weakness.

As a missionary, Elisabeth Elliot served the tribal people of Ecuador, including those who martyred her first husband. Her work as a speaker and author of more than twenty books is timeless (elisabethelliot.org). Schooling herself in the poetry of Amy Carmichael, Elisabeth often quoted Amy's poem "In Acceptance Lieth Peace." We may seek solace in denial, busyness, withdrawal, or defeatist attitudes (martyrdom), but God's peace comes from accepting the "breaking sorrow, which God tomorrow will to His [child] explain."

Often when we feel depressed, we want to hibernate and brood, but that does nothing to change our condition. Telling God we accept His will and timing pacifies internal chaos. Then, choosing to move—to do something useful—will improve our mood.

Evening – SING A LITTLE SONG

Is anyone among you in trouble? Let them pray.
Is anyone happy? Let them sing songs of praise.
JAMES 5:13 NIV

"Your face is giving you away."

"I know what you're thinking. I can see it in your expression."

Too many times, people allow their feelings to show on their faces. If we're mad, anger shows in the fiery darts coming from our eyes. Self-pity is portrayed by a turned-down mouth and an expression that says, "Poor me." When we disagree with someone, we often frown, wrinkle our forehead, or roll our eyes as a sign of disgust. We can't seem to keep from letting our thoughts show.

James teaches us how to respond to life's experiences. He says if you're in trouble, pray about it. We're much better off when we pray about what's bothering us, no matter what the problem, than to let it show for the world to see. Likewise, if we're happy, we can let those around us know it by singing. There's a gospel song that says, "I feel a little song coming on." When we pray about our troubles, we feel better and can then sing that song we feel in our hearts. Are you facing a problem today? Take it to God in prayer and let Him take care of it for you. Are you happy, then sing that little song you feel coming on.

Morning – THANK GOD

Praise the Lord! Oh, give thanks to the Lord, for He is good! For His mercy
endures forever. Who can utter the mighty acts of the Lord? Who can declare all His
praise? Blessed are those who keep justice, and he who does righteousness at all times!
PSALM 106:1–3 NKJV

Are you in the habit of thanking God? Taking one minute each morning to turn your thoughts toward thanks to God can change the outlook of your entire day. Maybe you woke up to the reminder of all the extra work on your plate this week. Maybe your children didn't sleep well last night, but you have a nonstop day today. Maybe you just don't feel like being in a good mood!

Stop. Just stop what you're thinking for a moment and focus your mind on God. Allow His Spirit inside you to remind you of His goodness. His love lasts. Always. Now thank Him for at least one great blessing in your life right now.

You are the only one in charge of your attitude. Many things will happen today. Some good, some maybe not so good, but all are outside of your control. You can control how you respond to everything that happens this day. Why not thank God no matter what? Think that might change how well your day goes? Why not give it a try and see what happens!

Evening – GRATITUDE

Devote yourselves to prayer, keeping alert in it with an attitude of thanksgiving.
COLOSSIANS 4:2 NASB

Gratitude is defined as the *feeling* of being grateful or thankful. Many times in our human bodies, our feelings don't match up with the truth. We may have all our needs met and a loving family, and still we struggle with a depression we don't understand. We may be married to an attentive and thoughtful husband, but we've lost that "in love" feeling.

Beth Moore says: "My feelings are—at times—such poor reflections of truth. Recount what you know to be true and before long, it will change what you feel." When you have trouble with your feelings, immediately run to the truth of God's Word and recount what you know to be true. Ask God to change your attitude. Write down truths from God and keep them in your regular line of vision:

- I am free and clean in the blood of Christ.
- He has rescued me from darkness and has brought me into His kingdom.
- I am a precious child of the Father.
- God sings over me.
- He delights in me.
- I am a friend of Christ.
- Nothing can separate me from God's love (certainly not my feelings!).
- God knows me intimately.
- God sees me as beautiful and I am wonderfully made.
- God is for me, not against me.

This is truth from His Word! And when you focus on truth, your confusing thoughts start to become clear. . .and amazingly enough, your feelings begin to turn back on!

Morning – PUTTING GOD TO WORK

Since ancient times no one has heard, no ear has perceived,
no eye has seen any God besides you, who acts
on behalf of those who wait for him.
ISAIAH 64:4 NIV

Prayer affects the three realms of existence: the divine, the angelic, and the human. God, men, and the angels are subject to the rules of prayer, which God has established. Prayer puts God to work in what is prayed for by His people. Prayer also puts us to work. If we do not pray, then God is not sent into action. Prayerlessness excludes God and leaves us at the mercy of our own circumstances. Understanding this, why would we not pray at all times and about everything?

Prayer puts the power into God's hands and keeps it there. Prayer is a privilege. It gives us the ability to ask the God of the universe for action. We should not hesitate.

Evening – THE LORD IS CLOSE

The LORD is righteous in all His ways, gracious in all His works. The LORD
is near to all who call upon Him, to all who call upon Him in truth.
PSALM 145:17–18 NKJV

Do you ever feel like you go to God in prayer with the same things over and over again? Is your prayer life in need of a little lift? The psalms are full of prayers and truth. To find a road map for prayers and promises, look to the psalms.

The authors of the psalms knew the truth of this scripture—that the Lord is close to those who pray to Him. They expressed their honest emotions to God—their joy, their fears, their praise. They understood that God loved them and wanted to have a personal relationship with them—just like He does with us.

If you're struggling with how to pray to God or what to pray about, use the psalms as your guide. Pray through a psalm every day. Add your own personal thoughts and feelings as you pray. Pretty soon, you'll realize that you have begun a personal friendship with the Creator of the universe.

Morning – GLORIFYING GOD

Do you not know that your body is the temple of the Holy Spirit. . .
and you are not your own? For you were bought at a price;
therefore glorify God in your body.
1 Corinthians 6:19–20 nkjv

Godly Christians desire to glorify God with their lives. We imagine this will involve significant accomplishments and praiseworthy acts of service. But we also glorify God through less desirable means. Paul's earnest expectation and hope was to magnify Christ in his body, even by dying (Philippians 1:20).

Jesus told Peter he would "glorify God" by a death he did not want and could not control (John 21:18–19). He was actually crucified as a martyr. Why did Jesus tell him he would die a horrible death? Perhaps to assure him that he would never again deny knowing Christ. He would be faithful unto death, thus glorifying God.

The way we suffer also brings God glory. Jesus said a man was blind from birth so that "the works of God should be revealed in him" (John 9:3). First Peter 4:16 tells us to glorify God when we suffer as a Christian.

Also, we glorify God in our bodies when we resist sexual immorality (1 Corinthians 6:18–20). Because the Holy Spirit dwells in our bodies, they belong to God, not to ourselves. We magnify God by how we treat our bodies.

The way we face death, endure trials, resist sin, and keep God's temple pure—these all glorify God as much as bearing fruit does.

Evening – A PRINCESS MINDSET

For God is the King over all the earth. Praise him with a psalm.
Psalm 47:7 nlt

You are a daughter of the King of kings, true royalty! In spite of that fact, it's often difficult to see yourself that way, isn't it? When you're feeling bedraggled and tired, when you're facing mounting bills, when your enemies rise up against you, it's easier to feel like a little peasant girl.

It's time for a princess mindset! You've got to remember several things: First, the King welcomes you into His presence. In fact, He bids you to come as often as possible. Second, you're going to live forever with the King! You'll walk on streets of gold and live in a mansion. Third, the Prince of Peace lives in your heart. Accepting Jesus as Savior assures you of a personal, day-in, day-out conversation with the one who spun the heavens and the earth into existence.

You. Are. Royalty. Of course, that also means you have to live like a daughter of the King! You're representing Him, after all. So, chin up. Put all whining and complaining aside. People are watching you so that they can know how a daughter of the King lives. Lead by example, princess!

DAY 248

Morning – OFFENSE

"Isn't this the carpenter? Isn't this Mary's son and the brother of James, Joseph, Judas and Simon? Aren't his sisters here with us?" And they took offense at him.
MARK 6:3 NIV

I'm so offended!" How many times have you felt like crying out these words? Probably more times than you could count. We all go through periods of offense, especially when we feel like there's a target on our back. Some people wear offense like an out-of-season garment. It's always with them, but it's not terribly pretty or appropriate.

Jesus certainly knew what it felt like to be rejected, but He wasn't one for offense. The same couldn't be said about the religious zealots who had it out for Him, though. They took offense at everything! If Jesus healed someone on the Sabbath, they got offended. If He spoke the truth about His deity, they got offended about that too!

You know, there are some people who are just going to be offended. You can tip-toe around all day trying to protect their feelings, but it's a waste of time. Instead of worrying about hyper-sensitive people, try turning your focus to God. Make sure your life, your words, your actions aren't offensive to Him. As long as you can answer in good conscience to your heavenly Father, He can take care of the feelings of others. And while you're at it, lay aside any feelings of offense you might be carrying. They will only weigh you down.

Evening – A PATTERN OF FORGIVENESS

"Therefore, my friends, I want you to know that through Jesus the forgiveness of sins is proclaimed to you. Through him everyone who believes is set free from every sin."
ACTS 13:38–39 NIV

Forgiveness means to pardon another who has wronged you. Forgiveness needs to be extended without and released from within so bitterness will not grow and consume you. And there is no doubt that this can be difficult. As Christians we are commanded to do so by scripture. We often show pity and compassion to others and let a situation go, get over it, apologize. However, all too often we look in the mirror and anger surfaces at ourselves.

Forgiving ourselves is the hardest step in the forgive pattern. Popular Christian speaker Joyce Meyer stated, "Forgive yourself for past sins and hurts you have caused others. You can't pay people back, so ask God to." It's a choice. When tempted to dredge up the wrongs, the sins, which you have asked the Lord to forgive, make a concerted effort to erase those thoughts. Lay aside all that "stuff." When you are embittered against yourself, forgive! If Jesus doesn't remember it, why should you?

Scripture tells us you are forgiven from every sin when you ask! So once you've prayed for forgiveness, face yourself in the mirror and say, "I'm free!"

Morning – YOUR CHILD'S SALVATION

*"Ask, and it will be given to you; seek, and you will find; knock,
and it will be opened to you. For everyone who asks receives,
he who seeks finds, and to him who knocks it will be opened."*
MATTHEW 7:7–8 NKJV

When John Spurgeon returned home from a ministry trip, he found the house quiet except for the voice of his wife from behind the bedroom door. She was pleading for the salvation of all their children, but especially their strong-willed firstborn son. The young man she carried such a burden for later became one of the greatest preachers and evangelists of all time, Charles Spurgeon.

We spend so much time disciplining our children for social behavior and so little time in prayer for their souls. A relationship with God can't be earned by good works or a sweet disposition. It can't be passed down through bloodlines or learned like a language. Salvation is a gift from God.

Jesus said in Matthew 21:22 (NIV), "If you believe, you will receive whatever you ask for in prayer." So we must ask the giver to grace our children with His endowment of salvation. Don't take it for granted that because kids are raised in a godly home or go to a Christian school they will have a personal relationship with Christ. Instead, sincerely, humbly, and relentlessly pray to God, who is generous in His gifts and waits for a people who are desperate for His work in their lives.

Evening – PRAY FOR CHRISTIAN HOUSEHOLDS

When she speaks, her words are wise, and she gives instructions with kindness.
PROVERBS 31:26 NLT

Is there a Christian woman whom you admire, someone who has helped you grow in your faith? In Paul's second letter to Timothy, he mentioned two special women in Timothy's life: "I am reminded of your sincere faith, which first lived in your grandmother Lois and in your mother Eunice and, I am persuaded, now lives in you also" (2 Timothy 1:5 NIV). How precious it is in God's sight when children are raised in households where He is the foundation and family is the priority.

In Christian households, children learn about God's love and faithfulness. Discipline is administered out of loving-kindness not anger, and love is taught through the parents' example. It is a home in which Christlike wisdom is passed from generation to generation.

In Timothy's household, he learned from his mother and grandmother's faith, and according to Paul, those seeds of faith grew in young Timothy and led him to become a servant of the Lord.

Whether you are married or single, have children or not, you can plant seeds of faith through your own Christian example and prayer. Pray for all children that they will grow up in godly homes, and pray for women everywhere that they will raise their children in Christian households and remain always faithful to God.

DAY 250

Morning – LIKE LITTLE CHILDREN

*And they were bringing children to Him so that He might touch them;
but the disciples rebuked them. But when Jesus saw this, He was indignant
and said to them, "Permit the children to come to Me; do not hinder them;
for the kingdom of God belongs to such as these. Truly I say to you, whoever
does not receive the kingdom of God like a child will not enter it at all."*
MARK 10:13–15 NASB

Have you ever heard a child pray from his heart? Not just a memorized prayer that he repeats before lunch but a real, honest prayer? A four-year-old boy prayed this:

"Dear God, I really don't like all the bad dreams I've been having. Will you please make them stop?"

His prayer was so pure and honest. He prayed, believing that God would listen to his prayer and do something about it. He wasn't afraid to say how he really felt.

This passage in Mark tells us that no matter how old we are, God wants us to come to Him with the faith of a child. He wants us to be open and honest about our feelings. He wants us to trust Him wholeheartedly, just like little kids do.

As adults we sometimes play games with God. We tell God what we think He wants to hear, forgetting that He already knows our hearts! God is big enough to handle your honesty. Tell Him how you really feel.

Evening – AN ANCHOR FOR THE SOUL

*But when you ask him, be sure that your faith is in God alone.
Do not waver, for a person with divided loyalty is as unsettled
as a wave of the sea that is blown and tossed by the wind.*
JAMES 1:6 NLT

Imagine being on a life raft in the middle of the ocean. When the storms come, the seemingly weightless raft is picked up and tossed wherever the wind chooses to take it. There is no ability to steer, no sail to work with the wind, certainly no protection from the storm. When the storm ends, the raft's destination is really left up to chance.

James tells us that this is how unstable we become when we do not have a strong foundation. When our loyalty is divided—between serving God and pleasing others, for example—we are as unstable as a raft in a storm on the raging sea. The writer of Hebrews speaks of our hope in Jesus as "a strong and trustworthy anchor for our souls" (Hebrews 6:19 NLT). Faith in God anchors us and braces us against the raging storm. When we are firmly anchored, the winds may whip us around, but ultimately we cannot be moved. Anchor your faith and loyalty on Him.

Morning – THREE GOOD THINGS

*Concerning this thing I pleaded with the Lord
three times that it might depart from me.*
2 CORINTHIANS 12:8 NKJV

When bad things happen to us, we often ask God to show us why. But God is not obliged to reveal His reasons this side of heaven. We trust His character even when we don't understand His ways. It may be that He wants us to rest in Him, not figure Him out. When we cannot know *why* (Psalm 44), we can still know *who* (Psalm 46).

Afflictions have benefits when we accept them as what God wants. They prune us, develop our character, and help us relate to fellow sufferers. Tears teach lessons we could not learn any other way. Sometimes we get dependence on God, not deliverance by God.

When Paul wrestled with his thorn in the flesh, he eventually stopped asking God to remove it. He realized a "messenger of Satan to buffet" him resulted in at least three good things. Because of how God was using him and giving him revelations, he would be tempted to exalt himself, but this piercing barb extinguished pride (12:7). He experienced God's sufficient grace (12:9), and it made him exchange his weakness for God's strength (12:10). Therefore, Paul delighted in his infirmities (12:10). Instead of hindering his ministry for God, somehow they enhanced what God accomplished through him.

It might be a good spiritual discipline to think of three good things for each of the irreversible circumstances and physical ailments we experience.

Evening – SPIRITUAL CPR

*How long, O LORD? Will You forget me forever?
How long will You hide Your face from me?*
PSALM 13:1 NASB

Our feelings do not determine our relationship with God. Since euphoria is not necessarily spiritual joy, feeling numb is not a sign of unspirituality—it's a grief emotion. Nevertheless, Psalm 13 gives a formula for times when we feel like God is gone—two verses each for Complaints, Petition, and Resolve (CPR!).

While we should not question God as if He goofed, it is okay to ask God questions. He may not answer, but He can handle our complaints. The writer asks God how long his suffering will continue. He feels like God is absent, his heart is filled with sorrow every day, and his enemies are winning.

So he petitions God to hear and answer, to put light back into his eyes, or else he will continue to feel dead, and his enemies will gloat over him. He *complains*, he *prays*, and then he *resolves* to trust God now as he has in the past. By remembering God's loving-kindness and rejoicing in the way God will deliver him, he can count on God's bountiful nature.

Two exercises will help us when afflicted—rejoicing in the Lord and singing to the Lord (Psalm 13:5–6). List things you are thankful for or think about God's attributes A to Z. Choose a praise song to play or sing throughout the day.

Suffering can cause doubt and fear to attack our hearts, but performing CPR will revive our weak faith.

Morning – EMPTINESS

*"You have made known to me the paths of life;
you will fill me with joy in your presence."*
ACTS 2:28 NIV

Imagine you're looking at a full-to-the-brim rain barrel. You've been in a season of abundant rain. It never occurs to you that a dry season might be around the corner.

Now picture yourself, weeks later, staring down into the barrel, noticing that it's bone dry. Drought has taken its toll. Now you have a picture of what it's like when you go through a season of spiritual wholeness and spiritual drought. Your rain barrel—your heart—is only as full as what's poured into it.

Did you realize that God can refill your heart with just one word? When He sees that your well is running dry, it breaks His heart. The only solution is to run to His arms and ask for a fresh outpouring of His holy water, the kind that will replenish your soul and give you the nourishment you need to move forward in Him.

It's up to you. God is waiting to meet with you. His everlasting water is prepped and ready to be poured out on you. All you need to do. . .is run to Him.

Evening – INHALING HIS WORD

"But the word is very near you, in your mouth and in your heart, that you may do it."
DEUTERONOMY 30:14 NKJV

God has given us His Word to encourage, strengthen, and energize us. It lifts us up when we are down and prods us into action when we feel incompetent. It gives us courage when we are afraid and provides us with effective ammunition against the enemy of our souls. With God's Word, we can replace Satan's lies with God's truth. One woman who memorizes scripture says that the practice helps her "take every thought captive *immediately*."

Are you intimidated by memorization? Pick two or three scriptures and write them on index cards. Put them in the places you will see them often, such as the car, bathroom mirror, or on the fridge. Don't force yourself to memorize. Simply inhale them like air (because they are life-blood for your soul). Sing them if you want to; there are apps—like the "Fighter" app by Desiring God ministries—that will put music to verses.

You'll be amazed how God will use those truths to shine the light in dark places of your spirit.

Jenna Lang says she "accidentally" memorized scripture by declaring promises of God out loud when she needed an emotional and spiritual boost. It paid off in unexpected ways, she says, because "being able to recall [verses] during times of intense trial helped me not give in to utter despair."

Morning – HEART SMART

Above all else, guard your heart, for everything you do flows from it.
PROVERBS 4:23 NIV

Words have such power. In fact, God's words created the entire universe. And it's the words we hear, see, and plant within that create *our* universe. Unspiritual thoughts and words are to stay out of our hearts. God's thoughts and words are to stay in. For the entire course of our lives is determined by what flows out of our very core. As we keep our hearts guarded, making sure they neither are hurt nor hurt others, we will also be watching our mouths, making sure our words are good, encouraging, and positive (v. 24). Our guarded heart not only helps others but also aids us in retaining the wisdom needed to keep our eyes focused on God and His Word (v. 25) and our feet on His path (v. 26).

So be heart smart. Watch what you're putting in so that you'll only get the best out. For, as Jesus said, "A good man out of the good treasure of his heart brings forth good things, and an evil man out of the evil treasure brings forth evil things" (Matthew 12:35 NKJV). What's in your heart?

Evening – SPEAK WORDS OF LIFE

The tongue can bring death or life;
those who love to talk will reap the consequences.
PROVERBS 18:21 NLT

During a conversation with her mom, Laura expressed her frustration with appointments and doctors. The irritation she felt could be heard in the words she spoke. Instead of dropping the matter, she continued grumbling and complaining.

As she prepared dinner that evening, Laura thought about what she had said and realized she had complained and grumbled for no reason. She realized her words might cause her mom some anxious moments and have a negative effect on her mom's decisions. Laura regretted her hastily spoken words and critical attitude. She had grumbled when she should have let the situation pass. She called her mom and apologized. Her mom didn't seem to be upset about their conversation, but Laura's earlier words could not be changed.

Words are powerful and once spoken can never be erased. The words we speak affect other people for either good or bad and, according to the writer of Proverbs, can bring death or life. The apostle James tells us in his writings that the tongue can start a big fire if we aren't careful. If we're one of those people who loves to talk and we allow ourselves to criticize or complain, we will reap unpleasant consequences. We should strive to speak life-giving words to those around us.

DAY 254

Morning – GRACE IN THE WORKPLACE

Always be humble and gentle. Be patient with each other,
making allowance for each other's faults because of your love.
EPHESIANS 4:2 NLT

According to a 2014 survey conducted by Nielson and Everest College, 80 percent of Americans (that's 8 out of 10) are stressed out by at least one thing at work. One of the reasons cited for the stress was annoying coworkers.

Do you clash with someone at work? There are a lot of possible reasons. It could be anything from a difference in basic temperament to opinions of neatness to a radically opposite approach in doing the inventory. We all have our own ideas and opinions, some of them good and plainly beneficial; others sounding ridiculous to the people who work with us. And sometimes the clashes result from sticking to one's Christian testimony. How do we handle these awkward moments?

Gentleness. If it's not a big deal, let it go. If you can give in to the other person's way of doing it without having to be untruthful or go against policy, then do it.

Humility. We don't always have to have the last word or prove our point to the letter.

Mercy. We can choose to get along, even if we don't agree, and refuse to let the irritations become huge tension points.

Let's not be holy snobs or know-it-alls, but rather let's practice the traits of gentleness, humility, and mercy and make the workplace a better place to be.

Evening – RELATIONSHIP WISDOM

Who is wise and understanding among you? Let them show it by their
good life, by deeds done in the humility that comes from wisdom.
JAMES 3:13 NIV

If you are having relationship trouble, here are some truths to ponder. Wisdom produces good conduct, and you can recognize it in your relationships because, according to James 3:17, it is:

- Pure
- Peaceable
- Gentle
- Open to reason
- Full of mercy and good fruits
- Impartial
- Sincere

But jealousy and selfish ambition (both self-centered in nature) produce bad conduct in relationships; they create disorder (see James 3:14–16). Both jealousy and selfish ambition create passions in us that are not guided by wisdom. You can recognize these evils in your relationships because they result in quarrels and fights.

If you have a consistent history in your relationships of quarreling, fighting, and relational disorder, check your heart for selfishness or jealousy. If you need to confess sin in your heart, do, then ask God for wisdom and empowerment from the Holy Spirit to practice good conduct. If you are aligning with those who are characterized by selfishness, ask God to give you the wisdom on how to proceed in your relationships. It all comes back to the heart.

Morning – BLESSING OTHERS

*Therefore if thine enemy hunger, feed him; if he thirst, give him drink:
for in so doing thou shalt heap coals of fire on his head. Be not
overcome of evil, but overcome evil with good.*
ROMANS 12:20–21 KJV

Susan glanced out the window to see her husband bending over a lawn mower in their driveway. The neighbor from across the street stood nearby. *He must be fixing something for her again*, Susan thought. She sighed, perplexed about this neighbor who asked for their help one day and yelled mean remarks at them the next. She treated everyone in the neighborhood the same way. One day she had scared a young boy who had dropped something in the street in front of her house and stopped to pick it up. His presence had aroused her dogs, who started barking furiously. She spoke harsh, unkind words to the boy, who was innocent of any wrongdoing.

Regardless of the woman's actions and her attitude, Susan knew they had to be obedient to God's Word. They could not repay evil with evil. They shared vegetables out of their garden and helped her with problems such as the lawn mower repair. At Christmas, Susan had walked across the street with a gift basket. At times it all seemed in vain, but they could not allow themselves to be overcome of evil. The outcome lay in God's hands.

Do you have someone who treats you badly? Resolve in your heart not to let that person's evil overcome you. Turn it over to God and let Him handle the situation. His solution is always best.

Evening – A POTENT PARADOX

Do not be overcome by evil, but overcome evil with good.
ROMANS 12:21 NASB

There's an old adage that says, "Don't get mad, get even." Unfortunately, that's going expressly against what Romans 12:21 would have Christ followers do. So if revenge is out, what other ways of dealing with evil could a woman take? Well, she could either allow it to taint and dictate everything in her life, or she could run and hide in fear. None of these ways seem very empowering, do they?

Jesus and New Testament writers give Christians many paradoxes. And the above verse is no different. Like the text about turning the other cheek (see Matthew 5:39), Romans 12:21 instructs God's people not to bow down to, hide from, or return evil for evil, but to conquer it by doing good. Amazingly enough, it works! And, as a bonus, it will not only stop evil (and evil doers) in its (their) tracks but will relieve the flesh-filled human desire of revenge.

What a glorious day it would be if, instead of taking revenge for or hiding from evil, every daughter of the King faced the dark beast head on. Neither cowering in fear nor wallowing in self-pity, God's girls can count on His power to step boldly, repay evil with a kindness, and move on. What a paradox! What a Godsend!

Morning – A SACRIFICE OF PRAISE

"Call upon Me in the day of trouble; I will deliver you, and you shall glorify Me."
PSALM 50:15 NKJV

There are times in life when our faith wavers and we're not sure what we believe anymore. It's easy to trust God when everything in life is going well or when you've experienced a miracle. Maybe a loved one has been healed of a disease. Or maybe you've just witnessed the miracle of birth. Or had a mountaintop experience with God in His creation. It's easier to trust God when you can see the tangible evidence that He is working in your life.

But what about when life is dark? What about when a loved one isn't healed or financial burdens are wreaking havoc in your life? Is God still there?

In Hebrews 13:15 (NIV), God's Word tells us, "Through Jesus, therefore, let us continually offer to God a sacrifice of praise—the fruit of lips that openly profess his name." To sacrifice in worship means to have faith in God even when you don't feel like it. Even when you can't see Him anymore. The only way we can do that is through the power of Christ working in our lives in each moment. Because of the cross, we can rise above our circumstances and trust that the God of heaven has purpose for everything that comes our way. We are able to look at situations from God's perspective and trust Him no matter what.

Evening – SINGING TREES

*Let the fields be jubilant, and everything in them; let all
the trees of the forest sing for joy. Let all creation rejoice
before the LORD, for he comes, he comes to judge the earth.*
PSALM 96:12–13 NIV

What are your favorite worship songs? Are they slow and soft, or fast and bright? Do they bring peace or excitement? What would you do if your favorite song was performed by a chorus of trees?

It would certainly make for an interesting service. No one would sleep through that one.

But the interesting thing about this idea from Psalm 96 is not just the singing trees and fields. It's why they are so joyful that seems intriguing. They are rejoicing before the Lord because He is coming to judge the earth.

Judging doesn't sound like much fun. Judging sounds like something that might be followed by the word *sentence*, *punishment*, or *penalty*. And there's nothing joyful about any of that.

But the writer of this psalm is rejoicing in this event because of two things he is sure of: (1) his place before the Creator of the earth and (2) the truth that God is a just and righteous judge.

Are you sure of these two things? Do you trust God to judge fairly? Could you sing with joy about your judgment to come? If you answer no, what can you do today to start trusting God more? What do you need to do to be sure of your position before God?

Morning – DAUGHTER

And He said to her, "Daughter, your faith has made you well;
go in peace and be healed of your affliction."
MARK 5:34 NASB

The woman in this passage had suffered greatly from an affliction that made her ceremonially unclean; she was an outcast, not able to participate in society. In an act of desperation, she pushed through the thick crowd to Jesus and touched His garments. When Jesus turned around and asked who had touched Him, she fell in fear and trembling at His feet and told her whole story. This woman had probably been in shameful hiding for many years and now, in front of a large crowd, recounted her humiliating story. Probably some of the spectators were repulsed by her story, and yet Jesus, in front of the whole crowd, called her "daughter." Can you imagine how it must have felt to this rejected and shamed woman to hear herself called "daughter"—a term of belonging and love?

You also have been adopted and called a daughter of God. Don't hide your shame and struggles from Him. In circumstances where you can hardly stand up under the weight of your burden, fall at His feet as this woman did. You will not be rejected or shamed by Him. He calls you daughter. He loves you and is able to heal you.

Evening – PRAISE TO THE WOMEN!

After this, Jesus traveled about from one town and village to another,
proclaiming the good news of the kingdom of God. . . . These women
were helping to support them out of their own means.
LUKE 8:1, 3 NIV

When a coworker at her building trades job commented, "You're just a woman," Kristin got mad. Though she sold power tools, she was terrified of them because of every careless customer who came to the store with digits missing.

But Kristin couldn't be afraid of the noisy power tools that could cut 4x6x8 posts easier than slicing butter with a warm knife.

A few months later, when the teacher took attendance at Kristin's college shop class, he remarked, "Out of twenty-one students, only five are men! What impressive projects you ladies are building!"

A chessboard made with three kinds of beautiful wood. Music boxes. Jewelry cases. A rustic dining room table.

Kristin created shelving for her home office with edges rounded on a router table. She fell in love with tools. She celebrated by buying a compound miter saw.

In Jesus' time, women had few rights and little importance. Yet Jesus included them in His ministry: the women learned from Master Rabbi Jesus; they helped support the ministry. They fed the followers with meals from scratch. When Jesus disappeared from the tomb, the disciples doubted, but the women were the first to see the risen Jesus, and they believed Him to be the Messiah.

Though some may say, "You're only a woman," think of Jesus' take instead: "You're important enough to share in My kingdom!"

DAY 258

Morning – LISTENING CLOSELY

I will listen to what God the Lord says.
PSALM 85:8 NIV

There is an old hymn called "Speak to My Heart" that should resonate in a believer's life. "Speak to my heart Lord Jesus. Speak that my soul may hear." Doesn't that define our prayer life? In faith, we talk with the Lord, and He wants to answer and wants us to listen.

In today's hurried world, with all of the surrounding noise, it's easy to ignore the still, small voice nudging us in the right direction. We fire off requests, expect microwave-instant answers, and get aggravated when nothing happens. Our human nature demands a response. How will we know what to do/think/say if we do not listen? When we are "yielded and still," then He can "speak to my heart."

Listening is a learned art, too often forgotten in the busyness of a day. The alarm clock buzzes, we hit the floor running, toss out a prayer, maybe sing a song of praise, grab our car keys, and are out the door. If only we'd slow down and let the heavenly Father's words sink into our spirits, what a difference we might see in our prayer life. This day, stop. Listen. See what God has in store for you.

Evening – QUIET TIME

He says, "Be still, and know that I am God."
PSALM 46:10 NIV

As you were growing up, how many times were you told to sit or stand still? And honestly, they were "tells" even if the adult added a "please." It may have seemed like you were merely being asked to be quiet, or not fidget, or not bump into another child, or not kick the seat in front of you. Could we as children have misread these dictates to be still? Were we actually being told to calm ourselves so that we might hear or learn something important rather than just as a control of our outward behavior?

Our earthly parents told us to be still just as our heavenly Father has instructed us to be still. When we calm ourselves physically and mentally, we are better able to focus our minds and listen with our hearts. We become open to hearing the Lord's direction for our lives. We allow ourselves to feel the peace that comes with the presence of the Holy Spirit within us.

Quiet time is a precious commodity. With mobile electronic devices, it seems we are constantly communicating via phone, text, or social media. Consider making time to put the electronics down and give yourself the gift of being still.

Morning – GREAT EXPECTATIONS

Now there was a man in Jerusalem called Simeon, who was righteous
and devout. He was waiting for the consolation of Israel, and the Holy
Spirit was on him. It had been revealed to him by the Holy Spirit that
he would not die before he had seen the Lord's Messiah.
LUKE 2:25–26 NIV

Simeon was an old man. He was righteous and devout. But surely there were other old men hanging around the temple who were righteous and devout. Of all the Pharisees and Sadducees nearby, of all the truly devoted, religious people of that day, why Simeon? Why did God choose this man to welcome His Son into the temple and proclaim His coming to all who would listen?

One key phrase offers a clue: "He was waiting for the consolation of Israel." In other words, Simeon knew God's promises, and he was looking for good things to happen.

What a lesson we can learn from this old saint! God has promised many good things to His people. But often, we mope around, stressed and anxious, worried that things won't go well for us. Why do we do that? Like Simeon, we should wake up each morning looking for God to do great things. We should greet each new day expecting God to work, to fulfill His promises.

Evening – GOD'S GOT A PLAN

"Here is a boy with five small barley loaves and two
small fish, but how far will they go among so many?"
JOHN 6:9 NIV

So often in life we want to know the whole plan up front. And if God doesn't give us the plan, we start making it up on our own. We get ten steps down the road and decide what can and can't be done. We think we are limited by our resources of time, talent, and finances.

But as today's verse shows, Jesus simply needs us to trust Him with a little and then let Him work. He doesn't need us to do His work, but He allows us to be part of His process. In the story, not only was there plenty to eat, but there were leftovers besides. These people had a physical need for food, and He gave them spiritual food as well.

Spiritually, Jesus gives us everything we need to be satisfied and then even more, so it spills over onto others. When we seek God and put His kingdom first, He provides for our physical and spiritual needs. He is our satisfaction. He is the ultimate answer.

Surrender to Him and see how He works beyond your limited thinking. He always exceeds our expectations.

DAY 260

Morning – ANCHOR

This hope we have as an anchor of the soul, both sure and steadfast, and which enters the Presence behind the veil, where the forerunner has entered for us, even Jesus, having become High Priest forever according to the order of Melchizedek.
HEBREWS 6:19–20 NKJV

We have this hope, not "we will" or "we had." As children of God we possess Christ as the anchor of our souls. The "veil" referred to was a physical, thick curtain that separated the holy of holies from the rest of the tabernacle. Only once a year could the high priest enter after being cleansed. Christ tore that veil in two with His sinless life, death, and resurrection. He opened the gates to a relationship with His Father. This is the good news that we now have a Redeemer who has brought us in relationship with the Father. Not a relationship that brings superhuman powers, but the defeat of sin. We can now enter the Lord's presence and, because of Christ, be seen as blameless. None of us has led a blameless life, which is why God sent His Son to do so for us. The debt that God demanded He also paid. What wondrous love is this that He would pay what we owe!

In Christ, we face each day redeemed. Have you taken the time to praise Him?

Evening – NO GREATER LOVE

For God so loved the world that he gave his one and only Son, that whoever believes in him shall not perish but have eternal life. For God did not send his Son into the world to condemn the world, but to save the world through him.
JOHN 3:16–17 NIV

Probably the most memorized passage of scripture, John 3:16 is the gospel in one sentence. We memorize it at an early age so our ears become accustomed to hearing it. But have you allowed it to completely change your life?

God didn't send Jesus to condemn us! He came to save us by giving up His life for ours. John 15:13 (NLT) says, "There is no greater love than to lay down one's life for one's friends." That is the very foundation of Christianity. As C. S. Lewis said, "Christianity, if false, is of no importance, and if true, of infinite importance. The only thing it cannot be is moderately important."

The next time you hear a child recite John 3:16 or listen as this verse is being read aloud, allow the words to truly seep into your soul once again. Thank God for His amazing gift of life and His unfailing love for us.

Morning – UNCHANGING MASTER

Jesus Christ is the same yesterday, today, and forever.
HEBREWS 13:8 NLT

It's said that the one thing we can count on is change—within and without. This is especially true for women because our bodies are constantly in flux, ruled by our hormones as they work to maintain a twenty-eight-day cycle. But that's just the beginning. A woman who experiences pregnancy embarks upon another process as a new life grows within. Then, once baby is born, mom's breasts begin producing nourishment for her offspring. When the child is weaned, her body goes back somewhat to its former self and the cycles begin all over again. After a handful of decades, her body takes on an entirely different pattern. Hot flashes and even more bizarre mood swings become the rule of the day as her estrogen decreases and testosterone increases.

Needless to say, for a woman, it is sometimes difficult to determine from one day to the next who she'll wake up as or what will rule her day—her hormones or her heart. Amid these seemingly endless fluctuations, it's good to know there's one constant: Jesus Christ. No matter what cycle your body is in—or out of—you can count on the anchor of your faith in the never-changing Jesus. In Him you have a Master of waves and wind, one who can calm your storms within and without. Allowing Him to rule your day, heart, body, and mind, is a sure course to a safe haven of peace.

Evening – GOD EQUIPS THE CALLED

I will instruct you and teach you in the way you should go; I will counsel you.
PSALM 32:8 NIV

As Patricia approached retirement, she asked the Lord for direction. She expected Him to give her peace about spending more time with her grandkids—which He did. What she hadn't expected was to feel the Lord leading her to write Christian fiction.

Patricia had done a fair amount of technical writing throughout her career. And she had been successful in writing grants and newsletters as a volunteer. What she didn't have was expertise writing inspirational stories.

Patricia didn't understand why the Lord was asking her to do something outside her comfort zone. Could she do it? After talking with her family, Patricia enrolled in online writing classes and joined a Christian writing organization. Three years, four classes, and five workshops later, Patricia received a writing contract. She still lacked confidence in her ability to write for Him, but Patricia was confident that her writing journey was being led by the Lord.

When Patricia saw her work in a bookstore, she felt a peace that could only come from God. Patricia hadn't been equipped to write for Him when He called her. With God as her counselor, she had been able to develop the skills needed.

DAY 262

Morning – THE LORD GIVES VICTORY

"See, God has come to save me. I will trust in him and not be afraid.
The Lord God is my strength and my song; he has given me victory."
ISAIAH 12:2 NLT

The first time we see the phrase "the Lord is my strength and my song" is in the book of Exodus in the song Miriam and the women danced to as Moses and Miriam and the children of Israel sang. The reason for their rejoicing was their deliverance from Pharaoh and his army. When the Israelites left Egypt, they came to the Red Sea. They realized the army of Egypt had followed them. Then the Lord opened the Red Sea, and the Israelites crossed on dry land. The Egyptians followed. But once the last Israelite was safe on the other side, the Lord closed the waters over the Egyptians who had followed them. It was a great deliverance, and the people celebrated.

Later, Isaiah not only predicted God's judgment on the people of Israel because of their sin and desire to go their own way, he also predicted that God would send salvation and deliverance once their time of judgment was complete. As God had delivered the nation of Israel in ancient times, so would He deliver His people in the future. All would know His name; all would trust Him and not be afraid; all would find strength in praise and rejoicing. And therein lies true victory.

Evening – TRUST GOD, BE BLESSED

"But blessed are those who trust in the Lord and
have made the Lord their hope and confidence."
JEREMIAH 17:7 NLT

The believer's hope is founded on Jesus Christ alone, for He alone was able to pay the sin price for all mankind. Implicit trust in God's provision should be a natural result if a person has trusted in Christ for salvation. But sadly it isn't always. In Jesus' parable of the sower, He tells of four different kinds of ground the seed falls on and compares it to sowing the seed of the gospel on human hearts.

Jesus told the parable of the wise man and the foolish man, saying all people go into one of those categories. The wise woman listens to Jesus' teachings and follows Him. Her life is built on a solid foundation so that when the storms come with the high winds and floodwaters, she will not collapse and wash away. She stands firm in the hope of the Lord. But the foolish woman is the one who hears Christ's words but doesn't obey them. Her foundation is laid on shifting sand, so that when the winds and storms come, her house collapses and she has nothing to hope for.

Determine to be the wise woman and be blessed because you place your confidence in Jesus Christ alone for salvation and a future.

Morning – SEEK PEACE

*Turn away from evil and do good. Search for peace, and work
to maintain it. The eyes of the LORD watch over those who
do right; his ears are open to their cries for help.*
PSALM 34:14–15 NLT

If something is worth searching for, it is often very valuable. Pirates search for treasure. A lady may search for just the right dress for a party or the perfect pair of shoes to match an outfit.

Children playing hide and seek search for the participant who is hiding. To find this hidden person and capture him is to win the game!

God's Word, in the psalms, tells us to search for peace. Peace is more valuable than all of the wealth on earth. To lay your head on your pillow at night and know that you are at peace with God and with those around you is a tremendous blessing. True peace is known only by the Christian. The world offers counterfeit versions, but only God can give true and lasting peace that passes all understanding. Seek peace. Search for it. Protect its presence in your life at all costs. If you are on a path that does not bring you peace, you are on the wrong path. Ask God to give you the strength to say no to the things that curtail peace in your life. Peace is essential.

Evening – A HEART OF PEACE

*Look at those who are honest and good, for a
wonderful future awaits those who love peace.*
PSALM 37:37 NLT

Before the sun came up each Friday morning, Shanna was in her car driving toward the hospital. She spent the thirty-minute drive talking to the Lord about her time there. She entered the hospital with great anticipation of what God would do in the hearts of the tiny patients in the neonatal intensive care unit. "Father, consume me with Your peace this morning, so that I am a comfort to the babies today."

As a "cuddler," she took her opportunity to comfort the tiny ones with the love and peace of God. She whispered words of encouragement, hummed songs of faith, and offered a calm and soothing peace as they rested in her arms. "It's my greatest hope that the Lord Himself will minister peace and healing to these little ones," Shanna said.

Our lives are stressful and full of day-to-day struggles. People in general are moving forward at a hurried pace, frenzied when others get in their way. God desires for His peace to strengthen you and for you, like Shanna, to share His peace with others.

DAY 264

Morning – OPEN UP!

Who is the King of glory? The LORD, strong and mighty; the LORD, invincible in battle. Open up, ancient gates! Open up, ancient doors, and let the King of glory enter.
PSALM 24:8–9 NLT

It's so easy to get focused on the things of this world. But that's how we get dragged away from Jesus, forgetting His saving grace, strength, love, and presence.

Today's verses give us an Old Testament picture of the ark, which contained God's glory, being brought into the temple. These same verses can apply to us today if we consider how much Jesus longs to be in our hearts, His temple on earth.

Jesus pleads: "Look! I stand at the door and knock. If you hear my voice and open the door, I will come in, and we will share a meal together as friends" (Revelation 3:20 NLT).

Jesus is outside the gate of your heart, waiting for you to open up your total being—mind, emotions, and will—to His saving presence. He, strong and mighty, invincible, is knocking at the door of *your* heart. He wants you, His temple, to open up your gates so He can spend time with you. Do you hear His knock? Are you willing to let Him into not just a small corner of your life but your *entire* life? He will not force His way in, for it must be your decision. He will be gentle and loving, only wanting the best for you. Will you open up?

Evening – GET ABOVE IT ALL

Set your mind on the things above, not on the things that are on earth.
COLOSSIANS 3:2 NASB

If you've ever taken a trip by airplane, you know with one glimpse from the window at thirty thousand feet how the world seems small. With your feet on the ground, you may feel small in a big world; and it's easy for the challenges of life and the circumstances from day to day to press in on you. But looking down from above the clouds, things can become clear as you have the opportunity to get above it all.

Sometimes the most difficult challenges you face play out in your head—where a struggle to control the outcome and work out the details of life can consume you. Once removed—far away from the details—you can see things from a higher perspective. Close your eyes and push out the thoughts that try to grab you and keep you tied to the things of the world.

Reach out to God and let your spirit soar. Give your concerns to Him and let Him work out the details. Rest in Him and He'll carry you above it all, every step of the way.

Morning – THE MAYPOLE

*Even the wilderness and desert will be glad in those days. The wasteland will
rejoice and blossom with spring crocuses. Yes, there will be an abundance
of flowers and singing and joy! The deserts will become as green as the
mountains of Lebanon, as lovely as Mount Carmel or the plain of Sharon.
There the LORD will display his glory, the splendor of our God.*
ISAIAH 35:1–2 NLT

Mingled with the sweet laughter of children, crepe paper streamers floated around the Maypole in Marie's kindergarten classroom. The teacher instructed them to hold gently onto the end of their streamer as they circled together around the metal support pole that tethered the whole scene together. Streamers twisted and twirled between them as they concentrated on their paper connection to it all, some arms held high, some lower, as requested. Then reverse, pay attention, twirl the other direction. Open windows blew in the hope of spring.

Recalling the scene, the colors floated somehow in her mind, blending perfectly with the aroma of drying finger paintings and cookies that someone's mother had baked. That day would stick in Marie's mind as one of joy and hope for years to come. She thanked God for moments like this one that pointed her to the great hope of Christ and now reminded her of the unfading hope that awaits her in eternity.

Evening – LIFE IS SHORT

So teach us to number our days, that we may gain a heart of wisdom.
PSALM 90:12 NKJV

A pastor tried to illustrate the brevity of life to his congregation. "Think of a straight line stretching into infinity on either end. Anywhere on the line, place a dot smaller than a pinprick. That is your life, your 'threescore and ten' years Moses spoke of."

James 4:14 (KJV) describes our life as "a vapour, that appeareth for a little time, and then vanisheth away." In reality, given our finite minds trying to wrap around an infinite concept, these examples don't really come close to describing the brevity of life. But in spite of that, God does have a purpose for each one of us, a purpose He designed uniquely for each individual.

As a new year stretches ahead, many tend to procrastinate, thinking that time stretches into enough time to accomplish their goals and still "enjoy life." But Moses likens our lives to grass that springs up fresh in the morning, but by evening it dries up and dies (Psalm 90:5–6). What seems a long time to us is really very little in the eyes of an eternal God. No wonder Moses' prayer was for wisdom to live a fulfilling and purposeful life in the brief time allotted to mankind. We would be wise to make this a daily prayer as we walk forward.

Morning – GOD'S GIFT OF WISDOM

*"Give me now wisdom and knowledge, that I may go out and come
in before this people, for who can rule this great people of Yours?"*
2 CHRONICLES 1:10 NASB

Dani suffered a miscarriage and a deep depression. Then she and her husband were blessed with demanding jobs, children—and bills. Life happened, and because of stress and busyness, Dani let her passion for Christ dwindle. She found herself consumed with diapers, dishes, and deadlines.

During a sermon that convicted her, she prayed for the desire to spend time with Jesus. Slowly it came, along with confusion about how to best fit Him into her demanding days.

But as Dani confessed her weakness, frailty, and disobedience to God and asked Him for fresh ideas, she felt peace as her loving heavenly Father whispered to her, "I'm so glad that you want to spend time with Me. I love it when you do." And He gave her a few creative ideas about how to seek Him in the midst of motherhood.

Now, Dani seeks the Lord daily—whether praying while she's in the carpool line, studying the Word during naptimes or music lessons, or staying up a few minutes after her children go to sleep. Dani prays that God will continue to give her a passion for Him, so that she can impart that love to her children.

Evening – EARNEST PRAYER

*If My people who are called by My name will humble themselves,
and pray and seek My face, and turn from their wicked ways, then I
will hear from heaven, and will forgive their sin and heal their land.*
2 CHRONICLES 7:14 NKJV

Another translation specifies how believers are to humble themselves and pray. We are to "seek, crave, and require of necessity" God's face (AMPC).

Have you ever watched children playing hide-and-seek? They look everywhere for the one they are after in the game! They put their whole hearts into it. We should *seek* God relentlessly.

Crave. The word brings about the thought of "fair food." Just inside the state fair entrance gate, tantalizing smells entice us. Cravings for pronto pups, funnel cakes, sweet cotton candy, or caramel apples are almost unavoidable. Our desire for God's presence in our lives ought to be strong and irresistible.

Necessity. What is it that you just can't live without? The cell phone with all its cool apps? That specially blended coffee each morning? Our hearts need God for survival. He is our one and only true necessity.

When you pray, call out to God with your whole heart. Prayer must be more than an afterthought to close each day, as eyelids grow heavy and sleep wins the battle. Seek God. Crave and require His face. Turn toward Him. He stands ready to hear, to forgive, and to heal.

Morning – THE WAY OUT

No temptation has overtaken you except what is common to mankind. And God is faithful; he will not let you be tempted beyond what you can bear. But when you are tempted, he will also provide a way out so that you can endure it.
1 CORINTHIANS 10:13 NIV

Everyone faces temptation. Scripture says that no one escapes it, and all become its victims (Romans 3:23). But don't be discouraged. God provides a way out.

Believers learn to endure and stand up to temptation by God's grace. When they rely on the power that comes from the Holy Spirit, then God provides them with strength to resist. Jesus said that this willpower comes by watchfulness and prayer. "Watch and pray so that you will not fall into temptation. The spirit is willing, but the flesh is weak" (Matthew 26:41 NIV).

As hard as people try, temptation sometimes wins. God has a plan for that too. He sent His Son, Jesus, into the world to take the punishment for the sins of everyone who believes in Him. Not only did Jesus suffer the consequences of sin but also through His sacrifice He provided God with a way to forgive sinfulness and to promise believers eternal life.

Watch and pray today that you don't fall into temptation, but if you do, then remember this: sin might win in the moment, but God's grace and forgiveness are forever.

Evening – WOMAN VERSUS THE DEVIL

Resist the devil, and he will flee from you.
JAMES 4:7 NLT

Satan is often depicted as a dark creature with spiny ears and pointy tail. But the Bible describes Lucifer as a beautiful angel, his mind full of wisdom and his brightness captivating. He is portrayed as an alluring work of art, not a monster. And that's what makes him dangerous.

Like the ring in Tolkien's Lord of the Rings trilogy, the offerings of Satan are attractive and appeal to the sense of power. Arthur Jackson wrote, "[Satan] conceals [his] hook in a godly bait, and like a skillful angler, he knows how to use the temptation best suited to our palate."

The devil is so subtle we often don't recognize the attack. He whispers thoughts and follows up with their justification. He includes emotional and biblical "proof," just as Satan said to Eve, "Has God not said. . . ," and used the same tactic to tempt Christ, saying, "It is written. . ."

The temptation can come in the form of begrudging your spouse, criticizing others, envying other women, or allowing bitterness to take root in your heart. These aren't just innocent flaws. These are satanic tools to hold you back from the abundant life and your full potential in kingdom work.

Ephesians 6:11 (NKJV) says, "Put on the whole armor of God, that you may be able to stand against the wiles of the devil." No matter what logical fallacies Satan whispers, be steadfast in prayer and Bible study. Seek the truth and you will find it.

Morning – PRAYING FOR UNBELIEVERS

"Make supplication to the Lord, for there has been enough of God's thunder and hail; and I will let you go, and you shall stay no longer."
EXODUS 9:28 NASB

Hannah frowned as she boarded the plane. The flight looked full, and she was tired. She wanted to read, drink a Diet Coke, and not talk to anyone.

Then the Holy Spirit reminded her of her pastor's words the previous Sunday: "Ask God to give you opportunities to share His love with others, wherever you go."

Hannah took her seat toward the back of the plane. "I'm available, Lord," she whispered.

Her seatmates included two people who didn't speak English. During the three-hour flight, Hannah prayed silently for them, smiling occasionally, and when the seat belt sign went off, she walked to the back of the plane.

After using the restroom, Hannah heard sniffling. A flight attendant sat in the jump seat next to the galley kitchen, crying softly. Hannah paused. "Are you okay?" she asked the woman.

"Not really," the attendant said, shaking her head. "I just got bad news before the plane took off."

"Can I pray for you?"

"I don't really believe in God, but I guess it couldn't hurt. . . ."

Hannah smiled, bowed her head, and quietly prayed on behalf of her new acquaintance.

Evening – PRAYER TOUCHES GOD

He was a devout, God-fearing man. . . . He gave generously to the poor and prayed regularly to God.
ACTS 10:2 NLT

In the book of Acts, a centurion named Cornelius received a vision from God. Though a Gentile, this man loved God, praying and fasting regularly. While he prayed, an angel of the Lord told Cornelius that God heard and honored his prayers. Accordingly, God instructed the centurion to go talk to Peter, God's servant.

Peter, having received a vision that God would cleanse and accept anyone whom the Jews deemed "unclean," agreed to meet this Gentile despite Jewish law. Cornelius invited his Gentile neighbors, friends, and family members when he met Peter in Caesarea. Realizing God orchestrated the meeting, Peter preached the gospel to Cornelius and all who joined him, and the entire group of Gentiles received the Holy Spirit (Acts 10:44–48).

Jesus takes note of a praying, giving heart like Cornelius had. Denominations mean little, while a contrite, teachable spirit touches God. Cornelius was a good, God-fearing man who needed to hear about salvation through Christ. So God honored his prayers and led him to the preacher—while teaching the preacher a thing or two at the same time.

Have you hesitated to share your faith with someone you think unseemly or beyond your realm of comfort? Begin now. Look what happened when Peter did.

Morning – ALL ABOUT ME

*My frame was not hidden from You, when I was made in secret, and skillfully
wrought in the lowest parts of the earth. Your eyes saw my substance,
being yet unformed. And in Your book they all were written, the days
fashioned for me, when as yet there were none of them.*
PSALM 139:15–16 NKJV

Have you ever considered how matchless you are in this world? No one is created in exactly the same way. We each have our own personalities, gifts, ideas, and dreams. C. S. Lewis wrote, "Why else were individuals created, but that God, loving all infinitely, should love each differently?"

Accepting our individuality is a lifetime lesson since there will be many times we will want to compare ourselves to others. But God has shown His love through the unique manner in which He creates and guides our lives. We are distinct, one from another. His presence in our lives keeps us on a path He created just for us. It's hard to fathom that kind of love.

With that knowledge, we can learn to love ourselves and others with Christlike love and enrich our relationship with Him. Ever-growing, ever-learning, we can trust the heavenly Father to mature us into what He created us to be: "Just ME."

Evening – KNOWING WHO YOU ARE IN CHRIST

*We are made right with God by placing our faith in Jesus Christ.
And this is true for everyone who believes, no matter who we are.*
ROMANS 3:22 NLT

Sometimes we measure our value by "what we do" (our work or our talents), but this should never be. Who you are is more than a name. More than a face. More than the job/work you do. You are uniquely created, a true one of a kind. You are God's kid. His. Loved. Cherished. Blessed.

What does the Bible say about you? You are: a new creation. A royal priesthood. A holy nation. The righteousness of God. A holy temple. A member of the body. A citizen of heaven. Saved by faith. Raised up by Him. The aroma of Christ. Filled with heavenly gifts. Delivered from the domain of darkness. Capable of doing all things through Him who strengthens you. On and on the descriptions go.

Wow! When you read all of those things, you begin to see yourself as God sees you. You're not "just" another person. You're a child of the one true King, and He delights in you! Today, take a close look in the mirror. Don't stare at your reflection in the usual way. Get God's perspective. Then begin to see yourself the way He does.

DAY 270

Morning – JOY VS. HAPPINESS

And the disciples were filled with joy, and with the Holy Ghost.
ACTS 13:52 KJV

There is a popular children's song about joy often sung in Sunday school or church. It goes like this: *"I've got the joy, joy, joy, joy down in my heart to stay!"* While it was written for children, it bears a wonderful message for all of us.

The difference between happiness and joy is that joy *stays*. If you are a believer in Christ, He resides in your heart. No matter what your circumstances, you can maintain a joy that is deep in your heart. You are a child of God and He will never leave you. You know you have the promise of eternal life. Happiness, on the other hand, is an emotion that comes and goes within minutes. Ever heard a baby crying loudly, but when he or she gets what she wants—a bottle, the mother, or a toy—the crying ceases immediately? Sadness has turned to contentedness. Temporary! Take the object of the baby's affection away and the tears return. As adults, we are not that different from these young ones. The breakup of a dating relationship or news that we are going to have to move due to a job transfer can zap us of our happiness. Not so with joy! Joy remains. Peace and joy go hand in hand. The Christian never has to lack either.

Evening – JOY FOR THE JOURNEY

The LORD is my strength and my shield; my heart trusts in him, and he helps me. My heart leaps for joy, and with my song I praise him.
PSALM 28:7 NIV

There are times when joy seems impossible. When you're going through a rough season, for instance, or when you're face to face with a proverbial Goliath. The enemy of your soul would like nothing more than to rob you of your joy. He's skilled at tripping you up, creating havoc.

But, guess what? It's possible to praise—to be joyful—even in the middle of the battle. There's a great story in the Old Testament about a man named Jehoshaphat who was facing a mighty opposition—an army, no less! He sent the Levites (the praise and worshipers) to the front lines. In other words, he led the way into the battle with praise on the lips of his warriors. And guess what? They prevailed!

The same is true in our lives. We must lead the way with praise. If we will maintain the joy in our hearts, even in the midst of our battles, we will be triumphant in the end. So, don't let the enemy steal your joy, even if you're walking through a difficult season. There are plenty of victories ahead if you don't give up.

Morning – AWRY

"For My thoughts are not your thoughts, nor are your ways My ways,"
declares the Lord. "For as the heavens are higher than the earth, so are
My ways higher than your ways, and My thoughts than your thoughts."
Isaiah 55:8–9 NKJV

There was so much Mary did not understand. The more she grew in her faith, the less she realized she knew. She had dear friends going through the terrible tragedy of losing their college daughter. A neighbor was dying of cancer just two doors down. Just waiting to die. A friend's rental home was bought by the city, citing eminent domain. His political views didn't line up with the city leader, and he was given a fraction of what the house was worth in the sale.

The list of injustices and things impossible to understand just kept growing.

One clear spring evening Mary looked up at the stars. The vastness is always striking on a clear night. She thought how small she was in the scope of it all and how God cares about it all. He not only cares, He intervenes in ways that she could not. Somehow, He knows what is best even when it all seems awry. He would take care of her and her friends, somehow, through it all.

Evening – TRUST AND OBEY

That they may set their hope in God, and not forget
the works of God, but keep His commandments.
Psalm 78:7 NKJV

From the time we were children, we knew the song: "Trust and obey, for there's no other way to be happy in Jesus than to trust and obey."

It's one thing to talk about trust, another to live it. And here's the problem: if you don't trust God, you probably won't obey His commands. So, these two things go hand in hand. Don't believe it? Here's an example: imagine the Lord asked you to take a huge step of faith, something completely outside of your comfort zone. You would likely hesitate. But would you eventually take the step, even if it made no sense to you? If you trusted God—if you had seen Him work time and time again in your life—you would eventually take the step of faith, even if it made no sense. Why? Because you trust that He's got your best interest at heart. (And you've probably figured out that He has something pretty remarkable up His sleeve!)

God is trustworthy. He won't let you down. When you settle that issue in your heart once and for all, obedience is a natural response.

DAY 272

Morning – GOD'S PROVISION

And my God will supply all your needs
according to His riches in glory in Christ Jesus.
PHILIPPIANS 4:19 NASB

Sometimes the littlest words in our language pack a lot of meaning into them. *All* is one of those words. Three letters encompass the total extent of the whole. Everything is in the word *all*.

In the letter to the Philippians, Paul is wrapping up a discussion of how God had used the church to provide for Paul's need while he was in prison, even though many of them didn't have much to give. Paul spoke out of experience when he told them God would supply all their financial needs because they gave sacrificially to help another person with a greater need.

But God meeting their financial need isn't all that is encompassed in the meaning Paul intended to convey when he chose this particular word. When Jesus taught this principle to His disciples, Luke recorded it in his Gospel: "Give, and it will be given to you: good measure, pressed down, shaken together, and running over will be put into your bosom. For with the same measure that you use, it will be measured back to you" (6:38 NKJV). Jesus indicated that whatever a person has to give, when they give it, they will receive as they have given. Emotional, spiritual, physical, material—whatever the need, God will supply it abundantly, "pressed down, shaken together, and running over."

Evening – HOW GOD MEETS NEEDS

And my God shall supply all your need
according to His riches in glory by Christ Jesus.
PHILIPPIANS 4:19 NKJV

Does God meet all your needs, or do you sometimes wonder if this verse is true? While our needs may be financial as they were for Paul and the Philippians, God's "riches in glory" are not limited to food, clothing, and shelter. We also need security, love, endurance, worthwhile goals, satisfying accomplishments, etc. Would God's promise extend to emotional cravings as well?

God knows that our deepest soul need is to know and love Him and to learn to be satisfied with Him. He has to be *enough*! To get us to that place, He may deprive us of things. He cares about our character more than our comfort. When we lack or long for things we consider vital, it can drive us to Him. A wife may pray for marriage harmony and start fighting more with her spouse. God centers on her *need* to deal with her selfish desire to dominate her husband. When she lets God prune out *her* faults, her *husband* will improve!

We may ask for healing, but our health worsens—weakness and disabilities highlight our need to depend on God. Personal failure can wean us from pride; sorrow and loss open us to God's comfort and increase our intimacy with Him. In other words, what God knows we need may not be what we want! God wisely supplies our needs not our greeds.

Morning – WOE BE GONE

*How long, O Lord? Will You forget me forever? How long will You hide Your face
from me? . . . But I have trusted in Your mercy; my heart shall rejoice in Your
salvation. I will sing to the Lord, because He has dealt bountifully with me.*
PSALM 13:1, 5–6 NKJV

One misconception our society has about Christianity is that Christians have to be happy all the time, no matter the circumstances. Is it biblical to question God? Is it biblical to mourn?

We see throughout scripture mourning, frustration, righteous anger, and tears. The shortest verse in the Bible is "Jesus wept" (John 11:35). Our goal as a child of God is to glorify our Savior, not wear a plastered smile around town. Being sorrowful or frustrated is not sin, but how you handle these emotions can lead to sin.

In Psalms, David asks the Lord many times if He has forsaken him. We watch David question the Lord, then explain his troubles, pain, and circumstances. Always near the end of a psalm, David revisits God's great character and works. Loving-kindness, salvation, bountiful. . .he reflects, remembers, and trusts in God. We must do the same when God appears distant. Reflect on the God of the scriptures and the wonders He has done in your life.

Evening – BITTERNESS

*"Don't call me Naomi," she told them. "Call me Mara, because the Almighty has made my
life very bitter. I went away full, but the Lord has brought me back empty. Why call me
Naomi? The Lord has afflicted me; the Almighty has brought misfortune upon me."*
RUTH 1:20–21 NIV

God has unseen beauty hidden in the midst of trials. Naomi, whose name means pleasant, poured out her sorrow to the women of Bethlehem, her hometown, in the scripture reference above. She lost her husband, two sons, and her home for a second time. However, God shows throughout history that He heals both physically and spiritually. He gives beauty for ashes and joy for the spirit in distress. For Naomi the answer was right beside her: her loyal daughter-in-law Ruth. Naomi, this old and tired woman, did not realize what happened would be used by God in His great rescue plan for humanity. In her confusion and despair, she was bitter, but El Shaddai, God Almighty, had everything under control. He used the death of Naomi's sons and her return to Bethlehem to bring Ruth and Boaz together. Otherwise God would have used another family to be the ancestors of Jesus. God once again brought pleasantness to Naomi by giving her a new home and hope. Although she did not personally see the blessing of kingship that came to Boaz's great-grandson David, Naomi was an important part of God's great plan for the little town of Bethlehem.

Morning – THINK ON THESE THINGS

*Finally, brothers and sisters, whatever is true, whatever is noble, whatever
is right, whatever is pure, whatever is lovely, whatever is admirable—
if anything is excellent or praiseworthy—think about such things.*

PHILIPPIANS 4:8 NIV

Single-minded. Such an interesting word! When you're single-minded, you are hyperfocused on the goal in front of you. Your gaze doesn't shift to the right or left. Picture a target shooter, aiming at her mark. She's got the bow and arrow in hand, but she's not looking at them. No, her eyes are fixed on one thing. . .that center mark. She's determined to hit it. That's you, unwilling to deviate for a second, lest you miss your opportunity. One of God's greatest desires is for His daughters to hyperfocus on good things: things that are noble, right, pure, lovely, and admirable. No more doubts, fears, or insecurities. From now on, single-minded aiming at a lovely target. Think on such things.

Evening – QUEEN OF THE HILL

*Though the fig tree may not blossom, nor fruit be on the vines; though the
labor of the olive may fail, and the fields yield no food; though the flock
may be cut off from the fold, and there be no herd in the stalls—
yet I will rejoice in the LORD, I will joy in the God of my salvation.
The LORD God is my strength; He will make my feet like deer's
feet, and He will make me walk on my high hills.*

HABAKKUK 3:17–19 NKJV

You haven't had a raise in five years. Your love life is dismal at best. Your kids aren't living up to your expectations. Your sister is ill. You've just totaled your brand-new car. Your mom recently passed away. And you don't have enough money for groceries this week. Your spirits are lower than low. What's a woman to do? It's simple. Change your lament of "Woe is me" to a song of joyful praise to God. Jump up and down; start skipping as you rejoice in your Lord. And before you know it, His strength will begin welling up within you. He'll make your heart truly sing. Instead of your being buried by your misfortunes, you'll be standing on top of them. Because of God and His amazing power, you are now queen of the hill. Your footing is sure. You have conquered your calamities! You are no longer a victim but a victor! Praise your Lord!

Morning – WHEN YOU CAN'T PRAY

*And the Holy Spirit helps us in our weakness. For example, we don't
know what God wants us to pray for. But the Holy Spirit prays for us
with groanings that cannot be expressed in words. And the Father who
knows all hearts knows what the Spirit is saying, for the Spirit
pleads for us believers in harmony with God's own will.*
ROMANS 8:26–27 NLT

Sometimes we literally cannot pray. The Holy Spirit takes over on such occasions. Go before God; enter into His presence in a quiet spot where there will not be interruptions. And just be still before the Lord. When your heart is broken, the Holy Spirit will intercede for you. When you have lost someone or something precious, the Holy Spirit will go before the Father on your behalf. When you are weak, the comforter will ask the Father to strengthen you. When you are confused and anxious about a decision that looms before you, the counselor will seek God's best for you. You are not alone. You are a precious daughter of the Living God. And when Christ ascended back into heaven, He did not leave you on this earth to forge through the wilderness on your own. He sent a comforter, a counselor, the Holy Ghost, the Spirit of Truth. When you don't know what to pray, the Bible promises that the Spirit has you covered.

Evening – LORD, HELP!

*"LORD, help!" they cried in their trouble, and he saved them from
their distress. He calmed the storm to a whisper and stilled the waves.
What a blessing was that stillness as he brought them safely into harbor!*
PSALM 107:28–30 NLT

Prayers do not have to be eloquent or majestic. There are no requirements for them to be long and labored. The only thing necessary is that you communicate with God. Your words can be heart-wrenching—rising deep from the very bottom of your soul—or calm and gentle as a whisper. However you speak to Him, you can know that He hears you and will answer.

Samuel Morse, the father of modern communication, said, "The only gleam of hope, and I cannot underrate it, is from confidence in God. When I look upward it calms any apprehension for the future, and I seem to hear a voice saying: 'If I clothe the lilies of the field, shall I not also clothe you?' Here is my strong confidence, and I will wait patiently for the direction of Providence."

The answer to your prayer does not depend on you. Your expressions of your heart spoken to your Father bring Him onto the scene for any reason you need Him.

DAY 276

Morning – GOD, THE ULTIMATE FASHIONISTA

Therefore, as God's chosen people, holy and dearly loved, clothe yourselves
with compassion, kindness, humility, gentleness and patience.
COLOSSIANS 3:12 NIV

Yesterday was the first day of fall. In some regions, the air will soon become quite frosty, and old fall jackets and sweaters will be making their way out of closets and drawers. Although such garments are one sure way to physically protect any woman from the colder weather, what can she wear to keep herself spiritually warm?

Colossians 3:12 contains a God-tailored list for His daughter. She is to clothe herself with the exact same characteristics her brother Jesus exuded when He walked this earth. First, she is to don compassion and kindness, the same emotions that moved Jesus to heal so many of the suffering. Then to apply humility, as Jesus did, being humble all the way to the cross. Next, she is to dress in the same gentleness Jesus displayed with the little children. Then to wear and bear His inexhaustible patience. And finally, on top of all of these great virtues, she is to "put on love, which binds them all together in perfect unity" (Colossians 3:14 NIV).

It's great to have nice, warm clothes in the house. But it may be time to get the spiritual garments out of the mothballs and try them on for size—today and every day.

Evening – SET ASIDE FOR GOD

And they made the plate of the holy crown of pure gold, and wrote upon
it a writing, like to the engravings of a signet, HOLINESS TO THE LORD.
EXODUS 39:30 KJV

The Israelites were on their way to the land promised to them by God in the book of Exodus. During their journey across the desert, they were continually brought to recognize that this God wanted them to personally know Him. God taught them how they should live differently from the surrounding nations: to be just, merciful, humble. He gave them instructions on how to set up a place of worship and on the activities and attire of the priests, so that the people could be in fellowship with God—as they were created to be originally. One aspect of the priests' clothing was a headpiece on which was written: HOLINESS TO GOD. It was a seal, like that of a king, which showed they belonged to the Creator and Lord of all. God also wants this for His children today. The image of Israel as set apart and of the priests as even further set apart symbolizes God's desire for the Church to be distinct and bear the seal of Christ. Christian women must show through their attitude, dress, words, and work that they honor an amazing God. When others see their testimony, they too will be irresistibly drawn to be set apart for God.

Morning – AS PURE AS RAINWATER

Hatred stirs up conflict, but love covers over all wrongs.
PROVERBS 10:12 NIV

Have you ever seen a rain barrel filled after a good storm? That water is clean and refreshing. But if you take a big stick and whip up the contents, soon the dregs will rise and whorl. Suddenly what was clean is now a dirty mess. That visual is a good one for Proverbs 10:12, which reminds us that hatred stirs up old quarrels.

When we choose to hold on to grudges, then hatred seeps into our hearts. It's like we're carrying around a big stick, and we're more than ready to whip up some dregs by bringing up an argument from the past. This is a common way to live, but not a godly or healthy one.

What's the answer?

Love.

When we love others, we will overlook insults, whether they are intended or not. Does that seem like an impossible task using these feeble shells of ours?

It is impossible in our own humanness.

But with the supernatural power of the Holy Spirit, we can overcome this need to stir up trouble, and we can forgive freely and love abundantly—just as Christ has done for us. So let us come not with a big stick but with a spirit as refreshing and as pure as rainwater.

Evening – I FORGIVE YOU

A man's discretion makes him slow to anger,
and it is his glory to overlook a transgression.
PROVERBS 19:11 NASB

Great power comes in these three little words: *I forgive you.* Often they are hard to say, but they are powerful in their ability to heal our own hearts. Jesus taught His disciples to pray, "Forgive us our trespasses as we forgive those who trespass against us." He knew we needed to forgive others to be whole. When we are angry or hold a grudge against someone, our spirits are bound. The release that comes with extending forgiveness enables our spirits to commune with God more closely, and love swells within us.

How do you forgive? Begin with prayer. Recognize the humanity of the person who wronged you, and make a choice to forgive. Ask the Lord to help you forgive the person(s). Be honest, for the Lord sees your heart. Trust the Holy Spirit to guide you and cleanse you. Then step out and follow His leading in obedience.

By forgiving, we can move forward, knowing that God has good things in store for us. And the heaviness of spirit is lifted, and relief washes over us after we've forgiven. A new sense of hope and expectancy rises. *I forgive you.* Do you need to say those words today?

DAY 278

Morning – A LOVING FATHER

*For the Lord corrects those he loves, just as
a father corrects a child in whom he delights.*
PROVERBS 3:12 NLT

Not many people would walk up to an unruly child in the grocery store and correct or discipline him. Not only is this socially unacceptable, but really, unless you know the child and, more importantly, love the child, it is impossible to provide correction. While the child may respond, he likely would do so out of fear—fear of a stranger stepping into his world.

Children respond to correction best when it comes from a loving parent. A loving parent doesn't discipline a child because they are embarrassed about the behavior, but because they love the child and long for a better future. They want to protect their child from unnecessary pain and teach them the way they should go. Our Father corrects us because He delights in us. We can listen and respond to His correction because we know, beyond a shadow of doubt, that everything He does springs from His deep, deep love for us.

Evening – PERFECT LOVE

And he will be called. . .Everlasting Father.
ISAIAH 9:6 NIV

There seems to be a newly recognized realization in our culture about the power fathers have on their children's lives. Whether by their presence or absence, by their nurturing or neglect, fathers have a profound influence on their children. Unfortunately, many men did not have good role models in their own fathers. So they do the best they can, often using their own flawed father as the default model.

As women, we gather much of what we believe about ourselves from our fathers. If he thought we were beautiful, deep inside, we know we're beautiful. If he was loving and nurturing and present, we feel worthy of love, worthy of others' time. But if he was highly critical or distant, we can carry around a deep sense of shame and low self-esteem.

No matter what kind of earthly father we had, he was imperfect. In God, we find a perfect, Everlasting Father, who has perfect, everlasting love and acceptance for us. Never again should we gauge our value by what our flawed, human fathers may have made us feel. We can look into the mirror of God's eyes and see ourselves through the reflection of the one who made us, who adores us, and who loves us beyond measure. He will never leave us. He will never forsake us. And no matter what we do, He will always welcome us into His presence with open, loving arms.

Morning – THE BREAD OF
LIFE IN A FEEDING TROUGH

"I am the bread of life."
JOHN 6:48 NIV

Jesus taught people they must believe in Him for eternal life. He illustrated His messages with object lessons, references to the Hebrew scriptures, and analogies. In John 6, He called Himself the true bread of life which came down from heaven, and referred to bread three ways: (1) the loaves of bread He had miraculously multiplied the previous day (John 6:26), (2) the manna that God sent from heaven in Israel's history (John 6:32, 49, 58), and (3) His body which would be broken for sin (John 6:50–51). Jesus spoke in spiritual terms (John 6:63), but many did not understand. They interpreted His words as cannibalism and stopped following "Rabbi Jesus" (John 6:66).

When Jesus said those who "eat His flesh and drink His blood" will have eternal life (John 6:53–58), He was giving an analogy for believing in Him. Believing means being convinced of a truth so that you fully trust in it. Jesus' other analogies for believing included receiving, being born a second time, looking, coming, entering, etc. Jesus said, "Very truly I tell you, the one who believes has eternal life" (John 6:47 NIV).

Believing what Jesus said is like "ingesting" Jesus into your whole being. In Ghana, Africa, the word for *believe* means "take God's words and eat them." How significant that God's Son had a manger—an animal feed box—for His cradle.

Evening – PLEASING GOD

*Let the words of my mouth and the meditation of my heart be
acceptable in Your sight, O LORD, my strength and my Redeemer.*
PSALM 19:14 NKJV

The Christian's life should be a prayer and a walking testimony to Christ's redemption. The way that others around you know that you are a Christian is through your words and your actions. God sees even beyond these to your heart. He knows your thoughts, your motives, and the secret feelings that no one else is able to discern. He hears the words that come from your mouth, but if they do not match what's in your heart, He knows. Both should be pleasing to the Father. As you walk and talk, consider Jesus. The popular slogan "What Would Jesus Do?" has come and gone. At one time it was on bracelets and billboards. Imagine that it still is. Would you desire that every interaction you have with another, each decision you make at work or school, and every thought that crosses your mind be pleasing to the Lord? You can only accomplish this through being in close fellowship with Christ, reading the Word, and allowing the Holy Spirit to enable you where you are weak. Ask God today to help your words and actions be pleasing to Him.

Morning – GOD SEES AND HEARS

"You shall call his name Ishmael, because the Lord has heard your affliction." . . . Then she called the name of the Lord who spoke to her, You-Are-the-God-Who-Sees.
GENESIS 16:11, 13 NKJV

Scripture gives the account of a woman who was marginalized, who had no voice, who was used sexually and treated harshly. Yet God met her in the wilderness. He spoke to her and let her speak. Then He told her what to do and she obeyed. Who was it? Hagar—a maid servant, an Egyptian not a Hebrew, a woman of no social status, and yet she was the first person in scripture to whom the Angel of the Lord appeared. He sent her back to the place of her suffering but gave her promises regarding her unborn son: he would become a great nation; he would be free and independent, hold his own in conflict, and live in the presence of his brethren. Believing what God said and knowing that Ishmael would not be a servant like she was gave her courage to face her conflicts back home.

She obeyed because of who God was. He was the *Ishmael*—God-who-hears—and the *El Roi*—God-who-sees. Other Bible people named the place where God encountered them; Hagar alone gave God Himself a new name.

When we are stuck in undesirable circumstances and wish we could run away, we can endure suffering if that's what God wants because He has promised never to leave us or forsake us.

Evening – JOY IN TRIALS

Consider it pure joy, my brothers and sisters, whenever you face trials of many kinds, because you know that the testing of your faith produces perseverance. Let perseverance finish its work so that you may be mature and complete, not lacking anything.
JAMES 1:2–4 NIV

James begins his letter by encouraging his brothers and sisters in Christ to find joy in their trials. The word *consider* tells us to move this discussion about trials out of our emotions and into our heads.

Stop and think about this for a minute. Trials are going to come. That is a fact of this life. We can't waste our time trying to avoid them. So instead, let's remember we have the ultimate victory in Christ. Nothing that happens on earth will take away our heavenly reward and the joy we will have in heaven.

With Christ, the fruit of our trials can be growth, maturity, peace, and the fruit of the Spirit instead of despondency, discouragement, depression, and hopelessness. Ask God for wisdom for the next step. Draw close to Him. Let perseverance finish its work to increase your maturity. Take real steps of obedience and faith, because the key to joy is obedience.

Morning – SAVORING THE WORD

Jesus answered, "It is written: 'Man shall not live on bread alone,
but on every word that comes from the mouth of God.'"
MATTHEW 4:4 NIV

Casseroles are veiled in gently rising steam; gelatin salads wobble temptingly. Like a net, the smell of fresh rolls draws the guests to the table. Potlucks are meals of chance, roulette for the taste buds. The strategic guest fills her plate with a small bite of everything. There are surprises—what everyone thought was lemon meringue turned out to be a gelatinous banana pudding, while an untouched sauce swelled with savory, meaty flavors.

Studying the Bible's sixty-six books can feel like a potluck, and our reading habits might be picky too. The Psalms and Proverbs might be sweet and easy to read, but the book of Numbers might have the attraction of week-old dry bread. The "good stuff" gets scooped up and the other books are overlooked.

As unsavory as they might seem, don't be so quick to pass on challenging sections of the Bible. Jesus said that men and women live by *every* word that proceeds from the mouth of God, not just some of them. Unlike a hit-or-miss potluck dish, all of scripture is meant for the Christian's nourishment (Romans 15:4). Seek the Father as you chew on the book of Judges or contemplate the life of the prophet Ezekiel. All His Word is sweet when you can see Him in it.

Evening – UNDERSTANDING THE BIBLE

So Philip ran to him, and heard him reading the prophet Isaiah,
and said, "Do you understand what you are reading?" And he
said, "How can I, unless someone guides me?"
ACTS 8:30–31 NKJV

Ravi Zacharias said that people today hear with their eyes and think with their feelings. We all tend to believe pictures more than words and accept truth based on our feelings more than facts. Philip did not ask, "How do you feel about that scripture?"

To know what God has communicated, we study the Bible like literature, seeking the central truth of a passage and never divorcing a verse from its context. For example, many Christians take Philippians 4:13—doing all things through Christ who strengthens us—as a promise that God will give us power to accomplish anything we desire. However, the context involves Paul learning to be content with little or much because he has Christ. By application, we can be content in our relationship with Christ, despite our circumstances. A misapplication would be having this verse as a T-shirt slogan for running a marathon!

We often distort God's truth by adding our own ideas to a verse and ignoring its context. We should first discern God's meaning to the original readers, then we can understand what He is saying to us. Interpreting scripture correctly allows the Holy Spirit to customize the application of God's truth to our needs at the time.

Morning – NO REGRETS

*Be diligent to present yourself approved to God
as a workman who does not need to be ashamed.*
2 TIMOTHY 2:15 NASB

Bonnie Ware nursed patients in the last twelve weeks of their lives. She recorded their dying epiphanies and compiled this top five list:

1. I wish I'd had the courage to live a life true to myself, not what was expected of me.
2. I wish I hadn't worked so hard.
3. I wish I'd had the courage to express my feelings.
4. I wish I had stayed in touch with my friends.
5. I wish that I had let myself be happier.

God has given us a great gift—life. Some use it well and others waste it.

William Borden was a college freshman when he started a prayer group with three young men. It grew to thirteen hundred by his senior year. He cared for widows, orphans, and drunks and sought hard souls who needed the gospel. He later pursued missions to Chinese Muslims, but Borden contracted spinal meningitis and died at age twenty-five. Inside his Bible, he had written: "No reserves. No retreats. No regrets."

In the parable of the sower, the master referred to the one who buried his money as a "wicked servant." But to the one who invested, he said, "Well done." Consider the investment of your life. If today was your last, would you be able to say, "No reserves. No retreats. No regrets"?

Evening – SLOW TO SPEAK

*So then, my beloved brethren, let every man be swift to hear, slow to speak,
slow to wrath; for the wrath of man does not produce the righteousness of God.*
JAMES 1:19–20 NKJV

How quick are we to give an opinion or proffer our observation? How eager are we to hold our tongues, listen, and discern, like a cautious child crosses the street? More times than we realize or care to admit, our tongues run away with our hearts, and we find ourselves saying dishonoring statements.

This need to be right and to be heard comes from a selfish and unbelieving heart. With a selfish mindset, we blurt our thoughts out before thinking them over. Without realizing it, we can consider our opinions of more importance than the Lord's Word. If we truly believed that God is all-powerful and all-knowing, then why do we jump in and verbally take the reins? Perhaps, though we confess it with our mouths, we do not believe the Lord is at work in the matter.

Ask the Lord to empty you of words and thoughts that do not glorify and honor Him. We need forgiveness when we have spoken harshly, acted foolishly, and disobeyed. Our disobedience is a great grievance and it does hurt our Father, like a disobedient child who strays from her parents. As scripture says, the wrath of man does not produce righteousness. We need help to not fall into the temptation of gossip and slander. Ask the Lord to teach you how to be slow to speak and quick to listen.

Morning – UPHELD

And so it was, when Moses held up his hand, that Israel prevailed; and when he let down his hand, Amalek prevailed. But Moses' hands became heavy; so they took a stone and put it under him, and he sat on it. And Aaron and Hur supported his hands, one on one side, and the other on the other side; and his hands were steady until the going down of the sun. So Joshua defeated Amalek and his people with the edge of the sword.
EXODUS 17:11–13 NKJV

As God placed Aaron and Hur at Moses' side, so He places our friends and family to support us when we simply can't lift a hand. We were created to be a part of the body of Christ, whether that be a large church in Tennessee or an underground gathering in East Asia. There will be numerous times in our lives when the Lord doesn't stop our personal battles; instead, He gives us the resources to finish the fight.

Isolation is a dangerous way to live. We are most vulnerable when alone and most susceptible to temptation. Satan wants you to think that no one else in the church can relate to your circumstances. He wants you to continue in silence; it's where he is most effective. But, if like Moses we allow our fellow brothers and sisters in Christ to support us and we lean on them for encouragement and wisdom, we can endure the suffering. Do not estrange yourself from the body of Christ; it is one way the Lord continually calls to us and provides for us.

Evening – LONGING TO BELONG

You are citizens along with all of God's holy people. You are members of God's family. Together, we are his house, built on the foundation of the apostles and the prophets. And the cornerstone is Christ Jesus himself. We are carefully joined together in him, becoming a holy temple for the Lord.
EPHESIANS 2:19–21 NLT

Clad in orange and navy blue, Danny and Kim made their way to their seats at the Detroit Tigers game with their three young sons. As they made it up the last two flights of stairs, two young men with blue face paint ran happily by.

Finally at their seats, the national anthem was just beginning. They remained standing and reminded the boys to remove their ball caps, which they did proudly. Kim noticed a whole group of paint-faced people directly across the stadium from them, cheering and having a great time together. With each runner advancement and run scored during the game, they ran the aisles cheering. Other fans had cow bells and pom-poms. They stood exuberantly with each successful play, celebrating. Some started a crowd wave, getting most everybody to their feet. It was a great experience to be part of something much bigger than themselves. There was a feeling of belonging for each one pulling for the team.

Kim thought about how we all long to belong, and our culture provides a lot of places to do that. Thankfully, God provides a place for us to belong that doesn't depend on this world's circumstances, and our admission has already been paid.

DAY 284

Morning – THE BLESSING BLUES

Bless those who persecute you; bless and do not curse.
ROMANS 12:14 NIV

"Roger's not even part of the family. He's adopted! He shouldn't get part of Mother's property!" Rena complained. "I want my share and everything else I deserve!"

Normally calm, Roger was rattled. Chosen by their mother for his financial expertise, he was astonished when his stepsister stopped probate. Now that their mother's house was in escrow, Rena stopped the sale. Her actions hurt all the family, including her children.

The next morning, Roger prayed, "Lord, get her good!" Then he realized his mistake in Jesus' words, "Love your enemies, do good to those who hate you, bless those who curse you, pray for those who mistreat you" (Luke 6:27–28 NIV).

"You're kidding, Lord. I've got the blessings blues and You want me to pray good things for her!" He began with clenched teeth, "Lord, bless Rena and her attorney. Let this come out Your way." As he asked God for a blessing on Rena day after day, Roger felt his own resentment melt away. He could smile. His sense of humor returned. He became willing to let God handle the situation entirely. He let go of worry and let God manage the issue.

Blessing those who mistreat you is impossible—except with God. In His strength, we can overcome.

Evening – LOVE YOUR ENEMIES

"Love your enemies, do good to them, and lend to them without expecting to get anything back. Then your reward will be great."
LUKE 6:35 NIV

These words, spoken by Jesus, are some of the hardest words we have to consider. Love our enemies? Really?

The thought of loving those who do us harm just doesn't sit right. The thought of giving kindness in return for malicious intent makes no sense and causes our stomachs to knot up, our shoulders to tighten. Love our enemies? Please, God, no.

Isn't it enough to avoid our enemies and do them no harm?

Sometimes. Maybe. But most of the time, God calls us to a love so brave, so intense that it defies logic and turns the world on its side. He calls us to love like He loves.

That means we must show patience where others have been short. We must show kindness where others have been cruel. We must look for ways to bless when others have cursed.

Something about that just doesn't feel right to our human hearts.

But God promises great rewards for those who do this. Oh, the rewards may not be immediate. But when God promises great rewards, we can know without doubt that any present struggle will be repaid with goodness and blessing many times over.

Morning – BRIMMING WITH WORSHIP

Therefore, since we receive a kingdom which cannot be shaken,
let us show gratitude, by which we may offer to God an acceptable
service with reverence and awe; for our God is a consuming fire.
HEBREWS 12:28–29 NASB

Author and pastor Louie Giglio said that all of us have the same testimony. We were dead. . .and now we're not! The rest of our story is details.

Do you see what we've got? New life! Does that bring a sense of wonder and thankfulness to your heart? If not, ask God to fill you with His wonder and thankfulness. For those of us who have grown up in the church and have heard the gospel twice a week for our entire lives, it can become just more words instead of the life-giving truth of who God is and who we are.

If you aren't brimming with worship, ask God to wake you up and change you from the inside out! Remember, God's Word tells us that we have not because we ask not (see James 4:2). . .so why not ask? If our prayers are in line with God's will, He longs to give us the desires of our hearts (see Psalm 37:4).

The presence and power of God In your daily life will change you. Even if you're in the middle of a dark time, God wants to give you His peace that goes beyond your understanding. He will. . .if only you will let Him!

Evening – THANK YOU

As for me, I will always have hope; I will praise you more and more.
My mouth will tell of your righteous deeds, of your saving acts
all day long—though I know not how to relate them all.
PSALM 71:14–15 NIV

Those in the workplace, be it an office or at home, really appreciate a "thanks—well done" every now and then. Kudos can make the day go smoother. And when others brag on us a tad, it perks up the attitude. Think then how our heavenly Father loves to hear a hearty "thank You" from His kids.

Our lives should be filled with praise to the Living Lord and King of kings. He is a mighty God who created us and watches over us. We ought to tell others of the deeds He has done in our lives. For the power of our testimony is great. Tell how He is our Savior and our hope. The psalmist exhorts us to hope continually because we know even in the darkest days, He has given us a promise to never leave our sides.

Synonyms for praise include: *admire, extol, honor, glorify,* and *worship.* This day take one or two of these words and use them to thank your heavenly Father. Don't take Him for granted. Give Him the praise He deserves.

DAY 286

Morning – TOUCHING JESUS

*When she had heard of Jesus, [she] came in the press behind, and touched his
garment. For she said, If I may touch but his clothes, I shall be whole.*
MARK 5:27–28 KJV

The woman with the issue of blood suffered for twelve years, and even though she had seen several physicians and spent all her money, she wasn't any better. She must have felt she was at the end of her rope. Then she heard about Jesus.

Sometimes we're at the end of our rope. We've done all we know to do and it hasn't solved a thing. We're so confident we can handle the situation, we have missed the secret this woman discovered. When she heard of Jesus, she made her way to Him. It wasn't easy. A crowd followed Jesus as He taught and healed people. She had to make her way through the throng of people who jostled and pushed against one another in their eagerness to be near Jesus. They may not have wanted to give way to her, but she pressed in, and when she reached Jesus, she touched His clothes and received healing.

The secret to solving any problem is to touch Jesus. We can't see Him in the flesh, but we can touch Him through prayer and His Word. Like the woman in this story, we must press through whatever may hinder us. Don't give up! Touching Jesus is all that matters.

Evening – A CONTRAST OF TWO LIVES

*"Behold, I am laying in Zion a stone, a tested stone, a costly cornerstone for
the foundation, firmly placed. He who believes in it will not be disturbed."*
ISAIAH 28:16 NASB

Kelly called herself a Christian. She attended church on holidays and thought of herself as a good person. When her husband died of cancer, the pain and suffering she felt awakened her, and she questioned her faith. Then a thought crossed her mind—had she ever really known God?

Soon Kelly was attending church and studying the Bible and devotionals. Even though she struggled through grief, her newfound relationship with Christ gave her hope.

Renee was another young widow struggling through grief. Unlike Kelly, Renee was considered a strong Christian. Until her husband died, she was highly involved in Bible studies and church leadership.

Like most, she also questioned her faith, but instead of seeking the purpose, she shut down, wanting more than anything to die and join her husband. It wasn't long before Renee took her own life.

Both women loved their husbands deeply, and the tears fell long and hard. But when tragedy struck, Kelly found purpose and beauty in her suffering because Christ became the cornerstone of her life. But Renee followed her sorrow into despair because the foundation of her life was her husband.

How sturdy is your foundation? Continually test the strength of your spiritual footing so you can be prepared when tragedy comes.

Morning – IF AT FIRST YOU DON'T HEAR...

The LORD came and stood there, calling as at the other times, "Samuel!
Samuel!" Then Samuel said, "Speak, for your servant is listening."
1 SAMUEL 3:10 NIV

Have you heard the anecdote about the man who wouldn't leave his home when asked to evacuate as a flood approached? When a van stopped for him, he said, "I'm a good Christian; God will take care of me." As the waters rose, the man went to a second-floor window. When a boat stopped for him, he again declined help. Eventually, he took refuge on the roof as the floodwater filled his home. A helicopter lowered a ladder to him, but he again refused to evacuate. He knew the Lord would save him. Unfortunately, the man drowned. In heaven he said to God, "I lived a Christian life; why didn't You save me?" God replied, "My son, I tried three times, but you refused My help."

Do we listen and respond when we hear something new or unfamiliar? Do we heed timely warnings of danger? Do we accept Christian help from others? If we at least try to listen for God and respond the best we know how to do, He will reach out to us more than once. Just as He did when he called to Samuel in the temple, God will keep trying to reach those who are listening for Him.

Evening – HEAR GOD'S WORDS

Naaman's servants went to him and said, "My father, if the prophet
had told you to do some great thing, would you not have done it?
How much more, then, when he tells you, 'Wash and be cleansed'!"
2 KINGS 5:13 NIV

Janet was in awe when someone at church would report that the Lord had talked to them. Janet didn't think the Lord had ever "talked" directly to her.

She decided to privately ask how people knew the Lord had talked to them. Andrew told Janet he heard the Lord tell him this girlfriend would become his wife. How? When both his sister and his best friend told him, "She's the one," he just knew. Lucia said, "The Lord told me to attend this church." How? The third time her roommate invited her to attend, she just knew. Rose told Janet that the Lord told her she should relocate. How? One evening Rose told her daughter that she still hadn't decided where to move. Her daughter responded, "I think you have." After Rose repeated that she hadn't yet decided, her daughter repeated her opinion that Rose had. The following morning Rose just knew the Lord had spoken to her.

As with the story of Naaman, we need to listen to those who care about us. God can use those who serve Him to deliver His messages. God may use a servant who appears to us as a family member or friend.

DAY 288

Morning – A TIME FOR EVERYTHING

*There is a time for everything. . .a time to search and a
time to give up, a time to keep and a time to throw away.*
ECCLESIASTES 3:1, 6 NIV

Learning to tell time when we were children wasn't easy. Understanding the clock face and the function of the little hand pointing to the hour was simple. But it was confusing to learn that it's ten minutes after the hour when the big hand is on the 2 or that it's a quarter till the hour when the big hand is on the 9. At least now with digital clocks, when it's ten past the hour, the digital display shows 10.

Eventually we all learned the essential lesson of telling time and understanding that time passes. As the Bible tells us, there is a time for everything in life. There are times when we need to search for answers and times to give up and surrender to the Lord. There is a time for us to hold fast to ideas and things, and a time to let go and throw away goals from our past.

Sometimes we cling to old priorities that actually drag us down. If we find that certain items or relationships are pulling us away from our Christian walk, we need to consider giving those up and letting go for our own good.

Evening – REFINED BY GOOD

*Let us not become weary in doing good, for at the proper
time we will reap a harvest if we do not give up.*
GALATIANS 6:9 NIV

One cartoon shows a man digging in a mine. We can see from a cutaway that he is inches from striking it rich. But he drops his pick and walks away, thinking he'll never get anywhere.

It's easy to get discouraged. Sometimes it feels like we are the only ones doing the right thing. Sometimes it seems doing the right thing works against us. We want to give up and just go along. We aren't getting anywhere. But many times people give up just before the fruit begins to show. God wants to encourage us to keep on going. He promises that we will see a harvest of our actions.

Galatians 6:9 reminds us that there are seasons. Just like a farmer plants her seed in one season and harvests the crop in the next, so it is with our actions. We don't necessarily see the benefits of doing the right thing right away. Some benefits we might not see until we get to heaven.

In the meantime, doing good benefits us. It refines us, getting our hearts aligned with God's. We act on His interests instead of our own, and we start seeing the world through His eyes. Keep looking for opportunities to do good and don't give up. Trust in God's promises.

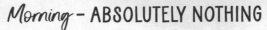

Morning – ABSOLUTELY NOTHING

*For I am convinced that neither death nor life, neither angels nor demons,
neither the present nor the future, nor any powers, neither height
nor depth, nor anything else in all creation, will be able to separate
us from the love of God that is in Christ Jesus our Lord.*
ROMANS 8:38–39 NIV

Sometimes, when our circumstances spiral downward and we feel like we're living a nightmare, we wonder where God went. His love, which is supposed to be never-ending, seems out of reach. We pray, but our words seem to bounce off the ceiling and fall flat on the floor.

But it doesn't matter how we feel. God promised that nothing can separate us from His overwhelming, magnificent, powerful love. And though our circumstances may numb our sensors, making it seem like His love is absent, we can fall back on faith in God's promises. His love is there, enveloping us, whether we feel it or not. Nothing in this world can keep His love from us. Absolutely nothing.

Cancer may destroy our flesh, but it won't destroy God's love. Bills may deplete our finances, but they can't deplete His love. Relationships may break our hearts, but they will never break His love. We don't have to face any of life's difficulties alone, for our Creator loves us. He will hold our hands through it all. And when we are too weak to face another day, His love will carry us.

Evening – LOVING ALL

*Beloved, let us love one another, for love is of God;
and everyone who loves is born of God and knows God.
He who does not love does not know God, for God is love.*
1 JOHN 4:7–8 NKJV

Love. What an amazing force! It is the greatest power of all—in heaven and on earth. Love cannot be defeated, lost, or destroyed. Why not? Because love is God—and God is love.

The love a newborn has for his mother is incredibly strong. In his eyes, she is the sun, moon, and stars. As a newborn views its mother, God's daughters are to view their God, looking at Him with total adoration, expectation, and inspiration. He alone nurtures the nurturer. It is His dedication to her in every way, shape, and form that gets a woman through the day. It is His Word that helps her to rise above the material pain and plain. It is His death-defying adoration that will never leave nor forsake her—in this life or the next. It is His love that flows out from her to all others. And the more she allows herself to be the conduit of His love, the more she understands the source of that love—the one and only God and song of her life.

DAY 290

Morning – WHERE YOU ARE, THERE I AM FREE

I sought the Lord, and He heard me, and delivered me from all my fears.
They looked to Him and were radiant, and their faces were not ashamed.
PSALM 34:4–5 NKJV

Ana could barely read when she came to faith, but her husband's passion for God and for His Word encouraged her to seek His presence. She struggled with each syllable as she studied her Bible between caring for her seven children. On the hills where she took Viorica, the milk cow, to graze, she would often read and pray. The worries of being the wife to an itinerant preacher, who could be arrested at any time due to the political climate of the country, were many. She sought God and petitioned Him for peace. The Lord heard and brought deliverance countless times—from financial provision to physical protection.

Now an elderly woman in her late eighties, Ana has lost sight in one eye, making it even harder to read. She still seeks her Maker in daily conversation and in listening to Bible teachers expound the Word. Her face radiates peace when she hears the words of Jesus, holding nothing back as she retells it to her grandchildren. She sought and beautifully found Him. Through her diligence in faith, she broke from the fears and constraints of illiteracy, of poverty, of social marginalization, and of political repression. Adonai delivered her. Seeking Him requires persistence, but it leads to freedom.

Evening – MY REFUGE

The Lord is my rock, my fortress and my deliverer; my God is my rock,
in whom I take refuge, my shield and the horn of my salvation, my stronghold.
PSALM 18:2 NIV

Here's the scene. You're snorkeling not far from the shoreline in a sparkling turquoise sea. You're enjoying the gentle sway of ocean waves and the pretty fishies. But you soon discover that you've drifted beyond the confines of the quiet bay. Suddenly, swells are heaving around you, and land looks like a distant memory.

You gulp some water and cough. You fight the waves, but your arms and legs quickly tire. Panic rises inside your belly. Adrenaline pumps. Fear becomes a living thing inside you as you shout, "Help me!" Someone on the shore sees you, but can they reach you in time before you're overcome by the waves?

You pray. Harder than you've ever prayed.

Then you see it. A big hulk of a stone, jutting out of the sea. You swim toward it, and in a few moments you are climbing onto that rock. You're clinging to that bit of sanctuary with every fiber of your being. Refuge never felt so good.

That is like God, our deliverer. He is our rock when we call out to Him, when we're in any kind of need—physically, mentally, or spiritually. Jesus may not rescue us in the way we want or in our timing, but He will never forsake us. It is His steadfast promise to us. Count on it.

Morning – BE STRONG AND COURAGEOUS

*"So be strong and courageous! Do not be afraid and do not panic
before them! For the LORD your God will personally go ahead
of you. He will neither fail you nor abandon you."*
DEUTERONOMY 31:6 NLT

In *The Horse and His Boy*, one of the books in the Narnia series by C. S. Lewis, we see a beautiful picture of how the Lord gives us strength and courage to do His will. The boy, Shasta, runs away from home. Along the way he meets up with a talking horse from Narnia and a nobly born girl, Aravis, with her talking horse. They decide to take their horses to Narnia, but their plans fall apart when they have to go through the Calormene capital city, Tashbaan.

Several times as they travel, they are chased by lions, harassed by cats, and generally persecuted by various members of the cat family. Finally, on one particularly dark night, Shasta crosses over a mountain pass alone. In the dark and fog, Shasta senses rather than sees a creature walking along beside him. And he's terrified.

Later, when he meets Aslan, Shasta learns that all the cats were Aslan, guiding them, pushing them, and yes, terrifying them into doing what they needed to do. Aslan was also his protector as he crossed the steep and dangerous mountain pass in the dark. Shasta is angry until he realizes that Aslan did everything out of love, even hurting Aravis when her pride was keeping them from the mission they'd been given.

Evening – FOLLOWING GOD'S SCHEDULE

The blessing of the LORD, it maketh rich, and he addeth no sorrow with it.
PROVERBS 10:22 KJV

Shelley pulled into Kaitlyn's driveway. She was right on time, but prepared to move as slow as necessary since Kaitlyn was a new mom and it never seemed their plans ever came together "on schedule" anymore. She had even brought an extra shirt, just in case the baby "erupted" onto her shoulder sometime throughout the day.

Forty-five minutes later, Shelley clipped the car seat into place and dropped the diaper bag behind the driver's seat of her car. Although she had somehow avoided the spit-up, mom and baby had changed clothes twice.

Finally on their way to the mall for shopping and lunch, the six-lane road slowed to a crawl. The entire intersection was blocked with fire trucks, ambulances, and tow trucks. The accident included a motorcyclist and several cars. Firefighters and police officers had formed a line around someone laying on the ground, a clue that the accident had probably resulted in at least one fatality.

As Shelley steered the car around into the detour, she said a prayer for everyone involved in the accident. Then she looked at Kaitlyn. "We could have been in that accident if we'd come along much earlier. I was sure we were on the baby's schedule, but apparently, we are on God's schedule."

Morning – PERFECT PEACE

You will keep in perfect peace those whose
minds are steadfast, because they trust in you.
ISAIAH 26:3 NIV

Peace is an elusive thing. We allow our emotions to control us and then wonder why peace rarely follows. Strangely, peace has nothing to do with emotions. Ponder that for a moment. Your peace—or lack thereof—isn't controlled by an emotional puppeteer. You can choose peace in the middle of the storms of life.

What's robbing you of your peace today? Take that "thing" (situation, person, etc.) and write it down on a piece of paper, then pray over it and shred it. Release it to God. Keep your mind steadfast on God, not what was written on the paper. It's no longer the driving force in your life. Your trust is in God, and He cares even more about your situation (or that person) than you do, anyway.

Letting go. . .taking your hand off. . .will bring peace. It's never easy to release something that's had a hold on you, but you will be blessed with supernatural peace once you do.

Evening – PEACE LIKE A RIVER

"I have told you these things, so that in me you may have peace. In this
world you will have trouble. But take heart! I have overcome the world."
JOHN 16:33 NIV

It was starting out to be a rotten day. Beth overslept and got a speeding ticket on the way to work. Upon arriving, she found that the receptionist had called in sick and the other assistant was on bereavement leave. Beth was responsible to cover everything in her small office. The sales team didn't seem to understand why she couldn't keep up with their rapid-fire requests. On the brink of tears, Beth felt overwhelmed and discouraged.

Life often feels like a stormy sea instead of a calm, peaceful river. Circumstances have the capacity to upend us, making us feel unstable and out of control. True, flowing peace comes from Jesus. It is in Jesus that we can have confidence and a mind that is calm, tranquil, and unmoved. The events of life can cause us to take our eyes off Jesus. Our river of peace lies in our Savior.

Morning – FLOWERS FALL

"The grass withers and the flowers fall,
but the word of the Lord endures forever."
1 PETER 1:24–25 NIV

It's funny how people try to make things last that were never meant to do so. For example, people hold on to mementos of special occasions, sometimes keeping the flowers that were worn on the day or that decorated the scene. They will press flowers, dry them, and preserve them in various ways. And when that isn't enough, they have silk renditions created. Or they take photographs and hold on to those instead.

We want good things to last. We want people to live long lives and relationships to endure hardships. We root for the longsuffering hero who finally wins in the end. We hold detailed ceremonies to remember those we have lost.

Though these bodies of ours were not meant to continue forever, when we have accepted Jesus as our Savior and Redeemer, we become "born again, not of perishable seed, but of imperishable, through the living and enduring word of God" (1 Peter 1:23 NIV).

It's this contradiction—forever souls bound in temporary houses—that makes us long for all good things to never die. But peace and contentment—a cure of sorts for that longing—can be found in the enduring Word of God. The more time we spend there, the more we realize we have all the time in the world.

Evening – FOCUSING ON TODAY

Don't brag about tomorrow, since you don't know what the day will bring.
PROVERBS 27:1 NLT

What do you have on your plate today? What about tomorrow? Do you remember those plans you have next week? And that trip you have later this month? What about the work thing you have next year?

If we take an honest look at this verse, we see there is no point in worrying about tomorrow, just as there is no point in worrying about next year! *Nothing* is set in stone. Even today is a fluid river of moments, susceptible to change.

We will find that we can be happier in life by simply taking each day as it comes. If we are not focused on our calendar of events, and instead decidedly focused on each moment of *this* day, we will have the ability to enjoy moments that otherwise would have passed us by. The hilarious thing your child just said that bubbles into laughter. The sweet message from your husband that warms your heart. A lunch date with a friend that encourages your soul. These are all moments we can revel in and enjoy, rather than thinking about the next thing on the list or schedule.

Today, let's keep our focus on only the events of *today*. We will find fulfillment, laughter, and a reduction in stress if we refuse to borrow the worries of tomorrow.

Morning – ENCOURAGE YOURSELF

David encouraged himself in the LORD his God.
1 SAMUEL 30:6 KJV

David and his army went off to fight, leaving their families behind in Ziklag. While they were gone, their enemy the Amalekites raided the city, burned it, and captured the women and children. When the men returned, they found just a smoking pile of rubble. Enraged and weeping uncontrollably, some blamed David and wanted him killed. What did David do when no one was around to encourage him? He encouraged himself in the Lord (1 Samuel 30:1–6).

David had a personal relationship with God. He knew the scriptures, and He relied on God's promises. Instead of giving in to discouragement, he applied those promises to his own situation and found strength. David relied on God to build him up. Many believe that he wrote these words in Psalm 119:15–16 (NLT): "I will study your commandments and reflect on your ways. I will delight in your decrees and not forget your word." *I will delight myself in Your decrees.* In the middle of his grief and loneliness, David delighted himself in the Lord.

Christians never have to face discouragement alone. As they trust God, they can also recall past times when He brought them success. They can communicate with Him through prayer and find support in His Word.

Remember, God is always on your side, always there, and always ready to lift you up.

Evening – THE LORD HIMSELF GOES BEFORE YOU

"The LORD himself goes before you and will be with you; he will never leave you nor forsake you. Do not be afraid; do not be discouraged."
DEUTERONOMY 31:8 NIV

How comforting and freeing when we allow God to go before us! Stop and consider that for a moment: you can relinquish control of your life and circumstances to the Lord himself. Relax! His shoulders are big enough to carry all of your burdens.

The issue that has your stomach in knots right now? Ask the Lord to go before you. The problem that makes you wish you could hide under the covers and sleep until it's all over? Trust that God Himself will never leave you and that He is working everything out.

Joshua 1:9 tells us to "be strong and courageous. Do not be afraid; do not be discouraged, for the LORD your God will be with you wherever you go." Be encouraged! Even when it feels like it, you are truly never alone. And never without access to God's power.

If you've trusted Christ as your Savior, the Spirit of God Himself is alive and well and working inside you at all times. What an astounding miracle! The Creator of the universe dwells within you and is available to encourage you and help you make right choices on a moment-by-moment basis.

Morning – REVIVAL BEGINS WITH REPENTANCE

"Produce fruit in keeping with repentance."
MATTHEW 3:8 NIV

A. W. Tozer said, "Have you noticed how much praying for revival has been going on of late—and how little revival has resulted? I believe the problem is that we have been trying to substitute praying for obeying, and it simply will not work."

Could it be that Jesus is waiting for His church to repent? To the Ephesian church, He said, "Consider how far you have fallen! Repent and do the things you did at first" (Revelation 2:5 NIV).

Why do we sit back in our comfortable darling sins and wonder why God hasn't sent a fresh wind of His Spirit? Could it be that our desire for revival is only rhetoric? Do we really want to see the power of God moving among us?

William Gurnall said, "Holiness has a mighty influence upon others. When this appears with power in the lives of Christians, it works mightily upon the spirits of men; it stops the mouth of the ungodly."

In a country where the majority is Christian, our light should be brighter than it is. Now is the time to wipe off the cobwebs of our stained-glass windows and let the light and beauty of Christ shine through.

Evening – BLINDED HEART

And David's heart condemned him after he had numbered the people. So David said to the LORD, "I have sinned greatly in what I have done; but now, I pray, O LORD, take away the iniquity of Your servant, for I have done very foolishly."
2 SAMUEL 24:10 NKJV

God knew David's heart. He knew David's prideful and selfish motives in numbering the Israelites. We are fools to think that our motives go unnoticed. Sin is alluring. Though from the outside we may be giving of our time and resources, if we act out of false motives, it is abominable in the Lord's sight. We become the ultimate weasel.

David's response to his sin is utter humility and repentance. When at the feet of the holy God, one who has granted mercy and grace, the only thing we can do is stand in horror of our sin. David pleads with the Lord, not as a groveling slave but as a convicted, sincere servant. "Take away my iniquity" is David's cry, because if we truly know and love the Lord, our sin will be odious to us.

Don't keep old and comfortable sins at arm's length. Plead for the Lord to take them away and remove them as far as the east is from the west. The Lord will not draw near to those whose hearts are far from Him.

Morning – WE ARE ALL MISSIONARIES

And on the sabbath we went out of the city by a river side,
where prayer was wont to be made; and we sat down,
and spake unto the women which resorted thither.
ACTS 16:13 KJV

When Jesus ascended after His resurrection, He instructed all of his followers to "go and make disciples" (Matthew 28:19 NIV) out of the nations. Every Christian is a missionary, whether he/she realizes it or not.

Joy is a Christian schoolteacher. One day on the way to work, she thought, *My mom is a kindergarten teacher in a public school in West Virginia. How cool would it be if my class called her public school class and sang to them?* She said, "When I arrived at school, I told my eighteen students that a missionary is someone who tells people about Jesus. We also talked about where West Virginia is. I thought it was humorous when one student asked what language they spoke! Then we called and sang 'Jesus Loves Me' to students at Kanawha City Elementary. They sang us the peanut butter song."

Joy had longed to teach her students about witnessing and was faithful to follow up on a creative idea. Let's pray for new places, times, and ways to share the gospel—and encourage others to do the same.

Evening – YOU ARE THE LIGHT OF THE WORLD

"In the same way, let your light shine before others, that they may
see your good deeds and glorify your Father in heaven."
MATTHEW 5:16 NIV

Edna, an elderly widow, frequently received family help with "the heavy work." She figured that just gave her more energy for the Lord's work. Edna was a tireless prayer warrior for her church and family. She baked and gave away cookies every week. She was committed to loving others however possible.

When a sixty-year-old lady with health issues from church lost her job, Edna offered her a home. Although she knew the Lord led her to make the offer, theirs was not a match-made-in-heaven. Edna tried to reflect God's love to her guest, even though the lady wasn't outwardly appreciative. Edna thanked God for letting her show the woman Christian love—even though she looked forward to again living alone.

Fast forward ten years. Edna has joined God in heaven. Now a thirty-year-old lady with health issues at Edna's church is going through a divorce. Her job is secure, but the direction for her life is not. Alice, a recently widowed friend of Edna's, invites the young lady to move into her home. Alice believes she's reflecting God's love the same way she had seen Edna do. She knows through Edna, God prepared her to make this invitation a decade ago.

Morning – JOY ANYWAY

For with the heart a person believes, resulting in righteousness,
and with the mouth he confesses, resulting in salvation. For the
Scripture says, "WHOEVER BELIEVES IN HIM WILL NOT BE DISAPPOINTED."
ROMANS 10:10–11 NASB

Connie and Josh had made three offers on three different houses in three months. There wasn't a lot of inventory in their price range and people wanted to purchase before Christmas. Although they felt God had impressed on their hearts they would be in this community for a long time, it seemed He had other plans for them for a permanent home.

They had moved their family several times throughout their marriage as the Lord led them and Josh's career grew. "We've never had a problem buying a house—until now," Connie stated.

"We have to trust that God will lead us to exactly what He wants us to have. He's always exceeded our expectations," Josh replied in an attempt to comfort Connie. Their prayer with each contract they signed was God's perfect plan be revealed to them. And each time the contract fell through—closing the door to their dream of owning their own home again.

When believing for God's very best, disappointment can come to steal your joy during the times of waiting. Disappointment can wear away your faith and enable your doubt. Instead, you can choose joy in the midst of your disappointment. God never fails—His best is yet to come.

Evening – CHOOSE HAPPY

A merry heart does good, like medicine,
but a broken spirit dries the bones.
PROVERBS 17:22 NKJV

Feeling gloomy, blue, out of sorts? Do you have an Eeyore personality, always "down in the dumps"? Scripture exhorts us to choose joy, to choose happy. And it's not always an easy task.

When a person is ill, a gloomy spirit can make it difficult for God's healing power to work. William J. Parker, a theologian, stated, "Let the patient experience an inward awareness of [God's] healing force and let him overcome his heaviness of heart and he will find his new outlook to be like medicine." Despite the sickness, we look to our heavenly Father for encouragement and strength, a heavenly tonic. A smile and a glad heart heal us from within and also help those who come into the circle of its influence.

At times it might seem impossible to cultivate a cheerful outlook on life, but in our Christian walk, it should become an intentional act as much as learning to control our temper or be kind. This new spirit within grows from a faith that all things can work together for good when we walk in God's light and look to Him for everything.

Morning – HAVE THINE OWN WAY

Know that the LORD is God. It is he who made us, and we are
his; we are his people, the sheep of his pasture.
PSALM 100:3 NIV

"Thou art the potter, I am the clay." Those are ringing words from the song "Have Thine Own Way" that stirs up emotions and a desire to allow God to mold us and make us in His image. But what a hard thing to do. We strive to create our own worlds, to make a plan, to fix it. However, God asks us to allow Him free rein.

Sheep follow their shepherd and trust in him for provision. "As in his presence humbly I bow." Submissive to their masters, they quietly graze the hillsides, knowing the shepherd knows best. What a wonderfully relaxing word picture: relying on God's guidance and timing, following His lead.

It is a simple prayer to ask Him to help us give up control, yet not a simple task. In obedience to His Word, we can bow our heads and ask for the Holy Spirit's direction and take our hands from the steering wheel. Then wait. Quietly on our hillsides, not chomping at the bit; hearts "yielded and still." We wait for the still, small voice. This day, resolve to listen and follow.

Evening – LASTING TREASURE

"Sell your possessions and give to those in need.
This will store up treasure for you in heaven!"
LUKE 12:33 NLT

In Luke 12, a rich man wanted bigger barns. Jesus told this parable to warn "against every kind of greed" (12:15). He said we are foolish to store up earthly wealth but not have a rich relationship with God (12:21). Greed is an obscure sin, but it causes many perils:

- We may become proud of our cleverness instead of crediting God with our material blessings. Jesus said the man's fertile ground (not his work or ingenuity) had "produced fine crops" (12:16).
- We can become more focused on storing (12:18) than on sharing (12:33).
- It tempts us to self-indulgence (eat, drink, be merry) rather than to meeting others' needs (12:19).
- The greater our wealth, the greater our worry (12:25–26).
- When our possessions possess us, we start to trust in our finances instead of depending on God (12:29–31).

The rich man was preparing for the wrong thing. Like him, we can spend our income acquiring more instead of spending our lives laying up heavenly treasure by being generous (12:33). When we give of our finances and sacrifice ourselves to help others, we invest in eternity. Treasure in heaven never loses value or disappears, and it keeps our hearts rich toward God (12:34). Loving physical treasure can lead to spiritual poverty. Loving what God loves makes us eternally rich.

Morning – WINNING BIG

"He who is faithful in what is least is faithful also in much."
LUKE 16:10 NKJV

Why shouldn't I play the lottery? If I can exercise self-control and spend only a few dollars a month on tickets, what is the harm? Even if I never win, I am not losing a lot of money, and I am certainly not keeping food out of my children's mouths. Why can't I take a small risk and keep the door open to winning big?

Our culture has become so accustomed to the lottery mindset that the idea that playing the lottery might be biblically wrong is unheard of. While there is no verse that specifically mentions the lottery, God gives us some principles in His Word that can guide us.

All the earth's resources belong to God, and He will give them to us if we need them to fulfill His will. ("The earth is the LORD's, and the fulness thereof" [Psalm 24:1 KJV]; "The silver is mine, and the gold is mine" [Haggai 2:8 KJV]; "Every beast of the forest is mine, and the cattle upon a thousand hills" [Psalm 50:10 KJV].)

Accumulating wealth is not to be our focus. (Matthew 6:19–24)

Coveting is a sin. (Luke 12:15; 2 Timothy 3:2; Colossians 3:5; Exodus 20:17)

Moneymaking schemes are like traps and usually lead to sin. (1 Timothy 6:9)

We are to trust Him, not in "uncertain riches." (1 Timothy 6:17; Proverbs 11:28)

God will take care of our needs if we honor Him. (Matthew 6:31–33)

Evening – I GIVE UP

God so loved the world that he gave his one and only Son,
that whoever believes in him shall not perish but have eternal life.
JOHN 3:16 NIV

God encourages us to surrender to Him. How does God expect us to do that? *Merriam-Webster* defines *surrender* as "to give (oneself) over to something (as an influence)." God has given us free will, so the choice becomes ours: to surrender or maintain total control.

When we make the decision to surrender, we give ourselves over to God and allow His authority in our lives. We place our hope in the God who runs the universe. Oswald Chambers said, "The choice is either to say, 'I will not surrender,' or to surrender, breaking the hard shell of individuality, which allows the spiritual life to emerge."

Isn't that an amazing thought? Our Creator God cares enough about us to delve into our everyday lives and help us. Through the Holy Spirit within, God's gentle hand of direction will sustain each of us, enabling us to grow closer to our Father. The closer we grow, the more like Him we desire to be. Then His influence spreads through us to others. When we surrender, He is able to use our lives and enrich others. What a powerful message: Give up and give more!

DAY 300

Morning – CREATE A "SMILE FILE"

There is nothing better for a man than to eat and drink and tell himself that
his labor is good. This also I have seen that it is from the hand of God
ECCLESIASTES 2:24 NASB

A woman's job—whether she's a mom, physician, schoolteacher, CFO, or artist—can be tiring and discouraging. Workplaces can be competitive, and children and husbands aren't always appreciative.

Be honest: Don't you, at times, feel trapped beneath the weight of expectations, to-do lists, and fatigue? To avoid burnout, it's important to regularly take note of your successes—especially when others don't notice your tireless efforts.

Emmy, an aspiring songwriter, decided that for every rejection she received, she'd note in her journal three productive things she had done that same week to hone her craft. Administrative assistant Bianca created an email folder specifically for affirming notes she received from her boss, kids, and husband. And Shelley, an executive director of a nonprofit, keeps a hanging file of silly cartoons, jokes, and pictures. When she is stressed or overwhelmed, she takes a moment to read something fun. It never fails to lift her spirits.

Why not keep a "Smile File" of your own? Take a simple shoebox or organizing bin and place encouraging cards, emails, and photos inside. You never know when it might come in handy.

Evening – THANKFUL, THANKFUL HEART

I will praise You, O LORD, with my whole heart;
I will tell of all Your marvelous works.
PSALM 9:1 NKJV

If you live from the perspective that 10 percent of life is what happens to you and the rest is how you respond, then every situation has a side—positive or negative. Say you're late to work; every stoplight on your way is a red one; and you feel like you just can't make up the time. Instead of complaining, consider the delay was one that God appointed to keep you safe.

When you choose to approach life from the positive side, you can find thankfulness in most of life's circumstances. It completely changes your outlook, your attitude, and your countenance. God wants to bless you. When you are tempted to feel sorry for yourself or to blame others or God for difficulties, push PAUSE. Take a moment and rewind your life. Look back and count the blessings that God has given you. As you remind yourself of all He has done for you and in you, it will bring change to your attitude and give you hope in the situation you're facing. Count your blessings today.

Morning – ROOTED AND GROUNDED

And that you, being rooted and grounded in love, may be able to comprehend with all the saints what is the breadth and length and height and depth, and to know the love of Christ which surpasses knowledge, that you may be filled up to all the fullness of God.
EPHESIANS 3:17–19 NASB

Pray these verses over yourself. Pray that God's love would ground you and make you secure. Pray that the roots of His love would reach deeper and deeper into your heart, leaving no room for fear, guilt, or sin. To be rooted and grounded in His love is to fully understand that He is for you and that He desires you to walk more closely with Him.

Pray that you would be able to comprehend the love of Christ that surpasses knowledge. What an interesting oxymoron to think that you could understand something that surpasses understanding. His love for you is so overwhelming that you *can't even imagine* its breadth and length and height and depth. Pray to comprehend even a fraction of His love for you so that it will transform your life.

Pray that you would be filled up to all the fullness of God. Being filled up to the fullness of God leaves no room for anything else. That God would desire to condescend to fill us up with Himself is awe-inspiring. Ask Him to do just that.

Evening – PRAYING FOR WISDOM

If any of you lacks wisdom, you should ask God, who gives generously to all without finding fault, and it will be given to you.
JAMES 1:5 NIV

The prayers of the righteous are powerful and effective (see James 5:16). When we pray, we become a part of the solution and a part of the blessing. Prayer is a great mystery, but Jesus tells us to pray always. Our prayers are heard and somehow, in a powerful way, they make a difference.

As you pray today, ask God to help you make wise decisions. Be thankful for the key leaders in your life: your pastor, your mentors, your spouse and family members. Pray for your children and young relatives to grow up as strong leaders. Pray for your local and national leaders. Pray for wisdom as you help select those leaders who will make decisions for you. God will give you His wisdom if you ask for it.

God's Word also tells us that we "do not have because [we] do not ask God" (James 4:2 NIV). You've probably heard that said this way: You have not because you ask not. If you are lacking wisdom, it may be because you've never really asked for it. You can change that today. Spend time with God, asking Him to fill you with truth and wisdom.

Morning – THE WHOLE TRUTH

But speaking the truth in love, we are to grow up in
all aspects into Him who is the head, even Christ.
EPHESIANS 4:15 NASB

When someone gives testimony in a court case, they are sworn in with the question "Do you swear to tell the truth, the whole truth, and nothing but the truth, so help you God?" Sadly, it can take a court case to cause someone to tell the whole truth.

Physicians at the University of Michigan were counseled by risk-management executive Richard Boothman and his colleagues to own up to mistakes early. When they chose a more honest approach, the number of malpractice claims fell; they were esteemed by patients for their transparency; legal expenses went down; and patient satisfaction increased. Interestingly, patients seemed to recover faster.

Everyone makes mistakes. When we admit them and take responsibility—even asking for forgiveness—we build integrity in our relationships. It also opens doors when we offer grace to others when they make mistakes. Make a choice to tell the whole truth and build strong relationships in your life today.

Evening – STARTING OVER

Then Peter came to Jesus and asked, "Lord, how many times shall I forgive
my brother or sister who sins against me? Up to seven times?" Jesus
answered, "I tell you, not seven times, but seventy-seven times."
MATTHEW 18:21–22 NIV

Picture this: You're in the middle of a heated conversation with a friend. The two of you are at odds. You say something. She says something back. You respond, determined to make your point. She does the same, her jaw clenched. Things escalate, and before long you spout something mean-spirited and completely out of character for you. *Ack.* There's no taking that back, is there? Words stick. At times like this, you really wish you could have a do-over. If only you could hit the REWIND button! The good news is, you can. With God's help, you can have countless do-overs. Sure, there will still be a mess to clean up, but He's pretty good at that part too! Why else do you think He told Peter there would be so many opportunities to forgive?

Morning – IN HIS PRESENCE

Let us therefore come boldly unto the throne of grace,
that we may obtain mercy, and find grace to help in time of need.
HEBREWS 4:16 KJV

Abigail was only three, but she knew that when she was at Grandpoppa's house, he made the best playmate ever. Sometimes she only had to ask twice to get him to play tea party with her and several of Grandmama's stuffed animals or special dolls. He was usually pretty quick to turn on the sprinklers so Abigail could run through the grassy yard in her bare feet. More than anything, she enjoyed crawling up in his lap with her favorite book and presenting it to him to read. If he ever got tired of the same old story, he never let on. Instead, he read it each time with surprise and sincerity—like he'd never seen the words before.

What a joy to know that, just like Abigail, we can come into the presence of God and make our requests known to Him. Just like a grandparent loves to see joy in his grandchild's eyes, God loves to give us gifts and see us delight in time spent with Him. Whatever we have need of, we can come in and sit down with our heavenly Father and tell Him everything.

Evening – GOOD GIFTS

"If you, then, though you are evil, know how to give good
gifts to your children, how much more will your Father
in heaven give good gifts to those who ask him!"
MATTHEW 7:11 NIV

It's a natural, God-bred instinct to care for our children. Even parents who seem to have little parental aptitude usually try to provide the basics. Yet where parents sometimes fall short, God never will.

God loves us, and He delights in caring for us. When our own children are tired or hungry or hurt, we don't want them running to some stranger for comfort. We want them to run to us, snuggle into our arms, and trust us to care for them. God is no different.

Sometimes, though, our children ask us for things we know might hurt them. A two-year-old boy might seem fascinated by the sharp knife Mommy is using to fix dinner, but she won't give it to him, and he may throw a tantrum. He won't understand that it's out of love his mother withholds the knife.

We become distracted and enamored with shiny things too. Often we see something that seems exciting and good, and we want it for ourselves. We get frustrated when God won't give it to us. But we can always trust God's heart. We can know that even when He withholds things we think will bring us happiness, He does it out of love.

Morning – PREPARING FOR THE BATTLE

*A final word: Be strong in the Lord and in his mighty power. Put on all of
God's armor so that you will be able to stand firm against all strategies of the
devil. For we are not fighting against flesh-and-blood enemies, but against
evil rulers and authorities of the unseen world, against mighty powers in
this dark world, and against evil spirits in the heavenly places.*
EPHESIANS 6:10–12 NLT

Putting on the armor of God does not mean that all of a sudden we are safe and the enemy will not threaten us. On the contrary, Paul did not tell us to hide in a cave, but to fit our bodies with the armor of God. In this way we will be able to stand firm against everything the enemy tries against us.

Let's take a look at our shield. The devil shoots fiery arrows at us, but we have the ability to lift our shield—our *faith*—to keep them from taking us out. It is through engaging our faith that we are able to remain standing. The devil will still throw lies, threats, and condemnation at us, but we believe by faith in the truth that the Lord has told us.

Life is a very real battle, but the Lord has given us everything we need to stand firm and conquer. We need to put on His armor and walk and fight with confidence in our Savior.

Evening – THE SHIELD OF FAITH

*Above all, taking the shield of faith, wherewith ye
shall be able to quench all the fiery darts of the wicked.*
EPHESIANS 6:16 KJV

When Paul wrote to the church at Ephesus about the shield of faith, he used the word *thureos,* which means "door." Roman soldiers' shields were large, rectangular, and door-sized. In other words, they covered every single part of the soldier's body. It's the same with our faith. The salvation we've been given in Christ covers us from head to toe. And because He is lavish in love and steadfast in keeping His promises, we'll always have enough for every situation we encounter.

The Roman soldiers' shields had one other distinctive quality: they were made of several hides of leather sewn together. This meant that every morning, a soldier would have to rub oil into the shield in order to keep it pliable and to prevent it from drying out and cracking. This daily renewal was the difference between life and death. . .literally!

In our own faith-walk, we must daily allow God's Holy Spirit to refill and reenergize us. The Spirit replenishes our joy, rebuilds our faith, and redirects our thoughts so that we can live boldly and courageously for Jesus. This begs the question: What have we done today to oil our shields? Let's not get complacent and allow distractions to deter us from our duty! In Christ, we have a true shield that won't ever let us down. Praise the Lord!

Morning – EMBRACING PAIN

*But he said to me, "My grace is sufficient for you, for my power is
made perfect in weakness." Therefore I will boast all the more gladly
about my weaknesses, so that Christ's power may rest on me.*
2 CORINTHIANS 12:9 NIV

Theologians have speculated on the nature of Paul's thorn in the flesh. We don't know much about it except that it must have tortured him. Paul says in Corinthians that he begged God—three times—to remove this thorn from him.

God always answers prayer, but often not in the way we want Him to. God could have healed Paul of this thorn, but He chose not to. Why? So His power could be felt profoundly—"so that Christ's power may rest on me," Paul says. Physical and emotional pain have a way of quickening our hearts toward God. When we are pain-free and trouble-free, we tend to think we can handle things on our own. We acquire a false sense of strength. On the other hand, pain gets our attention. If you are in pain, whether physical or emotional, be reminded that God hears your prayer. Our pain can be a literal reminder to trust in God's strength.

Evening – YET

"Though he slay me, yet will I hope in him."
JOB 13:15 NIV

There are many who know the meaning of these words better than the rest of us.

The family living in Tornado Alley whose house has been torn to shreds no fewer than five times in the last fifteen years.

The mother whose sons and husband were all lost on the field of battle.

The family of the woman who survived a long, wearying struggle with cancer only to be sent back into the hospital by a megavirus.

Have you ever felt under attack? Have you ever felt perhaps God was testing your mettle? How do you hold on to hope when there seems to be no reason to do so? What does that even look like?

Though his case seems extreme, it's unlikely that many of us would react much differently than the course Job took. People going through difficult periods of their lives cycle through anger and bitterness, anguish and sorrow, resignation and confusion, just as Job did. Though they probably don't sit and cover themselves with ashes, they may hole up in their bedrooms with quilts over their heads.

But in the end, what leads Job to hope is God. God is still there. Even through all of Job's complaints and cries and angry accusations, God does not leave. God does not change. God provides no excuses. Bad things will come. But so will God.

Morning – I SURRENDER

I will rejoice in the Lord! I will be joyful in the God of my salvation!
The Sovereign Lord is my strength! He makes me as surefooted
as a deer, able to tread upon the heights.
HABAKKUK 3:18–19 NLT

Sometimes life seems like an uphill battle and we certainly don't feel like celebrating. We find ourselves frustrated by the demands of the day and worried about the future. It's just too difficult to stay the course—keep on keeping on. We're tempted to throw up our hands in frustration and quit. That's when we must realize we're in the perfect position: hands raised in surrender.

Learn that God's promises are true. When we relax in His care and focus on Him, He will be with us in all our difficulties. He didn't promise a life with no problems. He did promise to carry us through. In Proverbs 3:4 in the Amplified Bible, the word *trust* is extrapolated: lean on, trust in, and be confident in the Lord. Are we leaning on the Lord? Do we trust Him with our future and the future of those in our care? Have we become confident in His Word?

Surrender and *trust*. Two words that lead to life and joy. Choose to surrender and trust this day. He'll then bring you safely over the mountains.

Evening – LOOK TO THE PROMISE

Let us hold unswervingly to the hope we profess,
for he who promised is faithful.
HEBREWS 10:23 NIV

"I promise to pick up the dry cleaning." "The check is in the mail, I promise." How lightly we use the word *promise*. We toss it around with very little meaning attached. The definition of *promise* is a statement telling someone you will definitely do something or that something will definitely happen in the future. The use of the word means you can hang your hat on it! This some *thing* is coming. Oh how often we fail to carry through with our word. It's wonderful we can know for sure—definitely—that God's promise is eternal.

God's Word contains promises upon which we can and must depend. The Bible is a priceless gift, a tool God intends for us to use in our lives. Too often we look away from "The Manual."

Are you tired and discouraged? Fearful? Be comforted in the promises God has made to you through His Word. Experiencing worry or anxiety? Be courageous and call on God. He will protect you and then use you according to His purposes. Are you confused? Listen to the whisper of the Holy Spirit, for our God is not a God of confusion.

Talk to Him, listen to Him, trust Him. Trust His promises. He is steadfast, and He will be by your side. Always.

Morning – ACTIONS SPEAK LOUDER WITH WORDS

Dear children, let us not love with words or speech but with actions and in truth.
1 JOHN 3:18 NIV

Everyone knew they could depend on Georgia for help. Her talents were as extensive as the tools she owned. If Georgia didn't know how to do something, she was willing to learn. Georgia described herself as a doer, not a talker.

Even though Georgia worked alongside others, she often felt lonely. Volunteers on a work team would be courteous and appreciative of her contributions, but she didn't feel she connected on a personal level. Georgia assumed that others didn't really like her.

While helping her sister strip wallpaper, Georgia mentioned that she often felt isolated when she was volunteering with a group. Robin gently probed, and Georgia gradually shared examples as they worked. When they sat down for a glass of tea, Robin asked if Georgia wanted her thoughts.

After an affirmative nod, Robin took her sister's hands and turned them palm up. "Georgia, you do so much good with these talented hands. But showing Christian love requires you to share your heart with actions *and* words."

Just as we develop a personal relationship with God through talking with Him, Georgia needed to speak from her heart to develop personal relationships. In 1 John 3:18 we're instructed to give love through actions and truth. To show love with truth, Georgia needed to become a doer *and* a talker.

Evening – A SOFT ANSWER

A soft answer turneth away wrath: but grievous words stir up anger.
PROVERBS 15:1 KJV

In the blink of an eye, a discussion can turn into a heated argument. This often happens with spouses if one blames the other for a problem or incident. Suddenly, the man you love is accusing you of something you didn't do or making an observation that puts you on the defensive. It's natural to want to defend yourself or get in the last word. Feeling hurt, you strike back in fiery indignation with harsh words. And just like that, you're in the middle of an argument that could have been avoided if you had simply refused to argue or given a soft reply to his accusation. Many broken relationships might have been saved if one of the participants had communicated their feelings in a quiet, gentle manner.

Do you often find yourself saying words you wish you could take back, words you would never have spoken under different circumstances? Do you hate the arguments that cut a rift in your relationships? Solomon in all his wisdom must have known about the old saying "It takes two to argue." He said a soft answer would turn away someone's anger, but harsh words would just stir it up. God is able to give us soft answers even in the middle of painful discussions. Ask Him to change your speech and your attitude.

Morning – NEVER ALONE

*For He Himself has said, "I WILL NEVER
DESERT YOU, NOR WILL I EVER FORSAKE YOU."*
HEBREWS 13:5 NASB

Life is full of disappointments, broken promises, failed relationships, and loneliness. It may seem like you are the only person you can really trust. But the Lord will never desert you or forsake you. He promises to be with you through this life and the next. When all else feels hopeless, know that He remains steadfast.

For those who have trusted people in the past but have been let down, this may be a hard concept to accept. But this is no idle promise based on the feeling of a moment. When Christ hung on the cross, He was forsaken by God. The sin that was laid on Him was so horrific and abhorrent that the Father, who was one with Jesus, could not look at Him. In the most heart-wrenching act of history, the holy Father turned His face away from His once blameless Son. Because Christ was willing to be forsaken and utterly alone, you never will be. God won't ever have to turn away from you—you now bear the pure innocence of Christ. Christ took your sins upon Himself so you would never have to experience what it's like to be completely alone and forsaken by God.

Evening – PRAY THROUGH LONELINESS

*The widow who is really in need and left all alone puts her hope in
God and continues night and day to pray and to ask God for help.*
1 TIMOTHY 5:5 NIV

Susan's loneliness ended when she married Frank. They had met and married in their fifties. The couple had no children or siblings, and their parents had all passed away. It was loneliness that brought them together, but their strong love for each other soon filled the emptiness that had been in their hearts. Then, sadly, after only three years together, tragedy struck. Frank became ill with leukemia and died several months later. Once more, Susan faced life on her own. But this time she faced it differently.

When they began dating, Susan hadn't been a believer. It was Frank who led her to the Lord, and together, throughout their marriage, they relied on their heavenly Father for help. They turned all of their hopes and problems over to God in prayer and trusted in His wisdom. Following her husband's death, instead of becoming lost in loneliness and grief, Susan turned to the one who would never leave her, the one who would comfort her and lead her forward. She turned to God to fill up her heart with His love.

Do you feel alone sometimes? Then, like Susan, give it to God in prayer. He will lift you up and lead you on.

Morning – LOVE THE UNLOVABLE?

"Bless those who curse you. Pray for those who hurt you."
LUKE 6:28 NLT

Do you know of anyone like this? Lydia was demanding, incorrigible, and cynical. She manipulated every situation, and if she couldn't, she whined and complained. Gossip was the norm for her, and she'd often spread unsubstantiated rumors. Some family members and coworkers accommodated her shifting moods and bursts of unrestrained anger in an effort to keep peace. Others simply distanced themselves.

So how do we bless those who curse us as Jesus commands? Ralph Waldo Emerson once said, "If you would lift me up you must be on higher ground." Christians stand on higher ground. We stand in our faith in Jesus Christ and His Holy Word. We stand on Christ's shoulders to lift up others to receive the same saving grace and forgiveness that we embrace.

That's how and why we can bless those who curse or hurt us. Because Jesus based everything He did, and does, on His love for us, how can we do anything less? That doesn't mean we need to befriend every unconscionable person or accept unacceptable behavior. But it does mean that we are to pray for and attempt to understand and love the unlovable, because God loves them.

The Lord never calls us to a task without equipping us to fulfill it. As we pray, He helps us to see that person through His eyes.

Evening – DIFFICULT PEOPLE

"You have heard that it was said, 'Love your neighbor and hate your enemy.' But I tell you, love your enemies and pray for those who persecute you, that you may be children of your Father in heaven."
MATTHEW 5:43–45 NIV

It's easy to thank God for the people we love who bring joy and peace and laughter and all sorts of other good things to our lives. We thank God for our husbands, our children, our extended families, and our friends.

But what about those people we don't like? What about the people who are all-stress-and-no-bless? Are we supposed to thank God for the people who put knots in our stomachs, who make us cry, or who leave us fist-clenching, smoke-breathing angry? We know we're supposed to pray for our enemies, but do we really need to thank God for them?

Well, yes. God wants us to love our enemies, and it only stands to reason that we'd thank God for the people we love. It is through the difficult people in our lives that we grow and stretch, for they often test our faith in ways the easier relationships can't. Even though we may not see a lot of good in some people, God looks at every person and sees someone He loved enough to die for. And apart from Christ, we can be difficult people too.

DAY 310

Morning – PLANTED BY THE WATER

"But blessed are those who trust in the Lord and have made the Lord their hope and confidence. They are like trees planted along a riverbank, with roots that reach deep into the water. Such trees are not bothered by the heat or worried by long months of drought. Their leaves stay green, and they never stop producing fruit."
JEREMIAH 17:7–8 NLT

While trees don't get to choose where they're planted, the ones growing by the riverbank have it made. Their roots are free to reach deep in the water. They never have to worry about drought or blistering hot days. They are in the ideal position for growth.

This familiar analogy, also found in Psalm 1, paints a beautiful picture of what it means to stand steadfastly with the Lord. Trees don't get to choose where they're planted, but we do, and we must choose carefully. For maximum growth, we must plant ourselves near a source of living water. . .close to the body of Christ. We must immerse ourselves in prayer, feed ourselves with God's Word, and be fertilized and challenged by the companionship of other believers. When we do this, we can be assured that we will stay healthy and never stop producing fruit.

Evening – COMMUNE WITH ME

The cup of blessing which we bless, is it not the communion of the blood of Christ? The bread which we break, is it not the communion of the body of Christ?
1 CORINTHIANS 10:16 KJV

Oh, what a blessed privilege, to commune with the Lord. To spend time with Him. To break bread together. To remember the work that Jesus did on the cross. Yet how often do we do this without really "remembering" the depth of its meaning?

The night that Jesus was betrayed—the very night before some of His closest followers turned on Him—He sat down for a special meal with them. He took the bread and broke it, then explained that it, symbolically, provided the perfect picture of what was about to happen to His very body on the cross. Then He took the cup of wine and explained that it too had pertinent symbolism, for it represented His blood, which was about to be spilled on Calvary.

The disciples surely couldn't comprehend fully what Jesus was talking about, but less than twenty-four hours later, it was abundantly clear. And now, two thousand years later, it's clearer still. And Jesus still bids us to come and commune with Him. He longs for us to remember—to never forget—the price that He paid on the cross that day.

Commune with me. Such simple words from God to mankind. Run to Him today. Spend time in holy, sweet communion.

Morning – AWAKEN THE DAWN

Awake, lute and harp! I will awaken the dawn. I will praise You, O LORD, among the peoples, and I will sing praises to You among the nations. For Your mercy is great above the heavens, and Your truth reaches to the clouds.
PSALM 108:2–4 NKJV

A hiker preparing to climb Mount Rainier begins her journey in the wee small hours of the morning. She is awake before the dawn to see the majestic swirls of sky, earth, and rolling mountains. After the terrific toil of the morning, she reaches the top and declares along with His handiwork the awesomeness of the Creator. There she is, so close to the heavens and among the clouds spoken of in today's psalm.

David may not have done something as impressive as climb Rainier when he penned this, but his poetic lines reveal intentionality in starting the day with an attitude of praise. He writes of waking up early to thank God for His mercy and of wanting to make everything around him sing because of God's goodness. Sometimes the heart may be too hurt for such feelings. The only balm is spending time with Him and remembering He is at work before the rising of each new day. Like the lute and harp that David summons, we are all part of God's orchestra—each with their unique sound, all created to be in a harmony of praise.

Evening – HE KNOWS YOU

How precious are your thoughts about me, O God. They cannot be numbered! I can't even count them; they outnumber the grains of sand! And when I wake up, you are still with me!
PSALM 139:17–18 NLT

Did you know that you have a history with God? Your relationship is ever growing, ever changing, and He knows you. He knit you together in your mother's womb. He's watched as you've grown up. He's seen every good day. Every bad day. Not a moment passes that He's unaware of what you're up to.

And He still loves you. When you live in relationship with Him, covered by the sacrifice of Christ, He doesn't see the things you've done wrong. Don't walk into this day feeling the weight of your failures and imagining there is no way He could continue to love you. He does love you, even through the worst of times. Sending His Son while we were still sinners is proof of that love.

So instead of coming before Him full of shame and with a heavy heart, come before Him in humble thankfulness and confidence that He loves you so much. When you come before Him, He is pleased to see His daughter—spotless and whole. He is willing—and desires—to have a deep and thriving relationship with you.

Morning – A TIME FOR SADNESS AND A TIME FOR JOY

A time to weep and a time to laugh, a time to mourn and a time to dance.
ECCLESIASTES 3:4 NIV

Solomon has been declared the wisest man who ever lived. The third chapter of Ecclesiastes, which Solomon authored, tells us that there is a time for everything. Do you find yourself in a time of weeping or a joyful time today? You may be mourning a deep loss in your life. You may ache to your very core with disappointment and sorrow. There is a time to be sad. You don't have to put on a show or an artificial happy face. It is okay to grieve. It is appropriate even. There are times in our lives when we must rely on God's grace just to see us through another day. We may need to lean on other believers and let them carry us for a time. But the good news is that there are also joyful occasions. Psalm 30:5 says that weeping may last for a night but that joy comes in the morning. If you are in a sorrowful period, know that joy is just around the corner. You may not be able to imagine it today, but you will smile and even laugh again. If you are joyful today, know that even when you face sad days, the Lord will be there walking with you. He never leaves us alone.

Evening – WISDOM'S CRY

*Wisdom calls aloud outside; she raises her voice in the open squares. . . .
"How long, you simple ones, will you love simplicity? For scorners delight
in their scorning, and fools hate knowledge. Turn at my rebuke; surely I
will pour out my spirit on you; I will make my words known to you."*
PROVERBS 1:20, 22–23 NKJV

The first psalm in the Bible has the personification of wisdom, a woman, calling out in the streets in the style of the prophets (a type of pre-Jeremiah jeremiad). She chastises the people for being simple. Simplicity can be a virtue in this world filled with desire for material goods and always wanting to acquire more and more. Humbleness and beauty in simplicity are rare. However, Wisdom speaks here against complacency in regard to spiritual truths.

God has so much He wants to teach us—to make us understand why certain things are the way they are or even to help us understand why we cannot have complete knowledge at this time. Too often people are content to remain in their state of rebellion because they choose their own simple or narrow-minded arguments over the words and wisdom of God. Yet God offers us a chance to repent so that He can pour out His Spirit of comfort and understanding on us as He makes known to us His words.

Morning – CONSTANT AND SHIFTING

*When I look at the night sky and see the work of your fingers—the moon
and the stars you set in place—what are mere mortals that you should think
about them, human beings that you should care for them? Yet you made them
only a little lower than God and crowned them with glory and honor.*

PSALM 8:3–5 NLT

Rachel's brother sent her a postcard from his international business travels. He was somewhere in Italy this time and wrote, "It's amazing that I can look up at the stars wherever I am and know that the people I love can see them too." It warmed her heart, and she never looked at the night skies the same way again.

She thought about how steady the stars were for people, a sure guide to stay on course or to find their way when they are lost. Constant as they are, they still shift all year long, and yet even that is predictable. Stars die and are formed continually too, yet the ever-changing lineup doesn't change the order that God has placed in the universe. What comfort Rachel felt thinking on how God had it all in His hands. Furthermore, He had given her a place in it all, a place where she was loved and cared for by the God of the Universe Himself.

Evening – FILLING IN THE BLANKS OF GOD'S PROMISES

Your love, LORD, reaches to the heavens, your faithfulness to the skies.

PSALM 36:5 NIV

Sometime ago a woman contacted me to tell me about a man she was interested in. She wondered if she should move cross-country to live near him. As we talked, I realized she didn't have a relationship with her love interest. "But I know he likes me," she said.

"How do you know?" I asked.

"Because I ran into him one night when I was out with friends and he said, 'I remember you. I met you last summer.' "

Of course, this woman had no basis for moving cross-country. It's just that she wanted this man so badly that she was filling in the blanks of what she didn't know with information that comforted her longing heart.

Sometimes we fill in the blanks with God too. Maybe He reveals something He is going to accomplish in our lives, such as a new job or the birth of a child. We then make the mistake of filling in the blanks of what He said with details He never gave us. We will get a job living in Cincinnati, or we'll have two boys and a girl.

We need to be careful not to add on to what God said lest we become discouraged and blame Him for being unfaithful. When life doesn't make sense, we can hold firmly to the certain promises He has given. He will always do what is absolutely best for us according to His agape love, and His perfect character and love demand the perfect handling of all that concerns us.

Morning – FORTRESS AND FIERCE WINDS

*"Do not fear, nor be afraid; have I not told you from that time,
and declared it? You are My witnesses. Is there a God besides
Me? Indeed there is no other Rock; I know not one."*
ISAIAH 44:8 NKJV

Just as Gael looked out the window to assess the strong winds whipping up outside, her neighbor's heavy trash can blew down the street. A bike in her driveway on its kickstand crashed onto its side. The dog was whining.

Gael quickly went down to the basement while she looked at the weather on her phone for emergency alerts. It turned out to be just very strong winds that day, gusts of over sixty miles per hour. They lost a few shingles from the roof, and everything that wasn't nailed down outside fell over.

It was a real blessing to have a safe place to go even though she wasn't in real danger that day. It was encouraging to think how this paralleled God, by analogy only, of course—the way He was always a rock for her no matter what came her way. Whether weather or a storm of life, He is truly our stronghold.

Evening – THERE'S NO PLACE LIKE GRANDMA'S

"The eternal God is your refuge, and underneath are the everlasting arms."
DEUTERONOMY 33:27 NIV

"There's no place like Grandma's," ten-year-old Ben piped up. "I can hardly wait to see what fun she has cooked up for us today!" he told his mother as she was driving him there.

Though Ben's room overflowed with souvenirs from theme park vacations, Grandma offered no such extras. What she did share was her time, home, encouragement—and fun!

"After I have a bad day," Ben continued, "Grandma hugs me and says, 'Ben, you're still going to grow up to be a wonderful man.' I feel better then."

When Ben arrived at Grandma's at the same time as two cousins, Grandma hugged the boys and ushered them into the kitchen where she was making flour paste. She smiled and said, "We're making piñatas today! When they're dry and done, we'll fill them with candy and toys!"

The unanimous response: "Hooray!"

Like Grandma's investment in her grandsons and her provision of a refuge through good days and bad, God believes in us and gives us safe places to rest.

God's refuge of strength and protection has stood unchanged for millennia. He's worth our trust. Though the world pulls us to trust in money, careers, causes, all become shaky invest-ments of time and effort. But trusting in God never fails. He provides the solid foundation that stands for all time—and is a safe place always. Just as at Grandma's, God supports and encourages us inside hugs from His strong arms.

Morning – CLUED IN

This book of the law shall not depart out of thy mouth; but thou shalt meditate therein day and night, that thou mayest observe to do according to all that is written therein: for then thou shalt make thy way prosperous, and then thou shalt have good success.

JOSHUA 1:8 KJV

God clues Joshua in on a few things, things he'll need to know now that he's Israel's new leader. The Lord tells Joshua that everywhere he steps, whatever land his foot touches, God has *already* given him (1:3). It's a done deal! God also tells him that he will not be defeated, that God will be with him no matter what and that Joshua should never be afraid or discouraged. (God repeats that last one two more times in this chapter alone!)

But then God mentions *success*, a word that appears only once in the King James Version. To have good success and to prosper, Joshua needs to speak, think about, and obey God's Word. After hearing these instructions, Joshua remains true to them and becomes the conquering hero God created him to be!

Today's daughters of the King can have the same victory! God has *already* given His princesses all they need to be successful—as a mom, a career woman, a wife, a sister, a friend. Keeping that in mind, as well as God's Word on her tongue and obedience in her actions, she cannot be anything other than prosperous in everything she does!

Evening – OVERCOMERS

For everyone born of God overcomes the world. This is the victory that has overcome the world, even our faith. Who is it that overcomes the world? Only the one who believes that Jesus is the Son of God.

1 JOHN 5:4–5 NIV

Earlier in the letter, the apostle John writes that there should be no fear among believers. But there is so much brokenness in the world and so much weakness that it is easy to succumb to fear. The hope Christians have, however, is greater than this because the perfect love of Christ casts out fear. When Christians follow Jesus with their whole being, they are new people who have become children of God. He works in and through His children to bring an end to the things that are distorted and perverted. It is faith, belief, and trust in God and His Word, which God builds up in His children, that gives Christians the ability to overcome. Only by faith in Jesus as God in the flesh, come to save humanity, can people overcome the darkness in the world. Whenever problems seem unbearable, daughters of the King of kings should always remember that God has planned a way out and that Christians are more than conquerors because of the sacrifice of Jesus who loves us. Jesus Himself said that the world would hate His followers but that they should take heart because He has overcome the world.

DAY 316

Morning – THE GIFT OF PEACE

"Peace I leave with you; my peace I give you. I do not give to you as the
world gives. Do not let your hearts be troubled and do not be afraid."
JOHN 14:27 NIV

Watching the news every day is enough to make anyone uneasy and restless, especially if the news stories are happening nearby. People disappear every day, children are abused, and cities are torn apart by rioting and looting. There seems to be no end to the evil that abounds in every city and town across our country. How can anyone live in peace under those circumstances?

As Christians, we can have peace even in the face of all the tragedy happening around us. Jesus made a promise to His disciples and to us as well. He was going back to the Father, but He was giving us a priceless gift. He gave us His peace. The world can never give us the peace that Jesus gives. It's a peace that we, the recipients, can't even understand. It's too wonderful for our minds to grasp, but we know it comes from Him.

Whatever is happening in your world, Christ can give you peace. None of the problems you're facing are too big for Him, whether it's trouble in the city where you live or pain in your own home. He is saying to you, don't let your heart be troubled about these things, and don't be afraid.

Evening – FINDING PEACE

And he will be called. . .Prince of Peace.
ISAIAH 9:6 NIV

We all long for a peaceful place. The desire for peace is etched into our genetic code. . .perhaps because we're made in God's image and He is full of peace. When we think of peace, our minds fill with images of calm, quiet serenity. We picture a hilltop, surrounded by lovely gardens, with birds singing and the gentle laughter of loved ones.

While it's good to seek out a peaceful, tranquil existence, that's not always possible. In this world, stress finds us. War happens. People can be mean and selfish. Diseases appear, accidents occur. So how can we have peace when the pressures and tensions of life seem to hunt us down?

It's possible to have peace in the midst of chaos when we understand where peace is found. God's peace isn't confined to a specific location or a specific set of circumstances. His peace isn't something we have to maneuver and create. Jesus Christ is the Prince of Peace. Peace is His kingdom, and as long as He lives within us, that is where His peace dwells.

It's important to walk away from stress when we can. But when stress finds us, we can extinguish it—or at least diminish it greatly—by calling on the Prince of Peace within our hearts. When we respond with the calm, quiet assurance that comes from Christ alone, we will find peace.

Morning – OUR COACH

*Show me your ways, Lord, teach me your paths. Guide me in your truth and
teach me, for you are God my Savior, and my hope is in you all day long.*
PSALM 25:4–5 NIV

As any good team knows, what happens off the field is just as important as what happens on the field. Young players first learn by watching the older ones play, longing for the day when they will be old enough to get in the game. They take notes and pay attention. When it's time to suit up, they are under the teaching and authority of their coach. A good coach will demonstrate the behavior he expects from his players, then watch closely as they do the drills and learn the plays. A coach analyzes, encourages, and corrects, over and over again, until the players get it right.

Our heavenly Father does much the same for us. He is a model, coach, and cheerleader. He shows us what he wants for us through His Word. He teaches us, using pictures we can understand. When we stray, he lovingly corrects us and guides us to a better way. Good coaches win games and lead their team on the right path. When we testify that God is our Savior, we can trust Him to teach us and guide us and never lead us astray.

Evening – GOING IN THE RIGHT DIRECTION

*Your commandments give me understanding; no wonder I hate every false way of life.
Your word is a lamp to guide my feet and a light for my path. I've promised it
once, and I'll promise it again: I will obey your righteous regulations.*
PSALM 119:104–106 NLT

As Maggie turned right, her friend Jenna, sitting in the passenger seat, squealed, "Oh, no! That was supposed to be a left turn, not right." Maggie let out a deep sigh. "It seems like I'm always headed in the wrong direction—not just physically—but with my life!"

She quickly made a U-turn that set them in the right direction based on the instructions they'd been given to the birthday party. "Well, we left early, so we have plenty of time," Jenna encouraged. "We'll be all right."

Maggie didn't respond. Jenna knew she was still thinking about the wrong turns she'd made in her life. Her voice softened. "Maggie, now that you are back in church and really looking to God for wisdom and direction, you can trust that He will show you the way."

"Yes, I know you're right," Maggie mused. "Each time I open the Bible, I discover something new. I feel encouraged when I read it, and I'm learning to make decisions based on what God's Word says is good and right for me." She smiled at Jenna. "Thanks, friend!"

Morning – A CLOUD OF WITNESSES

*Since we are surrounded by such a huge crowd of witnesses to the life
of faith. . .let us run with endurance the race God has set before us.*
HEBREWS 12:1 NLT

Does it seem like the Bible gets less respect today than twenty years ago? Religious leaders point to humanistic thought and increased secularization as causes for this trend. How have viewpoints that marginalize God become popular? Perhaps they grew from the contagious desire to do what is right in our own eyes. We resent being told what to do, even by God's Word. The Bible is like an instruction manual for life, and although its principles show how life works best, we prefer running our own lives, thank you very much. So when God's Word calls us to holiness and to pleasing Him rather than ourselves, we desire an easier way.

Following Christ involves discipline. It can be hard to deny ourselves something like sexual gratification outside of marriage when media and culture say "Go for it!" "You deserve this," or "It's no big deal." Sometimes we wonder if following Christ is worth it. The Hebrews 11 believers testify that it is.

Take this challenge—read Hebrews 11 and list every mention of reward, inheritance, and what the saints looked forward to. You will discover their motivation, which enabled them to bear life's grueling challenges with steadfast faith. They witness to us that living for eternity is worth every sacrifice and struggle we endure on earth.

Evening – LIFE ISN'T FAIR. . .THANK GOD

Walk in the way of love, just as Christ loved us.
EPHESIANS 5:2 NIV

Dartanyon Crockett and Leroy Sutton were high school teammates. A legally blind Crockett was often seen carrying Sutton, a double leg amputee, on his back.

ESPN's Lisa Penn reported their story, but wanted to help. She raised donations and coordinated events, helping Crockett win a bronze medal in the Paralympics and Sutton to become his family's first college graduate.

Leroy once asked, "Why did you stay?" Lisa responded, "I stayed because. . .we don't truly live [life] until we give it away. . . . I stayed because I love you."

Dartanyon and Leroy didn't deserve Lisa's love. She knew they could never repay her, but it wasn't fairness she wanted. Jesus said, "There is no greater love than to lay down one's life for one's friends" (John 15:13 NLT).

It's easy being on the receiving end of grace, but much harder to be the sacrificial lamb. In the face of tragedy, will you shake your fist at God, crying, "That's not fair!" or will you react like the martyr Polycarp? When given the option to reproach Christ or burn at the stake, he said, "Eighty-six years I have served him, and He never once wronged me. How then shall I blaspheme my King who has saved me?"

There will be times when God calls upon us to sacrifice, but Jesus gave up His throne, His glory, and His life for you. No, life isn't fair, and aren't you glad?

Morning – PRESSING ON

I press on to take hold of that for which Christ Jesus took hold of me.
PHILIPPIANS 3:12 NIV

We all need a lot of work when it comes to fulfilling God's perfect plan for our lives. We get sidetracked, we mess up, life distracts us. . .and progress is slow. No matter how sincere our desire to live out God's purpose for us, we fall down again. And again.

But that's okay. God knows us better than anyone, and He knows we're not perfect. He knows we'll make mistakes and have setbacks. All He asks is that each time we fall down, we get back up and keep moving forward.

Think about it. Christ saw potential in us—so much that He died for us. He didn't say, "Oh good grief, look how slow they are! Look at how many times they goof up. Never mind. It's not worth it." Nope. He paid such a high price for us because He knew we were made in His image. And He knew that as long as we trust Him and don't give up and keep pressing forward, our likeness will become closer and closer to His.

That's what He wants for us—for our spirits to mirror His. He wants us to love, for He is love. He wants us to be kind and gentle and compassionate, for He is all those things. He longs for us to be His representatives in this world. And we will be, as long we keep pressing on.

Evening – IN THE IMAGE OF GOD

Then God looked over all he had made, and he saw that it was very good!
GENESIS 1:31 NLT

God started with light, and His finishing touch was mankind. He created the heavens and the earth and everything in them. God was pleased with His creation. After He created the ocean and dry land, the plants and animals, He said that it was all *good*. But then He created man, and He said this was *very* good. Mankind is different from all of the rest of God's creation. We have intellect beyond that of animals. We have souls. We are made in the image of God. He is creative. We have a bit of creativity within us. Each of us is unique, and our creativity is displayed in a variety of ways. He is loving. We are capable of love. We are His children, and we are to reflect who He is. Just as a child looks somewhat like their earthly parents, we bear God's image. We are to look like our heavenly Father. When others listen to you, do they know that you are a child of the King of kings? When they look at how you carry yourself, do they see humility and yet confidence? You are a child of the Creator of the universe. Made in His image, you represent Him on this earth.

Morning – JOYOUS LIGHT

*Whom having not seen, ye love; in whom, though now ye see him not,
yet believing, ye rejoice with joy unspeakable and full of glory.*
1 PETER 1:8 KJV

Artist Thomas Kinkade was called the "painter of light." His work reflects light shining from the canvas, brightening his pictures. Wouldn't it be wonderful to be known as someone who lightens the places he or she goes? Most often those who light up a room do so because they contain such a measure of love and joy, often contagious joy. Light-filled people who love the Lord are infectious with a dazzling light illuminating the darkness.

Jesus is the light of the world. When we accept Him, the light is poured into us. The Holy Spirit comes to reside within, bringing His light. A glorious gift graciously given to us. When we realize the importance of the gift and the blessings that result from a life led by the Father, we can't contain our happiness. The joy and hope that fill our hearts wells up. Joy uncontained comes when Jesus becomes our Lord. Through Him, through faith, we have hope for the future. What joy! So let it spill forth in love. Be a contagious, light-filled Christian spreading your hope, joy, and love to a hurting world.

Evening – SMILE, SOMEONE NEEDS IT

A merry heart maketh a cheerful countenance.
PROVERBS 15:13 KJV

The gas station attendant whistled and smiled as Phyllis paid for a purchase.

"Nice to hear someone so cheerful this early in the morning," Phyllis said.

"Well, my Christian dad always said that no matter how bad you feel inside, keep a cheerful attitude," the man replied. "People think I'm always happy, but my heart is breaking," he confessed as he bagged her items. "As we speak, my twenty-three-year-old son is standing in a courtroom for sentencing. I bailed him out many times, so I told him that this time he'd have to face it alone. But it hurts."

Touched, Phyllis encouraged the man, saying, "No matter what, know that God's hand is on your son's life."

The man smiled and said, "Thank you. That's why I can smile."

One quote reads, "Some pursue happiness, others create it." Everyone has a story, and often it's a sad one. Who knows what the store clerk is facing, or the person sitting alongside you in the church pew? A smile or kind word can diminish their sorrow even for a split second. It may be the only "hug" they receive all day.

Phyllis prayed for the father who whistled despite his pain—the man who had learned that no matter what happened, God would encourage him to smile.

Morning – KNOWING CHRIST MEANS OBEYING HIM

We know that we have come to know him if we keep his commands.
1 JOHN 2:3 NIV

When we trust in Jesus as our Savior from sin, we believe in Him for eternal life. This decision guarantees that we will live forever with Him in eternity (John 3:14–17). Our assurance is based on God's promise (John 5:24), not on our behavior. However, God wants His children to live for Him during their time on earth. Paul's life goal was to magnify Christ with his life (Philippians 1:20–21). He called it "knowing Christ" and knowing the power of His resurrection, participating in His sufferings, and becoming like Him in His death (Philippians 3:10).

How do Christians *know* Christ? By obeying His Word and living as He did (1 John 2:5–6). How do Christians *obey* Christ? By loving. Jesus said all the commands hang on these two: "Love the Lord your God with all your heart and with all your soul and with all your mind" and "Love your neighbor as yourself" (Matthew 22:37–40). God knows that life works best when we obey, and that means loving God and people.

Christ's resurrection power enables us to obey. "Becoming like Him in His death" means living the self-denying life of the cross—death to being selfish, to indulging sinful passions, and to demanding our own way.

Evening – LIVE OUT THE WORD

"Keep this Book of the Law always on your lips; meditate on it day and night, so that you may be careful to do everything written in it. Then you will be prosperous and successful."
JOSHUA 1:8 NIV

When Joshua becomes the leader of Israel, God gives him one thing to do: immerse himself in scripture and do everything written in it.

James gives a similar directive in the New Testament (James 1:22) when he tells us not to just listen to the Word but to be *doers* of it. In Acts, the Greek word for *doer* can be translated as "poet" or "performer." We can think of it as a command to act out the Bible, to live it on the stage of our lives.

What do our lives look like when we live out God's Word? We have examples in scripture. All scripture is God-breathed, not just the commands. So all of it is instruction for modeling our lives. We can read in the Bible about people like Stephen, David, Mary, Mary Magdalene, the Prodigal Son, the Good Samaritan, and many more. These are people who acted in godly ways as they worked to live out God's Word in their lives, and they serve as examples for us.

God promises to be with us and that obedience brings prosperity and success. We just need to take Him at His Word and obey.

DAY 322

Morning – PRAYING FOR THE PERSECUTOR

"You have heard that it was said, 'Love your neighbor and hate your enemy.' But I tell you, love your enemies and pray for those who persecute you, that you may be children of your Father in heaven."
MATTHEW 5:43–45 NIV

"I can't believe she threw me under the bus that way," Sherri told a friend at work. "My boss stood up in the meeting with the president and senior leadership and told everyone how I had botched the budget presentation." The truth was Sherri had done everything correctly. She had every right to hate her boss at that moment. Instead, she prayed for her. What allowed her to pray for her boss was a love that was inhumanly possible.

What situations have you been in where it would have been much easier (and perhaps more fulfilling) to lash out against someone who had wronged you? At those moments, we should ask the Holy Spirit to fill us with love so we can pray blessings over those who hate us. That is the love of Christ—to love each person, not because of her actions but because of her humanity.

Evening – PRAYER TARGETS SELFISHNESS

Do nothing out of selfish ambition. . . . Rather, in humility value others above yourselves, not looking to your own interests but each of you to the interests of the others.
PHILIPPIANS 2:3–4 NIV

Every workplace seems to have one. A slacker: the person who sweats and toils when the boss is present but loafs, chats, and avoids work when unsupervised. As a result, the workload of truly industrious people increases.

People who strive to appear better than others give little thought of how their self-absorption affects their coworkers, friends, or family. They are difficult to tolerate, let alone pray for.

The above scripture discourages selfish ambition and encourages us to look to the interests of others. As believers, God expects us to take the high road. That means, despite someone's behavior, we are called to pray. Pray for her salvation; pray for God to work on her heart and mind; pray that when approached with the truth, she will receive it with a humble, open spirit.

God targets every heart with the arrow of His Word. It travels as far as the power of the one who thrust it on its course. Prayer, coupled with God's Word spoken to the unlovable, never misses the bull's-eye.

But we must first pray to see beyond the selfishness and view the needs behind it. When we do, God equips us to pray for others. Then the arrow of transformation is launched.

Morning – SO-CALLED WISDOM

Such "wisdom" does not come down from heaven but is earthly,
unspiritual, demonic. For where you have envy and selfish
ambition, there you find disorder and every evil practice.
JAMES 3:15–16 NIV

"Oh, she *knows* how to get what she wants." That statement isn't usually meant as a compliment. Unfortunately, women often have the reputation for being manipulators, passive-aggressive, and gossipers. Tearing down others is an effective way to gain status and relational power.

The early Christians who received James's letter were guilty of the same power-play. In chapter 2, James rebukes them for showing favoritism to the rich in their meetings and demeaning their poorer members (vv. 1–13). In this and other sins, the church had been following "earthly" wisdom—the wisdom that believes it has to tear down others to get what it wants, using any "evil practice" necessary. Disorder resulted—they were harming their relationships and the church body in the process.

These Christians had forgotten a vital truth. Their worth did not come from being richer or wiser than anyone else, but instead it came only through humbly accepting what they *couldn't earn*—their salvation through faith in Christ.

Jesus' acceptance of us is what allows us to give up struggling to maintain our status in comparison to others. What Christ thinks of us matters most, and He makes us free to walk in God's "heavenly wisdom" where humility and love reign (James 3:17).

Evening – AMAZING LOVE

"See, I have engraved you on the palms of my hands;
your walls are ever before me."
ISAIAH 49:16 NIV

We do all sorts of things to keep reminders of our loved ones around us. Children's handprints are memorialized in plaster of paris or in paint. We keep letters and mementos tucked in drawers. Flowers are dried and pressed. But most often we put up their pictures: on walls, on the refrigerator, on our computers, in our wallets, even on our phones.

Now think about how many times a day you look at your hands. We wear wedding rings, class rings, and mother's rings to remind us of our connection to our loved ones in a most obvious way. When God says He has tattooed our faces on His hands, He is telling us we are never out of His thoughts. He thinks of us constantly.

The phrase "your walls are ever before me" refers to the walls of a city. In ancient times, a city without walls was vulnerable to attack. God's keeping an eye on our walls means that He is keeping us under His protection. He never takes His eyes off us.

As humans, there is a limit to our love, our attention, our protective eyes. But God's love is limitless. He loves us in a deep, amazing way with an attention that never strays.

Morning – HE CAN DO ALL

*Then Job answered the LORD and said: "I know that You can do everything,
and that no purpose of Yours can be withheld from You."*
JOB 42:1–2 NKJV

Do we live in the knowledge that the Lord can do all things? Or do we walk each day hesitantly, as though He won't provide or will not answer our call? So very often we doubt, and our faith is small. How is it that we can worship such a great, vast God and have such a tiny belief?

Our unbelief robs God of His due glory and honor and it chains us to insecurity. There is nothing more powerful than the Lord; do we live as though this is truth? We store up so much knowledge of God's Word and promises in our heads, but we never let them settle and grow in our hearts. We keep them stashed away as nice facts that we can access when sorrow sets in, like aspirin for muscle pain, but we do not live by them. We need the Lord to help us place them in our hearts, as a seal. We need Him to help us bind them around our necks so that we are ever conscious of the Lord.

Evening – ARE YOU SURE?

*Yet, with respect to the promise of God, [Abraham] did not
waver in unbelief but grew strong in faith, giving glory to God.*
ROMANS 4:20 NASB

Doubt and uncertainty can upend us if we let them. When we are unsure of something, our steps falter, our words stutter, and our hearts rattle in our chests. Fear can set in. We must guard against this anxious spirit and trust the word God has spoken. To protect against an onslaught of concern, we must learn to lean on Him and allow the Holy Spirit to flow within us.

Paul wrote about doubting God's promises and said that feeling can only be combated by rejoicing. He who was chained, in prison, shipwrecked, and often in danger speaks of singing praises and being full of joy! But how, in our world, are we able to overcome our moods and rejoice? It is difficult, most certainly, and has to be a conscious choice. Steeping your heart in the Word of God, knowing verses that will comfort you, is a great beginning.

A doubting spirit is not of God, for He is not the author of confusion. Theologian Matthew Henry stated, "God honours faith; and great faith honours God." To truly give Him the glory, we must trust. Of this we are sure.

Morning – CAN'T YOU HEAR HIM WHISPER?

He says, "Be still, and know that I am God."
PSALM 46:10 NIV

Our society is so fast-paced there is little time to take care of our mental and physical health, let alone our spiritual health. We are beings created for eternity, and we are made in the image of a supernatural God, and yet paying attention to our spiritual journey gets put off and off and off.

Until something terrible happens. Like a financial crisis. Or infidelity in our marriage. Or bad news at the doctor's office. Or a death in the family. Then we do far more than pause. We go into a full-body panic mode, drenched in fear, racing around, grasping at anything and everything, desperate for answers. For peace.

But had we been in close fellowship with the Lord all along, we wouldn't be so frantic, our spirits so riddled with terror. What we need to do is to be still and know that He is God. Know that He is still in control, even though we think the bad news is in control. It's not. God is.

Life would be more peaceful, more focused, more infused with joy if we were already in the midst of communion with God when troubles come.

Can't you hear Him whisper to you, "Be still, and know that I am God"?

Evening – WE WON'T BE SHAKEN

*"I know the LORD is always with me. I will not
be shaken, for he is right beside me."*
PSALM 16:8 NLT

When crisis strikes, people often drift away from the Lord. Heartbreak doesn't heal overnight. As each day passes, another part of them either dies or regains life. Though they may believe nothing ever could have prepared them for such pain, the everyday choices they've made throughout life determine what they will be like on the other side.

Every day we have a choice to trust God and the opportunity to put things in His hands and look eagerly for the way He will work them out. Every day we are developing a relationship with Him. We are choosing whether we will invest or neglect. Build up or break down. Draw closer or walk farther. It is how we handle ourselves in our daily lives that determines the amount of faith we'll have when a crisis comes.

Maybe our hearts will still break, but we will know who to turn to. We will trust and believe when everything is dark, because we have walked many roads with Him. We know His character. We know He is good. We know that though we don't understand, *He does.* And because He does, we can rest in His love. We don't need to know the reason, only that He is with us.

DAY 326

Morning – EXUDE ENCOURAGEMENT

*Let us consider how we may spur one another on toward love and good
deeds, not giving up meeting together. . .but encouraging one another.*
HEBREWS 10:24–25 NIV

Soon after reading specialist Janey hired Sheila Thomas as a classroom aide to help children with learning problems in reading and writing, Janey realized Mrs. T.'s heart was wounded.

"I left home in my senior year," she confided in Janey privately. "My stepfather wouldn't leave me alone and Mom didn't believe me."

Sheila's success as an aide, mother, wife, and scout leader was legendary. Yet her journaling—no matter what the topic—bled with pain. With Janey's daily encouragement, Sheila became more confident. She began to visualize a different future ahead.

At the end of Sheila's first school year with the reading teacher, Janey encouraged Sheila to write her life story and enter it in a statewide contest. She didn't just place. "Wow, Mrs. T.! Grand prize! You won over everyone in the state!"

At Janey's urging, Sheila enrolled in college and graduated with honors. Sheila became the teacher she had always wanted to be.

Encouragement promotes growth and confidence. Everyone benefits from words that lift and nourish. Everyone needs encouragement to hurdle the negatives that hit them in words, situations, and relationships. Look for the gifts in others. Compliment others on the things they do well, their progress, and their achievements. Give others the vision God sees in them. Sincere words can change a life. God will show you how.

Evening – DOUBLE-SIDED TONGUES

*But no man can tame the tongue. It is an unruly evil, full of deadly poison.
With it we bless our God and Father, and with it we curse men, who have
been made in the similitude of God. Out of the same mouth proceed
blessing and cursing. My brethren, these things ought not to be so.*
JAMES 3:8–10 NKJV

There is a problem with the speech of this generation. It can be crude, unloving, and terribly profane. Yet it can also be affirming, positive, and churchy. And many people see nothing wrong with this dichotomy.

But God's Word says that there is something really awry with this kind of person. James compares speech to the fruit hanging on trees and water coming from specific sources. Everyone is fully aware that figs grow on fig trees, not olives, and that salt water cannot come from a fresh spring. Yet today, we don't blink our eyes when a Christian uses a bad word here and there. We make excuses on the grounds that "she was really upset" or "everyone slips once in a while." But what is really alarming is that our mouths reveal what is in our hearts. In Luke 6:45 (NKJV), Jesus said, "Out of the abundance of the heart [the] mouth speaks."

So is it really okay to use bad language once in a while? Only if it is okay to harbor evil in your heart once in a while! God wants to cleanse and renew our hearts so that our speech will reflect the good treasure that is inside us.

Morning – WRITTEN ON HIM

"Can a mother forget the baby at her breast and have no compassion on the child she has borne? Though she may forget, I will not forget you! See, I have engraved you on the palms of my hands; your walls are ever before me."
ISAIAH 49:15–16 NIV

God's people, during the life of the prophet Isaiah, were under threat of captivity, and they saw impending doom. They knew their dark and rebellious hearts brought this about, and they feared that Jehovah would forget or forsake them. God responded by likening Himself to a mother—the ultimate symbol of love and devotion. Mothers care for their children to guide and protect them. However, in this fallen world there are also women who abandon their children. God says that unlike weak and broken earthly parents, He will remain steadfast. He can do no less when He says that He engraved His children on the palms of His hands. Carved into His hands! This image comes to life when Jesus took nails through His hands to save sinners and make them children of God. What a powerful promise: He will never leave us or forsake us.

Evening – SAFE AND SAVED

*I will call upon the LORD, who is worthy to be praised;
so shall I be saved from my enemies.*
PSALM 18:3 NKJV

In Christ we are safe and saved. How do we know? The truth in God's Word tells us this:

We are hidden with Christ in God (see Colossians 3:3).

"He will cover you with his feathers, and under his wings you will find refuge; his faithfulness will be your shield" (Psalm 91:4 NIV).

"God is our refuge and strength, always ready to help in times of trouble" (Psalm 46:1 NLT).

"God is a dwelling place, and underneath are the everlasting arms" (Deuteronomy 33:27 NASB).

"For in the day of trouble He will conceal me in His tabernacle; in the secret place of His tent He will hide me; He will lift me up on a rock" (Psalm 27:5 NASB).

"The name of the LORD is a fortified tower; the righteous run to it and are safe" (Proverbs 18:10 NIV).

God gives us His Word so that we won't be afraid. He is closer to us than we think. Whenever you feel afraid or lonely, call on His name. Ask Him to make Himself known to you. Copy these scripture verses on note cards and read them again and again. God's Word is living and active, and the Spirit of God will remind you of these truths when you need them most. Don't be ashamed when you feel afraid. . .just take your fears straight to the only one who can free you from them. He will comfort you and cover you with His loving-kindness. .

Morning – LOVE GOD, LOVE OTHERS

And [Jesus] said to him, "'You shall love the Lord your God with all your heart, and with all your soul, and with all your mind.' This is the great and foremost commandment. The second is like it, 'You shall love your neighbor as yourself.'"
Matthew 22:37–39 NASB

It was Saint Augustine who said, "Love God and do what you will," meaning that if we're truly loving God, everything else will come together as it should (Romans 8:28). We'll make the choices He wants us to make as He guides us. We'll delight in Him and do His will. The entire Word of God is summed up in Jesus' response to the Pharisee who asked Him to tell which commandment was greatest. That's simple. Our purpose and mission in life is this: love God and love others.

The scripture goes on to say that the entire "Law and the Prophets hang on these two commandments" (Matthew 22:40 NIV). If you're obeying God's command to love Him above all else and to love others, then you are fulfilling all the rest.

How can you live a life of love? Ask God to be the very center of your life. Get to know Him on a moment-by-moment basis. Both His power and presence are constantly available to you. As you relate to others, remember the preciousness of each person. Even the difficult ones. They are created and loved by God.

Evening – KINDNESS

"Here is my servant, whom I uphold, my chosen one in whom I delight."
Isaiah 42:1 NIV

Jackie and her daughters celebrated Advent in a unique way. They decided that every day they would perform little acts of kindness. They wrote their ideas down, and with much excitement they planned to surprise friends, family, and strangers with unexpected blessings. They paid parking meters that were about to expire, sang carols at nursing homes, gave hot chocolate to the mail carrier, babysat for free, and did many other things anonymously or expecting nothing in return. The result? They were blessed with smiles, thank-yous, and even a few happy tears; and they hoped that their acts of kindness would prompt others to do the same.

In 1 Peter 5:2 (NIV), the Bible says, "Be shepherds of God's flock that is under your care, watching over them—not because you must, but because you are willing, as God wants you to be; not pursuing dishonest gain, but eager to serve."

God calls His people to serve, and service comes in many forms. Some work actively in the church as ministers and missionaries. Others volunteer in their communities through homeless shelters, fund-raising projects, food banks, and other causes. And every day, Christians like Jackie and her girls work silently in the background performing little acts of kindness.

Can you encourage someone today through a little act of kindness?

Morning – SET YOURSELF UP

"Now set your heart and your soul to seek the Lord your God. Therefore arise and build the sanctuary of the Lord God, to bring the ark of the covenant of the Lord and the holy articles of God into the house that is to be built for the name of the Lord."
1 Chronicles 22:19 nkjv

So much of our work and service for the Lord is attitude. When it comes to money, the difference between saving and hoarding is attitude. Here in 1 Chronicles, David, a man after God's own heart, instructs Israel to "set" their hearts and minds to seek the Lord before preparing His temple. Do we take the same mindset when going to church on Sunday or doing daily devotions? Or have these times with God become a check box on our schedules?

There is a fine line between worship and obligation. You know when someone is simply going through the motions; how much more does our Lord? Seeking God does not come naturally for us; we must prepare ourselves. There will always be something seemingly urgent when you sit down to pray or read scripture. There will always be a distraction. These are Satan's tactics; he wants nothing more than to distract you from precious time with God. In those moments, cry out to your Father and ask for focus. This is not weakness; it is intimacy—intimacy that we desperately need.

Evening – REMEMBERING WORKS

Sing to Him, sing psalms to Him; talk of all His wondrous works! Glory in His holy name; let the hearts of those rejoice who seek the Lord! Seek the Lord and His strength; seek His face evermore! Remember His marvelous works which He has done, His wonders, and the judgments of His mouth.
1 Chronicles 16:9–12 nkjv

We as selfish sinners really enjoy singing our own praises. It is fun, seemingly fulfilling, but is it healthy? When we don't see God's hand in small and significant events, we inevitably take credit or give credit to the wrong source. The kings prior to David took the credit and utterly disregarded God's hand in their lives and Israel's triumphs.

Our Lord is much too great, holy, righteous, and wise to not be recognized. As we see throughout scripture, the Lord does not honor a prideful heart. Once we realize our complete dependence on God, this is when we truly seek Him. In today's passage David calls us to seek His presence continually. Why? Because there is nothing that exists outside of our Lord. If we are to find strength, purpose, and wonders, they are to be found in the Lord. We might find counterfeits in other areas, but they ultimately lead to a dead end and emptiness. At these hollow moments, we are like the prodigal son. We have the choice to run back to our Father, repent, and trust His sovereign character, or we search and find another false god. Satan is all too willing to give us another false god—a lifeless alternative. Will you abandon your pride, selfishness, and unbelief and run back to your Father, singing His praises?

DAY 330

Morning – NOT WITHHOLDING

For the Lord God is a sun and shield; the Lord bestows favor and honor;
no good thing does he withhold from those whose walk is blameless.
Psalm 84:11 NIV

Gina's cat wanted to go out again as he did every evening. He pawed at the glass as if Gina didn't know the routine.

"It's raining out, kitty. Trust me, you don't want to go out tonight," she said, picking up her eighteen-pound, brown-and-black-striped feline that looked more like a bobcat. She held him calmly and looked in his beautiful green eyes. He promptly hissed at her.

Gina laughed and put him down, where he proceeded to paw more aggressively at the glass, as if to say, "Have you heard nothing that I've asked of you?"

I'm like that with God, Gina thought. *I ask Him to do something for me. I see He is completely able to do it. I also see His love for me. He clearly adores me. Yet He does not give me what I ask for. I forget that He sees beyond the door I am asking Him to open, and He knows when the time is right to either open it or redirect me.*

Evening – WAITING

Wait patiently for the Lord. Be brave and
courageous. Yes, wait patiently for the Lord.
Psalm 27:14 NLT

Waiting is rarely easy. Waiting means that something we desire is being delayed—postponed—and we don't know when it will arrive. It can be even harder when we are waiting for news that could be terrible—news that could change our lives for the worse.

Isn't it interesting that David linked being brave and courageous to this act of waiting? He is telling us that even though we don't know the timing or outcome of whatever it is we're waiting on, we should be brave in the face of it! We should not cower in a corner but move forward with courage! He also says to wait *patiently.* Here are some other words for *patient: calm, composed, enduring, uncomplaining,* and *understanding.* Waiting is not a passive thing! There is a call to action during this time.

There is good in waiting. Take this opportunity to lean into God. At first you may find that spending time with Him is hard, because you feel like He is keeping things from you. But soon you will find that waiting on God is one of the most rewarding things you could ever do.

Morning – A FOREVER LOVE

But I trust in your unfailing love;
my heart rejoices in your salvation.
PSALM 13:5 NIV

The Bible tells us that God's love for us is unfailing. The dictionary defines unfailing as "completely dependable, inexhaustible, endless." Our hearts can truly rejoice knowing that we can never exhaust God's love. It won't run out. We can completely depend on God and His love for us at all times and in all situations.

Many people—even Christians—go through life believing that God is just a grumpy old man at the edge of heaven looking down on us with disappointment and disgust. That couldn't be further from the truth! Through Jesus Christ and His power at work within us, God sees us as *holy* and *dearly loved* (Colossians 3:12 NIV) children. His love is unfailing, and that can never change! Check out the following verses:

- "In your unfailing love you will lead the people you have redeemed. In your strength you will guide them to your holy dwelling." (Exodus 15:13 NIV)
- "Many are the woes of the wicked, but the LORD's unfailing love surrounds the one who trusts in him." (Psalm 32:10 NIV)
- "How priceless is your unfailing love, O God! People take refuge in the shadow of your wings." (Psalm 36:7 NIV)

The next time you start to think that God is upset with you, remember His unfailing and unchanging love.

Evening – HIS DELIGHT

"The LORD your God is with you, the Mighty Warrior who saves.
He will take great delight in you; in his love he will no longer
rebuke you, but will rejoice over you with singing."
ZEPHANIAH 3:17 NIV

Delight. What a wonderful word! The connotations of enjoyment and pleasure, joy and gladness. You are usually delighted when something has pleased you. Maybe it's the song of a bird; the chatter of your child; or simply a quiet, starry night that soothes your senses and fills your heart with satisfaction.

Scripture tells us the Lord will take delight in us and will rejoice over us with singing. Imagine that! The very mighty warrior of the universe relishing His creation. And that creation is you. It's hard to imagine when we have our dirty faces or are out of sorts that He could care for us at all. But it's true. Our God saves and loves. Our God is truth and mercy. He loves His children.

Take a deep breath and carve out some time to appreciate and bask in the truth of the Bible. God loves *you* and He delights in *you*. You are the apple of His eye. Reach out a hand to Him this day, knowing full well He will interlace His fingers with yours and never let go. Selah. Pause and reflect.

DAY 332

Morning – SAFE AND SECURE

In thee, O Lord, do I put my trust: let me never be put to confusion. Deliver me in thy righteousness, and cause me to escape: incline thine ear unto me, and save me. Be thou my strong habitation, whereunto I may continually resort: thou hast given commandment to save me; for thou art my rock and my fortress.
PSALM 71:1–3 KJV

Rae had gone with her young sons for a couple days to visit her brother. He was a brave single man to have her crazy crew stay the night. After they all ate macaroni and cheese dinner together, the boys settled in with a movie while Rae and her brother sat in the kitchen with dessert and caught up.

Lost in good conversation, she suddenly realized that three-year-old Dexter was nowhere to be seen. She quickly walked the short hall of the three-bedroom apartment scanning each room until she found the sweetest scene she had ever found him in. In her brother's room, there lay Dexter snuggled in the center of the large fluffy bed, tucked under the down comforter, surrounded by a little cloud of pillows. When he saw her, he giggled and cuddled in with the toys in his hands.

Rae felt so good to see her child so happy, safe, and secure. It made her think how much God must love protecting and blessing her too.

Evening – THE BATTLE IS REAL, BUT SO IS OUR REFUGE

Keep me safe, O God, for I have come to you for refuge.
PSALM 16:1 NLT

Have you ever had days, weeks, or months when this was all you could pray? Or maybe in the heat of the battle, the intensity of the chase, the thought of running to Him for safety never even crossed your mind. Perhaps you believed this was a battle you could win on your own! And yet with each swing of your sword, you felt your strength fail.

Life is hard, and it's okay to admit that. The enemy we face on a daily basis is cunning and unrelenting. How wonderful it is that David looked to the Lord for his protection. And it wasn't protection in a spiritual sense—David's very life was at stake! He prayed to the Lord to keep him safe.

Maybe it feels like the Lord is far away—too intangible to be sought out for emotional strength, much less physical needs. My sister, He is not too far. He is a physical God who is able to keep you secure. He is ready and waiting to be your refuge. Whether your need is tangible or emotional, go to Him.

Morning – GOD WILL RESCUE YOU

He brought me out into a spacious place;
he rescued me because he delighted in me.
PSALM 18:19 NIV

God miraculously delivered the Israelites from the waters of the Red Sea. He took them to the Promised Land of Canaan, which was rich and flowing with milk and honey. But He did not do this immediately. The Israelites had been in bondage for forty years in Egypt. God heard their cry. He saw their oppression. The Bible tells us that the Lord came down and rescued them. He does the same for us today. It may be that you have been in a hard place for a long time, so long that you have nearly given up on God. You may not believe that He will come for you, that He even wants to rescue you. The Israelites felt this way also. God is still in the business of rescuing His own today. When He saves you out of a depressed and sorrowful situation, He will take you to a new place. From Egypt to Canaan, so to speak. Have you sought God's deliverance? Be diligent in prayer. In His timing, God will answer your plea, just as He did for the Israelites. You are His child. Even while you remain in the desert, He can refresh your soul. Seek Him. He delights in you.

Evening – OUR STRONG ARM

But LORD, be merciful to us, for we have waited for you. Be our
strong arm each day and our salvation in times of trouble.
ISAIAH 33:2 NLT

At times we may feel weak and discouraged. We don't even have the energy to lift our heads up and take on the next challenge. But God can turn us around. When we go to Him, when we seek His face, when we put all our cares on His shoulders, He comes to our rescue. He not only willingly takes our burdens away but also becomes our arm of strength. Through Him, we find more than enough energy to change the next diaper, tackle another project at work, seek a new path for our lives, deal with our teens and aging parents, cope with an illness, and find a way through a difficult relationship. Only God can turn our challenges into opportunities for Him to show His power. Just be patient. Wait on Him. And He will do more than see you through.

DAY 334

Morning – PEACE PLACEMENT

*And He shall stand and feed His flock in the strength of the Lord,
in the majesty of the name of the Lord His God; and they shall
abide, for now He shall be great to the ends of the earth.*
MICAH 5:4 NKJV

Shepherds were not society's most desired company. They tended to be rough, ragged, scrappy men who lived in the wilderness with the livestock. When the prophet Micah prophesied about the coming Messiah, he used language that the Israelites would not have guessed; Jesus will shepherd, be great, be their peace.

What is your peace? Do you place peace in your work, accomplishments, talents, or money? There are numerous things that offer peace, though they are not peace. Christ doesn't just bring peace; it's who He is. What a remarkable God we have who is the essence of peace and love—two things we strive to gain. When we strive, we feel compelled to work for peace, love, or righteousness, and all our works fall short. Christ did not come to earth and die and rise again so that we could meet Him halfway in a bargain. No, His incarnation, death, and resurrection were to pay the full price for our sins.

Evening – MAKING IT TO THE TOP

*I once thought these things were valuable, but now I consider them worthless
because of what Christ has done. . . . I press on to reach the end of the race and
receive the heavenly prize for which God, through Christ Jesus, is calling us.*
PHILIPPIANS 3:7, 14 NLT

The world believes who you know can take you far in life. You need the right contacts with clout to make it to the top. You need to run with the right crowd to be successful. You may even be expected to do unethical or immoral things to move up in the company. Women are sometimes asked to have affairs with their superiors. You may be asked to lie for your boss, dress a certain way, or flirt with potential customers. This lifestyle is degrading and results in unhappiness and tragedy for many.

God's Word teaches a different example. Knowing Christ is the best decision we can make as we go through life. He will never ask us to do anything immoral but will give us a pure heart and teach us to respect ourselves and others. It may mean we don't run with the popular, successful crowd. We may get passed over for a promotion or a raise, but knowing Christ gives us hope for the future. As we press toward the mark for a higher calling in Him, we find peace and wisdom in our daily lives.

Morning – STEP TWO: TRULY FOCUSING

*"O our God, will You not judge them? For we have no power
against this great multitude that is coming against us;
nor do we know what to do, but our eyes are upon You."*
2 CHRONICLES 20:12 NKJV

Even with a great army coming against him, King Jehoshaphat of Judah kept his faith in God. Even more importantly, Jehoshaphat knew enough to humble himself and go to the "guy" who was really in charge—his own King, the Lord God, the one whose spiritual muscle was a tremendous force in the material world.

In his prayer, Jehoshaphat reminded himself *and* his people of several things: (1) that no one can withstand God's power; (2) that time and time again, God has saved His people—as promised; (3) that God would hear his prayer and save Judah from her aggressors; and (4) that although Jehoshaphat and his citizens had no idea what to do, all would be well because their eyes were on the Lord—front and center.

The same holds true to this day! With her eyes on God, today's woman is not cognizant of the crashing waves. She no longer feels the sting of the wind. She refuses to allow her mind to wander with what-ifs. She looks away from storms, fears, and enemies as she determines to keep her eyes on the prize she knows is hers—the power, peace, and presence of God.

Evening – STAYING ON TRACK

I have fought a good fight, I have finished my course, I have kept the faith.
2 TIMOTHY 4:7 KJV

In our hustle-bustle world, it's easy to get so busy we forget our priorities. Hopefully, as believers, we've established our priority list with God at the top. Staying in touch with Him and walking in His will should be our number one goal.

Paul knew this when he exhorted the churches to stick closely to the teachings of Jesus. He knew the fickle heart and how easy it would be for them to stray. In his letters to Timothy, he reminded the young man of the importance of drawing close to God, hearing His heartbeat. Despite the pain and afflictions Paul suffered in his life, he kept his eyes on Jesus, using praise to commune with God.

Likewise, we can keep in constant communion with the Father. We are so blessed to have been given the Holy Spirit within to keep us in tune with His will. Through His guidance, that still, small voice, we can rest assured our priorities will stay focused on Jesus. As the author A. W. Tozer wrote, "Lord, guide me carefully on this uncharted sea as I daily seek You in Your word. Then use me mightily as Your servant this year as I boldly proclaim Your word in leading others."

DAY 336

Morning – THE GIFT OF FRIENDS

The seeds of good deeds become a tree of life; a wise person wins friends.
PROVERBS 11:30 NLT

During a long, boring presentation, Hillary saw the text from her friend LeeAnne and smiled. LeeAnne often texted funny pictures or silly quotes to Hillary on Wednesdays, because she knew Wednesdays were particularly stressful days for her best friend.

"Thank u!" Hillary replied. As she hit SEND, she thought of a joke she could send to LeeAnne after the meeting was over. She looked forward to their weekly lunch date, when they talked about their families, jobs, and relationship with the Lord.

Thank You, Lord, that You placed LeeAnne right in my path. Help me to be as good a friend to her and other women as she's been to me. And forgive me for not looking past the surface sometimes.

Hillary regretted that she had often misjudged other women. While the speaker droned on, she pondered how God had brought LeeAnne into her life. Before they'd met, Hillary thought LeeAnne was too pretty, wealthy, and successful to be real or down-to-earth. However, at a women's ministry event, they ended up sitting next to one another and discovered that they had quite a few things in common. Their friendship had been growing ever since.

Evening – GOOD OL' AUNT MABLE

Be kind and compassionate to one another,
forgiving each other, just as in Christ God forgave you.
EPHESIANS 4:32 NIV

Some days it can be fairly easy to don a smile and carry a basket of sweetness and light to scatter everywhere we go.

That is, until your aunt Mable shows up. Wow, when that woman walks through the door, it's as if a pit bull has had its tail pulled and you're the one with the guilty look. Aunt Mable will twist your words, offer you a few backhanded compliments, point out all your latest transgressions, and judge you within an inch of your life. When she's done with you, there will be nothing left but tears.

Yes, with Aunty Mable around, being a Christian becomes anything but easy.

We all have an Aunt Mable in our lives. And the only way to deal with the Aunty Mables is to pray for them. We must have compassion for them, love them, forgive them. Why, you may ask, should we bother? Because that is what Christ has done for all of us. While we were yet sinners, Christ died for us.

He even died for Aunt Mable. He even died for me and you. Because whether we want to admit it or not—there is a little Aunt Mable in all of us.

Morning – CAN OTHERS COUNT ON YOU?

The Lord is not slow about His promise, as some count slowness,
but is patient toward you, not wishing for any to
perish but for all to come to repentance.
2 PETER 3:9 NASB

Jessica grew up in a home filled with lies. Her parents made promises and very seldom kept them. Trusting others was extremely difficult for her. When someone broke a promise, the childhood wounds caused her heart to bleed once again.

There was a time when a person who made a promise refused to break that promise—even if keeping it cost them large sums of money. For the most part, society sees a lie as a normal, everyday part of life. In general, white lies are acceptable because there is a misconception that no one gets hurt. Lies are lies, and when promises are broken, someone suffers the consequences.

The Bible says that Satan is the father of lies and there is no truth in him, but that God will keep all of His promises. You are born again to reflect God's character and nature. People should be able to count on you like you count on God. Carefully consider the cost before you make a promise—and then keep it at all costs.

Evening – A MATTER OF CONSCIENCE

The integrity of the upright will guide them, but the
perversity of the unfaithful will destroy them.
PROVERBS 11:3 NKJV

Donna had been so excited the last three weeks about her newest and most prominent client, but this morning something had changed. The owner of the company she now represented had asked her a difficult question as he sat across from her desk. He had asked her to "fudge a little" and say that "they had been with her organization three years instead of three months" when others inquired about their business relationship. He even went as far as requesting she "doctor up" a few dates.

The client immediately recognized that his question made Donna uncomfortable, yet he pressed her for an answer. She squirmed a little and thought, *This is the biggest client I've ever brought on board.* She took a deep breath and looked her client in the eye. "No," she told him. "That's not the way I do business. If I fudged for you, then you could not trust anything that ever came out of my office. If you can't work with me, then I understand."

Her client smiled. "Good! I like that answer. I want to be able to trust you and this company to represent me in honesty and truth!" Donna relaxed. *It had been a test—a test of her ethics and of her faith.* She stood to shake her client's hand. "It will be a pleasure doing business with you, sir."

Morning – LAUGH TODAY!

A happy heart makes the face cheerful,
but heartache crushes the spirit.
PROVERBS 15:13 NIV

Some researchers say that a positive attitude can actually help you to live longer! Isn't that amazing? Did you know that laughter can do the same thing? Find something to laugh about today. Abraham's wife, Sarah, laughed when she discovered she was pregnant at an old age after longing for a baby for so many years. God surprised her when she had given up! Perhaps God has granted you an unexpected blessing. If so, laugh with joy today! If you have trouble with this, read the comics in the newspaper. Watch a humorous Youtube video of a dog or cat. Rent a movie that has some good, clean comedy. Read a few entries in a joke book. Do whatever it takes to find some humor in this day. Often, the greatest laughs come when we are free enough to laugh at ourselves. Have you done something really silly lately? Have you made a mistake that left you chuckling? Laughter is good for the soul. The book of Proverbs says that if your heart is happy, your face will show it. Are you going around with a long face? Do people look forward to seeing you or are you a "Debbie Downer"? If you find yourself complaining today, try replacing negative words with cheerful ones. Everyone enjoys being around someone who wears a smile.

Evening – A JOYFUL HEART

Sarah said, "God has brought me laughter,
and everyone who hears about this will laugh with me."
GENESIS 21:6 NIV

Kayla and her husband attended the funeral for the elderly mother of one of his business associates. Afterward, Kayla complained to her husband about how some of the grieving family members had behaved.

"Did you see the two daughters standing at their mother's casket, laughing? I couldn't believe my eyes."

Kayla's husband quickly came to their defense. "Yes, I heard them talking," he said. "They were remembering their mother's good sense of humor and some of the funny things she did when they were children."

In the Bible, King Solomon says, "There is a time for everything, and a season for every activity under the heavens" (Ecclesiastes 3:1). He adds this piece of wisdom: "All the days of the oppressed are wretched, but the cheerful heart has a continual feast" (Proverbs 15:15). While the daughters' laughter might have seemed inappropriate, it was exactly what they needed to start healing their broken hearts.

Are you or someone you know unhappy? A little laughter might help. Begin with a smile. When you hear laughter, move toward it and try to join in. Seek the company of happy friends, and invite humor into your conversations. Most of all, praise God. Praise is the best way to heal a hurting soul. Praise God joyfully for His many blessings.

Morning – OBEY WITHOUT DELAY

I will hasten and not delay to obey your commands.
PSALM 119:60 NIV

Belinda felt compelled to personally deliver the shawl her church was praying over. The hand-crocheted shawl was intended for her friend Cheryl, who was now in hospice care near her family over one thousand miles away. After worship, Belinda asked the pastor if there was a plan for getting the shawl to Cheryl. When she learned there wasn't a plan, Belinda knew what she needed to do. Amazingly, there was a reasonably priced round-trip flight available that very day.

By making the impromptu trip and taking the shawl, Belinda was able to personally share the love and prayers of their church with her dear friend Cheryl and her family. Soon after Belinda returned home, she received a call from Cheryl's husband. He told her that Cheryl had gone home to be with the Lord, wrapped securely in the prayer shawl. When she heard the peace in his voice, Belinda understood why the Lord had needed her to immediately make the trip to Cheryl's bedside.

Often we rationalize why we can't do something we feel called to do. We tell ourselves we don't have enough time, money, or skill. As Christians, we need to use our talents to determine how to accomplish the tasks our Lord asks us to accept. We need to be prompt "can do" Christians, like Belinda.

Evening – HARVESTTIME

"You know the saying, 'Four months between planting and harvest.'
But I say, wake up and look around. The fields are already ripe for harvest."
JOHN 4:35 NLT

When we notice a task that needs to be done, could it be a nudge from God? It's easy to think someone else will take care of it—whatever *it* is. We may believe we're not qualified or our schedule is too full, or we might even think it's beneath us. Whether it is a job at church or in the community or within our families, finding excuses is simple.

Sometimes when we wonder how we can work in the spiritual harvest Jesus mentions, we get grandiose ideas, beyond what God intends. He may ask us to serve in a food pantry when we thought we should preach the gospel in some remote country and lead hundreds to faith in Christ. Or He might want us to go to another nation, but what we're to do there is play with children or carry concrete blocks to help build a one-room school.

The only way our work will matter eternally is to allow God to direct our plans every day, and ask Him to show us exactly what will touch someone's life. Most often, He will tell us simply to show His love in some uncomplicated way that comes naturally. Obeying in those effortless situations prepares us for the times when the Lord directs us to do something that requires total dependence on Him to accomplish.

DAY 340

Morning – PRAYER OR BREVITY MANIA?

God knows how often I pray for you. Day and night
I bring you and your needs in prayer to God.
ROMANS 1:9 NLT

Our language is laden with abbreviations, or as one called it—brevity mania. Organizations are known for their acronyms—MADD, CARE, WAVES—and abbreviations like the AMA, ADA, NRA, and AFT abound. And how about texting—using symbols and letters to translate whole phrases or emotions? Crying equals :'-(and FWIW means "for what it's worth."

Although abbreviations—designed to lessen verbiage—are in vogue, they puzzle the over-fifty crowd. Is it too much to ask for the vocalization of a phrase for those of us who find stopping for an MAIB (mental abbreviation interpretation break) distracting?

Likewise, our prayers are often lost in the obscurity of brevity. We love fast food and instant success. All the while we struggle to take the time to utter a few extra syllables to God. We shoot "arrow" prayers while expecting God's response ASAP. We expect the Lord, who knows all, to interpret our every need.

Although arrow prayers are sometimes needed, God asks us to pray *specifically* and often for the person or problem just as Paul did. God made us to fellowship with Him. That includes open communication void of brevity mania!

Evening – SENDING GOD'S FAVOR

You help us by your prayers. Then many will give thanks on our behalf
for the gracious favor granted us in answer to the prayers of many.
2 CORINTHIANS 1:11 NIV

"I'll pray for you." Why is it those words seem weak, almost trite at times? It's what we say when we don't know what to say. When we don't know what to do, but we long to do something.

Yet, those four words are probably the most powerful words we can speak, as long as we follow through. When we pray, we call upon all the power of the King of heaven. When we pray, we see results. When we pray, miracles happen.

When we pray, people are blessed.

Friends, the power of prayer is better in a crisis than a casserole. It's better than being there, holding someone's hand, or doing their laundry. The power of prayer does more for a missionary on the other side of the world than a box of clothes or even a check.

Prayer brings peace. Prayer brings wisdom and clarity. Prayer is powerful.

Next time we offer to pray for someone, we can say it with the confidence that our prayers will be heard. They will be answered. And they will make a beautiful difference in the lives of those for whom we pray.

Morning – NO SHAME

Those who look to him for help will be radiant with joy;
no shadow of shame will darken their faces.
PSALM 34:5 NLT

Adam and Eve had the perfect home—a beautiful garden. Every plant, tree, and animal was theirs. Their perfect Father met every one of their needs. His rules were clear. All the garden belonged to them—except the fruit of the one tree. Adam was told plainly by God: eat the fruit of this tree, and you will surely die (Genesis 2:16–17).

Of course, the one thing they couldn't have was the one thing that captured their attention. When the serpent presented an opportunity, Adam and Eve took the bait. What followed was a feeling known to all of us thereafter—shame. They hid their faces and their bodies from God, covered with the profound awareness that they had failed Him. In the cool of the garden, Adam tried to avoid God and hide from Him further. Yes, the consequences were severe, but God demanded Adam and Eve look to Him so He could remove their shame.

No matter how we disappoint God, we never have to hide from Him or cover our faces in shame. All we need to do is turn to Him and ask for His forgiveness, mercy, and grace. One look at the Father and our faces can be radiant with joy.

Evening – BEAUTY FOR ASHES

To appoint unto them that mourn in Zion, to give unto them beauty for ashes, the oil
of joy for mourning, the garment of praise for the spirit of heaviness; that they might
be called trees of righteousness, the planting of the LORD, that he might be glorified.
ISAIAH 61:3 KJV

Repentance calls a believer to mourn for her sin. This mourning requires a Christian to recognize their sin and to feel remorse for their actions that offended God. God will use this humility and love of Him to give His children freedom and joy. Ashes were a sign of death and mourning—of being overcome by grief. However, God takes away death and the destruction of sin and instead gives the beauty of His presence. He molds the hearts of Christians to be more like the beautiful heart of Jesus. The second gift mentioned in the verse, oil, was an important medicine of antiquity; when Christians mourn their sin, God gives the medicine of joy by reminding His children that He cleanses them of the darkness in their hearts. When burdened by the cares of this world, He removes the spirit of heaviness and depression and clothes His people with praise and blessings. God then makes His children stand tall and firm like trees who have inherited the righteousness of Christ because they realize they have no righteousness of their own. The great gardener does this work of healing and reconciliation because He is good.

DAY 342

Morning – CLEANING UP

Draw near to God and He will draw near to you. Cleanse your hands,
you sinners; and purify your hearts, you double-minded.
JAMES 4:8 NKJV

Picture a muddy, unshorn sheep. A shepherd would have a job before him to clean up that animal because the fleece is quite deep. He must dig down with the shears layer by layer, tugging at the wool as he goes. In order to shear the sheep, he has to have hold of it, a firm grasp on a wiggling, uncooperative animal. Whatever it takes, the shepherd cleans the sheep.

Now picture us. Uncooperative, squirming, with insides that need to be cleaned. Our thoughts and actions have not been pure. Maybe we have lost our temper, taken advantage of another, or gossiped. Actions that are not what God wants of us. Actions that are called sin. Sin that blackens the heart. Like the sheep, we must be gathered in and cleaned.

Our most glorious God has promised He will do that for us when we ask. If we draw near to God and ask for His forgiveness, He will cleanse our hearts and make us part of His fold. Hallelujah. What a magnificent and overwhelming plan He has for us!

Evening – REASONING WITH GOD

"Come now, and let us reason together," says the LORD,
"though your sins are like scarlet, they shall be as white as snow;
though they are red like crimson, they shall be as wool."
ISAIAH 1:18 NKJV

Rabbi Isaac Lichtenstein starts one of his defenses for Jesus as Messiah with these words: "Come let us reason together." He cleverly invokes the very reasoning of God to prove to his Jewish readers that Jesus of Nazareth is indeed the Savior promised since the beginning of sinful time. For the rabbi, as a man, to propose such a dialogue is not too unusual, but for the Maker of all to approach and beckon humans into a similar discussion is breathtaking.

In the previous verse God instructs the people to "learn to do good; seek justice, rebuke the oppressor; defend the fatherless, plead for the widow." Knowing that they failed and will continue to fail, He laid that all aside and asked His people what they think of this: He will wash and whiten them. They only need to live in willingness to be obedient. They must recognize the darkness of their brokenness and break from it. How humbling that the Almighty would stoop to speak with us below. His call to come and then His proposition to deliberate together with Him reveals how deeply He cares for us. So let us come and let us listen to what He proposes: life.

Morning – ENCOURAGING WORDS

*Let no unwholesome word proceed from your mouth, but only
such a word as is good for edification according to the need
of the moment, so that it will give grace to those who hear.*
EPHESIANS 4:29 NASB

A talented puppeteer performs at elementary school campuses. His presentation is meant to decrease bullying. His simple message is taught through rainbow-haired puppets with silly voices. "Build others up! Don't tear others down!" It sounds easy, but is it?

Do you find yourself gossiping about coworkers or authority figures? This is, as the apostle Paul calls it in Ephesians, "worthless talk." It does nothing to build up but only to tear down. Imagine a young child playing with blocks. Such joy as the tower grows, block by block, taller and taller. But then, with a wrong placement, the whole thing comes crashing down! Are you a builder or a destroyer? Do your words add to others' welfare or are they destructive of it? As believers, our conversation should be wholesome and encouraging. Pray that God will remind you of this at the right moments so that you will not carelessly corrupt instead of intentionally encouraging.

Evening – ITTY BITTY WORDS

*The words of the reckless pierce like swords,
but the tongue of the wise brings healing.*
PROVERBS 12:18 NIV

Whoever started the childhood chant "Sticks and stones may break my bones, but words will never hurt me" lied. Plain and simple.

Words may seem itty bitty as they escape from our lips, but they have the power to make us cringe and cry and crumble into pieces. Pieces that may never come back together again the way they were meant to be.

Words can destroy a reputation. Break a tender heart. And a not-so-tender heart. Words can create an untold ripple effect of misery. And our words can grieve the Holy Spirit. Surely there is a better way to live. There is. It's with the power of the Holy Spirit. From Psalms comes a wonderful daily heart-prayer: "May these words of my mouth and this meditation of my heart be pleasing in your sight, LORD, my Rock and my Redeemer" (Psalm 19:14 NIV).

Our words can heal, comfort, challenge, encourage, and inspire. It's our choice, every minute of every day, which kind of words we will use. Those that heal or those that hurt. Let us always speak truth, yes, but let us do it with tenderness. Not with a mindset that feeds our egos, but with a caring spirit that pleases God.

DAY 344

Morning – SERVE THE LORD WITH GLADNESS

Make a joyful noise unto the LORD, all ye lands. Serve the LORD with gladness:
come before his presence with singing. . . . Enter into his gates with thanksgiving,
and into his courts with praise: be thankful unto him, and bless his name.
PSALM 100:1–2, 4 KJV

Many people in our culture think of Sunday as a day to relax and watch football, go fishing, or fire up the grill and spend time with their family. A great number of people no longer think of Sunday as a day of worship. As of 2014, the Barna Group stated that "churchless people"—those who hadn't attended a service anytime during the past six months—stood at 114 million.

Some people may find that statistic astounding, but how faithful are we to attend our local house of worship? Has Sunday become just another day? Do we consider it "our time" to unwind and rest from the stress and pressures of the week? Do we go only when it's convenient or on a special occasion? Are we becoming a part of that alarming statistic?

Worship is a time of acknowledging God in our lives and showing Him we're grateful for all His blessings, a time to make a joyful noise and sing praises to Him. It's a matter of getting our priorities straight, deciding to give back to God a little of the time He's given us. Keeping God first in our lives means setting aside time to worship Him.

Evening – A DAY FOR YOUR BEST

"Keep the Sabbath day holy. Don't pursue your own interests on that day,
but enjoy the Sabbath and speak of it with delight as the LORD's holy day.
Honor the Sabbath in everything you do on that day, and don't follow
your own desires or talk idly. Then the LORD will be your delight."
ISAIAH 58:13–14 NLT

Sunday has lost its special aura. The "come as you are" philosophy of many churches has made us lose the beauty of dressing up to attend God's house. The "early service" habit has let churchgoers get their duty done quickly so they can rush off to spend the rest of the day doing something other than worshipping and resting. The proliferation of restaurants open on Sunday has made us forget that Sunday dinner at home used to be the best meal of the week.

Now, in the days of the Old Testament, the people brought sacrifices to the Lord as an offering. These items had to be the best—the healthiest grain and produce, the most perfect lamb of the flock. There could be no defect or blemish in the offering presented to the Lord God.

Today, we are under the New Covenant, which did not abolish the old but rather fulfilled it, as Jesus said. One day in seven is still to be set aside for rest and worship, according to the pattern established by God at the beginning and set forth in the Ten Commandments. If we return to these values, perhaps we would see the beautiful benefits that accompany honoring this day of the week.

Morning – DIFFICULT PEOPLE

*"So be strong and courageous! Do not be afraid and do not panic
before them. For the Lord your God will personally go ahead
of you. He will neither fail you nor abandon you."*
DEUTERONOMY 31:6 NLT

Jennifer had been successful in her job at a large insurance company, but a shift in management turned her dream job into a nightmare. Jennifer and her new boss did not get along. Whatever she did, he seemed displeased. He called her into his office and complained about her work, and he stood at her desk and scolded her in front of her coworkers. Sometimes Jennifer went home and cried.

She didn't know what to do. There were several options. She could find another job; she could learn to put up with her boss's bad behavior; or she could confront him in a godly way. As she searched for answers through prayer and scripture, Jennifer decided to have a talk with her boss. The idea frightened her. Her mind raced with the consequences. She could lose her job! Still, it was what she needed to do. Jennifer carefully prepared what she would say. She planned her next steps if the conversation went badly, and she held tightly to the promise that the Lord would lead her.

Are you dealing with a difficult person? Then do what Jennifer did. Seek God's will. Act in faith, knowing that He will support you.

Evening – EXPECTATIONS

*"But love your enemies, do good to them, and lend
to them without expecting to get anything back."*
LUKE 6:35 NIV

Do you feel entitled to a certain kind of treatment from others? Think about that for a minute. Think about some of the most annoying things that happen to you on a regular basis. You have to wait in line longer than you like at the so-called fast-food restaurant. You order something online, and the store sends you the wrong thing. You do a good deed and no one notices. You give generously (so you think), and no one pays you back.

How much do you expect from others? From strangers? From friends? From enemies? From God?

Whatever your level of expectation, take a step back and evaluate what that says about your relationship with that person. It may be a good thing—for example, you expect faithfulness from your spouse because of the vows you've taken. But it may be that you have placed too much importance on your part in this equation. Should you get something simply because you have given something? Is that the requirement? Or rather, is the requirement to give cheerfully, with or without a reward?

Jesus came to turn the "eye for an eye" kind of justice on its head. He came to say that loving God with all your heart, soul, mind, and strength means giving differently. Giving big. And quite likely getting *nothing* back.

DAY 346

Morning – LET ALL THINGS BE SILENT

*"And the Lord will take possession of Judah as His inheritance in
the Holy Land, and will again choose Jerusalem. Be silent, all flesh,
before the Lord, for He is aroused from His holy habitation!"*
ZECHARIAH 2:12–13 NKJV

Throughout scripture we see the command to "be silent" or "be still." Have you ever taken a moment to meditate on and ponder this command? Why silence? In silence there is self-control, awareness, focus, wonder, awe, and deference. The God of the universe, all-powerful (omnipotent), all-knowing (omniscient), and all-being (omnipresent) deserves our thoughts and meditation. When we take the time to focus and listen, we glorify Him. No, there may not be a resounding voice that echoes in your soul, but when you dwell on God's character and His promises, you become more aware of and intimate with Him.

Intimacy with God is not easy. As women, we are highly relational, not in a groveling, clinging way, but we thrive on relationship. For some, intimacy with others has led to deep hurt. Intimacy involves vulnerability, and for some of us that is a tall order. We must be vulnerable with our Savior; it is the only way to grow closer to Him. Christianity is not a religion. It is a relationship with God that glorifies Him and fulfills our purpose.

Evening – YOU ARE WHAT YOU EAT

*Then Jesus declared, "I am the bread of life. Whoever comes to me will
never go hungry, and whoever believes in me will never be thirsty."*
JOHN 6:35 NIV

Jesus was talking to the disciples after the miracle of using five loaves and two fishes to feed five thousand people. Their focus continued to remain on the physical and natural world while He was talking about spiritual needs. He wanted them to know that He would provide for them not just physically but spiritually as well.

This was a new idea for them to grasp. They knew that God had provided manna and water in the desert for the Israelites. But they couldn't understand that through providing for a temporary, physical need, God was foreshadowing His coming ability to give us the bread of life, which would satisfy all our spiritual longings.

What we feed on is what nourishes us and determines how we grow. It becomes a part of us. Later, when Jesus is talking about how the branches must remain connected to the vine in order to live, He is talking about this same principle. If we are not connected to the one who gives us life, we cannot stay alive, let alone grow and flourish.

Are you staying connected to the one who gives you life? What are you feeding your soul? Does your life reflect a spiritually healthy diet?

Morning – JOY AND THANKFULNESS

*Then Hannah prayed and said: "My heart rejoices in the LORD;
in the LORD my horn is lifted high. My mouth boasts over my enemies,
for I delight in your deliverance. There is no one holy like the LORD;
there is no one besides you; there is no Rock like our God."*
1 SAMUEL 2:1–2 NIV

Hannah had prayed for years for a child. In those days, not bearing a child was a sign of disgrace, a sign that you had somehow displeased God. Hannah felt this stigma keenly.

God answered her prayers, and she followed through on her vow to deliver the child, Samuel, to live at the temple in service to the Lord. The name Samuel means "heard by God." And while it is difficult to imagine how a mother could give up her only child in this way, Hannah is rejoicing.

Hannah's focus is not on herself. She is praising God. She is telling others what He has done for her. She has surrendered all that is precious to her to the Lord and is trusting in Him.

How hard it is for us to do this! We worry and we fret and we wonder where God has gone when we don't see Him answering our prayers in the way we think it should happen. Let's follow Hannah's example and praise the Lord. And let's tell others of how He is working in our lives.

Evening – OPEN THE EYES OF FAITH

*"Therefore I tell you, whatever you ask for in prayer,
believe that you have received it, and It will be yours."*
MARK 11:24 NIV

At the conclusion of World War II and the end of the Holocaust, these words were found scratched on the wall of an abandoned farmhouse: "I believe in the sun even when it does not shine. I believe in love, even when it is not shown. I believe in God, even when He is silent." Sketched alongside the time-worn prose was the Star of David.

Have you ever prayed for something or someone, and God seemed to turn a deaf ear? One woman prayed for her son's salvation for seven years. Each day she knelt at the foot of her tear-stained bed, pleading for her child. But God seemed silent. Yet, what she failed to understand was that the Lord had been working all along to reach her son in ways unknown to her. And finally her son embraced the gospel through a series of life-changing circumstances.

The world says, "I'll believe it when I see it," while God's Word promises, "Believe then see."

Someone once said, "The way to see by faith is to shut the eye of reason." When we pray, rather than ask God why our prayers remain unanswered, perhaps we should ask the Lord to close our eyes so that we might see.

DAY 348

Morning – THIRSTING FOR GOD

O God, you are my God; I earnestly search for you. My soul thirsts for you;
my whole body longs for you in this parched and weary land where there is no
water. I have seen you in your sanctuary and gazed upon your power and glory.
PSALM 63:1–2 NLT

David wrote many of the psalms in the middle of difficult times. Biblical scholars believe this one was written when David fled Jerusalem when his son Absalom took the throne from him. Even in the midst of David's breaking heart, he sought the Lord with a deep, soul-parched thirst. He was the deer being hunted by his son; he was the one longing to be filled, to be completely satisfied through the only source who truly satisfies.

Many years later, Jesus said, "God blesses those who hunger and thirst for justice, for they will be satisfied" (Matthew 5:6 NLT). The thirst Jesus describes is the same thirst David spoke of. Charles Spurgeon, a nineteenth-century pastor in London, explained it this way in his *Treasury of David*: this thirst is "the cry of a man far removed from the outward ordinances and worship of God, sighing for the long loved house of his God; and at the same time it is the voice of a spiritual believer, under depressions, longing for the renewal of the divine presence, struggling with doubts and fears, but yet holding his ground by faith in the living God."

Evening – LOVE GOD FIRST

Take good heed therefore unto yourselves, that ye love the LORD your God.
JOSHUA 23:11 KJV

"I love my home. It's everything I've always wanted."

"I love new clothes. They make me feel special."

"I love my new diamond earrings."

"I love being a part of this group. It makes me feel important."

The word *love* is overused in the twenty-first century. If something is pleasing to us, we describe it by saying we love it. And we seem to acquire a lot of material possessions that we "love." There's nothing wrong with having nice things, but if we're not careful, our focus will center on things and not on God.

One reason we love all these possessions is because they feed a need in our lives—to have what others have, to feel important, to experience pleasure. Unfortunately, the need is bottomless. If we're not careful, we want more and more material possessions, which only satisfy on a temporary basis.

The scripture today cautions us to take heed that we love the Lord our God. Don't allow temporary pleasures to take the place of God in your life. He's the only one who can fill that bottomless hole and make you feel complete.

Morning – THE END OF YOUR ROPE

Do not be far from me, for trouble is near and there is no one to help.
PSALM 22:11 NIV

You can feel the desperation in David's prayer as you read Psalm 22. He feels utterly rejected and alone as he cries out to God.

Have you been there? Have you ever felt so alone and helpless that you are sure no one is there for you? Jesus meets us in those dark places of hopelessness. He calls to us and says; Don't let your hearts be troubled. Do not be afraid (John 14:27). I will never leave you or forsake you (Hebrews 13:5). You are never alone.

The late youth evangelist Dave Busby said, "The end of your rope is God's permanent address." Jesus reaches down and wraps you in His loving arms when you call to Him for help. The Bible tells us that He is close to the brokenhearted (Psalm 34:18).

We may not have the answers we are looking for here in this life, but we can be sure of this: God sees your pain and loves you desperately. Call to Him in times of trouble. If you feel that you're at the end of your rope, look up! His mighty hand is reaching toward you.

Evening – LET GOD FIGHT FOR YOU

"O our God, will You not judge them? For we have no power
against this great multitude that is coming against us;
nor do we know what to do, but our eyes are upon You."
2 CHRONICLES 20:12 NKJV

Sue was called as a witness in a robbery. Never having been involved in anything of this nature, she felt fearful of what might happen when she saw the young man who had robbed her. He was only fifteen, but he had an adult accomplice who had recently been released from prison. Would the perpetrator recognize her, and would he or his accomplice take revenge on her for testifying against him? She wanted to be brave, but fear threatened to paralyze her. She knew her strength came from God and prayed for His help.

When she was sworn in, Sue took her place on the witness stand. The adult was being tried for his part in the crime, but the juvenile needed to be identified. The judge turned to Sue and said, "We're going to bring in a young man. If he's the one who robbed you, all you have to do is shake your head yes or no." When it was over, she felt great relief and knew God had been with her in the courtroom that day.

No matter who or what we face in life, God will be with us. He supplies the power and strength we don't have. If we allow Him to fight for us, we will have victory.

DAY 350

Morning – PRESSING ON

Brothers and sisters, I do not consider myself yet to have taken hold of it. But one thing I do: Forgetting what is behind and straining toward what is ahead, I press on toward the goal to win the prize for which God has called me heavenward in Christ Jesus.

PHILIPPIANS 3:13–14 NIV

The Olympic games began in seventh century BC in Olympia, Greece, and were held every fourth year for nearly 1,200 years. In the third century BC, Alexander the Great required every region he'd conquered to speak Greek. Because of this, Paul and the people of that time were very familiar with Olympic terminology.

Paul uses the image of a marathon runner pressing onward, straining ahead, not looking back as he strives for the prize—a crown of laurel leaves. It was a great honor to wear that crown, and each participant kept his eye on that prize as he ran forward with all his might.

In the same way, we must keep our eye on the prize—the crown God will give each of us who has lived a life pleasing to Him. We can't look back, or we'll surely stumble. Each day, each moment, we must press ahead as we make choice by choice to live for Him.

The good news is, we're not competing against anyone but ourselves. It doesn't matter where the people around us are on the track. All that matters is where we are and that we keep moving forward.

Evening – DETERMINED TO WIN

"Fear not, for I am with you; be not dismayed, for I am your God. I will strengthen you, yes, I will help you, I will uphold you with My righteous right hand."

ISAIAH 41:10 NKJV

God loves you and desires to bless you; your adversary, the devil, wants to convince you to give up on ever receiving the promises of God.

Think about the last time God showed up and turned your circumstances around. Most likely in the midst of your celebration of the blessing, another challenge or difficulty hit you head on. It's the enemy's attempt to steal what God did for you and even convince you that God wasn't in it.

He wants to bring disappointment in the hope that you'll just give up. When John the Baptist baptized Jesus, God blessed Jesus by declaring Him as His Son. From there Jesus went into the desert to fast and pray for forty days. Immediately the devil came to tempt Jesus, trying to get Him to give up His blessing. Jesus refused to give up. Like Jesus, you can hold tight to the win God has promised you.

Satan, your adversary, wants you to give up and quit. But if you remain determined to win—refusing to let go of God's promise—you will always win!

Morning – PRAYING FOR PEACE

Pray for the peace of Jerusalem: "May those who love you be secure."
PSALM 122:6 NIV

With the news of yet another outbreak of unrest in the Middle East, this phrase comes to mind: "Pray for the peace of Jerusalem." One might think that King David had prophetically understood how war-torn this area of the world would be over the centuries. And, while it is good for us to pray for peace from war in Jerusalem and other places in the world, we should also be praying for peace with God.

As the Prince of Peace, Jesus overcame the world—its wars, pain, and evil. Jesus is the way to peace, both our inner peace and the peace of the world. But it all begins with us as we seek God's will for our lives; get closer to Him; quiet our minds; and listen to that still, small voice. There can be no lasting peace anywhere without being renewed day by day, praying for inner peace, growth of grace, and the love of ourselves and others.

Evening – PEACE WITH GOD

Therefore, since we have been justified through faith,
we have peace with God through our Lord Jesus Christ.
ROMANS 5:1 NIV

The type of peace this verse is talking about isn't a feeling. It's the kind of peace that's like a peace treaty. When we ask Jesus to be Lord of our lives, our status and relationship with God change. We go from being His enemies to being His friends. Additionally, we have a sense of relief that His wrath and the punishment for our sins are no longer hanging over our heads.

We also can celebrate that peace with God is not just a onetime event. Rather, it is an ongoing source of blessing. Peace *with* God leads to peace *from* God. And this peace is not just the absence of turmoil and trouble, but a real sense that God is in control. It's a small representation of heaven here on earth. His peace brings the confidence that He is working things out in our lives, even if we can't understand it all.

Satan would love to steal our peace. He can't change our relationship with God, but we can give Satan a foothold when we worry and ruminate and fuss over our circumstances instead of turning them over to God. Give your troubles to God and rest in His peace.

Morning – DISCOVER YOUR
DREAM ONCE AGAIN

Restore unto me the joy of thy salvation; and uphold me with thy free spirit.
PSALM 51:12 KJV

Have you ever looked at a small child and caught a glimpse of the possibilities of success that lay dormant within them. Perhaps you even picture just a little of who they might later become. Did you have a dream as a young person that has not yet been realized?

Life happens, and often those big dreams seem impossible. Maybe you went to school and started your career, maybe got married and started a family. Today that dream may be packed away in the garage, sitting on a shelf in the attic, or buried deep in a quiet, seldom touched part of your soul.

God has a plan. Even though you may have changed and gone in a different direction—that desire that He put within you can still be realized. The dream was still in there, and the ability to do what you once were passionate about can grow in your heart again. Dreams that God put in your heart are what make you who you were created to be. When you trust God to take your life and do with it what He purposed, He'll make your dreams a reality in His time. Just trust Him!

Evening – DETERMINED AND SURRENDERED

"And then, though it is against the law, I will go
in to see the king. If I must die, I must die."
ESTHER 4:16 NLT

Esther might have won the beauty contest in ancient Persia, but she also had guts to go with her glitz. Raised by her uncle Mordecai, a devout follower of Yahweh, she had principles that held her firm in the time of testing.

You know the story of her marriage to King Xerxes after the banishment of Queen Vashti and of her sudden introduction to royal life. You know also of the subplot of the wicked Haman who had a rabid hatred for the Jews and who despised one Jew in particular and secretly plotted his demise. And then there was Mordecai, who worked as an official in the palace and got the intelligence report to his niece that she was the only one who could save her people from extinction. She was the only one who had access to Xerxes. Well, actually, she only had access when he summoned her. But desperate times required desperate measures, and after days of fasting, Esther dressed to the nines and walked in to catch the king's eye and plead her case.

Of course, we know the end of the story, but she didn't know it at the time. She was completely surrendered to whatever her fate may be. This was the moment for which she had been summoned to the kingdom.

Like her, you are called to surrender yourself to God's purpose. Have the guts to surrender and do your part in His kingdom.

Morning – MUCH LOVE

"Therefore, I tell you, her many sins have been forgiven—
as her great love has shown."
LUKE 7:47 NIV

Scripture records the story of Jesus dining with Simon the Pharisee. At the dinner, a woman of loose morals came forth, kissed Jesus' feet, and washed them with her tears. Simon was incensed. He felt Jesus should reprimand the woman; after all, she had sinned greatly. Jesus didn't condemn her, but He forgave her. Her faith saved her because she poured out everything at His feet. The Interpreter's Bible states, "The significant difference between the woman and Simon is not that she had been a worse sinner than he. . .but that she has realized more truly and deeply the reality of her sin."

Often we feel we fall short in our walk with God. We plunge into the trap of measuring ourselves by another's yardstick. This isn't what God wants for us. He desires that we fall at His feet and worship Him—loving Him with an extravagant love. When sin enters our lives, as it will, we confess that sin and turn to His face. He's there in the darkest hours.

Others may know what you've done, but Jesus knows what you can become. Simon the Pharisee saw this woman as a weed, but Jesus saw her as a potential rose and watered it. When you fall in love with Christ, the first thing He opens is your heart. Be transformed by the Father's grace. Love extravagantly.

Evening – GOD'S YARDSTICK

"Do not judge, or you too will be judged. For in the same way you judge others,
you will be judged, and with the measure you use, it will be measured to you."
MATTHEW 7:1–2 NIV

Showing up in the late afternoon just before closing, the couple had traveled far to the home improvement store in town with their emergency.

"It's hot and we need to put an air conditioner in the window," the man began.

"What kind of window? Does it slide to the side or does it need to slide up?" Doris asked.

"The up kind," his wife responded.

"A casement," Doris remembered from her recent on-the-job training. "What size?"

The man pulled from his pocket a bootlace that was frayed on one end.

"Like this," he said as he stretched it across the counter. It could only be as accurate as elastic.

Doris thought, *Stupid! To come all this way without the window size!*

She looked up. They saw her attitude. "Sorry. You have to have the right measurement to fit the window. You don't want to have to rebuild the whole wall. Take this free yardstick and come back. We'll be glad to help you."

God's command not to judge is assessed by our own actions. When others know less than we think we do, give us a hard time, or don't agree with us, we must not judge them. Using our standard of measure, God will measure us—and reward us according to what we do.

Morning – THE BLUE AND THE GRAY

"No one lights a lamp and puts it in a place where it will be hidden."
Luke 11:33 niv

The Civil War is often recognized by the blue and gray uniforms that identify the opposing sides—blue for Union soldiers, gray for Confederates.

Few people know, however, that the colors were not assigned at first. Gray was often worn by Union volunteer units, and the opposite was also true. At the battle in Shiloh, the Orleans Guard Battalion wore blue dress uniforms into battle. The problem came when men would fire and kill their own soldiers. The Louisiana Guard wittingly made the decision to turn their coats inside out so the white lining would show.

Some Christians have suggested we should blend in with the world and find common ground. But just like with the Civil War uniforms, this theory has led to confusion not commonality. The non-Christian doesn't see any difference between the world and the church.

Rather than blend, we should be set apart. That doesn't mean aloof, but it does mean different. Paul said, "Don't copy the behavior and customs of this world, but let God transform you into a new person by changing the way you think" (Romans 12:2 nlt). We have been given a light in the darkness. Why would we hide that light in order to look like the world?

Evening – DO NOT BE CONFORMED

Do not be surprised. . .if the world hates you.
1 John 3:13 niv

Many Christians don't want to appear odd in "normal" culture, but history shows that those who live in stark contrast to the status quo accomplish great things.

In 1876 President Rutherford B. Hayes brought strength of mind and character to the White House. He also brought his unapologetically Christian wife, Lucy.

The couple began each day with prayer and devotions. Sunday evenings they sang hymns with the staff. Men in office and their wives were irritated when Lucy banned alcohol for her children's sakes, calling her "Lemonade Lucy."

Nevertheless, she was one of the most beloved First Ladies in history. She was well known for her care toward soldiers and compassion for slaves. She carried herself with confidence and kindness, and many called her "Mother Lucy."

The Bible encourages us not to be conformed to this world. We are called to stand out by our behavior like "aliens and strangers." "Live such good lives among the pagans," Peter wrote, "that, though they accuse you of doing wrong, they may see your good deeds and glorify God on the day he visits us" (1 Peter 2:12 niv).

Society saw Lucy's behavior as strange, even extreme, but they loved her.

The world needs Christians who will practice the convictions of their faith despite public criticism. Yes, the world will think you're strange. Yes, you will be mocked. But there will be others who find you inspiring.

Morning – CHANGE OF MIND

*Do not love this world nor the things it offers you, for when you
love the world, you do not have the love of the Father in you.*
1 JOHN 2:15 NLT

The world entices us with its fashion, beauty, and youthful preservation. But striving after and focusing on these things is not what God wants for us. He doesn't want us to become carbon copies of those who have facelifts, breast enhancements, and the most up-to-date wardrobe. For when we become so conformed to this world, we lose out on the most important thing of life: God's transformational power! To keep us from becoming conformed to a society that is often self-serving, rude, egotistical, vain, and violent, God wants us to renew our minds each and every day. He wants us to have attitudes and ideals that reflect His goodness. He wants us to change ourselves and the world from the inside out. For when we have our heads on straight, God will work to bring the best out in ourselves to the good of all. So fix your face on God's, focus on His light and way, and see how brightly you begin to shine.

Evening – RENEWING THE MIND

*Don't copy the behavior and customs of this world, but let God transform
you into a new person by changing the way you think. Then you will learn
to know God's will for you, which is good and pleasing and perfect.*
ROMANS 12:2 NLT

We are surrounded by technology that introduces us to new ideas all the time. No matter what your choice of electronic device, you have the world at your disposal. Sometimes the information isn't acceptable for Christians. We may not have asked for these bits of information, but they invade our world every day. No matter where we turn, evil is present on all sides. Paul wrote to the Roman church telling them not to be conformed to the world around them, but to allow God to transform them and renew their minds. Can we as twenty-first-century Christians do the same? Yes, we can.

1. Don't allow yourself to view or read everything that comes across the screen in front of you. If it appears suggestive or impure, it probably is.
2. Take time to read your Bible every day. Don't let the cyber world be your only source of information. Hear what God has to say to you personally.
3. Ask God to renew your mind and show you what is profitable for you as a Christian.
4. Don't accept something just because everyone else does it even if it's "politically correct." Choose today to be transformed by the renewing of your mind.

DAY 356

Morning – OBEDIENCE BRINGS PEACE

*So Joshua took the entire land, just as the Lord had directed Moses,
and he gave it as an inheritance to Israel according to their
tribal divisions. Then the land had rest from war.*
JOSHUA 11:23 NIV

Victory does not come without obedience. Joshua took the entire land because he followed God's instructions. Joshua battled enemies with greater numbers and better technology. In each battle, victory looked different, but in all of them God was faithful.

Our obedience will look different in each situation depending on what God wants us to do. We must ask for guidance. Obedience will keep us on the right track and away from contaminating influences. When we trust in our resources or the wisdom of the world, we will be led astray.

Additionally, obedience to those in authority over us is obedience to God. Joshua followed Moses' instructions. It can take more faith to see God speaking to us through other people.

Joshua battled for seven years. Obedience can take a long time. It's a daily choice, not a one-time act. Faithful obedience keeps our hearts soft before the Lord and keeps us out of a pattern of disobedience that leads to a hard heart that cannot hear God's voice.

Ultimately, obedience brings peace. We can't control our circumstances, but when we obey God, we will find peace in the midst of them. If you don't have peace, look for where you're not obeying. What are you trying to control that you should give to God?

Evening – RUN WITH ENDURANCE

*Let us strip off every weight that slows us down, especially the sin
that so easily trips us up. And let us run with endurance the race
God has set before us. We do this by keeping our eyes on Jesus.*
HEBREWS 12:1–2 NLT

Running was the first and, for many years, the only event of the ancient Olympic games. So it is no wonder that the New Testament writers use the metaphor to describe the Christian life. The first races were 200-yard sprints. These gradually increased in length as the Olympic games continued to develop. The modern marathon commemorates the legendary run made by a Greek soldier named Pheidippides, who ran from the battlefield outside Marathon, Greece, to Athens to proclaim a single word: *victory!* Then he collapsed and died.

The Christian race lasts a lifetime, with Christ Jesus as our goal, the prize that awaits us at the finish line in heaven. It can't be run all-out as a sprint or no one would last the course. Though there was one race in the ancient games where the runners wore full armor, most of the time the ancient runners ran naked, stripping away anything that would slow them down. Obviously the writer of Hebrews was familiar with the ancient sport of running when he advised believers to run with endurance the race God set before them.

Morning – AT ALL TIMES

With all prayer and petition pray at all times in the Spirit, and with this in view, be on the alert with all perseverance and petition for all the saints.
EPHESIANS 6:18 NASB

When giving instructions about important things, it's good to be specific. The more specific the instructions, the more likely the task will be done correctly. That's why when Paul spoke to the Ephesians about praying, he didn't leave any question about when to pray.

Prayer isn't a ritual to practice before bed or first thing in the morning or when the sun is at a certain place in the sky. Though it's great to have specific times of concentrated, focused prayer, our conversations with God shouldn't be limited to a certain time on our calendar. God wants us to pray *all the time.*

After all, God wants to be included in our days. He wants to walk and talk with us each moment. Imagine if we traveled through the day with our children or our spouse, but we only spoke to them between 6:15 and 6:45 a.m.! Of course we'd never do that to the people we care about. God doesn't want us to do that to Him, either.

God wants to travel the journey with us. He's a wonderful companion, offering wisdom and comfort for every aspect of our lives. But He can only do that if we let Him into our schedules, every minute of every day.

Evening – PRAY WITHOUT CEASING

Pray without ceasing. In every thing give thanks: for this is the will of God in Christ Jesus concerning you.
1 THESSALONIANS 5:17–18 KJV

Pray without ceasing. Pray continually. Never stop praying. Pray all the time. Regardless which translation of the Bible you choose, the command is the same. It seems impossible! How can one pray all the time? Consider this. You are young and in love. You must go to school and work. You may be separated by a great distance from your beloved. And yet, every moment of every day, that person is on your mind. You talk on the phone and text constantly. His name is always on your lips. So much so that some of your friends find it annoying! Is your relationship with Jesus like the one described here? He wants to be the name on your mind when you are daydreaming. He wants to be the first one you chat with each morning and the last one you confide in each night. He wants you to be so utterly absorbed in Him that it begins to annoy some of your friends! Pray without ceasing. Love Jesus with all your heart. He is crazy about you.

DAY 358

Morning – ASKING FOR IT

Therefore confess your sins to each other and
pray for each other so that you may be healed.
JAMES 5:16 NIV

Forgiveness is hard enough to grant, let alone to request. Taking responsibility for your mistakes and asking for mercy from the person you've offended are not easy things to do. It is especially difficult when you didn't know you'd hurt the person in the first place and they had to approach *you*.

Most people would rather make excuses for their behavior than own up to it. However, asking for forgiveness is one of the most powerful testimonies of your faith that you can demonstrate. When we ask for forgiveness, we acknowledge we have trampled the dignity of another human being. We admit that we have hurt God as well by sinning against a person He deeply loves. In asking for forgiveness, we humble ourselves and throw ourselves on mercy—the mercy of the person we've hurt and our Father's mercy.

It is a gift to be forgiven. Sometimes forgiveness is withheld—a "reasonable" human reaction to sin, but painful nonetheless. Even if the person in question refuses to forgive you, you must do all you can to make peace, and then leave it in the Father's hands—He can bring peace where peace seems impossible. Take heart: if you have confessed your sin to the Father, He has forgiven you and will never hold that sin against you.

Evening – GUILT REMOVAL

If we confess our sins, He is faithful and just to forgive
us our sins and to cleanse us from all unrighteousness.
1 JOHN 1:9 NKJV

Sometimes we don't feel forgiven. Even though we have believed that Christ's death and resurrection paid the penalty for all our sins and we now have eternal life, we still sin. First John 1:9 tells us believers to confess our sins to God, and He cleanses us. What if we still feel guilty? Some people say we should forgive ourselves. This is not a biblical concept, but it probably means accepting God's forgiveness. If feelings of guilt return every time we recall what we have done, perhaps we are still grieving the losses a particular sin has caused. Sin can be forgiven and restitution can be made, but most consequences are permanent. Something broke like an egg when we sinned, and it cannot be fixed in this life. Yet God can redeem it for good. Failures can keep us dependent on Him and give us empathy for others.

Two things will help us "feel" forgiven: (1) thanking God for His promise that we are cleansed "from all unrighteousness." The promise is as sure as God is. And (2) meditating on Galatians 5:1 (NKJV): "Stand fast therefore in the liberty by which Christ has made us free, and do not be entangled again with a yoke of bondage." Stand victorious in the truth that Christ has freed us from our sin and guilt. It cannot enslave us again unless we let it.

Morning – A JOY FOCUS

For the joy set before him he endured the cross. . . .
Consider him who endured such opposition from sinners,
so that you will not grow weary and lose heart.
HEBREWS 12:2–3 NIV

We cannot sustain emotional health without hope—something good to anticipate. Believers in Christ have a hopeful future even when our prognosis is death, because we will forever be with the Lord (see 2 Corinthians 5:8). Nonetheless, during trials, it takes determination and spiritual power to meditate on the joys set before us, like Jesus did.

One way to keep a joyful focus is found in Psalm 68:19–20 (NIV): "Praise be to the Lord, to God our Savior, who daily bears our burdens. Our God is a God who saves; from the Sovereign LORD comes escape from death." In the margin by these verses, I have listed the "escapes from death" God has mercifully granted our family—fifteen times so far we have been delivered from life-threatening accidents or potentially fatal illnesses. (What names and dates can you list in your Bible?)

What if God does not deliver *from* a trial? Then He will sustain us *through* the trial by bearing our burdens with us every day.

When we "grow weary" and find ourselves "losing heart," let's focus on God our Savior, our sovereign Lord, our burden-bearer. If the joy of the Lord is our focus, it will also be our strength (see Nehemiah 8:10).

Evening – "I LIKE THE DEPRESSION"

"Blessed are you who are poor."
LUKE 6:20 NIV

Sally Wall found her father's account of the Depression after he died:

> I LIKE the Depression. No more prosperity for me. I have had more fun since the Depression started than I had in my life. I had forgotten how to live, and what it means to have real friends. . . .
>
> I like the Depression. I am getting acquainted with my neighbors and following the biblical admonition to love them. Some of them had been living next door to me for 3 years; now we butcher hogs together.
>
> I like the Depression. I haven't been out to a party in 18 months. My wife has dropped all her clubs, and I believe we are falling in love all over again. I'm pretty well satisfied with my wife, and I think I will keep her. . . .
>
> I like the Depression. Three years ago I never had time to go to church. I played checkers or baseball all day Sunday. Besides, there wasn't a preacher in Texas that could tell me anything. Now I'm going to church regularly and never miss a Sunday. If this Depression keeps on, I will be going to prayer meetings before too long.
>
> Oh Yes! I like the Depression!

What is the Great Depression in your life? Could it be that, despite yourself, you're better off for it?

DAY 360

Morning – GREAT EXPECTATIONS

*Trust in the Lord with all your heart; do not depend on your own understanding.
Seek his will in all you do, and he will show you which path to take.*
PROVERBS 3:5–6 NLT

Let's face it. Sometimes we have such grand plans. And the great day comes and our expectations are dashed against the wall. Nothing has turned out like we'd envisioned. And we find ourselves angry, frustrated, horribly disappointed, and feeling sorry for ourselves. Our thirtieth birthday came and went with no one batting an eye. On back-to-school night, teachers had nothing but discouraging things to say about our kid. Our grown-up daughter's visit was spent with her visiting her friends instead of one-on-one time with mom. The dream job we had sacrificed everything for turned out to be the worst career move ever.

Fortunately, there is an upside to all these scenarios. For we have a God who has a great plan for our lives. He's working things out so that these great disappointments will work for our good. We simply need to trust in Him. So don't try to figure it all out on your own. Just head back into His arms. Cry on His shoulder. And ask Him to show you the next step. Leave it to Him to straighten everything out. And He will transform your great expectations into something beyond your limited imagination!

Evening – HE PLOWS OUR HEARTS

*Sow righteousness for yourselves, reap the fruit of unfailing love,
and break up your unplowed ground; for it is time to seek the Lord,
until he comes and showers his righteousness on you.*
HOSEA 10:12 NIV

Has God brought you through a season of growth and you thought you might get a break?

Sheri thought the same thing after losing both her parents within a year's time. She was finally moving through life on an even keel and quite content; then her husband lost his job. They had little in savings, and her job was not enough to pay all the bills.

Her husband was depressed about his prospects for another job and often unmotivated because of it. They quickly fell behind on rent and utilities. Vacations and dinners out became extreme luxuries. Sheri picked up a part-time job on top of her full-time job to help make ends meet. Even still, they began to fall into debt, and before long both of them teetered on the verge of despair.

Yet God gave them the strength they needed to get through each week and month and eventually provided better jobs for both of them. None of it was perfect, by any means. But what Sheri and her husband realized was that God was breaking up some unplowed ground in them that they hadn't known needed to be plowed.

Morning – LOVE MULTIPLIED

"For where two or three gather in my name, there am I with them."
MATTHEW 18:20 NIV

Sunday morning was cold and gray. Jackie would much rather have snuggled back under the covers instead of going to church. In fact, it was extremely tempting to sleep in. Jackie willed herself from the warm bed and got ready to leave. Within moments of entering the church, she was greeted by a couple of women friends who invited her to sit with them during the service. The bleak, cloudy day was immediately transformed by the blessings of love and friendship.

Sometimes it seems that attending church is a burden instead of a blessing. God reminds us with today's verse that we are meeting more than other people. We are meeting *Him* there! Whenever two or more are gathered to worship Him, His presence is experienced in an awesome way. Not only is this a blessing, it is also a privilege. Many in the world are not able to worship freely.

Evening – COMMUNITY AND SERVICE

*And let us consider how we may spur one another on toward love
and good deeds, not giving up meeting together, as some are
in the habit of doing, but encouraging one another.*
HEBREWS 10:24–25 NIV

"I don't need to attend church to be spiritual. My relationship with God is personal, and I can worship Him anywhere. Besides, on Sundays I need time for myself to catch up on loose ends at home." Lone Ranger Christians often express this justification for not connecting with a local church.

Yes, we can worship God anywhere and everywhere, but church involves more than worship. Church is about community (considering one another) and encouragement (spurring each other to love and goodness). We Christians need each other. As members of the body of Christ, we have spiritual gifts that God expects us to use "for the common good" (1 Corinthians 12:7). He has gifted us the way He wants (12:18). We cannot say we don't need each other (12:21) because what concerns one concerns all (12:25). We share each other's sufferings and successes (12:26).

Therefore, when we make the sacrifice of time to meet together weekly, we are fulfilling God's purpose for us. Isn't that more important than getting our chores done or having "me" time? Our membership in Christ's body includes benefits and responsibilities. Like coals in a fire, we keep each other warm and glowing as long as we're connected.

DAY 362

Morning – MAKE SOMEONE HAPPY

"Anyone who wants to be first must be the very last, and the servant of all."
MARK 9:35 NIV

The Christian life requires a servant attitude, even at home. It's easy to say, but difficult in practice. Like the young boy who vowed, "I have resolved this year not to fight my sister. . .unless she fights me first or makes me mad or I feel like it," we might say, "I have resolved to serve my husband unless he doesn't deserve it or makes me mad or I don't feel like it."

Katherine von Bora was a living example of servant love. She and Martin Luther shared a love that was sincere and expressive, but he was poor and often sickly. Katherine took care of the home and farm and even slaughtered the animals herself. Katie (as he called her) frequently nursed Luther through gout, hemorrhoids, and the like, all while raising six children.

"My Katie is in all things so obliging and pleasing to me," he wrote, "that I would not exchange my poverty for the riches of Croesus."

James 4:6 (NKJV) says, "God resists the proud, but gives grace to the humble." Jesus was the perfect example of servanthood, and He calls us to follow Him. An attitude of service and humility pleases God, and that includes during home life.

How glad we should be, how eager to follow Him, knowing that Christ didn't stop serving, even to the point of death for a people who didn't deserve it.

Evening – HAVE YOU THANKED SOMEONE TODAY?

*They have been a wonderful encouragement to me, as they have been
to you. You must show your appreciation to all who serve so well.*
1 CORINTHIANS 16:18 NLT

Have you thanked your pastor, friends, or family who have encouraged or helped you just when you needed it?

Paul wrote to the Corinthian church, explaining how Stephanas and his family were the first converts in Achaia and how they devoted themselves to serve others. He reminded them that when Stephanas, Fortunatus, and Achaicus arrived in Corinth, they supplied whatever needs the people had and they "refreshed my spirit and yours."

When true believers serve, they serve from the heart not an inward desire for outward praise. This is what Stephanas did, yet Paul still prompted the church to show appreciation for God's servant and what he did for them.

Do you ever feel taken advantage of? Do you labor and receive little to no recognition? As God's servants, we work because we love Christ; yet an occasional display of appreciation is always. . .well, appreciated. That's what Paul communicated. "Hey guys, let's encourage our brothers through showing our appreciation to them for all they did for us!"

Paul's suggestion holds true today. Thank someone who has refreshed your spirit. It will encourage them and you to keep persevering on life's pathway.

Morning – QUIET TIME

*"But when you pray, go away by yourself, shut the
door behind you, and pray to your Father in private.
Then your Father, who sees everything, will reward you."*
MATTHEW 6:6 NLT

Life is so noisy. Kids squabbling, televisions blaring, horns honking, people talking, coworkers arguing, phones ringing, computers dinging, text messages coming through. . .it can get crazy. Where can a woman go to find peace and quiet? Many have retreated to their bathrooms or even their closets for moments of alone time. Likely, you have your own special spot, meant for getaways. Of course, kiddos are probably beating on the door. In the middle of all the chaos, God longs for us to spend quiet time with Him. He doesn't care where this takes place or even if it's completely silent in that place. All that matters is that you draw near to Him and tune in to hear His still, small voice. What's keeping you from doing that now? Take a few steps away from the noise and spend a little time with Him.

Evening – REMEMBERING HIS PROMISES

*Tell everyone about God's power. His majesty shines down on Israel;
his strength is mighty in the heavens. God is awesome in his sanctuary.
The God of Israel gives power and strength to his people. Praise be to God!*
PSALM 68:34–35 NLT

Do you ever find yourself dreaming of a place of safety? A place where you can close your eyes, rest your head, and let go of the stress and angst that follow you around like a shadow? It rarely matters what kind of season you are in—busy or calm—you always seem to feel an inner longing to find a place where there is nothing but peace.

Before you move on to the next thing on the list, take a moment to close your eyes. Don't reach for a book. Refuse to look at your phone. Keep your thoughts from wandering away. And simply fix your heart on the one who loves you. Think about His compassion. Dwell on His promises. Consider His majesty and the army of angels He commands. Have faith in the one He sent so you can forever be with Him.

Whether you need comfort, encouragement, or protection, He is the answer. Look first in His direction for clarity and understanding. He is close at hand and forever unchanging.

DAY 364

Morning – "BE STILL" MEANS STOP STRIVING

God is our refuge and strength, an ever-present help in trouble.
PSALM 46:1 NIV

News broadcasts distress us daily. We may be living in the time of "wars and rumors of wars" that Jesus predicted in Matthew 24:6 (NIV). He added, "See to it that you are not alarmed. Such things must happen, but the end is still to come." Because God is our refuge (fortress) and strength, we need not fear. Even when natural disasters strike (Psalm 46:2–3 NLT). Even during national conflicts (46:6). Note the refrain in verses 7 and 11: "The Lord of Heaven's Armies is here among us." *Who could defend us better?* "The God of Israel [our personal God] is our fortress." *What better protection could we have?* God is also working to end all wars (46:8–9). He will win and be exalted in the end (46:10), which is sure to come.

In light of this, how should we respond? When verse 10 tells the nations to be still and know He is God, it means they should stop striving, lay down their arms. God will do the fighting and will eventually end all conflicts. Isaiah 2 is a parallel passage that describes the latter days when metal will be used for farming and fishing tools, not for weapons.

We can personalize this psalm by remembering to let God fight our battles. Stop striving and know that He is God, our refuge and strength.

Evening – LOOKING BEYOND EARTHLY REASSURANCES

Some nations boast of their chariots and horses,
but we boast in the name of the LORD our God.
PSALM 20:7 NLT

David, the writer of this psalm, did not find his hope in things that came from this earth—things he could see with his own eyes or create with his own hands. He did not find it through a solution his mind could conjure. He had faith in the Lord, and that was enough. We can only imagine how comforting it would be to look upon our defending army during a time of war, but he chose to look beyond the army and instead fixed his eyes on the Lord.

Through any trial or pain, the Lord sees all, and He loves his people in a deep, unfailing way. Although a thousand may fall, our fate and lives rest in Him and Him alone. We cannot look to earthly things to predict our future, finances, employment, etc. God's plans far exceed anything we could plan, and if we trust and follow Him, we will end up in a place we never would have come up with on our own.

Breathe in. Breathe out. Rest and believe. It is through fixing our eyes on God and looking to Him for direction that we are reassured and can experience peace.

Morning – UNCONDITIONAL LOVE

*Neither height nor depth, nor anything else in all creation, will be able
to separate us from the love of God that is in Christ Jesus our Lord.*
ROMANS 8:39 NIV

To try to compare God's love with human love is nearly impossible. We love our families and our closest friends. But is our love unconditional? Families have divided for incidents as minor as a lack of understanding or an unexpected flare-up. Disagreements, hurt feelings, or built-up anger have caused many people to sever precious ties.

God's love, however, is unconditional. His love isn't based on our good deeds. It isn't grounded in our personal goodness or faithfulness. When we sin, He forgives. If we fall, He lifts us up and helps us go forward. He isn't easily angered, and He doesn't turn His back when we do or say something disapproving.

What would happen if we exercised God's love toward others? If we didn't take offense when someone was offensive, if we forgave when wronged, if we prayed instead of accused, if we loved even when someone failed to love us?

As Christians, nothing can separate us from God's unconditional love that is rooted in a personal relationship with Jesus. God loves you no matter what. Go and do the same.

Evening – PRECIOUS BUNDLE

*But because of his great love for us, God, who is rich in mercy,
made us alive with Christ even when we were dead in
transgressions—it is by grace you have been saved.*
EPHESIANS 2:4–5 NIV

It's your first baby, and the nurse has just placed that precious newborn bundle in your arms. You count her wee little toes. You brush your lips against her cheek. You gaze into her eyes. Oh, such pools of delight. And you love her—that cherishing kind of love that makes your heart ache. You are filled with such wonder and sighing bliss that you think you might die of an overdose of pure joy.

Yes, you do indeed love your child profoundly, and yet it can't come close to the intensity of affection and care and devotion your heavenly Father has for you. He delights in you even when you're red-faced and wailing. Even when you're stamping your feet. Even when you stumble and fall into sin.

In fact, His great love for us is beyond human understanding. His love included sending His only Son to die for us so that we could know freedom from sin and death. Imagine. Now that is amazing love.

But just as parents long for their children to grow up and love them in return, so does God. He welcomes your company, not just for the here and now, but for all time.

SCRIPTURE INDEX

OLD TESTAMENT

GENESIS

1:1 . . . . Day 127
1:31 . . . . Day 319
13:3–4 . . . . Day 9
16:7, 9, 13 . . . . Day 197
16:11, 13 . . . . Day 280
19:17, 26 . . . . Day 85
21:6 . . . . Day 338
33:4 . . . . Day 70
39:2–3 . . . . Day 209

EXODUS

3:14 . . . . Day 132
9:16 . . . . Day 174
9:28 . . . . Day 268
14:13–14 . . . . Day 134
15:2 . . . . Day 201
17:11–13 . . . . Day 283
19:4 . . . . Day 213
39:30 . . . . Day 276

LEVITICUS

19:18 . . . . Day 82

NUMBERS

23:19 . . . . Day 91
27:4 . . . . Day 227

DEUTERONOMY

10:12 . . . . Day 137
11:13–14 . . . . Day 207
30:14 . . . . Day 252
31:6 . . . . Days 291, 345
31:8 . . . . Day 294
32:6 . . . . Day 32
33:27 . . . . Day 314

JOSHUA

1:8 . . . . Days 315, 321
1:9 . . . . Day 49
1:16–18 . . . . Day 81
2:3 . . . . Day 157

5:15 . . . . Day 87
6:1–2 . . . . Day 189
9:14 . . . . Day 146
10:8 . . . . Day 232
11:23 . . . . Day 356
14:9 . . . . Day 83
15:19 . . . . Day 200
23:11 . . . . Day 348

RUTH

1:16 . . . . Day 161
1:20–21 . . . . Day 273
3:9 . . . . Day 130

1 SAMUEL

2:1–2 . . . . Days 214, 347
2:8 . . . . Day 180
3:10 . . . . Day 287
12:24 . . . . Day 173
16:7 . . . . Days 25, 185, 202, 230
18:1 . . . . Day 123
23:28 . . . . Day 164
30:6 . . . . Day 294

2 SAMUEL

7:18 . . . . Day 58
20:16, 19 . . . . Day 138
22:30 . . . . Day 180
22:31 . . . . Day 121
24:10 . . . . Day 295

2 KINGS

5:13 . . . . Day 287
6:16–17 . . . . Day 234

1 CHRONICLES

4:9–10 . . . . Day 54
16:9–12 . . . . Day 329
16:34–36 . . . . Day 90
17:20 . . . . Day 192
22:19 . . . . Day 329
29:9 . . . . Day 149

2 CHRONICLES

1:10. . . . . Day 266
7:14. . . . . Day 266
16:9. . . . . Day 184
20:12. . . . . .Days 335, 349
20:15, 17 . . . . Day 242

NEHEMIAH

6:9 . . . . Day 171

ESTHER

4:16. . . . . Day 352

JOB

2:13. . . . . Day 52
3:25. . . . . Day 17
3:26. . . . . Day 203
12:10. . . . . Day 79
13:15. . . . . .Days 226, 305
22:22. . . . . Day 16
33:28. . . . . Day 158
40:8–9 . . . . Day 169
42:1–2 . . . . Day 324
42:3. . . . . Day 169

PSALMS

1:2 . . . . Day 228
4:1 . . . . Day 44
5:1–3. . . . . Day 43
5:3 . . . . Day 44
7:17 . . . . Day 12
8:3–5. . . . . Day 313
9:1 . . . . Day 300
9:10 . . . . Day 47
13:1 . . . . Day 251
13:1, 5–6 . . . . Day 273
13:5. . . . . Day 331
13:5–6 . . . . Day 167
16:1 . . . . Day 332
16:6 . . . . Day 215
16:7–8 . . . . .Days 43, 196
16:8. . . . . Day 325
17:8 . . . . Day 187
17:15. . . . . Day 217
18:2. . . . . Day 290
18:3. . . . . Day 327

18:19. . . . . Day 333
18:32. . . . . Day 133
19:1 . . . . Day 176
19:12–13 . . . . Day 218
19:14. . . . . .Days 223, 279
20:7 . . . . Day 364
22:2, 5. . . . . Day 163
22:11. . . . . Day 349
23:4 . . . . Day 149
23:6. . . . . Day 91
24:8–9 . . . . Day 264
25:4–5 . . . . Day 317
25:10. . . . . Days 9, 58
27:1 . . . . Day 107
27:13. . . . . .Days 19, 155
27:13–14 . . . . Day 65
27:14. . . . . Day 330
28:7 . . . . Day 270
31:14. . . . . Day 222
31:19. . . . . Day 141
32:8 . . . . Day 261
32:8–9 . . . . Day 206
32:8, 10. . . . . Day 46
33:21. . . . . Day 176
33:22. . . . . Day 128
34:1 . . . . Day 66
34:4–5 . . . . Day 290
34:5 . . . . Day 341
34:14–15 . . . . Day 263
36:5 . . . . .Days 147, 313
37:3–5 . . . . Day 171
37:5–6 . . . . Day 106
37:7–9 . . . . Day 119
37:23 . . . . Day 68
37:37 . . . . Day 263
40:10. . . . . Day 14
42:11. . . . . Day 40
44:26. . . . . Day 221
46:1 . . . . Day 364
46:1–2, 10 . . . . Day 1
46:10. . . . . Days 2, 258, 325
47:1 . . . . Day 163
47:7 . . . . Day 247
50:14–15 . . . . Day 208
50:15. . . . . .Days 165, 256
51:10. . . . . Day 55

51:10–12 . . . . Day 11
51:12 . . . . Day 352
53:1–2 . . . . Day 148
55:17 . . . . Introduction, Day 165
55:22 . . . . Days 95, 158
56:11 . . . . Day 171
62:7–8 . . . . Day 182
63:1–2 . . . . Day 348
63:3–7 . . . . Day 83
63:7 . . . . Day 171
68:34–35 . . . . Day 363
71:1–3 . . . . Day 332
71:14–15 . . . . Day 285
72:18 . . . . Day 201
73:25–26 . . . . Day 228
78:7 . . . . Day 271
81:1 . . . . Day 126
81:10 . . . . Day 239
84:11 . . . . Day 330
85:8 . . . . Day 258
86:4–5 . . . . Day 26
89:1 . . . . Day 101
90:12 . . . . Day 265
94:18–19 . . . . Day 21
95:1–2 . . . . Day 126
96:12–13 . . . . Day 256
100:1–2, 4 . . . . Day 344
100:3 . . . . Day 298
103:17 . . . . Day 39
103:12 . . . . Day 218
103:13–14 . . . . Day 230
105:4 . . . . Day 206
106:1–3 . . . . Day 245
107:1 . . . . Day 3
107:2 . . . . Day 57
107:28–30 . . . . Day 275
108:2–4 . . . . Day 311
119:32 . . . . Day 233
119:60 . . . . Day 339
119:104–106 . . . . Day 317
119:105 . . . . Days 133, 191
119:111 . . . . Day 57
120:7 . . . . Day 171
121:2 . . . . Day 171
122:6 . . . . Days 216, 351
127:4 . . . . Day 28

130:5–6 . . . . Day 150
130:7 . . . . Day 98
135:3 . . . . Days 132, 226
139:4 . . . . Day 151
139:13–14 . . . . Days 69, 231
139:14 . . . . Day 113
139:15–16 . . . . Day 269
139:17–18 . . . . Day 311
143:8 . . . . Day 45
145:17–18 . . . . Day 246
146:1 . . . . Day 178
146:6–7 . . . . Day 181
149:4 . . . . Day 69

PROVERBS
1:20, 22–23 . . . . Day 312
3:5 . . . . Day 18
3:5–6 . . . . Days 195, 212, 360
3:5–7 . . . . Day 96
3:11–12 . . . . Day 236
3:12 . . . . Day 278
3:13 . . . . Day 211
4:23 . . . . Day 253
8:10–11 . . . . Day 125
8:17 . . . . Day 237
8:33 . . . . Day 191
10:12 . . . . Days 116, 277
10:22 . . . . Day 291
11:3 . . . . Day 337
11:25 . . . . Day 161
11:30 . . . . Day 336
12:18 . . . . Day 343
13:15 . . . . Day 42
13:24 . . . . Day 154
14:15 . . . . Day 192
14:30 . . . . Day 100
15:1 . . . . Day 307
15:13 . . . . Days 320, 338
15:15 . . . . Days 97, 198
15:30 . . . . Days 13, 241
16:18 . . . . Day 142
16:24 . . . . Day 223
17:9 . . . . Day 114
17:17 . . . . Day 193
17:22 . . . . Day 297
18:10 . . . . Day 134

18:15 . . . . Day 59
18:21 . . . . Day 253
18:24 . . . . Day 224
19:11 . . . . Day 277
20:5 . . . . Day 138
23:7 . . . . Day 17
24:14 . . . . Day 33
27:1 . . . . Day 293
27:17 . . . . Day 80
28:26 . . . . Day 233
29:23 . . . . Day 115
29:25 . . . . Day 144
31:25 . . . . Day 62
31:26 . . . . Days 219, 249
31:30 . . . . Day 113

ECCLESIASTES
2:24 . . . . Day 300
3:1, 6 . . . . Day 288
3:4 . . . . Day 312
3:11 . . . . Day 60
4:9–10, 12 . . . . Day 30
4:12 . . . . Day 193
6:9 . . . . Day 50
9:10 . . . . Day 198
11:10 . . . . Day 125

ISAIAH
1:18 . . . . Day 342
9:2 . . . . Day 147
9:6 . . . . Days 232, 278, 316
12:2 . . . . Day 262
25:7 . . . . Day 164
26:3 . . . . Days 93, 292
26:3–4 . . . . Day 172
28:16 . . . . Day 286
30:18 . . . . Days 29, 229
33:2 . . . . Day 333
35:1–2 . . . . Day 265
40:10–11 . . . . Day 5
40:31 . . . . Days 45, 237
41:10 . . . . Days 234, 350
41:13 . . . . Day 222
42:1 . . . . Day 328
43:10 . . . . Day 177

43:25 . . . . Day 48
44:8 . . . . Day 314
49:15–16 . . . . Day 327
49:16 . . . . Day 323
55:8–9 . . . . Day 271
55:10–11 . . . . Day 28
58:13–14 . . . . Day 344
61:1 . . . . Day 109
61:3 . . . . Day 341
63:9 . . . . Day 10
64:4 . . . . Day 246

JEREMIAH
1:6–7 . . . . Day 146
4:1 . . . . Day 170
15:16 . . . . Day 34
17:7 . . . . Day 262
17:7–8 . . . . Day 310
17:8 . . . . Day 175
29:11 . . . . Days 96, 205
29:13 . . . . Day 86
33:3 . . . . Day 197
33:3, 6 . . . . Day 174
33:6 . . . . Day 79
33:10–11 . . . . Day 214

LAMENTATIONS
3:21–23 . . . . Day 221

EZEKIEL
32:26–27 . . . . Day 98
33:11 . . . . Day 8

DANIEL
9:23 . . . . Days 68, 135

HOSEA
6:3 . . . . Day 88
10:12 . . . . Day 360

JOEL
2:13 . . . . Day 179
2:28 . . . . Day 210
2:32 . . . . Day 203

JONAH
2:7 . . . . Day 66, 116

MICAH
3:8 . . . . Day 171
5:2 . . . . Day 202
5:4 . . . . Day 334
7:7 . . . . Day 166

HABAKKUK
3:17–18 . . . . Day 61
3:17–19 . . . . Day 274
3:18–19 . . . . Days 88, 306

ZEPHANIAH
3:17 . . . . Days 5, 84, 196, 331

ZECHARIAH
2:12–13 . . . . Day 346
3:9–10 . . . . Day 14
7:5–6 . . . . Day 115
14:20–21 . . . . Day 50

NEW TESTAMENT

MATTHEW
2:11 . . . . Day 243
3:8 . . . . Day 295
4:1 . . . . Day 53
4:4 . . . . Day 281
5:16 . . . . Day 296
5:43–45 . . . . Days 82, 309, 322
6:1 . . . . Day 64
6:6 . . . . Day 363
6:9 . . . . Day 143
6:11 . . . . Day 213
6:14–15 . . . . Day 186
6:15 . . . . Day 153
6:25 . . . . Day 152
6:28–29 . . . . Day 152
6:33 . . . . Day 24
7:1–2 . . . . Day 353
7:2, 5 . . . . Day 153
7:7–8 . . . . Day 249
7:11 . . . . Day 303
7:24–25 . . . . Day 78
8:13 . . . . Day 75
9:22 . . . . Day 75
9:37–38 . . . . Day 160
13:16 . . . . Day 159
15:25, 28 . . . . Day 229
15:28 . . . . Day 227
15:32 . . . . Day 181
18:20 . . . . Day 361
18:21–22 . . . . Days 114, 302
21:16 . . . . Day 109
22:37 . . . . Day 207
22:37–39 . . . . Day 328
24:12 . . . . Day 118
25:1–2 . . . . Day 2
25:23 . . . . Day 104
25:35 . . . . Day 124

MARK
5:27–28 . . . . Day 286
5:34 . . . . Day 257
6:3 . . . . Day 248
6:31–32 . . . . Day 187
9:23–24 . . . . Day 220
9:35 . . . . Day 362
10:13–15 . . . . Day 250
11:24 . . . . Days 189, 347
12:30–31 . . . . Day 38

LUKE
2:25–26 . . . . Day 259
2:34–35 . . . . Day 72
2:36–38 . . . . Day 199
6:20 . . . . Day 359
6:28 . . . . Day 309
6:32 . . . . Day 162
6:35 . . . . Days 284, 345
6:38 . . . . Days 20, 108
7:38 . . . . Day 108
7:47 . . . . Days 117, 353
8:1–3 . . . . Day 200
8:1, 3 . . . . Day 257
8:18 . . . . Day 121

10:40 . . . . Day 136
11:33 . . . . Day 354
12:33 . . . . Day 298
12:42–44 . . . . Day 94
14:28 . . . . Day 136
16:10 . . . . Day 299
18:1 . . . . Day 151

JOHN
1:12 . . . . Day 3
1:16 . . . . Day 73
3:2 . . . . Day 19
3:5–7 . . . . Day 111
3:16 . . . . Days 4, 188, 208, 299
3:16–17 . . . . Day 260
3:23 . . . . Day 104
4:28–29 . . . . Day 63
4:35 . . . . Day 339
5:6 . . . . Day 35
6:9 . . . . Day 259
6:35 . . . . Day 346
6:48 . . . . Day 279
8:7, 9–11 . . . . Day 41
8:32 . . . . Day 103
8:44 . . . . Day 143
10:10 . . . . Day 54
10:14–15 . . . . Day 170
11:35 . . . . Day 97
11:39 . . . . Day 144
13:9 . . . . Day 27
13:12–14 . . . . Day 55
13:18 . . . . Day 137
14:15–17 . . . . Day 59
14:16–17 . . . . Day 23
14:23 . . . . Day 49
14:27 . . . . Day 316
15:9 . . . . Days 120, 139
15:9–10 . . . . Day 139
15:12 . . . . Day 168
16:33 . . . . Days 120, 292

ACTS
1:8 . . . . Day 42
2:28 . . . . Day 252
2:44–45 . . . . Day 194
3:6 . . . . Day 243

8:30–31 . . . . Day 281
10:2 . . . . Day 268
10:4 . . . . Day 20
13:15 . . . . Day 160
13:38–39 . . . . Day 248
13:52 . . . . Day 270
16:13 . . . . Day 296
18:27 . . . . Day 15
24:3 . . . . Day 110

ROMANS
1:9 . . . . Day 340
1:21 . . . . Day 22
3:10 . . . . Day 71
3:22 . . . . Day 269
4:20 . . . . Day 324
5:1 . . . . Day 351
5:8 . . . . Day 199
5:16 . . . . Day 93
6:23 . . . . Day 81
8:1 . . . . Day 155
8:11 . . . . Day 242
8:13 . . . . Day 111
8:18 . . . . Day 172
8:26–27 . . . . Day 275
8:38–39 . . . . Days 90, 289
8:39 . . . . Days 168, 365
10:10–11 . . . . Day 297
11:33–36 . . . . Days 47, 106
12:1–2 . . . . Days 124, 150
12:2 . . . . Day 355
12:3 . . . . Day 142
12:6, 8 . . . . Day 177
12:9 . . . . Day 225
12:10 . . . . Day 30
12:11–12 . . . . Day 52
12:14 . . . . Day 284
12:15 . . . . Day 123
12:16–18 . . . . Days 224, 239
12:20–21 . . . . Day 255
12:21 . . . . Day 255
13:14 . . . . Day 12
15:4 . . . . Days 34, 159
15:13 . . . . Day 63

1 CORINTHIANS

1:8 . . . . Day 240
1:9 . . . . Day 216
2:5 . . . . Day 77
3:3 . . . . Day 215
3:6 . . . . Day 129
3:11–14 . . . . Day 51
6:18 . . . . Day 156
6:19–20 . . . . Day 247
7:17 . . . . Day 167
8:6 . . . . Day 86
10:13. . . . . Days 99, 238, 267
10:16. . . . . Day 310
11:3 . . . . Day 74
13:1 . . . . Day 194
13:4–7 . . . . Day 231
15:19. . . . . Day 65
16:18. . . . . Day 362

2 CORINTHIANS

1:3–4. . . . . Day 101
1:11 . . . . Day 340
2:15 . . . . Day 8
3:18 . . . . Day 17
4:1 . . . . Day 148
4:16–18 . . . . .Days 21, 190
5:17 . . . . Day 4
9:6 . . . . Day 241
10:3–4 . . . . Day 140
10:5. . . . . .Days 31, 105
12:8 . . . . Day 251
12:9 . . . . .Days 244, 305
12:9–10 . . . . Day 89

GALATIANS

3:2 . . . . Day 117
4:6 . . . . Day 242
6:4–5. . . . . Day 56
6:9 . . . . Days 92, 166, 288
6:9–10 . . . . Day 39

EPHESIANS

1:16. . . . . Day 122
2:4–5. . . . . .Days 76, 365
2:10 . . . . Day 130

2:19–21 . . . . Day 283
3:16–18 . . . . Day 131
3:17–19 . . . . Day 301
3:20–21 . . . . .Days 95, 210
4:2 .Days 102, 254
4:15 . . . . Day 302
4:29 . . . . Day 343
4:32 . . . . Day 336
5:2 . . . . Day 318
5:18–20 . . . . Day 1
5:19 . . . . Day 84
5:20 . . . . Day 13
5:21 . . . . Day 74
6:10–12 . . . . Day 304
6:16 . . . . Day 304
6:18 . . . . Day 357

PHILIPPIANS

2:3–4. . . . . .Days 122, 322
2:4 . . . . Day 225
2:5 . . . . Day 145
2:5–7. . . . . Day 27
2:15 . . . . Day 127
3:7, 14 . . . . Day 334
3:12 . . . . Day 319
3:13–14 . . . . Day 350
3:13–15 . . . . Day 61
3:20 . . . . Day 204
4:4 . . . . Days 40, 107, 195
4:8 . . . . Days 105, 145, 274
4:8–9. . . . . .Days 179, 211
4:11, 13. . . . . Day 89
4:19 .Days 18, 272

COLOSSIANS

1:9 . . . . .Days 23, 53
3:2 . . . . Day 264
3:12 . . . . .Days 71, 276
3:13–14 . . . . Day 80
3:17 .Days 87, 141
3:23 .Days 173, 205
4:2 . . . . Day 245
4:6 . . . . Day 209

1 THESSALONIANS

5:11 . . . . Day 36

5:16–18 . . . . Day 112
5:17–18 . . . . Day 357
5:18 . . . . Days 22, 110

2 THESSALONIANS
3:11–13 . . . . Day 236

1 TIMOTHY
1:14 . . . . Day 46
2:1, 3 . . . . Day 64
2:1–4 . . . . Day 24
5:5 . . . . Day 308
6:6 . . . . Day 183

2 TIMOTHY
1:5 . . . . Day 157
1:7 . . . . Day 6
1:9–10 . . . . Day 188
2:15 . . . . Day 282
4:7 . . . . Day 335

TITUS
2:12 . . . . Day 186
2:14 . . . . Day 41

PHILEMON
20 . . . . Day 16

HEBREWS
2:17–18 . . . . Day 10
3:13 . . . . Day 36
4:12–13 . . . . Day 11
4:16 . . . . Days 73, 129, 303
5:12 . . . . Day 175
6:19–20 . . . . Day 260
10:22–25 . . . . Day 37
10:23 . . . . Days 62, 306
10:24–25 . . . . Days 37, 326, 361
11:1 . . . . Day 212
11:1, 6 . . . . Day 119
11:16 . . . . Day 235
11:25–26 . . . . Day 204
12:1 . . . . Days 67, 318
12:1–2 . . . . Days 99, 356
12:2–3 . . . . Day 359
12:6 . . . . Day 154
12:28–29 . . . . Day 285

13:5 . . . . Day 308
13:8 . . . . Day 261

JAMES
1:2–4 . . . . Day 280
1:2–5 . . . . Day 190
1:4 . . . . Day 92
1:5 . . . . Days 31, 301
1:6 . . . . Days 184, 220, 250
1:12 . . . . Day 238
1:19 . . . . Day 219
1:19–20 . . . . Day 282
1:25 . . . . Day 78
3:8–10 . . . . Day 326
3:13 . . . . Day 254
3:14 . . . . Day 183
3:15–16 . . . . Day 323
3:17 . . . . Day 77
4:1–2 . . . . Day 56
4:7 . . . . Day 267
4:8 . . . . Day 342
4:14–15 . . . . Day 76
5:13 . . . . Days 32, 244
5:16 . . . . Days 72, 112, 358

1 PETER
1:4–5 . . . . Day 140
1:8 . . . . Day 320
1:15–16 . . . . Day 51
1:24–25 . . . . Day 293
3:3–4 . . . . Days 185, 217
3:4 . . . . Day 25
4:7 . . . . Day 94
4:8 . . . . Day 131
5:6 . . . . Days 15, 70, 102
5:7 . . . . Day 128
5:10 . . . . Day 48

2 PETER
1:3 . . . . Day 240
1:3–4 . . . . Day 67
1:19 . . . . Day 29
3:8 . . . . Day 7
3:9 . . . . Day 337

1 JOHN
1:9 . . . . Day 358
2:3 . . . . Day 321

2:6 . . . . Day 60
2:15 . . . . Day 355
3:1 . . . . Day 100
3:13 . . . . Day 354
3:18 . . . . Day 307
3:18–20 . . . . Day 85
4:4 . . . . Day 103
4:7–8. . . . . .Days 162, 289
4:16 . . . . Day 118
4:16, 18. . . . . Day 6
4:21 . . . . Day 156
5:4 . . . . Day 33
5:4–5. . . . . Day 315

3 JOHN
2 . . . . Day 35

REVELATION
3:19 . . . . Day 178
21:4 . . . . Days 7, 182, 235
22:12–13 . . . . Day 135

DAILY INSPIRATION FOR A WOMAN'S SPIRIT!

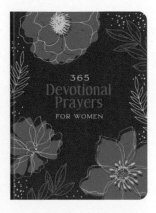

365 Devotional Prayers for Women

This daily devotional prayer book is a lovely reminder to bring any petition before your heavenly Father. Hundreds of just-right-sized prayers touch on topics that will help you grow a courageous faith.

DiCarta / 978-1-63609-744-2

Daily Devotions to Nurture Your Faith

This beautiful daily devotional collection will engage your spirit with Bible wisdom and encouraging devotions. Each entry includes a scripture, faith-nurturing devotional reading, and prayer.

DiCarta / 978-1-63609-722-0